The real voyage of discovery consists not in seeking new landscapes, but in having new eyes...

Marcel Proust (1871~1922)

# *Preface*

The Senator Robert F. Kennedy said, "Some men see things that are and ask 'Why?' and others see things the way they could be and ask 'Why not?'" This book is born from the vision of "Why not?" It's a vision of possibility about what education could be, not how it is. One where students run TO school instead of FROM school. One where students ask for homework instead of complain about it. It's a vision where teachers are heard, appreciated and respected. It's one where teachers have the power to affect decisions about the curriculum, their classroom, their students, and school policies. It's also a vision about partnership - where teachers learn and work with students, not teach "at" them and where teachers, students and administrators work as a team, sharing ideas, supporting each other and enjoying the privilege (not the burden) of being co-responsible for the quality of learning.

Sound like a dream? It's not. A dream is a vision without a plan. There is a plan and you are the most important part of it. The plan is almost too simple. Start right now, with yourself... start figuring out where you "are" with your role in education, what is needed and what you can do next to make education work around you. Where do you begin? With this book and yourself.

Make small changes at first. Build your confidence in new areas. Get comfortable with change. Then, begin to network and support others in growing. What will support you as you continue to impact education? You have your hands on it! This book is designed to be a companion, a traveler's aid and owner's manual for you, the educator with more than just a dream. It is for the educator with a vision, the you with a commitment to "make it happen." As partners, you and I can "break the back" of mediocrity in education. Step by step, one by one, we can make it happen. It's inspiring what a single person can do. Are you resigned to "the way things are?" Or, are you a 21st century "player?" If you're a player, you're holding the "playbook." Turn the page, the adventure is about to begin!

# Table of Contents

About Our World... Your Conversation Affects Your Results... There Are No Unresourceful Students, Only Unresourceful States... Each Person Does His Best... A Low Ego Works Best... Authenticity Works Better Than "Acts"... Teaching Is a Lifelong Process of Learning, Not an Event... Great Teaching Requires a Different Role... Teaching Requires a "Seize the Day" Attitude... Teaching Is an Inherently High-Risk Job... Teaching is a Fully Paid Personal Growth Seminar

## 6. *Taking Care of Business* 73

Preparation... The True Professional... Support... Parent Relationships... Handling Parent Conferences... Relationship-Building... Smart Ideas... Build Rapport... Report Card Success Tips... Avoid Labels... Distribution... Follow-up... Your Health... Physical Messages... Dress Standards... Your Self-Expression... Affirm the Positive... Take Acting Lessons... Set An Example

## 7. *Lesson Planning* 81

Lesson vs. Learning Planning... Moving From "Covering the Content" to "Uncovering the Learning"... Benefits of Strong Learning Plans... Clarify Your Outcomes... Three Major Learning Areas... Accelerating the Learning... Ingredients of Success... Skills Model... Planning the Content Learning... An Interdependent Approach: Thematic Learning Planning... Thematic Learning in a Nutshell

## 8. *Learning Environment* 99

Environments Can Teach... Read This First... How to Get Help... Safety is First... Room Preparation... Temperature Is Critical... Use of Color... Power of Peripheral Stimuli... Affirmations... How to Use Markers... Lighting... Room Arrangement... Open Space... Seating for Success... The Sounds of Learning... Ice-Breaking

## 9. *Presenting Skills* 109

Presenting or Communicating... Three Part Communication... General Guidelines... Planning and Organization... Notes and Prompts... OPENINGS: Well Begun is Well Done... Keys to Introductions... Start on Time... Tools for Openings... Non-verbal Attention Getters... Positive Greetings... SUCCESS TOOLS: Develop Rapport... Work the Group... Respect Gradient... Provide Key Information... Student Fears Addressed... Preview Coming Attractions... Guidelines for Success... Oral Contracts... State the Rules... Logistics... Elicit Needs, Provide Solution... Certainty Affirmations... Congruency is a Key... Different Types of Voices... Dramatize Your Point... Keep Sentences Brief... Positive Wording... Let's Get Physical... CLOSINGS: Parting is Such Sweet Sorrow... Advantages of Powerful Closures... Five Keys... Discover the Conclusions... Review Time... Using Mind-Mapping... Discussion... Feedback to You... Class Evaluation...Reconnect the Learning... Preview Coming Attractions... Congratulate & Celebrate... A Closing Ritual

## 10. *Powerful Listening Skills* 131

Two Ears, One Mouth... Worst Listening Mistakes... Listening is a Learned Skill... Use a Listening Voice... Learn What the Speaker Needs... Many Ways to Listen... How to Listen Successfully... How to Create a Listening Environment... Empathic Listening... Here's The Real Skill... Avoid These Listening Mistakes... Listen to the Person First... Reading Non-Verbals... Precision Listening... Clarifications... Generalizations Corrected... Unspecified

Nouns, Pronouns and Verbs Exposed... Limits Clarified and Exposed... Absolutes Exposed... Imposed Values Made Evident... Lost Performatives Retrieved... Distortions Challenged... Distortions Clarified

## 11. *Successful Interactions* — 145

It's All About People... The Key to Interactions Is the Process... Are They Just Common Sense?... Three Key Qualities... Use the Non-Verbals... Questioning Strategies... Should You Interrupt?... Personal Preparation... Your Actual Responses... Think Before You Ask... Hostile Questions... Asking Content Questions... Whom To Call On?... Before You Ask Questions... Types of Questions... When You Get the Answer You Like... What if the Answer Is Wrong?... Handling "Wrong" Answers... Student Sharing... How to Respond... Validate Student Contributions... Responding to Creativity... Discussion and Inquiry... Pre- and Post-Class Dialogues... Do You Make This Mistake?... Here's a Winner!... What If You Fail At It?

## 12. *Activities for All Ages* — 161

We Know Better Now... Advantages of Experiential and Cooperative Learning... Four Key Steps... Selection and Planning... Set-Up & Introduction... Group Selection... Operation & Maintenance... De-brief & Closure... Types of Activities: Grouped by Multiple Intelligences

## 13. *Learning Strategies* — 171

Keep Track of Yourself... Introduce Pre-Exposure... Use Visualization... Use Analogy... Discover Learner's Prior Knowledge... Goal-Setting... Mental Practice Boosts Learning... Chunk Up or Chunk Down... Relaxation Boosts Learning... Isolate Key Points... Board Skills... Modeling the Learning... The Flip Chart/Overhead Alternative... Use Colors Well... Presentation Cards... Discussion Cards... Peripherals: Posters, Signs and Banners... Multi-Modal, Multi-Media Sources... Use Guest Speakers... Better Notetaking... Add Music... Why Engage Emotions?... How To Engage Emotions... The Self-Convincer State... How We Get Self-Convinced... What To Do About It

## 14. *Rituals and Affirmations* — 185

Rituals Enrich Our Lives... Seasonal Rituals... Morning Rituals... Affirmations... Visual Affirmations... Auditory Affirmations... Kinesthetic Affirmations... What to Put On the Walls... Sample Affirmations Peripherals

## 15. *Multiple Intelligences* — 193

Teaching Content or Discovering Intelligence?... Intelligent People... Defining Intelligence... Who Is Intelligent?... Logical-Mathematical... Interpersonal... Spatial... Musical-Rhythmic... Intrapersonal... Bodily-Kinesthetic... Verbal-Linguistic... Additional Key Considerations... Your Action Steps... How to Reach Everyone... How to Nurture The Multiple Intelligences... Integrating Across The Curriculum... Assessing Multiple Intelligences... What Are Other Key Implications?... Where Do Gifted and Talented Programs Fit In?

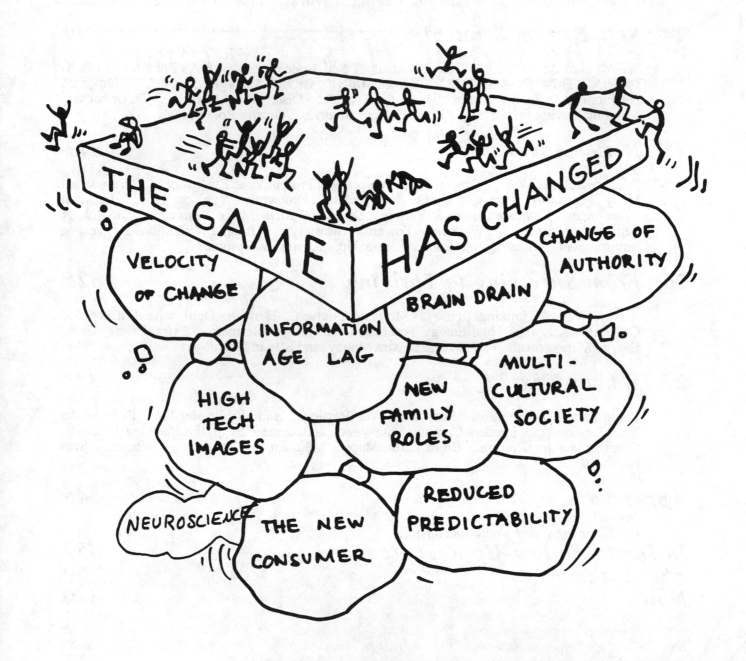

# *The Game Has Changed*

## What's Really Going On?

This book is not about the problems facing today's educators. It is about the vision and possibility that can be brought forth to make education work. After all, the problems we face as educators are, to a large degree, merely symptoms. Addressing the symptoms will not change education. New ones appear faster than we can solve the old ones. We are bailing water out of a boat that we already know has holes in it!

We've spent trillions of dollars in education since landing on the moon and many measuring sticks say the quality has remained the same or gotten worse. Teachers experience widespread powerlessness, bitterness and resignation. Teacher strikes have doubled in the last decade. Instead of a conversation about the joys of learning, education has become a conversation about dropouts, low test scores, school security, teenage pregnancy, vandalism, AIDS, teenage drunk driving, violence, drug abuse and suicides. Not that these areas don't deserve attention. They do. But somehow the focus of education has changed.

What's caused it all? What's putting us on such a treadmill? How can we get at the real source of the frustration? Why do we seem to be constantly behind at making education work? The questions we raise seem to point to something fundamental. The world has changed in many profound ways. We cannot play by the old rules and succeed. A return to the basics will not work. Another simple "band-aid" will not work. Why? The basic structures on which education was established are crumbling.

## The Game Has Changed

We cannot solve our problems at the same level of thinking that got us into them. Outcome-based education, cooperative learning, inclusion, cultural diversity or any other program, will not "fix" education. Nearly everything we've used so far may be adding to the problems. "Stand and deliver" is out. Old teacher roles are out. Clumsy bureaucracies are out. We simply cannot use the old behaviors and expect the same responses as before. Life is quite different now. Here are some of the more dramatic changes and their corresponding results:

# Greater Velocity of Change

Entire industries start and stop within a single decade. Schools are no longer preparation for a single job or career. Schools now must be a preparation for many careers. The average high school graduate in 2010 will have 3-5 careers (not jobs) compared to 1-2 for his or her parents. Jobs simply become extinct faster nowadays. Students need to learn HOW to learn, not WHAT to learn. Many students believe that their curriculum is outdated and does not provide them with the real tools for life. More and more students are getting home schooling, attending alternative classes, alternative schools, summer programs and taking "home study." Classroom enthusiasm is at an all-time low. Dropout rates are staggering: New York City-34%, Chicago-43%, San Diego-35%, inner city schools average 40-60%. Nationwide, one out of four students drops out of school!

Another result of the increasing rate of change is found in staff development programs. Many of the ideas and programs offered as solutions to problems are out of date immediately. Teachers have become tired of having to learn something new only to have it dropped and replaced by something even "newer." This constant "band-aid" approach leaves teachers burned out and cynical about additional teacher training since most programs continue to teach content - the WHAT rather than the HOW.

*It is the learners who will inherit the*
*future...the "so-called learned," who think they*
*"know it all" will find themselves frustrated*
*by a world that has passed them by*

Even if a program is useful, it often trains teachers in an area so specific that they exemplify the saying, "If what you hold is a hammer, you only look for nails."

# Information Age Impact Is Increasing

This creates a widening gap between what's known and what's implemented in schools. The research in psychology, sociology, neuroscience, biology, physics and education has an enormous lag time for individual educator implementation. The lag time for in-the-system innovation is usually 5-10 years for pilot programs and an 10-25 year lag for widespread implementation!

This wide gap creates a sense of hopelessness about staying informed. Teachers stop trying to stay updated. Textbooks are often out of date at print time. Students make an unfortunate distinction between what happens at school and the "real world." This reduces student motivation to participate in what many perceive as an irrelevant or bankrupt system.

*The new currency of our time is not factory skills,*
*but information and the ability to access it at will...*
*highly successful people know what's going on and*
*have the knowledge to navigate skillfully*

Since the new currency is information systems, how can our students become culturally, socially and economically wealthy if they are being taught out-of-date programs featuring recitals, "math facts," states and capitals, spelling drills and woodshop. We're in a world of calculators, CD-ROM encyclopedias and carbon-fiber plastics. But students, in many schools are still being taught a 1950's curriculum in a 1950's way. You can only input a limited amount of concrete knowledge in so many years of schooling. What's the solution? Switch our students from content-absorbers to "information navigators."

# Increasingly Advanced Technology

The sophistication of the information age means that we have created a new entity "The electronic authority." Students now turn to INTERNET, home computers, television, radio, CD-ROM, compact discs, and videotapes as their source of up-to-the-moment information. Perhaps creating an even greater impact is the additional learning students get electronically: trends, values, fashions, manners, customs, and ethics. Historically, this information was taught through the authority of parents, churches, or schools. Yet today, none of these seem to be primary sources of authoritative information for young people.

This trend creates fewer positive role model relationships and less sense of community, bonding and responsibility. Results are greater classroom discipline problems, delinquency and crime. There's less development of family relationships because the students don't HAVE to go to their parents for critical information as they did forty years ago.

*The teacher used to be the leader and provider...*
*today's teacher is the catalyst and navigator*

The power and charisma of the media has changed student standards for communication. The congruency of actors and impact of multi-media electronic presentations spoil students for unrealistic standards. Two generations ago, the classroom teacher was one of the most visible and powerful role models in a student's life. Now role models come from sports, theater, film and entertainment... celebrities made famous and visible by the media. Teachers simply can't compete, nor should they even try to compete.

Students bring the mindset of television to class each day. In comparison, students often see teachers as inadequate or boring. Thus, many students have less respect for their teachers, daydream more and participate less in class.

# The "Provider-User" Relationship Has Changed

In the past, school was designed as a "provider" of information for students who would be "users" of that information. This created a power structure with the teacher as dispenser of valuable information and the student as powerless receiver of the "pearls of wisdom." In this role, the student was passive, a vessel to be filled.

*The old model was that a teacher would stand and deliver...*
*That model is dead... you are a learning catalyst and*
*the students are now the stars of the class*

When the teacher controls the information, the student expects the teacher to "do it to him" rather than being in a learning partnership. The old method keeps students from being responsible for their learning. The information age has enabled students to become their own "provider." They are no longer at the mercy of teachers to get information. Hence the old "provider-user" relationship is obsolete.

Years ago, teachers had fewer demands placed on them. Today, the demands are extraordinary and the school structure is not set up to handle these needs. Our educational system simply does not support and nurture the teacher - teachers need both, especially now. There are insufficient pathways for teachers to express themselves and be heard. There is a chilling lack of acknowledgment and support for the job teachers do. Even in this day of reform, too many schools are still designed to bypass the teacher on some of the most important decisions teachers must live with: teacher-student ratio, class hours, curriculum and classroom design. To add to the insult, teachers' salaries have lagged behind other comparable professions.

This changing role has left the teacher with less prestige and respect in the community. The powerlessness, lack of respect, lack of support and nurturing, have left most teachers in a state of resignation. To survive, they have simply adapted to the problems and circumstances. The evidence is in both conversation and actions. The prevailing conversation in education is about problems and circumstances. It ought to be about possibilities and resources.

## Restructuring of the Economy and Social Family

In the industrialized countries, another shift is occurring. The voting tax base in the 1950's and for the next twenty years, was largely comprised of a husband and wife with one to three children. These taxpayers voted in their own and their children's best interests. If a community needed to raise bond money for schools, parents voted for it. But times have changed.

Today, the educated vote more than the uneducated. The middle class and upper class vote more than the lower class. But they vote for tax cuts, not educational bond issues. The traditional two parent family, with school children, now makes up less than 30% of the total population. The remainder is composed of seniors, parents with grown children, childless couples and singles. Those who would vote in favor of educational issues are now the minority. Today, the traditional or single parent family, who may truly want better schools for their children, may not be able to afford it. The tax rebellion has voters thinking of today's paycheck, not tomorrow's generation. Without a tax supported system of education, the future is being mortgaged.

In California's tax-supported university system, annual tuition was under $500 in 1965. By 1995, it was over $4,000. That's not inflation, it's a runaway anti-tax populist movement gone awry. The impact of this is simple: In a society where education is the passkey to opportunity, fewer and fewer students can afford to go to college. It's now up to those who can afford it, not who deserve it.

*Education used to be considered a right,*
*now it's becoming more of a privilege...*
*Expect learning to become more self-taught,*
*Anticipate more pay-as-you-go*

In 1960, 95% of all unwed mothers put their babies up for adoption. In 1994, a whopping 92% of all unwed mothers **kept** their babies. More mothers with more babies don't vote. Older parents and childless couples vote. That changes the dynamics of the electorate dramatically.

More and more mothers work outside the home than ever before. More and more children live with just one parent. Parents spend less and less time with their children. In addition, Jerald Bachman of the Survey Research Center in Michigan

4

says two-thirds of all high school students are working part-time. He adds that one-quarter of them work over 20 hours a week! The impact is staggering. We have "latch-key kids" who come home to an empty house in the afternoon.... child care centers bulging at the seams... kids without a sense of belonging and teens spending increased time on the job. There's no one left to give the emotional nurturing, the support, the sharing of values, the discipline and responsibility of our nation's children. Most parents' leave the job up to the schools.

*You cannot assume that your learners*
*will come from homes where they get*
*adequate food, nurturing & life skills*

Teenagers report experiences of alienation, feelings of separateness and painful loneliness. Suicide, drop-out, crime and drug abuse rates are at an all-time high. Runaways are increasing and so is teenage pregnancy. Working teenagers are frequently exhausted and unable to stay awake in class.

## Drain of Leadership from Education to Business

Years ago, some of the best and brightest people in the United States provided vision and leadership for schools. Now, the economic opportunities in business have attracted many of the leaders with vision. Today, schools often set aside "vision", hiring administrators for their ability to solve problems, reduce vandalism, raise test scores and manage disenchanted staffs. The role of principal is often compared to that of a police chief or fire-fighter.

The kinds of roles principals are asked to fill attracts fewer visionary and more of the problem-solver type of person. This creates a school environment that consists of conversations about problems, rather than vision. What most faculties and staff need is a visionary empowering them to create the kind of nurturing learning environment they know is possible.

## Increased Market-Driven Consumerism

The power of the media has grown so much that nearly anything or anyone can be the next "hot" item. There's a constant push for being rich, famous, healthy, happy, attractive and successful. Sports and entertainment salaries have become public record and making a million dollars a year seems commonplace. We've all become numb to megabucks, especially with athletes getting 100 million dollar contracts.

*Some kids act as if getting the latest pair of athletic*
*shoes is more important than getting an education...*
*in a way, they can't help it - they're brainwashed*

This emphasis on being rich or one of the "beautiful people" places tremendous pressure on our youth. Stress in children has become commonplace. It's just too difficult for them to keep an even keel in the "go for it" world of glitz and glamour. Unrealistic expectations are demoralizing our nation's youth. Kids don't see any way they can "make it" the way the system has it set up, so they simply give up. They can't win, and they know it. Teen suicides, drinking, and drug use have jumped up dramatically in the last ten years.

# An Increasingly Multi-Cultural Society

In many cities, the term "majority" or "minority" populations have reversed. For example, in New York, Los Angeles and many other cities, there are more non-whites than whites. This shift in ethnic percentages means that school staffs need to be more sensitive to a wider range of needs. In the Southwest, there's an increasingly greater Mexican-American and Asian population, while in other areas the increase is in Blacks. The old concept of "WASP-based" schools is obsolete.

*All motivation and learning is culturally driven... a multi-cultural school requires re-thinking of the learning processes and environment as much as the curriculum*

In short, you can't simply throw at your students an annual multi-cultural awareness day and be deluded into thinking that will solve the motivation and learning problems of non-Anglo learners. Culturally, Asians and Eastern Europeans are more likely to assimilate than Hispanics, Native Americans and African-Americans. The problems caused by cultural differences will not go away with time. It will take an honest concerted effort on the part of everyone to make it work. What's at stake is the future of our civilization.

In districts around the country, changes are happening far too slowly. Teachers need to learn how to be a learning catalyst in cultures other than their own. In cities like San Diego, there's an innovative Race and Human Relations Department to assist teachers who are wholly unprepared to deal with student populations of three to five ethnic backgrounds and for whom English is a second language. In some classes, teachers have reported ten to fifteen separate languages spoken at the same time - and remember, each language brings its own culture.

*We all are facing a critical decision: do we provide a fragmented, culture-specific education to please everyone who has the political power to request it that way... or do we sub-divide into culture-specific learning communities?*

Should teachers be asked to teach in other languages? Bilingual and trilingual education has had support for many years. But a backlash has formed. Now, many are saying, where has this all gotten us? As a country, are we all better off today than thirty years ago? Educationally, that's easy to answer. No, we are not. Inclusion and diversity are ethically correct. But they have created significant challenges for both faculty and staff. Teachers experience consistent communication failures, an increase in student tension and many mis-diagnosed learners. Many educators predict the problems will continue to increase with the present immigration policies.

# Less Predictability

The difficulty that education faces is compounded by a supremely complex society that constantly gives mixed messages. While ten trends are increasing, five others are decreasing. We have so many indicators and statistics available that even the simplest of issues are clouded.

For example, we are nearly paralyzed by the process of creating a responsible and authentic budget. The problem is not that we don't have enough money for education. We do. The problem is not that we don't have enough information. We do. The problem is that we are often unable to sort out the information in a way that tells us what we really need to know in order to spend the money responsibly.

*Countless research studies have suggested that there is enough money available in education for a quality learning experience... but few schools or districts are allocating money in a way that makes it happen*

This makes for missed opportunities, cost overruns, wasteful resource allocations and increased difficulty in assessing budget priorities. It means money gets wasted while other deserving programs suffer. We have larger budgets than ever before, yet there's constant conversation about scarcity of money. It's no wonder that teachers experience feelings of resignation about education.

## Job Market Changes

The information age is dramatically impacting the job market. As we move into the 90's and the 21st century, there are four dominant job markets emerging. They are: 1) manual-industrial 2) technologists 3) service providers 4) knowledge workers, also referred to by Robert Reich as "symbolic analysts." Ask yourself, "Which of these careers am I preparing my students to succeed in upon graduation?"

The industrial worker made up the largest single labor group in the 1950's. This gave under-educated workers a tremendous opportunity to join the middle class through decent wages. But those jobs, the assembly-line manufacturing jobs, are increasingly scarce. By 1990, they accounted for one fifth of the labor force. By 2010, they will account for just 12% of workers. The fastest growing occupation is that of the "technologist." They are the x-ray technicians, computer programmers, physical therapists, lab technicians, print production houses, nurses, technology repair workers, etc. These workers require some education and still use their hands. They are the 21st century version of the factory or farm worker. They are both a service provider and an industrial worker. These career options often need a college education, but some vocational colleges are also able to fill the requirements.

The second largest occupation is the service provider. These include doctors, lawyers, and all the occupations in sales, design, teaching, public relations, travel, retail shops, hotel management, airline personnel, car rental agencies and more. Of these jobs, most require a college education. This field has remained stable after the 1980's job market boom. But times have changed.

## Prepare for the Knowledge Revolution

The biggest boom is what social theorist Peter Drucker calls the "knowledge worker." This person is like an upscale "technologist." To succeed, the worker requires strong formal education and strong ability to apply theory in the practical world. This occupation includes producers, inventors, writers, publishers, marketers, executives, neurosurgeons and scientists. While this area of the job market will not become the majority in the near future, it will redefine what it means to be educated. In this case, it means one who continually updates knowledge and has mastered lifelong learning.

Those most interested in careers as a "knowledge worker" will value education very highly. Those considering occupations in service, industrial-manual or as a technologist will treat education as a means to an end, to get as little as needed just to get hired and keep the job. But the knowledge worker will constantly be learning, upgrading and trying to better position the learning they have in a global marketplace. They'll be learning by CD-ROM, cable channels, audiotapes, books and seminars. Their ability to learn will be their greatest asset.

## School as a Social Reformer

In the 1950's the traditional family structure and/or religion provided the primary sources of social policy. For better or worse, it was the family and church that created, reinforced and determined values. In the mid 1960's the school began to slowly become the primary carrier. How does it do it? Through a constant flow of programs that are "politically correct."

* multiculturalism
* AIDS awareness
* inclusion policies
* gender awareness

* drug awareness & prevention
* safety programs
* drivers education
* life skills

These programs may have great merit. But there is only a finite amount of time in each school day. For every program that's put in, something's got to be taken out. When school has to become a "second home" or in many cases the "only home" for students, the impact on traditional barometers of quality are tremendous.

Reading, overall achievement scores, or even SAT scores **will be lower** in spite of a more "watered down" test (Though test-makers deny it, the 1995 version of national and state achievement tests are clearly, definitely weaker than the 1965, 1975 or 1985 version. Should we lower our standards in education? NO! However, we might want to be more realistic in the diversity and quantity of what is expected from education. Instead of offering 25 separate programs for secondary schools, we might want to do a better job on 15 of them.

## Revolutions in Neuroscience

There's an explosion in brain research that threatens the existing paradigms in learning and education. New and dramatic theories may force all of us to look closer at what we are doing. We may even have to stop altogether and redesign what we do and how we do it. The new paradigm is emerging with spellbinding implications. It's a marriage of many powerful concepts and discoveries in neuroscience including the role of emotions, patterns, survival, environments, rhythms, positive thinking, assessment, music, gender differences and enrichment, in the way we learn.

In addition, shocking theories by top scientists assert that when we are learning something, we may only be discovering something that has already been genetically built-in or "pre-programmed" into our brains. In addition, our brains *may not at all be designed for formal instruction, but rather, only the learning necessary for survival.* New systems theories tell us how to successfully restructure our schools as a complete learning organization. If these postulates hold true, many of our conventional educational models will be shattered like glass. Some would say, it's about time. Many of these astonishing discoveries will be explored in chapter two.

# So What, Now What?

With all these changes occurring, where are we? What do we, as educators, need to do to make some sense out of this world in flux? There are no simple answers. Answers wouldn't help anyway. Answers don't empower people. Answers are dead-ends and typically, the quick end of much needed introspection. What's needed is continual inquiry. Who are we as educators and what do we bring to the party? We need to keep asking questions about ourselves. Questions such as:

"What is the rightful role of schools?"
"How are the roles of teachers changing?"
"What do I really know about learning?"
"How can I get the skills that are most needed?"
"Where is my own level of commitment in this job?"

You might say, "Pretty important questions." You're right. As a whole society, we might lack answers to these questions. Certainly many individuals ponder but, as a profession, teachers have much introspection to do. The education of our children is a critical job of staggering importance. Success will require that we be more than "who we are" right now. It won't be enough that we "try" our best. We'll have to do what's needed. That will require skills, knowledge, vision and a new spirit of empowerment. Our next chapter will be the beginning.

---

## *Additional Resources for Further Study and Follow up*

*Techno-Trends* by Burris
*The Learning Revolution* by Dryden & Vos *
*The Learning Imperative* by Howard (Harvard Business Review)
*Brain-Based Learning & Teaching* by Jensen (Turning Point)*
*Megatrends 2000* by Naisbitt (Warner Books)
*The Work of Nations* by Reich (Random House)
*Third Wave* by Toffler

* Items marked with an asterisk are available in the Appendix.

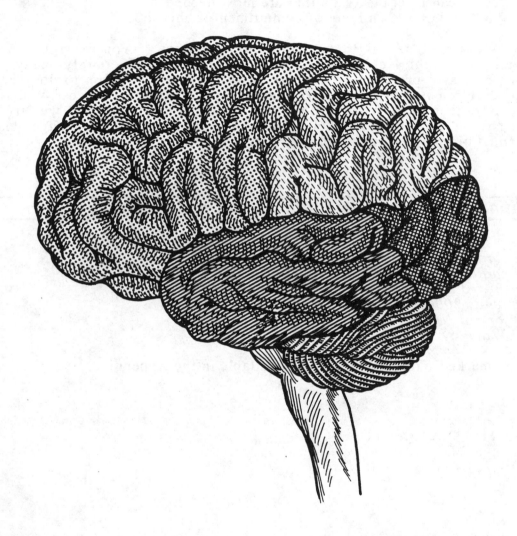

# 2

# Learning & the Human Brain

## It All Starts Between the Ears

Are you curious about how your students learn? You're not alone. Ninety percent of the books written on the human brain have been written in the last five years. There are literally thousands of them! What do you realistically and practically need to know? This chapter reveals the most important principles about the brain and how we learn.

## Our Unique Brain

Your brain is about the size of your two fists held next to each other. It's soft, pink, mostly water and weighs about three pounds. The brain of each of your learners is as individual as a fingerprint. It contains a lifetime of unique experiences, meanings, beliefs, models and data. This represents quite a challenge and shows the limitations in uniform group instruction. This unique brain develops on different but normal timetables which can be years apart in developmental stages.

*Lock-step, assembly-line learning violates*
*a critical discovery about the human brain:*
*each brain is not only unique, but is also*
*growing on a very different timetable*

In addition to the "in the moment" differences in physiology, neural wiring and biochemical balance, every brain is on a different timetable of development. For some brains, the "normal" time to learn to read is age two. For another, the "normal" time is age six. There can be, in fact, *a spread in differences up to two and even three, years in completely normal developing brains.*

## It's No Blank Slate

Are we born with a blank brain? No. Researchers have discovered how much of our survival learning is built-in, just as is an animal's ability to find food. It turns out the brain has been uniquely, genetically pre-programmed for a great deal of learning. Research suggests that our basic learning skills for math, language and physics models may be "hard-wired" into our brain. Part of our role, as teachers is to help draw out that learning. The word "education" comes from the Latin word, "*educare*," to draw out.

## Unlimited Potential

Your learners are far more capable than ever imagined. Each successive study of the brain's potential has documented that previous studies were often too modest. The brain has about one hundred billion (100,000,000,000) cells! When all linked together the number of connections our brain can make is variously estimated to be from $10^{14th}$ power (a hundred trillion), to $10^{800th}$ power (more than the estimated number of atoms in the known universe).

## A Biochemical Factory

The brain cells connect with other cells through branching out and connecting with nerve strands called dendrites. Learning is actually the split second chemical reactions of sodium and potassium at the moment of dendritic interaction. Bigger brains are not necessarily better. Einstein's brain was average sized. But he had more connections and more glial cells, the support cells that "lubricate" our thinking. The specific combination of nutrients, chemicals and hormones is the primary determiner of the quality of learning.

## Enriching the Brain

The brain is quite malleable throughout life. The brain can be nourished and developed well into old age. In fact, there's no reason to let up. Even at age 80 and 90, your brain can still be youthful and quick if you challenge and use it. The good news is that our brain is not fixed in it's ability to learn or think. You can improve it with physical or mental exercise.

In fact, you can physically change the structure of the brain through enriching experiences in as short as a week. Stimulate the brain with multi-sensory experiences, novelty and challenge. Our brains are also enriched by specific nutrition, positive social bonding and feedback in our learning environments. The effects of enriched brain development often diminish after 2-4 weeks unless challenge and novelty is maintained. Dull classrooms are out! Multi-sensory, colorful, intriguing environments are in!

## Feeding the Brain

There are specific nutrients that the brain needs for maximum learning. These include, as a beginning, sufficient water and physical rest. The brain also needs tyrosine-rich protein, selenium, boron, B vitamins, fructose and omega-3 fatty acids. These can be found in fish, eggs, wheat germ, brazil nuts and cottonseed oil. It is impaired by excessive carbohydrates (which triggers the release of serontonin, a relaxant), saturated fats (learning drops by 20%) and sugars (creates metabolic swings). In general, the brain loves exercise, fresh water, oxygen and protein.

## Left and Right Brain

The original work of left and right brain researchers has been updated by new research. We now know that we are usually using both sides of the brain in nearly every activity. It's just a matter of degree. Most people process music in their right hemisphere, but not musicians. They process more on the left side because they analyze the composition more. Avoid generalizations about left and right brain activities. We now know that most activities do use both sides of the brain. We do use the left brain to deal with parts, learning in sequences. The right brain is best with wholes and random learning.

We all have 90 minute cycles for deep and light sleep which continue throughout the day. It's just that we're more awake. Each peak signifies more dominate left or right hemisphere activity. This means every 90 minutes certain of your learners are more likely left hemisphere dominant, others more right hemisphere dominate. But every learner may be on a different timetable. You can affect their timetables through engagement of emotions and physical activity.

# Three Parts of Our Brain

Our brain acts as if we actually have three brains in one: the lower brain (often called "reptilian," it includes the brain stem and cerebellum), the mid-brain (often called "limbic or mammalian" area: amygdala, hippocampus, hypothalamus, pineal gland, thalamus, nucleus accumbens) and the neomammalian (the cerebrum & neocortex, often referred to as the "thinking cap").

While the three areas have some vagueness in their biological boundaries, their functions are clearly different. Dr. MacLean's triune brain theory provides a useful model for understanding and reaching the learner's brain.

The easiest way to understand the three parts of the brain is to think of an office building. Let's say the lower level has maintenance and custodial workers. They make sure the building has heat, electricity, air and is structurally safe. On the middle level we have the employees who provide the daily needs, the "what's real," the feelings, the energy, the motivation and the life-blood of the business. The top level contains the executive management who understand trends, forecasts, are the most creative and do the long-term planning. The brain itself is quite similar in its functions.

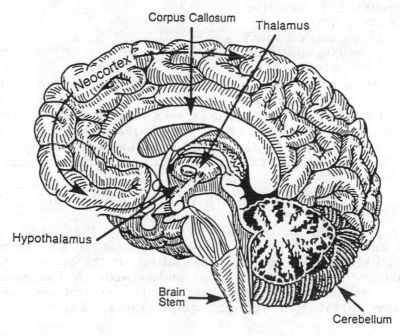

13

The lowest area, known as the reptilian brain, comes up from the spinal cord and is about the thickness of your middle finger. It's called that because its behaviors are very similar to those of a cold-blooded reptile. It is instinctive, fast-acting and survival-oriented. It's the part of the brain that's responsible for student behaviors such as:

- social conformity... common hairstyles, clothes, etc.
- territoriality... defending "my stuff, my desk, my room"
- mating rituals... flirting, touching, attracting another
- deception... often forms of subverted aggression
- ritualistic display... trying to get the social attention of peers
- hierarchies... the dominance of leaders, "top dog" behaviors
- social rituals... the repetitive & predictable daily behaviors

The mid-brain area is known as the mammalian brain. It contains the amygdala, hippocampus, thalamus, hypothalamus, pineal gland and some scientists believe several other key parts. It is the part of the brain most responsible for:

- social bonding and attachments from parental bonding
- our hormones, feelings of sexuality
- our emotions, both positive and negative
- what is true, valid and what we feel strongly about
- our contextual memories
- immediate expressiveness
- long-term memory

The cerebrum and the neocortex covering it are the upper 80% of the brain. The neocortex is about the size of a double-sided newspaper sheet, but it's wrinkled to fit around our cerebrum. We usually call this area of the brain our "thinking cap." It includes the frontal, occipital, parietal and temporal lobes and provides us with the abilities we often think are most human:

- thinking, reflection, consciousness
- problem-solving, computations
- language, writing and drawing
- long-range planning, forecasting
- visualizing, envisioning
- reading, translating and composing
- creativity in art, music and theater

Each of the three areas of the brain influences the other. The part of the brain with the highest priority for behavior (survival) is the brain stem or reptilian brain. If a brick is thrown at your head, the neocortex asks what is the size, color, origin and weight. The limbic brain feels afraid or angry but *the reptilian brain will always override the other two brains' tendencies when it comes to survival*. It simply says to your body, "Duck, now!" That's quite a useful survival response!

## The Brain Stem (Reptilian Brain)

Computer generated images show very clearly that under threats, anxiety, negative stress and induced learner helplessness, the brain operates differently. There is increased blood flow and electrical activity in the brain stem and cerebellum area and decreased activity in the mid-brain and neo-cortex. That means the brain has "minimized." You get more predictable, rote, knee-jerk reaction behaviors when the brain senses any threat that induces helplessness. Survival always overrides pattern-detection and problem-solving. This fact has tremendous implications for learning.

Since all areas of the brain are still being used (it's simply a matter of degree), the expression "minimized" may be much more accurate than "downshifted." It is less capable of planning, pattern-detection, judgment skills, receiving information, creativity, classifying data, problem-solving and other higher-order skills. It's as if your open, receptive arms suddenly close down to much new information. The brain is likely to "minimize" under the following conditions:

- potential physical harm from classmates, staff, family, others
- intellectual threats (ideas being attacked, questioning potential)
  a test or essay returned with derisive comments
  lack of information to meet the task requirements
- emotional threats (feelings or self-esteem under criticism)
  potentially embarrassing moments
  reward systems that threaten withdrawal if not achieved
- cultural-social threats (disrespect)
  isolated from peers, working by oneself
  unable to pursue personal values at school
  limited chance to utilize meaningful personal life
- resource restriction
  constricting time deadlines for performance

When your brain perceives "alarm" or "danger," the body reacts instantly. In these types of intense, stressful or threatening situations, the hormone adrenaline is released from the adrenal glands. They are right above the kidneys and inject adrenaline into the bloodstream immediately. This instantly speeds up your heart rate, making a greater blood supply available to the large muscle groups. The immune system is temporarily suppressed as are higher-order thinking skills. This process gets your body ready for immediate fight or flight - there is no higher-order behavioral choice being made. This is the reptilian brain in action.

You observe reptilian-brain behaviors when expressed as playful or taunting games, compulsion to follow daily routines, tropistic behaviors (fads, cliques), preening for better attractiveness, informal debates over meaningless subjects, competition for approval, informal role-plays, a learning environment which is "nested" like an animal's home - the "It's my stuff," and "I'm top dog" type behavior, learners flocking in teams, flirting with each other and adhering to group trends. Traditionally, teachers invest a great deal of energy combating the ever-evolving, counter-productive rituals. There are alternatives.

Rituals can fill the needs of the learners without being counterproductive to learning. Brain-based learning environments and teaching strategies avoid problems. They focus on understanding the brain and working with its natural tendencies instead of constantly suppressing and conflicting with them. You might focus on the following:

- Creating a brain-affirming learning climate
- More personally meaningful projects of choice
- The use of productive rituals
- An absence of threat, rewards and artificial deadlines
- Provide resources needed for learning
- Allow students multi-status learning with self-assessment

Some reptilian brain behaviors are going to occur regardless of what you do. Many of them can be destructive. Accept the need for these rituals, but not necessarily the content of them, especially if they are negative. You have the power to provide alternative productive outlets for what are basically powerful, biological expressions. Examples include:

1. Establish new, positive and productive rituals such as: arrival and beginning rituals (music fanfare, positive greetings, special handshakes, hugs, etc.)
2. Special organizational rituals (team or class names, cheers, gestures, games, etc.)
3. Situational rituals (e.g., applause when learners contribute), and closing or ending rituals (songs, affirmations, discussion, journal writing, cheers, self-assessment, gestures, etc.)

# Learning With The Limbic Brain

Our mammalian brain the mid-brain, is not one but several related areas including: the amygdala, hippocampus, thalamus, hypothalamus and the pineal gland. Some say it also includes the top of the reticular formation. The mammalian brain is complex, widely distributed, and powerful. Combined, these areas regulate our immunity, hormones, sleep cycles, appetite, sexuality, emotions and more. Our mid-brain area may be the glue that holds our whole system together. The carriers of our emotions are peptide molecules which are composed of a chain of amino acids (shorter than protein chains). *There is a far greater number of neural fibers extending FROM the mid-brain into the neocortex than there are going from the neocortex INTO the mid-brain.* From a survival viewpoint, this makes sense - when you feel strong fear, the brain places a priority on that emotion over any other information. This is important evidence that:

*Emotions are more important and powerful to the brain than higher-order thinking skills... learning and meaning is driven by feelings; the brain is virtually a "box of emotions"*

Maybe the most amazing thing about this part of the brain is: while all of us can be presented with evidence that something is true, it is not verified in our own world until we *feel* that it is true. In spite of all we have learned from reason, science, logic or common sense, we do not feel that anything is true until our mid-brain, the limbic portion which deals with emotions, says that it is true.

Many other researchers including McGaugh, Pert, MacLean, O'Keefe, Damasio and Nadel have written about the critical role of emotions in learning and the link between cognitive data and emotions. Dr. Paul MacLean, pioneer in brain research, says that the most disturbing thing about the way the brain is "wired up" is the limbic system which insists that ultimately the learner must *feel that something is true before it is believed.* MacLean says with puzzlement:

*"The limbic system, this primitive brain that can neither read nor write, provides us with the feeling of what is real, true and important"*

In a learning context, the engagement of emotions can help the brain to "know what it knows," to give the needed stamp of approval. Listen for expressions that let you know that others are processing the veracity of an experience. Someone says that "It just doesn't feel right." Another says, "I'll believe it when I see it." A third says, "Wait 'til he hears about this." These phrases indicate an attempt to feel

16

convinced about something. Only then will there be actual belief. The new research on emotions is that it is a key part of the logic and reasoning process. In other words, separating emotions from logic is not only nearly impossible but also detrimental to the brain. Here's what the newest research says about emotions: while too much emotion in our thinking can be detrimental, a lack of emotions can also impair clear thinking.

*We used to think of emotions and logic*
*as being opposites or a bad combination...*
*the new research validates the critical role*
*of emotions in the thinking process*

Increased learner self-confidence follows, along with intrinsic motivation for future learning. Many rituals that celebrate the learning can do more than just make the learning fun, they can also seal the information and experiences in the brain as real and worth remembering.

Include simple opportunities for learners to engage emotionally after a learning experience. It could be learner enthusiasm, "high fives," acknowledging their partner, dramas, role-plays, quiz shows, debates, impactful rituals and simple celebrations. It could even be as simple as an enthusiastic learner conversation about the topic. The key is simple, but critical: engagement of emotions leads to learners "knowing that they know it." That leads to self-confidence and the motivation to learn more.

# The "Higher Order" Brain

When you see a picture of the brain, or a brain in a jar, the bulk of what you see is mostly the wrinkled neocortex wrapped around the cerebrum. It has four dominant areas.

1. Frontal lobe: problem-solving, will power, planning
2. Parietal: reception of sensory information
3. Occipital: primarily deals with vision
4. Temporal: deals with hearing, language & some memory

This part of the brain is split into two halves, the left and right hemisphere. The cerebrum is covered by the neocortex. This "thinking cap", which is about the size of a rumpled up newspaper, is 1/8" thick and covers the cerebrum. The key characteristic of the neocortex is the ability to detect and make patterns of meaning. This process involves deciphering cues, recognizing relationships and indexing information. The clues that the brain assembles are best recognized in a Gestalt format, not in a digital "adding up" process. In short, the brain is not very good at handling isolated, sequential bits of information. Of course, many teachers offer a great deal of that. That is both boring and frustrating to the learner.

*The brain's capacity and desire to make or*
*elicit patterns of meaning is one of the keys*
*to understanding & promoting learning*

Hart reminds us that "...pattern recognition depends heavily on what experience one *brings to* a situation" (emphasis added). These patterns must continually be revised, altered or updated as new experiences add information, insights and corrections. In fact, Hart says that learning is the extraction of meaningful patterns from confusion. In other words, figuring things out *in your way*. Humans never really cognitively understand or learn something, with the exception of motor and procedural learning as a infant, until they can create a personal metaphor or model.

## Hormonal Influences

Our brain cannot maintain learning attentiveness continually. It is affected by normal fluctuations in nutritional and hormonal-related brain chemistry. These fluctuations occur in cycles of approximately 90 minutes across the entire 24 hour day. At night we all experience periods of "deep sleep," REM time, and light sleep. During the daytime, *these cycles continue, but at a level of greater awareness*. Even animals have these periods of basic rest and activity.

A woman's 28-day menstrual cycle may explain why some learning succeeds at specific times and some doesn't. During the first 14-day half of the menstrual cycle, the hormone estrogen alone is present. Estrogen specifically promotes more active brain cells, increases sensory awareness and increases brain alertness. The brain, flooded with this hormone, experiences feelings of pleasure, sexual arousal, well being, enthusiasm and self-esteem. Researchers suggest this may be the optimal time for female learning.

## Our Brain Needs Deep Rest

The brain can become more easily fatigued when conditions for learning are weak. To get the brain's best performance, it needs deep physiological rest, the kind in which you are "dead to the world." Students from abusive families, areas of high crime, those with high stress parents, in overcrowded homes, those affected by divorce, the death of a loved one, violence or poor nutrition are especially impacted. Other research indicates that sleep time may affect the previous day's learning. By cutting nighttime sleep by as little as two hours, your ability to recall may be impaired the next day. The rule holds truer for complicated and complex material than it does for familiar or simple material. Some scientists speculate that sleep gives your brain time to do some "housekeeping" and rearrange circuits, clean out extraneous mental debris and process emotional events.

These principles give you a better idea of what the brain is like. It's not at all like a computer. It's more like a rain-forest jungle. It has no central command center, no boss or ultimate authority. It has overgrown areas of "intellectual weeds" and can be encouraged to grow in many new areas. It has its own seasons, own systems of parasites and a whole set of complex interdependent relationships. Our brain is quite complex and the better we understand the complexity, the easier our job will become.

## Guidelines for Better Learning

How much do you need to know about learning to be an effective teacher? Some knowledge, it turns out, can be a powerful ally in your work. By understanding the brain's natural operating principles, you will be better able to teach to the brain. Learning will go up dramatically, discipline problems will drop and the joy of learning will stay intact. The basic profile of how we learn might be illustrated something like this:

## Personal History
*(beliefs, experience, values, knowledge)*

**+**

## Present Circumstances
*(environment, feelings, people, context, goals, moods)*

**+**

## Input (5 senses)
*(visual, auditory, kinesthetic, olfactory or gustatory)*

**+**

## Processing (learning preferences)
*(left or right hemisphere, limbic, abstract or concrete)*

**+**

## Meaning
*(To get it, we connect experience & form conclusions AND
we detect or create patterns, that gives us a feeling)*

**+**

## Response (7 intelligences)
*(verbal-linguistic, spatial, bodily kinesthetic, musical-rhythmic,
intrapersonal, mathematical-logical, interpersonal)*

Volumes of literature have been written on the theory of learning. It is not the purpose nor the scope of this book to duplicate or illuminate all the current theories of how we learn. However, you may find it quite valuable to discover some of the key principles of the brain's operation that encourage learning. For the sake of brevity and clarity, here are 11 key principles of our brain and learning.

## Stress and Threat Impair Learning

When we're happy, sad, stressed, fearful or experience any other emotion, our body releases into our bloodstream various chemicals to help us deal with the event. For example, under fear states, it typically releases adrenaline to prepare the fight or flight response. Because our brain is run by chemicals, it's impacted dramatically by changes in our moods. They reduce our brain's capacity for understanding, meaning, memory and higher order thinking skills. In short, a stressful and threatening class climate dramatically impairs learning. Learners are threatened by loss of approval, helplessness, rewards, criticism, lack of resources and what the learner feels is a hopeless deadline.

## Emotions Run the Brain

Learning is not just mental, our learning and meaning are run by feelings. Bad ones negatively flavor all attempts at learning. Good ones create an excitement and love of learning. The dominant determiner of our behavior is determined by our body's hormones; and they create the emotions. Emotions determine why we learn and if we are confident that we know it. Most importantly, we only believe something and give it meaning when we feel strongly about it. Our brain gives an attentional priority to all emotionally-charged information. Our emotional brain tells us what is true and what is not true. One researcher claims that our brain "...is just a box packed with emotions."

*Our "thinking cap" (the neocortex)*
*is strongly run by patterns, not facts*

Our upper brain, the neocortex, does what we call the "higher order" thinking skills. Yet it needs something very different than other parts of the brain. It is a pattern-detecting and pattern-making organ that is continually seeking meaning by organizing words, shapes, numbers and ideas into a meaningful pattern.

*The brain craves information only as a*
*means... the means of forming or creating*
*conclusions or patterns of meaning*

We learn best with larger learning themes, fuller, complete patterns and interdisciplinary relationships. We do most poorly when we "piecemeal" learning into linear, sequential math facts and other out of context information lists. In short, any lesson which is designed as a simplistic, "fact-oriented" lesson plan is poorly designed for today's learner.

## We Learn Multi-path &
## Simultaneous Multi-modal

The brain simultaneously operates on many levels, processing all at once a world of color, movement, emotion, shape, intensity, sound, taste, weight, and more. It assembles patterns, composes meaning and sorts daily life experiences from an extraordinary number of clues. This amazing multi-processor can be starved for input in a typical classroom. Why? It's capable of far more information, experiences and stimulus than it is given.

*Learning takes no time at all...*
*it's not learning that takes all the time*

Learning is visual, auditory, kinesthetic, conscious and non conscious. The brain is rarely over-stimulated in a classroom. The issue of learning styles is less important in this context. Why? The brain learns best on many pathways at once. The best learning is the immense variety of experience from rich, multi-sensory real-life stimulation. Your classroom is best when it is interesting, rich, noisy, busy and real-life. In fact, the best classroom is the outdoors. Can you take your students there?

## Our Brain is Not Designed For
## Typical Rote, Semantic Memory

Far too often, teachers are still using the old model: teacher teaches, students memorize for the test. That's a waste and a crime. The brain is very poorly designed for traditional textbook memory approaches. But it can recall well if you know how to use your natural recall. Our brain's memory is best in contextual, episodic event-oriented situations which include motor learning, location changes, music & rhythm. Ordinarily primary school teachers maximize this type of learning. It makes sense for ALL teachers of all ages.

Researchers conducted experiments to discover whether the time of day affects memory. They found that we incorporate two different types of memory into our learning: literal and inferential. In the morning we seem to favor literal memory and in the afternoon our brain is better at integrating knowledge with what we already know.

## All Learning is Mind-Body

The old model was to keep learning mental, our bodies separate. Researchers now tell us how important our whole self is to learning. Our mood, eye patterns and diet affect learning. Our physiology, state, posture and breathing also affect our learners. To learn to learn better, we'll want to learn more to use the mind-body relationship. You may want to manage and read states better and teach learners how to better manage their own states (feelings, posture, breath, etc.). Eye patterns affect our learning, so does nutrition and so does our hormone levels.

## The Brain is Poorly Designed
## For Formal Instruction

How much did you learn and retain from high school or college? Usually the answer is, "Just enough to get my degree." Everything else you learned, you chose to because it was fun. Our brain is genetically programmed to learn the behaviors needed to be learned for your perceived survival. Your survival may be physical, social, intellectual or emotional. Naturally, the brain can learn what it wants to learn when choosing to. Sound obvious? It's best that we focus on learning, not instruction or teaching, to encourage the brain to learn more and develop better thinking skills.

## Our Cycles and Rhythms

Our brain is designed for ups and downs, not constant attention. Hormones, diet, emotions and chemistry continually rigger fluctuations in attention, memory and learning. The terms "on" or "off" task are irrelevant to the brain. We learn best with *choices* of when to learn, since individual learners are on different chronological, biological and hemispheric timetables.

*Learning is best when alternating focused and*
*diffused activities... constant focused learning becomes*
*increasingly wasted over time... in fact, the whole notion*
*of "time on task" is biologically wrong and*
*educationally irrelevant*

The brain seems to have a natural learning pattern of a pulse. How long is best for a focused activity like a lecture? Use the age of the learner in minutes. The maximum, even for adults, is about 20-25 minutes, say researchers. The brain learns best when the learning is interrupted by breaks of 2-5 minutes for diffusion or processing. For example, a ten year-old is good for about ten minutes of focus time and 2-5 minutes of diffusion (group work, individual time). A six-year old is best with about six minutes of focus, 1-3 minutes diffusion (play time).

# Assessment

Most of what is critical to the brain and learning is tough to assess. The most valuable and best learning is often the creation of content and cultural biases, working models, weighted values, complex patterns, learning-to-learn skills and interdisciplinary relationships. These are rarely assessed and rarely included in traditional assessments. Later in the book, we'll talk about what the brain is really learning and better forms of assessment.

# Alternate Relax-to-Energize

Our brains are constantly running on two learning cycles, says one researcher. The first is a "low to high energy" cycle and the second is a "relaxation to tension" cycle. These two cycles dramatically affect our learning and perception of ourselves, he says. Thayer says learners can focus better in the late morning and early evening. Yet they are more pessimistic in middle to late afternoon. Our thinking can get unrealistically negative at certain low times and quite positive during high cycles.

Another researcher says the activation and suppression of cerebral/limbic structures is key to the success of a learner. He says the relaxing effects of a positively suggestive learning climate are key to "reducing the vigilance intensity to an optimum by activating the serontonin-energetic systems or suppressing the catecholaminegetic systems." Translated, this means the brain stays alert and relaxed for learning but not anxious and hyper-stressed.

# Learning is Holistic

For years, scientists gathered information about the role nutrition, exercise, attitude, lifestyle, posture and emotions play in learning. There are studies which consistently verify the role of background, beliefs and emotions in learning. There is research on the role of exercise and stimulation by Diamond and Greenough. Others claim that learning is linked to our hormones and biochemical rhythms. Connors and Healy remind us about the role of nutrition. The compilation of that research is persuasive and compelling:

*All learning involves our body, our emotions,*
*our attitudes and our health... brain-based learning*
*says that we must address these variables*
*more comprehensively*

Holistic learning means that we are learners with feelings, beliefs, food cravings, personal problems, attitudes and various levels of learn-to-learn skills. While the old academic model addressed primarily the intellectual part of learners, the new prevailing model says we learn with our minds, heart and body. It also says that the better we deal with all of these issues, the more effective we'll be in teaching and learning.

22

Recent brain research suggests we are far from a "learning machine." Instead, our learning and physical performance are dramatically affected by our biological rhythms. Orlock says that we have temporal cycles of the mind and body that correspond to lunar and solar cycles. We have a 24-hour solar cycle and a 25-hour lunar cycle that affect us in countless ways, including cell division, pulse rate, blood pressure, mood swings, concentration and learning ability. In addition, these cycles influence memory, accident rate, immunology, physical growth, reaction time and pain tolerance.

## Additional Resources for Further Study and Follow up

*Awakening Your Child's Natural Genius* by Armstrong (Putnam)
*It's All in Your Head* by Barrett (Free Spirit Publishing)*
*Use Both Sides of the Brain* by Buzan (Penguin)*
*Making Connections: Teaching & The Human Brain* by Caine & Caine (Addison-Wesley)*
*MindShifts* by Caine, Caine & Crowell (Zephyr)*
*Decartes' Error* by Damasio (Putnam)
*Quantum Learning* by DePorter (Dell)*
*The Learning Revolution* by Dryden & Vos (Jalmar Press)*
*Human Brain & Human Learning* by Hart (Books for Educators)*
*The Creative Brain* by Herrmann (Ned Herrmann Group)*
*Brain-Based Learning & Teaching* by Jensen (Turning Point)*
*The Learning Brain* by Jensen (Turning Point)*
*What Infants Know* by Mehler & Dupoux (Blackwell)
*Inner Time* by Carol Orlock (Birch Lane Press)
*The Amazing Brain* by Ornstein and Sobel (Houghton-Mifflin)
*Superlearning* by Ostrander & Schroeder (Dell)*
*Accelerated Learning* by Rose (Dell)*
*Open Mind, Whole Mind* by Samples (Jalmar)*
*Three Pound Universe* by Teresi and Hooper (Tarcher)

* Items marked with an asterisk are available in the Appendix.

23

# *3*

## Learning Styles Made Easy

### How Important Are They?

A learning style is a preferred way of thinking, processing and understanding information. If you had to learn biology, would you rather watch a video, listen to a lecture or work in a lab? Researchers found that learners scored "significantly higher" in the way that fit their own particular learning style. A report of the New York State Board of Regents' Panel on Learning Styles said that it is essential to alter teaching strategies to meet a more multi-cultural global society. Were you taught to present things in a logical, sequential order? That's the "kiss of death" for many learners.

*Seventy-five percent of teachers*
*are sequential, analytic presenters...*
*and 70% of all their students*
*do not learn that way*

Many studies have been done that suggest that certain student learning styles will virtually guarantee school success and others will doom a learner to failure. Learners who are field-independent and have a reflective cognitive style are far more likely to succeed in a traditional school context. Start with a more global overview, and then go to the sequential style. In order to reach both global and sequential types of learners, one must use both approaches.

*The easiest way to reach alll of your learners*
*is simple: provide both variety and choice*

There are many learning style profiles available today. Each of them have their strong points. The reason that they are so different is that they are assessing different things. Like the story of the six blind men and the elephant, each has a different opinion of what they are holding. Some are assessing the input process, others the cognitive filters, others the processing and others the response styles. The learners below exemplify many different styles. After you take a look at them, turn to the next page and get an overview of the five most well-known learning style models.

# Bandler-Grinder

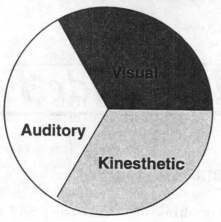

Visual

Auditory

Kinesthetic

# Herrmann

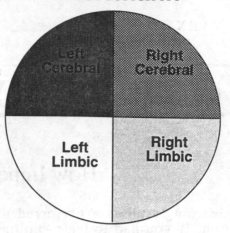

Left Cerebral

Right Cerebral

Left Limbic

Right Limbic

# Dunn & Dunn

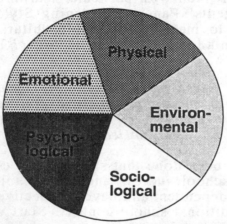

Physical

Emotional

Environmental

Psychological

Sociological

# Gregorc/Butler

Concrete Random

Concrete Sequential

Abstract Random

Abstract Sequential

# 4-MAT System

If (concrete to active)

Why (concrete to reflective)

How (abstract to active)

What (abstract to reflective)

The human brain actually does not just have a single "learning style." Humans are far more complex than that. We use many styles, depending on the circumstances and survival needs. To get a more accurate understanding of how we actually learn, it makes more sense to sub-divide the learning process into four appropriate categories. They are the following:

**1. CONTEXT.** The **circumstances surrounding the learning** provide important clues about what will happen during the learning. For example, are temperatures, social conditions or relationships important? The learning style profile that does this best is Dr. Rita and Kenneth Dunn's Profile.

**2. INPUT.** All learners have to have some **input to initiate the learning.** But we only have five senses. The input is most likely either visual, auditory, kinesthetic, olfactory or gustatory. Although all two month-old babies are gustatory learners, less than 1% of all child-, adolescent- or adult learners use it as their dependent or preferred source. The same can be said for olfactory input (example: dogs are great olfactory learners!). The input has to be either external (from an outside source) or internal (you create it yourself, in your own mind). Visual external would be you looking outward, visual internal would be you visualizing. The model that is the most useful for this information is the Bandler-Grinder model.

Samples says that we have many other senses including the vestibular (repetitious movement), magnetic (ferromagnetic orientation), ionic (electrostatic atmospheric charges), geogravimetric (sensing mass differences), proximal (physical closeness) and others. It is suggested that infants may actually possess all of these senses. Early conditioning tells them which ones are "socially correct" or "culturally appropriate." Perhaps in other societies, people would use different senses or a wider range of them.

**3. PROCESSING.** This is the way you handle the actual **manipulation of the data** which comes in. You can process in frameworks of global or analytical, concrete or abstract, multi-task or single-task, etc. This is dependent on relative hemispheric dominance, either right or left side. There are several options when it comes to HOW you process the learning. The two models that do this well are the Ned Herrmann Brain Dominance model and the Gregorc/Butler model.

**4. RESPONSE FILTERS.** Once you have taken in the information and processed it, you're likely **to do something** about it. But your mind's response filters will be your very first, nearly intuitive "reasoning" behind what you do. You'll react based on time, risk assessment, internal or external referencing. The models drawn from here are partially 4-MAT and Meyers-Briggs.

As you have discovered, each of the five dominant learning styles models has positive qualities. By themselves, none explain the full learning process. To put it all together, you'd have a new format called "The Global Learning Profile™."

# How Do We Learn?

**Contextual Factors**

Field dependent
Field independent
Flexible environment
Structured environment
Interdependent
Independent
Dependent
Relationship driven
Content driven

**Input Preferences**

Visual external
Visual internal
Auditory external
Auditory-internal
Kinesthetic-tactile
Kinesthetic-internal

**Processing Format**

Contextual-global
Sequential-detailed/linear
Conceptual (abstract)
Concrete (objects & feelings)

**Response Filters**

Externally referenced
Internally referenced
Matcher
Mismatcher
Impulsive-experimental
Analytical reflective

Is this a new learning styles profile? No. It's a more complete grouping of the variables. Right now, each of the terms above may be meaningless to you. Let's take a closer look at them. After each one is described, pause for a moment and reflect on the relationship of it to your own learning style and that of your family or your children. You may even think of a particular student in class you have had or currently teach. It will make each of them far more meaningful.

# Contextual Factors

**Field dependent:** prefers contextual cues; learning presented in natural contexts like field trips, experiments, real life - a street learner, not artificial; learns best in situations where the learning would naturally occur; learns about science by going to museums, doing outdoor experiments, field trips.

**Field independent:** learns in irrelevant contexts; uses computers, textbooks, audio tapes, books; can learn in libraries or classrooms; is comfortable with second-hand and third-hand learning.

**Flexible environment:** can learn well in a variety of different environmental conditions; variables include: lighting (natural or fluorescent), sound, temperature and furniture design, the noise of others talking or music played, sitting in chairs or on the floor, standing or given choice.

**Structured environment:** prefers a more structured environment; has very particular needs for exactly how to learn with minimal tolerances for variations; prefers learning with more certainty from rules, conformity & authority.

**Independent:** prefers to learn alone; can learn with others, but effectiveness is lessened.

**Dependent:** prefers to work with pairs, partners, groups and teams; can work alone but is less effective; works best in a busy, noisy talkative environment with others, where interpersonal relationships are valued.

**Relationship driven:** prefers to like the presenter (WHO delivers the information is more important than WHAT the information is); must build a relationship of trust, credibility and respect BEFORE listening or learning.

**Content driven:** prefers valuable content (it's MORE important than the source of the information); if the learner dislikes the teacher, learning will still go on, as scheduled.

# Input Preferences

**Visual external:** prefers visual input, keeps eye contact with a teacher, posture is upright, creates mental pictures, talks fast in monotones, wants handouts, uses visual terminology like, "See what I mean?" A visual learner is usually a good speller, would rather read than be read to, enjoys writing, prefers neatness, is organized, chin is up, and is less distracted by noise. Do you get the picture? They have a "personal space" and don't like others standing too close. If asked, "Are you hungry?" They might check their watch (to "see" if it's time for them to be hungry!

If we were to describe visual habits, we'd say they likely prefer colorful, thinner clothes. They love handouts, books, computers, overheads, art and photos. They buy a car based on its looks, not the feel. If you're in another room talking to them, they want to come into the room to see you as they talk. They are good at visualization and have trouble with verbal instructions.

**Visual internal:** prefers to "see it" in the mind's eye first. They want to visualize the learning before it's presented. They tend to daydream, imagine and let their mind make many mental pictures prior to more formal learning.

**Auditory external:** prefers input to be auditory, talks constantly, either to self or others, they are easily distracted, they memorize by steps and procedures, head bobs, eyes move to side, greater use of tempo, tonality, pitch and volume... answers rhetorical questions, wants test questions to be put in order learned, can mimic sounds of other's voices, they talk to themselves at night and before they get up in the morning, they often replay conversations in their head.

Math and writing are more difficult. They speak rhythmically, like class discussion, dislike spelling, like to read aloud, enjoy storytelling, remember what was discussed, often mimic tone, pitch, tempo and pace of the teacher. They like social occasions more than others and often are better at recalling jokes and conversations.

**Auditory internal:** prefers to talk to him or her-self before learning about it. "What do I know? What do I think about it? What will this mean to me?" They often hold nearly endless conversations with themselves and have difficulty making up their minds. They are also very strong in metacognition.

**Kinesthetic tactile:** prefers physical input. They want to learn by doing. They're a "hands-on" try it first, jump in and give it a "go" type of learner. They have a commitment to activity or comfort, are in touch with feelings, physical body, have minimal facial expression and talking, use measured words with pauses, slower breathing, like action novels. Can be very active, but the area is often a mess where they are. Uses words like "this feels good" or "let's get a handle on this." More likely to be a big eater. May like active events a lot. This learner is more likely to be relatively right hemisphere dominant. Proximity and personal attention has greater impact. This means learning by doing the task is more interesting than reading about it or hearing about it.

**Kinesthetic internal:** prefers inferential, intuitive, TV, stories and movies or those with a great deal of "heart" and feeling in them. Strong non-verbal communications valued (tonality, tempo, posture, expression, gestures). Greater emphasis on HOW something is said than on WHAT is said. It also means they need to have positive feelings about the task first. Kinesthetic internal learners are less verbally expressive, more physically expressive, less likely to be first to raise their hand in class (because they need to go "internal" to check out their answers before offering them).

Preferred input could also be kinesthetic internal (as opposed to external). That means the learner prefers to first experience feelings about something before learning about it or doing it. They want to experience them on their own, first. One can either feel their way into doing or act their way into feeling. This would be the former.

# Processing Format

**Contextual global:** prefers the big picture, an overview first, key concepts only, relates with all pieces together - holistic, gestalt. This learner wants the relevance, the thematic vision & purpose first. More likely to prefer multi-tasking... means learner prefers to work on many problems, problems and tasks at the same time... attend to one for a while, then switch to another, then back to the same or even another. More likely to be inferential and intuitive... infers meaning, uses kinesthetic internal cues to relate, prefers simple and quick approximation to measure, asks the question "Why be so exact?" They often have a "feeling" for the information.

This learner is often referred to as a "right-brain" learner. A more visual right-brain dominance means a preference for processing in pictures, symbols, icons and themes. This learner has external focus tendencies, with a high degree of distractibility. That encourages the mistaken "at-risk" label; in truth, the learner simply needs to be reached with more multi-tasking, non-verbals, global overviews and stronger relationships in learning.

**Sequential detailed/linear:** prefers things sequenced, small steps at a time, do one thing, then asks "What's next?" Also wants a menu, formula, list of upcoming events, subject material. More likely to be a single task learner... prefers to stay focused on a single problem or task... can work on several tasks only if done in order. More likely to be analytical and word-based, measuring, analyzing, asking Qs, compares, contrasts, knows why and how, wants to fully understand something before doing or deciding on it. Words have specific meanings and the teacher will usually be held to what is said, word for word.

This learner is often referred to as left-hemisphere dominant. It means that they prefer the world of the written word, want clear, detailed instructions and want structured lessons. They tend to focus internally, meaning a lower level of distractibility. They are oriented for the long-term and prefer to know what's coming up each day, hour by hour. These learners excel in math, language, computers and other sequential work.

**Conceptual (abstract):** prefers the world of books, words, computers, ideas, conversations, this learner enjoys talking or thinking but not much "doingness," very much "in the head." This learner often goes into more abstract professions such as writing, college professor or accounting.

**Concrete (objects & feelings):** prefers the world of the concrete: things that can be touched, jumped over, handled and manipulated. Also wants specific examples given, use of hands-on experiential, learns by doing an activity, wants to try things out, wants action, games and movement. This learner prefers to use their hands or body for work: dancer, sculptor, truck driver or actress.

# Response Filters

**Externally referenced:** responds primarily based on what others think. The question often asked is "What are others expecting me to act like, think or say?" They use society's norms and rules for sources of their behavior. Before responding, they ask themselves questions on topics like etiquette and family values.

**Internally referenced:** responds using him or herself as the primary judge or source for behaviors. Their own set of rules may or may not be the same as those of society. Very independent thinker and actor.

**Matcher:** responds by noting similarities, agrees more easily, likes consistencies, finds sameness in relationships, prefers things that belong, go together, make sense and enjoys consistency, habits. This learner will more likely approve of something that has been done before, that fits into an overall plan and that is generally consistent with the rest of the learning.

**Mismatcher:** responds by noting differences, what's off, missing, wrong or inconsistent. They say "But... why not?... or, what if?" They find flaws in the arguments, prefer variety and change; not negative, simply contrarian. More likely to sort incoming information by differences. Mismatchers tend to want to discover exceptions to the rule, find out what's missing, discover what's wrong, off or different. As a result, rules and laws are less potent and "testing" the rules is more common. Mismatchers are skeptical of words like "always, everyone, all, never and no one." Hence you'll hear more responses like, "Yes, but... " This learner wants more variety, enjoys experimenting and abhors traditional lesson plans, predictability and what everyone else is doing.

**Impulsive experimental:** responds with immediate action on thoughts, trial and error, experiential, the pattern is do it, then keep doing it until it is figured out. This learner is more likely to be present oriented.

**Analytical reflective:** responds internally, takes in information, processes it reflectively, a pragmatist, stays at a distance, the classic passive, "stand back and watch" learner. More likely to be past or future referenced. Wants to reflect on the possibilities.

# How To Reach ALL Learning Styles

The Global Learning Profile™ are your variables for teaching and learning. It's the variety of ways the brain is naturally inclined to learn. Don't we all use all of these, at one time or another? Yes, we do. That's why, instead of trying to teach every learner in their dominant learning style, we must remember to offer our students *both variety and choice.* It's that simple. The human brain is a multi-processor. It learns many ways, usually at the same time. Offer your students a variety of learning experiences, from computers to groupwork, from field trips to guest speakers, from independent work to role play. Variety and choice. It's that easy.

In experiments by Torrance and Ball, student learning styles were assessed, and then the students were put through a course to expose them to other methods. Through exposure to right-hemisphere, non-linear learning strategies (imagery, intuition, brainstorming, metaphors, etc.), the learners were able to make more use of their existing capabilities and extend into new areas. The results also showed that the students were able to "change their preferred styles of learning and thinking through brief but intensive training." All of us have altered our own learning style in cases where we simply had to in order to learn. While our dependent input would stay the same, we can be taught to utilize a greater variety of methods to input, process and respond.

Learners often change preferences for how information is presented to them based on the time of day. In a study by the University of Sussex in England, researchers found that detailed and literal learning was better in the morning, when performance was better on tests involving details and exact, precise information. In the afternoon, global learning improved, as did inferential and contextual material.

# Lifelong Learning Style

Another researcher, Grinder, says that while you might use several styles, your preferred (or dependent) style will stay with you for much of your life. Why? It's the one that you learned to use for survival as an infant, so your brain always gives it first priority whenever survival is threatened later on in life, too.
Let's use this example: a fire breaks out in a room. Your immediate, first reaction will be one of the following: 1) visual (quickly size up the situation, looking for exits, others in need, etc.); 2) auditory (start yelling "Fire", giving

directions or screaming); or 3) kinesthetic (start running for the exits or grabbing others to help them out). While you may do all three, one will be an instinctual first reaction. That's your dominant, dependent input preference.

Learning preferences are age-dependent. As a baby, up to six months, all of us were gustatory. Then, as an toddler, ages 2-5, most of us became more kinesthetic. All preferences are learned early in life; researchers believe ages 2-5 seal in our dependent profile. As a young child, ages 5-9, most of us became more auditory. About 40% of learners develop into visual learners by secondary schools. Those learners that remained kinesthetic often fell behind in instruction or became a behavior problem. Those are often labeled as "developmentally delayed" or hyperactive. More often than not, their brain is NOT delayed. It's just fine, there is simply a great range of what is normal for development.

## Detection and Diagnosis

One of the most often-asked questions is "How can I discover a student's learning strategy?" There are two easy answers: 1) provide choice and they'll choose their favorite; and 2) learn to pay attention to how students respond to what you do. Each one of the learning styles listed above gives clues. Visual learners follow you with their eyes as you move across the room, they watch for visual cues, they want notes and handouts. Mismatchers find differences in what you are doing versus what they think has or should have happened. Start with just one learning style. Identify as many students as you can who have that one. Then pick another and work with it. Over time, you'll have the process down to an art. As you develop your own eyes and ears for these learners, you'll find it increasingly easy to identify them, often non-consciously.

With so many learning strategies mentioned, and so many others still unrecognized, it could seem fruitless to pursue them all. Yet it's much easier than it seems. Remember the brain is a multi-processor and is good at integrating parallel, simultaneous inputs. The secret to satisfying your learners is simple. I didn't say it was easy, but it is simple:

*Provide choice in how learners can learn*
*& make sure you provide a variety of methods*
*when you don't offer choice*

Any time you get the least frustrated with an individual student, take a moment to learn what their learning strategy is. A few simple questions will uncover it.

- What is trying to be learned? (a skill, a concept, a value etc.)
- What are the essential components of it? (each of the micro-steps)
- What is a similar or parallel activity to the learning activity being attempted?
- Is it a type that the student has already done successfully?
- Apply the strategy that the student used before to succeed in the new activity.
- Utilize the same resources from the earlier success to the new one.

Here's an example of uncovering a learning strategy. On the playground, a student was afraid to climb up a tall slide. Even though the climbing was probably quite safe, he was too afraid to leave the ground and to do the activity. The teacher solved the problem like this:

TEACHER: "Is there any reason you don't want to climb the ladder?" (information gathering)

STUDENT: "Yes, it's too dangerous."

TEACHER: "But you'll be in a safe place." (attempts an obvious rebuttal to gather more data)

STUDENT: "It's still too dangerous." (Discovers it's not a matter of logic, it's something else - teacher needs more data)

TEACHER: "Have you ever done anything else that was dangerous?" (notice teacher has quit insisting that it's not dangerous - it is, to the student - teacher attempts to find a past parallel activity which included danger, but ended up fun)

STUDENT: "Sure, I ride my skateboard pretty fast." (just the reference the teacher had hoped for...he's a kinesthetic-tactile learner)

TEACHER: "So what. Lots of kids say fast, but HOW FAST?" (teacher challenges student's activity, attempts to elicit risk-taking, braggart part of student)

STUDENT: "Really fast!" (strategy worked)

TEACHER: "How in the world did you ever do that?" (teacher affirms student as a dangerous risk-taker in another context, then asks for the strategy)

STUDENT: "It easy. I start out slow, then just do it." (Jackpot! Student has given you the learning strategy, but teacher elects to verify)

TEACHER: "You mean you learned how to do it by starting slow and working your way up?" (he's a sequential learner, teacher realizes)

STUDENT: "Sure, it's easier that way." (strategy verified)

TEACHER: "Take a look at the ladder once again. Since you seem to learn best in chunks, if you were to climb up just part of the ladder, how far could YOU GO (emphasis on these two words) and still feel safe?" (teacher asks student to participate in selecting chunk size)

STUDENT: "About two steps. But that's all, no more." (chunk size given)

TEACHER: "OK, but do you have enough nerve to do even that much?" (challenge issued to complete first chunk, that appeals to mismatchers)

STUDENT: "Sure, anybody could do that." (student completes the first part of the climb and returns to the ground)

TEACHER: "You did great! Now that you've conquered that, how far could you get on your next time?" (reinforcement, further challenge issued)

STUDENT: "Well, about to there." (Student points to new goal, process continues until student successfully reaches top of ladder in four chunks)

The student here is linear, kinesthetic, mismatcher. He likes challenges, physical activity, but one step at a time. How did I know that? I just asked the right questions. How did I know which questions to ask? I already knew the possible choices of learning styles, so I simply asked the ones that might fit.

Once you know what style you are presenting with, you can begin to include other styles. The most common behavior is that teachers use the teaching style that fits their own learning style. In order to reach more students, you will need to present in a full multi-dimensional, multi-sensory mode that includes many of the major strategies. This comes with practice. When any of the most common ones fail, your experience will guide you to try some of the other possibilities.

# Culturally-Reinforced Learning Styles

All learning styles are culturally reinforced. While this does not guarantee that anyone in that culture will have those same characteristics, it does help you understand others better. In other words, the a higher percentage of that culture will have that learning style. Remember, a culture can be as specific as the middle-aged lumberjacks of Astoria, Oregon. It can be all women (now, that's a very generalized culture!) but remember there are some common values and experiences that cut across boundaries and all women have some shared cultural traits. Not a lot of them, but some.

The following generalizations are only guidelines and *will not* hold up under 100% specific-case scrutiny. Treat each individually - go by first-hand experience. There are many ways to define culture; by wealth, color, geography, genetics, values or simply gender. Women are more likely to be auditory than men. So are Southern Europeans. Northern Asians are more likely to be matchers, as are Midwesterners.

Research suggests Native Americans are strongly right-hemisphere dominant. But not every single one! A higher percentage of Hispanics are kinesthetic. Rural learners tend to be more field dependent. Israelis and Australians have a higher-than-usual percentage of mismatchers. Northern Europeans and Asians are more likely to prefer visual learning. These are merely generalizations and you will want to deal with each learner on an individual basis only. (Please don't write me racist letters about political correctness).

For example, you might discover that (as an example only) Asians are more likely to be "visual, future-referenced" learners. This implies the use of strategies such as reading and other visuals, and the use of future-based motivation ("If we do this today, what we can get tomorrow is...").

As another example (and only just an example), you might find Hispanics or Blacks to be more "present-referenced and kinesthetic learners." Often, a culture will encourage certain styles and have subtle reinforcements such as the "mañana attitude" ("take it easy, we can always do it tomorrow"). This infers the need for more immediate value in the classroom, not long-term benefits. It also infers more "hands-on" learning with a chance to learn-by-doing with less lecture.

Some cultures, such as the American Indians, are more likely to be "past-referenced, right hemisphere learners." In the classroom, this translates to a teaching strategy which builds heavily on tradition, our past and what we have learned from our ancestors. It is also important to deal in wholes, not parts; feelings, not facts; music and ideas, not texts and lists.

We have been vastly underestimating the capacity of the learner. In fact, our expectations may have been too low for all types of learners. Maintain high expectations regardless of the evidence. Teach in many different learning styles so that the potential of every learner is tapped. Then use alternative forms of assessment to provide avenues for those who learn differently. Provide a climate where every learner is respected and nourished. Avoid homogeneous ability grouping. Utilize multi-status and multi-age teamwork.

These groupings below are NOT how each member of these groups learn or act. What is listed is what each culture reinforces. Just because my own culture reinforces mathematics or music, that doesn't mean that I'll turn out to be strong in those. But it does help you understand where I'm coming from. In other words, these are not for you to use for stereotyping, they are for illumionation and insights.

## African-Americans
   field-dependent (use of relevant information in larger context as clues to learn)
   inter-personal relationships (people, personal stake in content vs. issue-only
       oriented)
   more likely auditory-kinesthetic (learns by talking, listening and doing)
   intuitive reasoning (versus inductive or deductive)..present referenced learner.
   majority mismatchers (learn by differences vs. similarities, exception vs. the
       rule)
   often peer pressure to not "act white"...to maintain cultural identity and
       integrity
   feelings & intuition valued (estimate & approximate vs. measure)
   strong non-verbal communications (tonality, tempo, posture, expression,
       gestures)
   high task variability (prefers diverse problem-solving angles, variety of
       stimuli)

## Asians
   more likely visual learners, future referenced with use of deferred gratification
   field-independent (less contextual clues used)..majority matchers (learn by
       similarities)
   intra-personal relationships (independent preferred)... more likely sequential,
       high-detail
   inductive & deductive reasoning (measure vs. estimate)
   low variability of task preferred (focused on fewer tasks)
   attributes failure to lack of effort vs. lack of ability

## Anglos
   more likely visual-kinesthetic learners...verbal communications stronger than
       non-verbal field independent (less use of contextual clues) intrapersonal
       (independent learners) object-oriented (vs. people oriented)...present-to-
       future referenced
   more likely to attribute failure to combination of a lack of effort and/or ability
   combination match-mismatch (learn equally by similarities & differences)
   low task variability-prefer single-item concentrated tasks
   likely to attribute failure to a lack of effort (if male) ability (if female)

## Hispanics
   field-dependent (use of clues in context)
   interpersonal relationships valued as learning strategy
   peer pressure to not "act white"...to maintain cultural identity and integrity
   more likely a kinesthetic learner... past-to-present referenced
   majority are matchers (learn by similarities)...low-variability of task preferred
   likely to attribute failure to lack of ability, not effort
   intuitive... estimate & approximate vs. measure
   more R-hemisphere dominant as learner

## Native Americans
   field dependent/ past/present/future referencing balanced
   peer pressure to not "act white"...to maintain cultural identity and integrity
   kinesthetic/R-hemisphere "wholistic" outlook...feelings to action oriented
   high non-verbal communications/extended family support
   matcher (learns by similarities)...attributes failure to lack of ability
   low-task variability/intuitive learners
   temporal orientation critically oriented towards strongly cued "cultural time"

A key part of the process is making sure that you work as partners with your students in discovering and eliciting the strategy. You'll learn the kinds of questions to ask and how to draw conclusions from them. Always check out your conclusions and recommendations with actual experience. Then make sure the student knows which strategy is best for her or him. Not only will you be more successful by cooperating with the student, but you are doing a long-term favor for your students when you teach them how to teach themselves. The next time a student is having trouble in a similar situation, chances are, they'll be able to handle it on their own.

## Three keys to understanding learning styles:

1. **The brain learns many ways at once; we do not have a single, dominant lifelong learning style.**
2. **Provide a variety of learning methods; use multiple intelligences as a model.**
3. **Provide choice for your learners so they can choose how they want to learn at least 50% of the time.**

Discovering your students' learning strategies and fulfilling them is both exciting and gratifying. It's an easy job as long as you keep in mind the three keys listed above. You'll be amazed at the difference it makes and it'll truly empower you and your students.

## Additional Resources for Further Study and Follow up

*Learning & Teaching Styles* by Kathleen Butler
*Teaching Students Through Their Individualized Learning Styles: A Practical Approach* by Dunn, Rita & Dunn, Kenneth (Reston Publishing)
*Righting the Educational Conveyor Belt* by Michael Grinder (Metamorphous Press)*
*The Creative Brain* by Ned Herrmann (Lake Lure Books)*
*The 4MAT System* by Bernice McCarthy (Excel )*

* Items marked with an asterisk are available in the Appendix.

38

# 4

# Diversity & Differences

## Learners Who March
## To a Different Drum

This chapter is also about the "square peg and round hole learner." It's about the learner who does not fit on the educational conveyor belt. It might be because of a discipline problem, ADHD, a learning style, a drug abuse problem or even gender differences. This learner is less likely to feel comfortable in a traditional group setting. They are less likely to get good grades. Surprisingly, they do have a chance of succeeding in society as long as you believe in them.

## Matchers and Mismatchers

Our brain either "matches" up with familiar data, "mis-matches" it (differentness, exceptions), or it creates combinations in-between. A learner may learn by similarities (familiarity) or differences (novelty) in varying amounts. Virtually no one does either type of learning 100% of the time, but there are tendencies. About 50% of Americans match and mismatch evenly - they do both with the same frequency. About 10% of the population mismatches constantly and 40% are habitual "matchers." The matchers work at the same job for years, keep the same friends, eat at the same restaurants and do many of the same activities year after year. They use generalizing phrases like "everyone, always, we, never, all." They make generalizing patterns quickly.

The "mismatchers" tend to prefer changes over sameness. They try out new things, go to a different restaurant, take a new route home, and experiment more. They find exceptions to the rule, they use phrases like, "but..." and "not always..." If a sign says "NO Trespassing," a matcher will obey. A mismatcher will wonder "What's in there?" Mismatchers are distinctly different from:

1) divergent thinkers (who tend to be more exploratory and creative, but not as contrarian)
2) skeptics (who tend to question things consistently but are either closed minded or impossible to sway)
3) age-related "phases" (almost all two year-olds say "NO!" to nearly everything, but that's a developmental stage)

4) delinquents (who simply want to be "bad" because of domestic problems, peer pressure, low self-concept, etc.)

The degree to which a nation's population or particular culture (urban, rural, men, women, etc.) matches or mismatches is entirely culturally reinforced. In some cultures, like Japan, it's simply bad etiquette to mismatch, so you have a nation which has a higher percentage of matchers. In Israel, the culture encourages asking questions, finding exceptions and mismatching. Australia has a higher percentage of mismatchers than most countries, to a small degree, because it was used as a penal colony by England. More importantly, it has what is known as the "California greener grass syndrome." That means those who emigrate are often self-selected as being "different thinking" and wanting a change. That's partly what self-selected California's diverse population. In America, more matchers live in the Midwest than any other part of the country. States with relatively high percentages of mismatchers include Vermont, Oregon, California and Washington.

Mismatchers in the classroom tend to focus on differences, exceptions and what is missing. You say to a group that you'll be done in ten minutes. After some time, a learner raises his hand and says "It's been eleven minutes." You pass out some paper. A student, having found the only misspelling on the handout, raises his hand and says, "How come this is spelled wrong?" You ask your students to begin an activity. One says, "Why aren't we doing this the way Mr. Jones's class did it last year?" If you say to them, "You've got two choices." They're thinking, "What's the third?" And those differences can drive matchers crazy (unless they've read this, first).

Most students respect the classroom rules, but mismatchers often break them, almost as if obsessed with trying to find out the answer to the question, "I know the rule, but is there an exception to it?" This kind of response is typical of that made by a mismatcher. Pull that student aside and tell him or her, "Creativity is wonderful. If you are creative in areas other than discipline, it'll keep us both happy and you out of trouble."

Again, rarely is anyone a total "matcher" or "mismatcher." Usually, you'll have learners who "match generally, with some mismatching," or "mismatch generally with some matching." The whole point is to realize that these learners are sorting patterns their way in order to learn. You can easily recognize learners as generally more "matchers" and "mismatchers."

**Those who are matchers tend to:**
   • agree with you more often
   • prefer the familiar, tried and true
   • be uncomfortable with novelty
   • follow rules, stay with the group
   • learn by similarities
   • do what is expected by others

**Those who are mismatchers tend to:**
   • disagree more often
   • prefer novelty, change, a bit of risk
   • sometimes ignore rules and boundaries
   • need differences to understand content

**To deal with those who are mismatching:**
   1) Don't try to "fix" them; they're not broken

40

2) Appreciate and respect their alternative point of view ("Thanks for pointing that out. I hadn't thought of that.")

3) Make sure that they follow the same rules as everyone else. Avoid labeling any learner, since they may vary preferences, depending on stress levels or circumstances. It's best to use "match" and "mismatch" as active, flexible verbs (e.g., "He was mismatching me again," or, "Good mismatch."

We may have labeled countless learners as troublemakers when, in fact, the way they learn is simply by trying to establish a pattern for meaning. Think of the question, "Is this person filling the mold (matching) or trying to break the mold (mismatching)?" The next time a student says, "Hey you misspelled a word on this worksheet," say "Thanks for finding that. If you'd like, you can be in charge of always finding any typos or misprints." Learn to appreciate that mismatchers love to learn, they simply learn by differences, not similarities.

# Multi-Cultural Diversity

Many learners feel that they don't fit in the system. It's easy to feel that way when the system was designed by a different culture than your own. The multi-cultural influence on our educational system continues to build on two fronts. There's the increased awareness as we acknowledge distinctive patterns in Black, Hispanic, Anglo and American Indian cultures. These patterns significantly affect your students' communications and learning styles. Although it's critical to avoid generalizations, you'll find that some background to fall back on is highly useful when a communication seems amiss or you get a response you're unprepared for. Use the following chart as a **guide** but use your own experience as a **rule**.

## *Examples of Conversational Styles*

|  | Blacks | Hispanic | Anglo | Am. Indian | Asian |
|---|---|---|---|---|---|
| Conversational Eye contact | Low | Low | High | Med | High |
| Assertiveness | Moderate | Low | Low-Moderate | Low | Low |
| Ways to Align | Call for unified expression | Call for silence | call for silence | Call for silence | Ask for silence |
| Conversation Style | Direct personal truth-issue oriented | Passive containment | Non-confrontive representative compromising peace oriented | Direct combination issue/truth compromise | Casual calm, historical |
| Use of Emotions | As a valid source of expression | To be held back until confront point | To be managed | To be contained as much as possible | To be avoided |
| Reaction to Heated Dialogues | As long as talking is going on, it's OK verbal threats rarely serious | Extremes: withdrawal or high response to verbal can lead to pent-up violence | Discomfort: threats taken seriously | Discomfort: avoidance | Discomfort: keeping emotion out |

As always, ask, ask and ask. Check things out. Avoid assuming. The purpose of this is to stimulate some openness on the subject, not create stereotypes. You're bound to face these issues: cultural diversity, inclusion and gender treatment inequity. They have been a source of friction and frustration for all sides for many years. In this chapter, we'll examine some of the issues and allow you to come to your own conclusions.

Today's culturally diverse population is a demographic reality, creating economic and social problems. Some also charge that it's a specific cultural problem with a political agenda. Let's take a look at both sides.

1. There are disproportionate school failure rates for students of color.
2. Students most likely to drop out and quit are students of color.
3. The percentage of students of color is increasing in schools.
   In 1995, 1/3 of all students in America were non-white.
4. The dominant educational, social-cultural structure is Anglo.
5. Society either reaps the benefits of educated citizens or pays the social, economic and criminal price of those who are disenfranchised.

There are other points of view to the issue of cultural diversity. While not very popular in many areas, these arguments are often used by those who are against it:

1. The movement is motivated by those who are out of power who simply want more power at the expense of others.
2. Things are not perfect the way they are, but they don't need an overhaul.
3. It's just a big political strategy to gain a political base.
4. The country is designed to absorb other cultures, not change to take on their culture.
5. Those who don't learn or stay in school are simply not motivated, or have weak character or the wrong family values.

What is the right approach to take? You have many considerations. First, how do you feel about the issue? Get informed and learn more about the history, culture and issues of other cultures. Second, what is the school policy regarding multiculturalism? Find out how textbooks are selected, how curriculum is created and what are the state mandates. How do we respond to our culturally diverse populations?

There is new evidence that what we call "race" is very different than what "race is genetically. The landmark book on the topic is *The History and Geography of Human Genes*. Its conclusion: once you remove the genes for skin coloration and physical stature, human "races" are nearly identical! In fact, the variations among individuals is so much greater than those among races, that *the whole concept of race is genetically meaningless.* Surprisingly, sub-Saharan Africans are closer to Southern Europeans than they are to Australian Aborigines. Native American tribes were of three blood lines, genetically, not one. Caucasians are genetically in between the Mongoloids and the Africans. The old ideas about white, yellow and black skinned origins are genetically meaningless.

If that issue is settled, there's only one issue left... the degree of cultural differences. There is no "black" culture, just as there is no "white" culture. There is no one "Hispanic" or "Native American" culture. Among blacks, you'll have urban, rural, liberal, conservative, lower income, middle income and upper income. You'll have the same groupings with every other people of color. In other words, blacks are not a definitive race culture, neither are whites, yellows or reds. Those have been and still are, political designations.

In one school, you'll have different cultures: the upper achievers, the socialites, the athletes, etc. Automatically grouping people of a single color into a culture together creates two things: 1) the illusion that there is a single culture of specified color; and 2) it is separate from the rest of the school. Be careful about assuming just because someone is Chinese that they will act, feel and live in a particular Chinese cultural way.

# Male and Female Differences

If people of color don't even define a single culture, how about genders? Is there a male and female culture? Yes, definitely. There are two points of view on the subject: the sociological and the biological (for the moment, we'll ignore the political one). For a sociological angle, read *You Just Don't Understand* by Deborah Tannen and *Men are from Mars and Women are From Venus* by John Gray. You'll find consistent and dramatic differences in the everyday lives of men and women. They do live in different worlds. Now, let's examine the biological angle for the moment.

There are obvious visible differences between the sexes (usually). Are there differences inside the brain? Much of the research on male and female brain differences has been done by females. In this chapter, it is drawn from many sources including Dr. Jere Levy of the University of Chicago, Dr. Marion Diamond of UC Berkeley, Dr. Doreen Kimura, Dr. Stewart of Concordia in Montreal, Dr. Kolb of the University of Lethbridge in Alberta, Canada, and Dr. LaCoste. All of them have reported clear-cut male-female brain differences. Although some things can safely be said about certain differences, there is still some dispute over the scope and magnitude of other differences. Taken altogether, the evidence suggests that male and female brains are organized along very different lines from very early in life. Variances within the same sex do exist, but certainly not to the same extent as those found between the opposite sex.

*While each brain will have different*
*amounts of sexually differentiated characteristics,*
*the generalizations about differences still hold*

The list below of sexually determined differences makes a strong statement. It seems that post-conception hormonal influences are the primary difference-maker. Not all females are five foot five and not all males are five foot nine. But on the average, males are taller than females. The range of the differences listed below is more like a continuum. In the same spirit of averages, neuroscientists have found many physical differences. Examples of sexually determined differences include:

- length of the nerve cell connectors
- nucleus volume in hypothalamus
- pathways that the neurotransmitters follow
- density of nerve cell strands
- shape of the nucleus in the hypothalamus
- thickness of left and right side of the cortex control centers
- the number of vasopressin neurons in hypothalamus
- thickness and weight of the corpus callosum
- location of control centers for language, emotions & spatial skills

# Different Developmental Stages

In the early years, brain growth rates among both genders may vary from as little as a few months to as many as three years. And there are definite differences in how the female and male brains develop. Therefore, assessing and grouping children chronologically is as ridiculous as it would be to group teachers or business persons chronologically by age in their jobs.

In a study of 200 right-handed children, the boys outperformed the girls on spatial tasks. But linguistically, the girls show earlier dominance than the boys. Boys often have trouble, because of right brain specialization, in learning to read early in life. Since reading is both spatial and linguistic, it makes sense that girls generally learn to read earlier than boys.

*Developmentally, girls learn to talk and read earlier, on the average, than boys do... does this make it right to label the boys "slow learners" or "hyperactive?"*

The brain not only grows differently, it decays differently. We now know that the right brain of females has longer plasticity than that of males. This means it stays open to growth and change for more years in girls than in boys. The degeneration of nerve cells in the male brain precedes that of females by 20 years. Although the rate of loss by females is greater than that of males, it is still not enough to overtake them. The researchers say that their estimates of cell loss are conservative.

There may be a reason why adolescent boys are more physical than adolescent girls. That part of the brain is much more developed in males at that time in their life. For females, the part of the brain used for interpersonal skills is more developed and plays an integral role in teenage girl culture.

# Gender-Differences in Thinking

Researchers report the female brain is very different from the male brain with regard to sensory perception. Males and females almost live in a different world created by the processing of very different sensory information. Females often report having experiences that males don't understand, such as intuition, food cravings or social interaction clues. Literally hundreds of studies have been done to eliminate cultural biases from experiments so that researchers can really tell what are the true differences, not what has been socially programmed.

While there are documented functional differences between females and males, there are still biases which affect infants' early brains. These continue to develop in response to cultural biases. Nature or nurture? It's both! Here is a summary of some differences between males and females:

**Hearing:** The female ear is better able to pick up nuances of voice, music and other sounds. In addition, females retain better hearing longer throughout life. Females have superior hearing, and at 85 decibels, they perceive the volume twice as loud as males. Females have greater vocal clarity and are one-sixth as likely as a male to be a monotone. They learn to speak earlier and learn languages more quickly. Three-quarters of university students majoring in foreign languages are female. Females excel at verbal memory and process language faster and more accurately. Infant girls are more comforted by singing and speech than males.

44

**Vision:** Males have better distance vision and depth perception than females. Females excel at peripheral vision. Males see better in brighter light; female eyesight is superior at night. Females are more sensitive to the red end of the spectrum; excel at visual memory, facial clues and context; have a better ability to recognize faces and remember names. In repeated studies, females can store more random and irrelevant visual information than males.

**Touch:** Females have a more diffused and sensitive sense of touch. They react faster and more acutely to pain, yet can withstand pain over a longer duration than males. Males react more to extremes of temperature. Females have greater sensitivity in fingers and hands. They are superior in performing new motor combinations, and in fine motor dexterity.

**Activity:** Male infants play with objects more often than females. Females are more responsive to playmates. The directional choice, called "circling behavior," is opposite for males and females. In other words, when right-handed males walk over to a table to pick up an object, they are more likely to return by turning to their right. Right-handed females are more likely to return by circling around to their left.

**Smell and Taste:** Females have a stronger sense of smell and are much more responsive to aromas, odors and subtle changes in smell. They are more sensitive to bitter flavors and prefer sweet flavors. Females are more susceptible to the damaging effects of alcohol than males.

# Learning Style and Problem-Solving Differences

Males and females have very different ways of approaching and solving problems. Here is a summary of the research on differences in problem-solving, broken down by gender.

**In general, females do better than males in the following areas:**

1) Mathematical calculation
2) Precision, fine-motor coordination
3) Ideational fluency
4) Finding, matching or locating missing objects
5) Use of landmarks to recall locations in context, on maps

**The problem-solving tasks that favor males are:**

1) Target-directed motor skills (archery, football, baseball, cricket, darts, etc.)
2) Spatial: visually rotating objects
3) Disembedding tests (locating objects, patterns from within another)
4) Mathematical reasoning, word problems
5) Use of spatial cues of distance, direction in route-finding

There are many activities in which females excel over males: assembly, needlework, precision crafting, micro-production, communication, sewing, nursing, pharmacy and many of the arts. On the average, developmentally speaking, girls read earlier than boys. If we actually accounted for differing brains, we'd suddenly find that up to 75% of all boys who are now considered "developmentally slow" would immediately be reclassified as normal. Think of the areas in which males excel: gross motor skills like sports, mechanics, construction and sculpture.

So, are these differences environmental or genetic? There is considerable research going on to determine this. So far, the consensus is that the answer indicates both factors play a role.

**In general, females are more:** multi-tasking, interpersonal, intuitive, matching, high non-verbal, and more likely to attribute failure to lack of ability.

**In general, males are more:** single-task, issue-oriented, visual-kinesthetic, inductive or deductive and more likely to attribute lack of success to opportunity or effort, not ability.

# What Can You Do?

Education should not try to be culture or "gender-bias free." Equal education does not mean that everything should be done the same; it means providing equal opportunity. There are real, physical differences among cultures and between the sexes. Many male-female behaviors make much more sense when considered in the context of brain development.

Eliminate groupings by age or grade. They tend to cause feelings of inadequacy. Learners are being measured against those with developmental advantages instead of by effort. Change expectations. Keep students in age clusters, such as ages 2-4, 5-7, 8-10, 11-13, 14-17.

Become informed. Learn the differences between culturally reinforced stereotypes and real physical differences. Keep expectations high and avoid stereotyping. Change some expectations about behavior and learning. Be holistic and ecological, using a "systems" approach to insure greater success. Educate others about the differences. Many problems may not be problems at all. They may simply be an expression of the "natural" way in which one sex or another really operates. Open up discussions with your colleagues about the research and its implications.

# Attention Deficit Disorder

There are many theories on the causes of ADHD, the attention-deficit hyperactivity disorder. This condition is most typically characterized by learners who are easily distracted, have short memory, are physically active, often talkative, have poor concentration and are low in achievement and productivity. Here are the latest theories on the cause and remedy for this prevalent problem.

The brain stem and limbic systems regulate attention and our brain's ability to pay attention is regulated by complex variations in the efficacy of chemical neurotransmitter molecules. Norepinephrine and dopamine (both catecholamines) are the principal neurotransmitter systems that process attention. Some researchers say that an insufficient number of these molecules may cause hyperactivity.

Learner attentiveness may be optimized with a "normal middle level" of these catecholamines. Stimulant drugs like Ritalin™ work to normalize the brain's reaction to distracting stimuli, improving concentration and focus. While the drug seems to work miracles, some parents are concerned about the principle behind prescribing behavior-altering drugs at an early age. Others are concerned about side-effects.

Barkley says that the disorder is a combination of a "rule-following disorder" (a dislike of following rules) a linkage in the linguistic-motor system created by a genetic disorder where words and actions match up poorly, and a high motivational threshold (it takes a great incentive for seemingly simple tasks). He adds, the disorder is so situational, we may want to redefine what attention deficit really is. In other words, take an ADHD child out of school and put him in a different setting, and his symptoms often disappear.

## Use of Drug Therapy

Some say that although 3-10% of the population supposedly has it, millions of others are undiagnosed. In fact, from 10-27% may have ADHD. More than 80% of the cases are caused by a malfunction within the inner ear system. That area regulates our balance and sensory motor responses, and affects vision. Up to 90% of all problems can be treated successfully by one to four years of drug therapy. While sometimes vitamin B-6 works, Ritalin™ and Cylert™ are the most popular, and they tend to be overprescribed.

By using MRI scans, it was discovered that ADHD children had a smaller corpus callosum, particularly in the region of the genu and splenium and its anterior. Hynd says that "subtle differences may exist in the brains of children with ADHD and that deviations in normal corticogenesis may underlie behavioral manifestations of this disorder." That's a fancy way of saying that "children with attention deficit disorder may suffer from a right hemisphere syndrome." Put simply, the left and right side of the brain don't talk to each other as well as they should.

## A Gender Issue

One neuropsychologist says that since most hyperactive behavior disappears in boys over time, it's a dubious sex-based label. She says that if you factored in the differences in male developmental stages, most boys would not be labeled a problem. There is, in fact, a considerable movement developing worldwide that wants to create more appropriate gender-based learning.

Grinder says that some students diagnosed as hyperactive may, in fact, simply be expressing their particular learning styles. A kinesthetic learner may want to move around, touch, tap, hit, try out and engage his body in almost everything. This learner is more likely to be a male. If the teacher is visual, the movement may be attention-getting and, at times, annoying. To the teacher, this is a "problem student" when, in fact, the student may be normal.

## The Ears Have It

Perhaps the most promising research on hyperactivity and dyslexia comes from researchers who have made strong correlations to inner ear problems. It seems that infection-related fluids (effusion) interferes with hearing which interferes with auditory perception and processing. Levinson's double-blind studies and research led him to discover a 96% incidence of cerebellar-vestibular dysfunction in dyslexics. He has successfully treated many dyslexics with motion-sickness drugs and repatterning exercises.

Some research correlates the disorder to excessive lead in the water supply, emotional problems stemming from inadequate family stability, food additives (especially red dye, aspartame, preservatives and artificial flavors), excess sugar, a couch-potato lifestyle, refined carbohydrates, and excessive television watching. Whichever turns out to be the cause, it will be some time before we know for sure. There is an understandably enormous difficulty in isolating specific behaviors and testing with all the variables.

For example, a student continually gets into fights and can't sit still for more than a minute. The student rarely does any class work, is distracted easily and has few friends. This student may have ADHD, or may not. The truth is uncertain. One doctor identifies a student as ADHD whom another would call "normal".

Many learners are just normal and they have been misdiagnosed and put on drug therapy. Many have serious other problems and the drug therapy is masking the real problems. For some, the drug therapy is a miracle cure. At this time, there is no consensus about the singular or true causes of ADHD.

Start with the simplest things first. Begin eliminating variables. Discover if the student is more kinesthetic or has a rule-following cognitive disorder. Then focus on diet changes. Stay open-minded about symptoms and treatment. If one method of treatment is not working, it's not a hopeless case. Switch to another professional and switch methodologies.

# Dealing With Dyslexia

Several researchers have reported on various different strategies for dealing with dyslexia. Each uses recent brain research to help the learner to manage the disability and learn successfully. Right now, there is no scientific consensus about how to deal with this troubling reading problem. However, there are several schools of thought regarding dyslexia.

## 1. The Influence of Color
Livingstone says that our brain processes sensory information on two separate parallel paths. The faster sensory system notes the location in the background. The slower system, in the foreground, processes what the objects are. In dyslexics, the faster system is sluggish and doesn't delete quickly enough the previous word or words seen. As a result, when eyes move from word to word, the reader experiences blurring and fusing of words. He says that special colored lenses (called Irlen) can help the reader successfully deal with this problem.

Others disagree. They say that the supposed benefits of tinted lenses are unsubstantiated. The literature is either unpublished or difficult to obtain. They also contend that recent experiments have proven that the intervention of colored lenses is insupportable.

## 2. The Influence of Sounds
Since dyslexics are frequently right hemisphere dominant, they miss out on many key sounds. In addition, a split second delay in the routing of information within the brain, when it has to cross hemispheres twice, creates a time delay in understanding oral instructions. This makes super-attentive listening a requirement for dyslexics. But that can get exhaustive when it has to go on for more than a few minutes. As a result, the child tends to lose attention, and gets further behind in learning.

### 3. Re-Training the Eyes

Davis says that the problem has to do with spatial orientation. He defines a point of perception in space which he calls the "visuo-awareness epicenter." The location of this epicenter varies among individuals. For example, a boxer's epicenter is 16 feet above his head; a race car driver's, 30 feet in front of him. For best reading, the epicenter may need to be within inches of the head - above and behind. By retraining the brain to be in control of this roving center of awareness, reading improves dramatically. Davis said his method is "not a panacea but a learning process". It takes about 35 hours of training and counseling to implement his method. He claims an 80-90% success rate.

One model states that hemispheric stimulation may be beneficial in treatment. In this model, many of the problems of dyslexia are treated by proper stimulation of the left hemisphere. In fact, Galaburda of Harvard says that the brains of dyslexics have different patterns of cell organization from those found in normal brains.

### 4. Inner Ear Problems

Some researchers have made strong correlations to inner ear problems. It seems that infection-related fluids (effusion) interferes with hearing which interferes with auditory perception and processing. That would make sense, since Berard reports that 85% of dyslexics have hearing difficulties. Why? A hearing defect in the range of 500 cycles per second prevents hearing the quieter, more easily-confused voiceless consonants, such as M, N, P and B. The left hemisphere is specialized for hearing clicks and other closed sounds, while the right is more sensitive to vowels.

Other research agrees that these differences occur prenatally during key times of cell migration. Certain groups of neurons end up in the "wrong" areas, causing poor reading but encouraging mechanical or creative abilities. In fact, many of the most creative artists, composers, producers, athletes, singers, and musicians will tell you that they are dyslexic including Cher, Muhammed Ali, Madonna, and Dustin Hoffman are dyslexic.

Never give up on learners who are having a tough time. A majority of those learners who have dyslexia can be successfully treated. Do some research to find local resources that are successful in treating dyslexia. Print a list of these resources and make it available to parents or students.

# Drug Abuse

The problems of drug abuse are surprisingly amazingly widespread. Not only in the type of drugs used, but who is affected. Suffice it to say anyone, even students from good parents in good neighborhoods, can have problems with drugs. In addition, the form of devastating poisons can be any of the following:

* cigarettes
* No-doz, Vivarin
* alcohol
* cocaine
* cold remedies, valium

* marijuana
* Ritalin crystals
* glue, paint, other inhalants
* amphetamines
* LSD, crystal, angel dust, etc.

Learn the behaviors of those who use those drugs. Have someone from the local police department come to your school and talk to your staff about the appropriate steps to take when you suspect someone is a user. Find out the school policy and be ready to act on it. When you have a student who you think is involved, take action. You may be the best hope he or she has to deal with the problem. Ignoring it will not chase it away. Be proactive; don't wait until a student overdoses and everyone says, "Why didn't anyone do anything?"

# Gifted and Talented Learners

Are there learners who are "more intelligent?" It depends on what you mean by intelligence. If you buy into the false notion of a fixed intelligence, you'd be right. But our intelligence is not fixed and can develop in many ways with proper enrichment. Gardner's theory of multiple intelligences says gifted and talented programs are, at their best, ignoring what we now know about the brain. At worst, they are very elitist and damaging. Why? The whole presumption about who is gifted and who is not is based on an outdated model. Here are some **false assumptions** about gifted programs:

**1. Giftedness can be measured or predicted** (False. The majority of society's greatest contributors were NOT identified as gifted in school.)

**2. So-called average (or below average) students would not benefit from an enriched gifted program** (False. Research suggests that all learners benefit.)

**3. There are only a few truly gifted learners.** (False. Master Japanese violin teacher Suzuki proved he could teach competent-level violin playing to any child. Drs. Glen and Janet Doman of the Institute for Human Potential in Philadelphia have been proving that you can teach nearly any baby math and reading skills before age three. Unless there is brain damage or a specific disease preventing it, each of us can develop some form of genius. It takes will and skill.)

**4. Special talents and abilities are genetic** (False. Research suggests it accounts for about 30%. That means that for the majority of your talent, intelligence and ability, it's up to you!)

**5. There's *something special* about gifted learners.** (Yes, this is true in a illogical way. Those who are more visual learners are more often mislabeled as the "talented and gifted." Visual learners are often quieter, read better, focus longer and pay attention to the teacher.) For many teachers, having a student like that is a real "gift" in their class!

That is an amusing definition of gifted! If that's a gifted learner, what would you call physicist Steven Hawking, producer/director Steven Spielberg, dropout Walt Disney, Martin Luther King, scientist Albert Einstein, musician Stevie Wonder, writer W.E.B. DuBois, singer Ray Charles, producer/director Spike Lee or producer Quincy Jones? *Every single one of them has been labeled, at one time or another, a problem student.* What does that tell you about the value of labeling? Everyone of them has made a significant contribution to our lives. Maybe it's time to bring our assessment of what's "gifted" into the real world.

Having said that there is no place for so-called "gifted and talented" learners in a multiple intelligences program, what about the other end of the spectrum? Should there be pullout programs for students with special needs?

Yes, but only a certain kind of program. There's a difference between teaching content and process. Many pullout (special education) programs teach primarily content. They simply teach it slower, using more flexibility and stronger relationships. By itself, that's not bad. But in the larger context of education, it does more of a disservice unless it's done right. The bad part is that students get stigmatized as "slow learners" and their self concept can be destroyed.

# There is a Better Way

Should we end all pullout programs? No. Doing it "right" means that all pullout programs should be teaching process and values, not content. Avoid teaching the spelling words, teach the new system of HOW to spell. Never put them in a good state for learning forever, teach them HOW to manage their own states. Teach them about eye accessing cues, learning style profiles, learn to learn skills, graphic organizers, communications skills and social skills. Give them self-confidence through skills not content. These students should be out of regular classes just long enough to get both content and process. The moment they can be mainstreamed and "included," arrange for them to be with the others.

---

## Additional Resources for Further Study and Follow up

*Creating Success* by Akin (Innerchoice)
*Planning & Organizing for Multicultural Instruction* by Baker
    (Zephyr Press)
*Beyond Language* by Bilingual Office (CSULA)
*Reclaiming Youth At Risk* by Brendtro, et. al. (National Educational Service)
*Many People, Many Ways* by Chris Brewer (Zephyr Press)
*History and Geography of Human Genes* by Cavalli-Sforza, Menozzi &    Piazza
*Respecting Our Differences* by Duvall (Zephyr Press)
*Linking Through Diversity* by Walter Enloe (Zephyr Press)
*Don't Accept Me As I Am* by Feuerstein (Plenum Press)
*Mediated Learning Experiences* by Feuerstein (Freund Publishing)
*Men are from Mars and Women are From Venus* by John Gray
*Righting the Educational Conveyor Belt* by Michael Grinder
    (Metamorphous Press)*
*Endangered Minds* by Healy (Simon & Schuster)*
*At Risk Students and School Restructuring* by Kirschner
    (Research for Better Schools)
*Everyday Genius* by Kline (Great Ocean Press)*
*From Rage to Hope* by Kuykendall (National Educational Service)
*Giving Up On School* by LaCompte & Dworkin (Corwin)
*Keeping a Head in School* by Levine (Educators Publishing Service)
*Brain Sex* by Moir & Jessel (Dell)
*Compassionate School* by Morrow (Prentice-Hall)
*You Just Don't Understand* by Deborah Tannen
*Smart Kids with School Problems* by Vail (E.P. Dutton)
*Why Black People Tend to Shout* by Wiley (Penguin)


* Items marked with an asterisk are available in the Appendix.

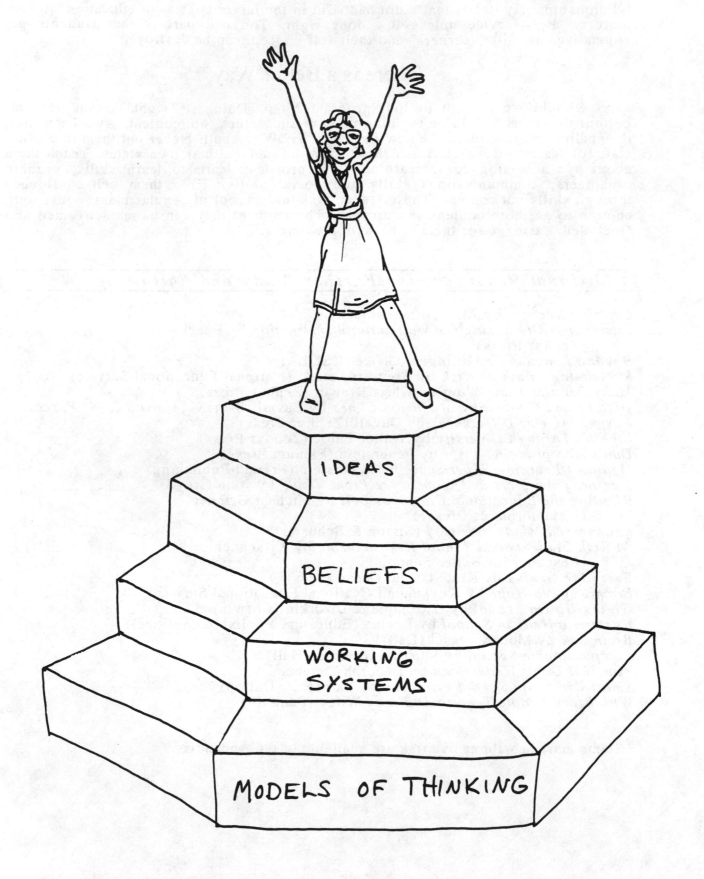

# 5

## *Mental Models of Success*

### Your Secret to Success

The secret to successful teaching is contained in "mental models." These are the frameworks, the belief systems, the thought patterns, the paradigms and sets of operating principles on which your thoughts and behaviors are based. A mental model in a successful teacher is similar, regardless of whether the teacher is a first year teacher or a thirty-year veteran. The mental model allows the teacher to make smart decisions most of the time, build or preserve student dignity and spark learning in an almost magical way. This chapter illuminates the "right stuff," the key ingredients for a successful teacher. How important are these ingredients?

The Harvard Educational Review discussed students educated in a poor neighborhood of Montreal. Despite the likelihood to the contrary, two-thirds of the former pupils of "Miss A" achieved the highest level of adult status, while the remaining third were classified as "medium status." None of her former students fell into the "low" group. Years later, the students remembered her unshakable faith in their ability to learn and the extra time and attention she gave. Both the students and the teacher remembered one another well and their special times together. Another teacher in the Washington D.C. area has had, among his students, four who later became Nobel Prize winners. One would be a coincidence, two would raise an eyebrow. Four is simply stunning.

To have that kind of long lasting influence, a teacher needs even more than great lesson plans, subject mastery and well polished presentation skills. One study asked individual teachers to describe values, beliefs, attitudes and their correlation (if any) to results in the classroom. It demonstrated conclusively that teachers with better classroom results had a certain set of attitudes about themselves, learning and their students. These upcoming values or underlying premises are literally HOW top teachers think of themselves, their job and their students.

### The Pygmalion Effect

In the classic book on teaching, *Pygmalion in the Classroom*, Rosenthal reminds us of the power of our own beliefs. A teacher was told that a group of students were highly intelligent. In fact, the students had tested well below normal and often displayed behavior problems. But the unknowing teacher figured that if these were gifted students, then she'd better treat them that way. You can guess the end of the true story. The more she treated them that way, the more they responded that way. She literally created gifted students. This study, forty years old, is still the most eloquent statement about the power you have over the success of your students. What you believe, you will create. Do you think you were given a class of "low ability" kids? If you do, *you will prove your beliefs true.*

Remember a time when you thought someone was prowling around your house. You probably felt fear. Then, later, you discovered that it was only the wind or the neighbor's pet. The "prowler" caused your reaction of fear, even though he didn't actually exist! Although it was an illusion, your mind and body reacted as if the prowler was real. You responded "as if" it were true. This could be called the "As If" principle: act as if something is true and you will get the same effect as if it is true. Teachers who believe that every one of their students are gifted will get the same results as those other teachers who teach the officially gifted students.

OLD MODEL

| |
|---|
| I Teach |
| Students Perform |
| I Assess |

**TODAY'S MODEL**

| |
|---|
| *I'm a Catalyst for Student Learning & Student Self-assessment* |

## Role as Catalyst, Not Teacher

Times, have indeed changed. Today's top teachers think of themselves as "learning catalysts" instead of teachers. After all, *teachers* are supposed to teach. The old definition is basically *more of the same,* top-down, "I'm in power, you are lesser." Instead, a learning catalyst *changes the role to promoting learning in whatever form is appropriate.* They are fully skilled in the use of multiple intelligences and the learning styles models (like Dunn & Dunn, Gregorc, Herrmann, GLP, 4-MAT, etc.). They are skilled at reading student states and managing them appropriately. They utilize and integrate technology, mind mapping, accelerated learning, peripherals, music and art across the curriculum. They give learners choice and variety, with plenty of feedback. And more importantly, they've not only had exposure to these methods, *they use them consistently and with confidence.*

## The "Demand Model" versus "Discovery Model"

One way of teaching commonly used is to figure out the behaviors you want from your learners. Then, measure all the behaviors, from outset to completion, reward the positive ones and punish the negative ones. You might say, "That's not bad... everyone does that." That model is known as B.F. Skinner behaviorism.

## OLD "DEMAND" MODEL

Behaviorist theories: Student as subject... identify, demand & measure all the desired outcomes... reward the desired ones and punish the undesired ones

## TODAY'S MODEL

*This approach asks, "How does the human brain naturally, intrinsically, learn best and what can we do to encourage more of its best learning?"*

# You Make a Difference in the World

You are a biological miracle. Unless you are an identical twin, there never has been, nor ever will be another person like you in human history. Until genetic cloning is perfected, you are a solitary gift to humankind. You bring a unique package of mind, heart, spirit and skills to your learners. No one before you and no one since will have that special package. With that unique package, you have a unique responsibility to share it with others. You are a once-in-forever celestial event. Be responsible and bring forth your gifts to others.

Some have the erroneous attitude that only CERTAIN people really matter, and that the rest are simply pawns on the chessboard of life. On closer inspection, every so-called important person has many others who support and make possible what he or she does. Every one of us does matter and because of that, everything we do, small or large, adds to the sum total of all the effects and nationwide contributions. We are the pebble that redirects the flow of water that alters the flow of a stream that changes the riverbanks that alters the landscape that fills the lakes that provides water for thousands that evaporates into clouds that changes the weather that affects the fate of humanity.

Because you do make a difference, every part of your life is worth attention. For example, does it matter if you say "hello" to the student in the back of the room? Absolutely! It does matter if you take the extra moment to prepare your presentation better. Everything you do, in some way, contributes to your students, as well as to the educational system. This attitude also says that the value you add to the lives of your students will also enrich your own life.

Here's an example. As a teacher, if you excite and inspire just ten students from your class, and each of those kids relates their enthusiasm to ten other kids, how many have you actually affected? The answer is obviously ten times ten or 100 students! Can you imagine the cumulative effect over a period of years? That's why every student is valuable, unique and important. Each student is deserving of both your time and respect.

OLD MODEL
```
Some People Make a Difference
Some Don't...
Let's Invest More in Those
That Matter
```

**TODAY'S MODEL**
```
Either None of Us
Make a Difference Or
All of Us Make a Difference
Therefore, I Do Make
A Difference
```

# You Have the Power of Choice

Top teachers have the attitude (whether true or not) that they have free choice to feel and experience exactly what they choose. After all, if you're not in charge of your own thoughts and experiences, who is? There are those who believe that someone or something else made them feel a certain way. It's easy to tell by their expressions: "You make me so happy!" "You make me mad." "You frustrate me!" "The way you do that makes me nervous." All of these statements are born out of a belief that someone else can force you to have certain feelings or experiences. A super-teacher chooses his or her own feelings, and chooses the appropriate ones for the situation. Instead of "you make me so frustrated," a super-teacher accepts responsibility by saying "I feel so frustrated." In order to be able to manage your student's behavior and learning in class, you must have control over your own attitudes and responses.

OLD MODEL
```
Laying Blame:
"I'm a Victim of Circumstances
Beyond My Control"
```

**TODAY'S MODEL**
```
I Can't Control Everything,
But I Can Control
My Responses To Everything
```

# You Are the Cause of Your Own Experience

You can't control everything in life or in your classroom. But you do have the power to control how you respond to what happens. The essence of your humanity is your power of choice. That power resides in the moment between a stimulus and your response. In that split second (what may seem like an eternity) you either have a knee-jerk reaction or react responsibly. You also have a choice over both what you experience externally and internally. It means you can choose how to feel regardless of whether you are in a traffic jam, a rainstorm or a class of so-called problem students. It is your choice to feel frustrated, happy, sad or peaceful - you have the power to run your own life. You are choosing your job, your friends, your spouse, your foods, your activities, what you read, and the TV programs you watch. It's all up to you and you are not a helpless victim. It means that, at any point on life's merry-go-round, you can change horses, enjoy the one you've got or get off the ride.

An interesting corollary of this belief is it can allow you to make the shift from considering yourself responsible-guilty (as in "Who's to blame?") to being responsible-accountable (as in "You can count on me"). Being accountable as a teacher means that you are the one who makes the choices that lead to the results. When there is credit to be given out, give it to others - especially your students. When there is accountability to be considered, raise your hand high.

If every year you have lazy unmotivated students, and every school or grade level you teach at has lazy unmotivated students, guess what the common element is in all those situations? It's you! You are the one that is making it possible (creating the opportunities) for motivation and high energy to be present in your students OR making it impossible for those qualities to manifest in your presence. Truly, accountability is one of the most important qualities a teacher can have.

## It's Your Job to Enter the Student's World

Successful teachers approach the student from the student's point of view. If a student's interest is motorcycles, the teacher would relate the course materials, in some way, to motorcycles. What's more, if the student does not understand the material, the teacher adjusts the approach. Does this sound like more work? Initially, it is. Does it work? Dramatically well. It should be added that the students also need to know how to teach themselves so that the teacher's job, in the long run, gets easier.

The old model was to teach, then assess if students got it. If they didn't, then teachers would repeat the instruction or figure that the learner was a bit slow. The new model is different. You provide the environment for learning. You bring out the learner's intrinsic motivation. You then engage their curiosity about a particular subject. You create support systems and make resources available. Then you challenge the learner to discover new worlds. Then you get out of the way of the learner so he or she can learn at their own exciting, engaged pace.

Does this mean that all the responsibility is on the teacher? No. First, you assume full responsibility. Then, as soon as it is appropriate, help the student assume his or her share of responsibility. You start, then empower the students.

```
OLD MODEL
Teacher Presents His or Her View
of The World As The Truth....
Students are Expected to Conform
to Their Model
```

```
TODAY'S MODEL
You Ask Learners,
"What is Your Model? How
Do You Think... and Why? I'll
Enter Your World So We Can
Talk to Each Other."
```

# The Meaning of Your Communication
## is the Response You Get

If you explain photosynthesis to your students and they don't understand it, you have several choices. You could assume that they are a bit slow or didn't do their homework. You could assume that the topic is too tough for their understanding, or that it's an off day because of the weather. The problem with any of those choices is that none will accomplish the objective of insuring that your students understand photosynthesis.

The solution? Acknowledge that regardless of how clearly you THINK you explained it, the students didn't understand. Remember, your commitment is to do what will make the students successful. Then choose to "repackage" or re-format what you just said until they get it. If you say "green" and they hear "red," simply try something else until they receive what you mean to put out. That's flexible teaching!

The only problem with this belief is that it means that you will be constantly re-formulating what you say because you have ceased to blame it on the students. Yet something exciting happens when you adopt this belief: the quality of your communication and success in class goes up dramatically. The shift to make here is from blaming others or justifying poor results, to being accountable for them. It's a much more exciting way to teach and it certainly will produce better results.

# There Are No Failures:
## Only Outcomes and Feedback

If you accept responsibility for your communications as well as what goes on in the rest of your class, you could begin to feel that you fail a lot. Unless, of course, you had a belief that each time you "fail" at something you learn something... and that each learning experience is valuable and needed. If your belief is that learning something new is more important than "looking good" or avoiding failure, you begin to enjoy former so-called failures and see them as gifts. Or, at worst, see them as simply a result to be learned from.

What's a failure? When you don't get your desired results or outcome? What if each time that happened, you learned important information? What if each time you had a so-called failure, it actually provided you with a valuable and useful lesson which made you a better person? That's exactly what top teachers believe. They believe that regardless of what happens in their classroom, they can learn, grow and excel from the experience.

Therefore, a failure is as good as a success. Each and every happening builds successes. It adds to the knowledge necessary for success and increases the chances of the next event being more closely aligned with the desired results. Are we turning lemons into lemonade? Absolutely! It's highly effective in gaining personal excellence because it forces you to learn and to find a lesson in every so-called failure. There's nothing wrong with "failures" - it's only when you don't learn from them that a result is truly a failure.

Could you imagine how much fun you'd have in life if this was a belief of yours: every adversity carries with it the seeds of an equal or greater gift! It's a well-worn cliché, but it's as true as ever: what you look for, you shall find. Look for the negative and you'll find it. Look for a gift in your mistakes, and you'll find it, too. Welcome mistakes because any person who doesn't make mistakes certainly is risking very little.

OLD MODEL

| |
|---|
| Avoid Mistakes... |
| They're Bad. |
| Mark students |
| Down for Failure |

TODAY'S MODEL

| |
|---|
| **Mistakes Are Feedback & an Opportunity to Grow... We Can Use Them Positively & Learn From Them** |

# Feedback Is Critical to Successful Teaching

What follows from the previous belief is that feedback and correction are absolutely essential to classroom mastery. Your progress towards mastery could be measured by your willingness to allow yourself to be coached. To the degree that you allow input from qualified others and you do something about it, you'll improve. Teaching means you must be willing to be a student yourself. In fact, your students will learn from you at the rate you learn from them.

Once in the classroom, if you're trying new things, you can expect to have lots of learning experiences. You begin each class knowing very little about how each student thinks and organizes their "reality." The only way you'll find out is to ask, or try something and risk making mistakes at it. Due to the unlikely odds of successfully hitting every student's communication and learning strategy the first time, you're going to have many unsuccessful outcomes.

Yet, failure is a label put on an event in which you don't get your outcome. You might as well put on another more useful label: feedback. Now success comes easier knowing that failure is no longer possible, only outcomes. Failures and mistakes are simply feedback you need to be successful; hence they are valuable and useful. Correction, without invalidation, it is indeed, one of the real keys to mastery. Masters use such phrases as "Wow, I learned how not to do it that time!" or, "Boy, is this an apparent mess. What can I learn from this?" You can re-frame the meaning of the word failure, and replace it with the word lesson or gift.

With many types of students in your classroom, you'll need many different techniques and that requires plenty of flexibility. Each so-called failure gets you closer to your outcome, so the greater your flexibility, the greater your chance of success. It means a complete and total detachment from any method you use. After all, you may need to abandon it in seconds. It also means that you'll be doing more on-the-spot thinking than ever before. Less planning, more coaching.

# Inflexible Teaching Is
## Primary Cause of Learner Failure

You may be saying "That's going too far. I know how important planning is!" You're right. But times are changing. Remember, *whether this belief is or is not true is not the issue.* The real question is: If you act as if this belief were true, will your results go up? There is much evidence that they will. In other words, if you believe it is your responsibility to get through to the students, you will become a better teacher. If you claim that it's 100% the student's responsibility to get the material, you might as well just mail a book to him.

If, on the other hand, you accept that you have something to do with how the student performs, then it will allow you to use the students successes and so-called failures to learn from and become a far superior teacher. It means a total suspension of any unresourceful or negative judgments about your students. After all, they are simply responding to your level of teaching skills.

As a corollary to this, there are also no resistant students, only inflexible teachers. No student gets up in the morning and says to himself, "I think I'll resist learning today." The natural tendency is to want to learn, since most learning occurs non-consciously. Our job is to make learning as much fun for our students as it was in kindergarten. With greater flexibility in teaching strategies, there would be no more tracking, grouping, or hierarchies of so-called intelligence. Bellamy's experiments at the University of Oregon discovered that it inflexible teaching led to the labeling of mentally retarded as "untrainable." His results proved that with FLEXIBLE teaching strategies, you could not only teach, but job-train students with IQs below 50. That's super-teaching!

OLD MODEL

| Some Are Going to Fail |
| No matter What Is Done |
| It's Just The Way It Is |

*TODAY'S MODEL*

| *Instill Success Attitudes* |
| *Increase Your Own Flexibility* |
| *& Your Success Rate Will Soar* |

# All Students Are Gifted:
# The Context Determines the Evidence

The work of Harvard Psychologist Howard Gardner suggests that we have not one or two but multiple intelligences. He says each of us has our own unique package of intelligences and all of us have gifts worth developing. Traditional teaching focuses on two of them in the grades from 6-12. But rarely does a kindergarten student fail. Why? Because teachers think of their children as potential astronauts, writers, dancers, fathers, scientists, engineers, nurses, teachers, designers, mothers and leaders. The classroom is full of music, movement, reading, drawing, interacting and song. That's what is too rarely found in a sixteen year-old's science, English, math or history class.

The same student who flunks the math test at school may be a top surfer, socialite or car mechanic. The student who writes poorly may be a good video game player, actress or chef. The student who is doing poorly in all of his classes may be the most creative, resourceful and powerful neighborhood gang leader. Treat your students as if they were gifted - you'll make discoveries about their resources in creativity, flexibility, social skills, leadership and problem-solving abilities.

All of your students have talents and gifts; it's your job to find useful applications in the classroom. Create opportunities for responsibility and success in the classroom for students so they can use "street skills" in an academic setting. Soon they'll begin to re-assess their potential to succeed scholastically. Students want to succeed. Give them the chance by letting them use, inside the classroom, what they already do well outside school. The rural student who does home chores and looks after his siblings has developed the attributes of perseverance, commitment, dedication and loyalty. Enhance those qualities in the classroom. Top teachers assume that every student is gifted. They simply act "as if" it was true to get better performance from the student. The result is a student who enjoys learning and has strong self-esteem.

61

```
OLD MODEL
Let's Test Students
To Find Out If They
Are Gifted Or Not
```

```
TODAY'S MODEL
Let's Bring Out the
Giftedness in Every
Learner We Can
```

# We Are Conditioned By Our Beliefs About Our World

Over time, each of us has learned what can be done and what cannot be done. Yet each person seems to produce different results. This tells us that our beliefs and attitudes, which have conditioned us very powerfully, vary widely from person to person. That variance of beliefs about what can and cannot be done is subtle, but easily measured in the classroom. Translated into teacher expectations of student performance, those beliefs can dramatically affect behavior. When you believe your students will do better, they usually do.

As teachers, we are all biased. There are no "objective" teachers. In an exhaustive review of teacher behaviors, it was discovered that some of the most powerful influences contribute to a subjective bias which in turn, affect student performance. Here are four of them:

- **Unconscious reactions.** You may dislike or like a student simply because he or she unconsciously reminds you of your own child or a neighbor's. All it takes is an action, a comment or look that you associate with another child, and the instant association is made.
- **Cognitive Dissonance.** We often have a tendency to ignore evidence which is inconsistent with our expectations or prior experience. Your least-liked student can make a brilliant deduction and you're much more likely to ignore it than if it was from your class "genius."
- **Halo Effect.** We often allow one characteristic to overshadow others as an umbrella or behavioral "halo." If your favorite student has a small annoying habit, you are more likely to discount it and be more forgiving.
- **Projection.** One tendency is to see in others the things we like or dislike the most about ourselves. This creates a strong subjective "filter" through which you evaluate behaviors.

These other factors make it difficult to single out any one variable as the reason for student changes in performance. As a top teacher, your goal is to reduce your bias and subjectivity as much as possible. Although many factors are present, at least start with the awareness that you are likely to be biased! The bottom line is that teacher subjectivity is a dominant influence in student performance.

# Your Conversation Affects Your Results

It's both interesting and exciting to discover the distinctions between average and true master-level teachers. One key difference is in the conversations, both internal (what you say to yourself) and external (what you say to others).

*The single greatest difference is that great teachers have conversations about possibilities and less effective teachers talk about complaints, problems and limitations*

In other words, top teachers talk about how they want things to be, what could happen, openings for success, student breakthroughs, new ideas, potential within students and the opportunities for their work. The less effective teachers have conversations about the limitations of their students, how bad things are, how no one listens to them, how they were right all along, what's wrong with education and who is to blame for the problems at their school.

Possibility or complaint? That's the distinction to be made in your conversations. What's the possibility that your students could actually be twice as smart as they appear to be, but you are actually stunting their growth? What's the possibility that homework could be a joy instead of a punishment. What's the possibility that learning could be fun instead of a routine?

Teaching well is a conversation with students about their possibilities, not complaining that they are not meeting them. As a conversation, teaching needs to be empowering and exciting. Very few people get empowered out of complaints or limitations. Beginning now, begin to monitor your conversations about education and teaching. You may be surprised to discover that in your life, you will get the result of your conversations. They are THAT powerful!

# There Are No Unresourceful Students, Only Unresourceful States

Every teacher has encountered the student who appears slow, unmotivated or incapable. Yet that same student can rebuild a motorcycle from scratch or write magnificent love letters to a friend. A key principle, one that super teachers know and live by is this: all behavior is state-related. What your students do has more to do with the momentary state that they are in than their abilities or capacity. All of us go through moments when we are exhausted, tired, depressed or doubting. In those moments, even the most well-trained and professional educator can be unresourceful. Obviously, students have unresourceful moments, too. To change behavior, change the state. Some of the most effective ways to alter states are presented in later chapters.

OLD MODEL

| Label Students |
| :---: |
| Based on |
| Classroom Performance |

# Each Person Does His Best

Evidence shows that successful teachers are compassionate and understanding. How can you teach another teacher those traits? The answer is simple. It's a matter of whether or not you believe that every student is doing his or her best. Super-teachers, those who teach with compassion, understanding and care have a different belief about people than average or below-average teachers. The belief is this: Each person's behavior makes total and perfect sense when understood from the context of that individual's reality.

Since each student has had a different upbringing, different parents, different information, experiences and in fact, lives in a different world from you, the behavior exhibited is totally appropriate - regardless of how illogical, bizarre, stupid, crazy or sick it seems. If you had the exact same everything (parents, home, history, etc.) as your students, your behavior would have to be very similar to theirs. In reality, we'll never know if this belief is true or not. We don't have a control group to study. But if you follow this belief and its implications, you'll be much more successful.

The expression "doing their best," refers to the best for that student, not for you. There should be something more added: "everyone is always doing their best GIVEN: (1) the context (2) the perceived choices available and (3) the intended outcome. Given those three qualifiers, people are always trying to, meaning to, and actually doing the best that they can. YOU might be able to do better, but your students are not you. If you keep reminding yourself of this, you'll gain much peace of mind and compassion for others in a world of seemingly wacky behavior.

> *The teacher's mission is to*
> *re-discover the childhood joys of learning*
> *with students as their partners*

Because each student is always doing their best, there's a positive intent to all behavior. You may ask, "But what about the student who defaces materials, assaults others, destroys property?" The answer is the same: the intent is positive, even though the method used to achieve that outcome is deplorable. When a student assaults another, the positive intent may be to clear out his anger, resolve a feud, gain peer acceptance or build a sense of importance. When defacing property, the positive intent is to release anger or feel important. When you ask why a person exhibits delinquent behavior, there's always a good reason, to that person. Because of this, super-teachers are constantly trying to create outlets, avenues and alternative methods for the positive intents to get the positive behaviors they really want.

# A Low Ego Works Best

Your teaching can take many different paths and options. The difference between having a low ego and a high ego is enormous and shows up in many ways. Teachers with high egos could be described as having these actions:

- Wanting to let students know when they make a mistake
- Resisting picking up the trash on the floor in your room
- Wanting students to remember you at the end of the year
- Wanting to be right about something in debate or discussion
- Hoping students will like you and think highly of you
- Having it be important to look smart, witty or charming
- Making students wrong for forgetting something
- Having your own life be more important than your student's
- Keeping things the same, protecting status quo

The above actions all radiate from a point of view - that of high ego. The ego is the part of us that tries to protect us from looking bad, being wrong or to blame. High ego is not high self-esteem or self-confidence. It is a concern for what others will think and operating from a basis of "How can I cover my act?" There is a better way.

Having a low ego means that you are more concerned about what is true to yourself and your own integrity instead of what others think. Low ego means others come first, not in the sense of harming yourself, but in the sense of allowing others to be "the star." If we re-did the list from above, a low ego person might take actions like these:

- Letting your own humility and mistakes set an example
- Never being too proud to do "whatever it takes" to help
- Wanting to allow others to be heard and acknowledged
- Wanting students to experience how great they are
- Having it be important to make *others* look good
- Making it safe for students to admit their own mistakes
- Getting satisfaction by helping others make their life a success

One of the easiest ways to determine where your ego is at is to ask a simple question: "What am I committed to, getting credit or having my students get credit?" The person with a low ego will answer that the commitment is to his or her students. Another simple way to measure ego is by the amount of change you are comfortable with in your life. The ego wants to protect status quo and resists new ideas and changes. The ego wants you to be comfortable with no upsets, changes or threats to your teaching. But quality teaching requires risk and change. And that means a low ego.

| OLD MODEL |
| :---: |
| The Teacher As<br>The Boss, The Star, The Autocrat<br>of the Classroom |

## TODAY'S MODEL

| Your Learners As<br>Proactive, Responsible,<br>Stars of The Classroom |
| :---: |

# Authenticity Works Better Than "Acts"

All of us have our "acts." These are roles that we play, hats that we wear and personalities that we have. The good part of our act is that it can provide us with great flexibility in our behaviors. It is also convenient because if someone rejects us, they are not really rejecting us, only our act. The bad part comes when we start believing our acts and think that we ''are'' our acts. Often we have acts as a protective device to protect our ego against the attacks and criticism that life brings us. Other times our act is an attempt to be interesting, cute or theatrical instead of being genuinely interested in others. In either case, acts can present problems.

As an example, if you act aloof or "cool" when it's time to admit a mistake (that's the act called "I'm so perfect I don't make mistakes. I just change my mind."), the risk is that students will never get to know who you really are. That's because they are responding to your act and not who you are underneath the act. Many teachers think they are friends with their students when, in fact, they are not. Their students don't even know who you are; they only know the act.

Don't try to be perfect or totally "together" for your students. If you do, your students will feel uncomfortable around you and will be afraid to make mistakes of their own. Your students will miss out on really knowing who you are if you take your acts too far. The solution is to be authentic. Always let your students in on what is your act and what isn't. And never believe your own act.

# Teaching Is a Lifelong Process
# of Learning, Not an Event

One does not "become" a great teacher - one simply commits to it as a path. There's no big "ta-da" or end point of skill level to celebrate. This means that it's an on-going and expanding path of growth and "becoming." One of the best ways to stay on the path of commitment and growth is to reinforce your philosophy with the writings of Lao Tzu. Translated, Lao Tzu's *Tao Te Ching* means "the book of how things work." Written in the fifth century BC., it has long been a classic in both Chinese and world literature. Its much-loved wisdom has withstood the test of time well.

In fact, many of its sayings are familiar to you: "The journey of a thousand miles begins with a single step." Not surprisingly, the best teachers seem to include ancient wisdom as well as modern tools in their teaching. The best updated version to study is *The Tao of Leadership* by John Heider. Here is an adaptation of its philosophy:

*A wise teacher lets others have the floor. A good teacher is better than a spectacular teacher. Otherwise, the teacher outshines the teachings. Be a mid-wife to learning - facilitate what is happening, rather than what you think ought to be happening. Silence says more than words, pay much attention to it. Continual classroom drama clouds inner work. Allow time for genuine insight. A good reputation arises naturally from doing good work. But do not nourish the reputation, the anxiety will be endless; rather nourish the work. To know what is happening, relax and do not try to figure things out. Listen quietly, be calm and use reflection. Let go of selfishness; it only blocks your universality.*

*Let go of your ego, and you will receive what you need. Give away credit, and you get more. When you feel most destroyed, you are most ready to grow. When you desire nothing, much comes to you. The less you make of yourself, the more you are. Instead of trying hard, be easy: teach by example, and more will happen. Trying to appear brilliant is not enlightened. The gift of a great teacher is creating an awareness of greatness in others. Because the teacher can see clearly, light is shed on others. Teach as both a warrior and a healer; both a leader and a yielder. Constant force and intervention will backfire as will constant yielding. One cannot push the river; a leader's touch is light. Making others do what you want them to do can become a failure. While they may momentarily comply, their revenge may come in many forms. That is why your victory may be a loss. To manage other lives takes strength, to manage your own life is real power.*

With insights, you may discover that the way things are is "the way they actually are" instead of "why aren't things different?" Much of an ineffective teacher's time is spent trying to MAKE things go differently or DISPUTING what actually is occurring. An unwise teacher is PUSHING or FORCING and is ANNOYED at the processes of life. For you to grow as a master teacher, you must know what teaching really is about. It is about serving others, discovery of each person's highest self, humility, acknowledgment and allowing others the respect and love they need to grow.

## Great Teaching Requires
## a Different Role

The old model of a classroom teacher "filling up" students with knowledge is obsolete and damaging. The role which works in today's world is that of a coach - that is "one who uncovers talent and learning, instructs, inspires in the fundamentals." It's a delicate shift, but it may be the most important one a teacher can make. In sports, the top names and biggest winners in sports coaching history all taught much more than the sport. The legends, Vince Lombardi, Don Schula, Red Aurbach, Don Coryell, "Bear" Bryant and John Wooden all built character and had a powerful affect on the personal lives of their athletes.

Coaching means that the teacher is more interested in providing direction in learning than the learning itself. It means the teacher is a guide, not an authority. It means that the personal, philosophic and emotional part of the learner is coached and directed as much as the intellectual part. Yet, in order to do it, the teacher must have his or her own life in order. That's a tall order for any occupation, much less one that puts personal growth at the bottom of budgetary priorities.

Old Model

| Fill up the Students With KnowledgeLike A Container |
| --- |

**Today's Model**

| **Be a Catalyst So Learners Can Learn How To Gain Skills & Knowledge** |
| --- |

# Teaching Requires a
## "Seize the Day" Attitude

Many students find school boring and tedious. This can often be reinforced by their parents who might find their jobs either stressful or unfulfilling. But with student's academic (and sometimes, personal) lives at stake, teachers must role-model a real "carpe diem" attitude. That means making the most out of today, finding the jewel or the gift in every opportunity and if life gives you lemons, learning to enjoy making lemonade. Life isn't a certain way. Life is created, on the spot, every day, by real people who make it their way. Something disastrous happens to two different persons; one becomes stronger, the other falls apart. Why? Their mental models say either life is a wondrous gift or it's a kick in the butt. Each attitude brings different results.

# Teaching Is an Inherently
## High-Risk Job

The notion of teaching as a safe, comfortable easy-going job is changing. Many years ago, elementary education teachers needed mainly a lot of love, secondary and college teachers needed lecture skills. Elementary teachers still need a lot of love, but that's about all that's the same. Teaching is far more rigorous than it ever has been.

It's a front-lines position for courageous and committed learners willing to take risks and make mistakes. It's a dangerous job because teachers must confront whatever ideas, systems or relationships not working in their personal or professional lives and change them. It's a place where consistent performance breakthroughs are needed just for survival. It's an intense on-the-edge line of work which requires that you set a public example of integrity, love, commitment and awareness for up to six hours a day with your "dirty laundry" on display.

It also requires an extraordinary commitment to change, learning and being coached. Just as teaching is a coaching job, it is also critical to have a willingness to be coached yourself. One of the greatest baseball players who ever lived was the Japanese legend Sadahara Oh. In spite of his unparalleled success, Sadahara was so committed to growth, that he went to his teacher to get coaching after each ballgame. This meant being up, after a day's workout and a night game, from midnight until two in the morning to get tutored!

Ask yourself what you do that acts as a stand for your commitment to being coached and learning new things. How do you respond to suggestions, changes and new policies? When was the last time you tried out (and committed to mastery) an entirely new teaching methodology? It takes that kind of openness in order to be effective. It takes that kind of role modeling for your students - the more they find you being willing to being coached, the easier it will be for them.

# Teaching is a Fully Paid
## Personal Growth Seminar

There is no other occupation which requires such rigor and such exemplary behavior. There is also no other occupation which has provided such possibility to our children and the planet as a whole. In your classroom, you can break the back of classroom "deadness." You can put an end to the boredom of learning and make it into a real joy. You can build nurturing relationships that can last a lifetime. You can break the back of any of your own limitations in life, using the classroom as your own education. Learn to live with more love, more integrity and more vitality by being the very embodiment of it in the classroom.

Accordingly, consider very strongly whether or not you want to play by the game one hundred percent. Because once you call yourself a "teacher" you must, out of fairness to yourself and your students, play the game as if it mattered. Because it does. Your students may become a success or failure in life depending not on how you teach, but who you are in the classroom.

OLD MODEL

| Teaching is a Safe, Easy, Low Risk Secure Profession |
| --- |

**TODAY'S MODEL**

| **Successful Teaching Requires Constant Personal Growth & Professional Risk-Taking** |
| --- |

This chapter has provided the prototype of the "Super-Teacher." It included many ways of thinking about yourself, others and teaching. If any of these ways are new to you, you may want to review to be sure you understand them. Check to see if you agree with them. If you don't, gather evidence to support the possibility that they may be true. Or, simply "act as if" they are true. Have the desire and faith necessary to make them a part of you. You might repeat them to yourself or write them up on 3" X 5" cards and put them in plain view for daily review. Use mental pictures to rehearse the actual activity, allowing yourself to become more comfortable with them.

And finally, the most important step... use them. Integrate these patterns of success in your behavior and you'll be pleased with the results. You can begin the path to mastery with these successful ways. Now is a good time to start, and here are a few affirmations. Make a copy of this next page on a nice quality colored paper. Post it up or distribute it. It'll be your daily inspiration.

*Dream your dreams*
*Enjoy the gift and privilege of life*
*Envision excellence*
*Cherish and support your friends*
*Give enthusiasm to others*
*Be inspiring*
*Know that you make a difference*
*Take manageable risks*
*Tell those that you love how you feel*
*Live with passion*
*Discover the gifts of everyday life*
*Aim for the stars*
*Smile and radiate your love*
*Recognize your inner beauty*
*Think and live healthy*
*Think bigger than ever before*
*Appreciate the good things in life*
*Take pride in yourself*
*Be greater than your highest thought*
*Live your vision every day*
*Practice what you preach*
*Appreciate yourself*
*Live with integrity*
*Think only the best of others*
*Enjoy the journey*
*Live for today*
*Make your dreams come true*
*Begin it NOW!*

## Additional Resources for Further Study and Follow up

*Seven Habits of Highly Effective People* by Covey (Simon & Schuster)
*Maps of the Mind* by Hampden-Turner (MacMillian)
*The Tao of Leadership* by Heider (Humanics New Age)
*Playful Perception* by Leff (Waterfront Books)

* Items marked with an asterisk are available in the Appendix.

# 6

# *Taking Care of Business*

## Preparation

Teaching has many facets: the attitudes, skills, knowledge, experience, relationships... and the business side. This chapter is on the role of you as a professional. The more you think of yourself as a professional, just like an attorney, doctor, counselor, engineer or producer, the better prepared you'll be for a successful work experience in the business of education.

Learn about the job you have. Learn the various cultures of your school. Discover the past - find old newsletters or newspaper articles. Ask about the traditions and rituals. Who were the legends, the key people of yesterday and today? Find out who has power and who doesn't. Find out who plays the role of "victim" and who plays "hero." Meet other teachers, locate sources of supplies, key people at school like the secretaries, cafeteria workers, custodians, etc.

## The True Professional

Those who complain about "getting no respect" would do themselves a favor by respecting themselves first. If you want to be treated like a professional, act like one. Dress professionally. Be on time. Read professional journals. Keep up in your subject matter. Get on school staff development committees. Invite other teachers to read *SuperTeaching*. Get business cards. If a school does not provide you with a business card, get one. Full service copy shops can make them for you for very little money. Put your credentials and your specialty on the card and carry it with pride.

## Support

Find a true friend who is also a great mentor teacher in your school. Sign up for every workshop you can... be a hungry learner. Get specific feedback from the principal and other teachers. Set up an audio tape and videotape of yourself. Ask the students to give you written evaluations once a week. Teach them how to evaluate you to get the kind of specific, accurate quality you want and need.

# Parent Relationships

Help parents become an ally. Ask questions. Be affirming, not adversarial. Ask for their opinions (you don't have to take their advice, just listen!). Stay calm when confronted with anger. Take three deep breaths and work to preserve the relationship you have with them. Keep your integrity.

# Handling Parent Conferences

Be prepared. Do all of your research before the conference. Have notes and any test scores available to support your concerns. Make it available for the parents to see at the moment. This could include work that the student has done recently to support your concerns. Make copies if the work must go with the parent. Parents are interested in the best for their child. Approach this meeting as a great opportunity to assist this young person. Bring a calendar of the school year to the meeting so that you can each talk about dates for goals and student commitments.

# Relationship-Building

Strong relationships will serve you and the student throughout the school year. Start with the comfortable and familiar territory. Small talk is of big importance for the first 60 seconds. Purposely make eye contact and smile. Create and maintain rapport. Use "we" and "us" instead of "I" and "me." Talk in approximately the same pace, tempo and volume as the parent. Find areas of common agreement. Match conversational predicates like "I see what you mean." Learn as much as you can about the particular culture of the family, regardless of the ethnic background. Everyone's culture affects their own learning.

# Smart Ideas

If you are limited to the amount of time you have available for the conference be sure that you have a clock visible from where you are sitting, with the parents' backs to the clock. This creates a natural way for you to monitor time. Start and conclude the conference at the scheduled time. You have a busy schedule, as do the parents. Have a list of a half dozen things you like in the student and want the parent to reinforce. Give the affirmation so that the parent knows you look for the good. Avoid comparisons with other students.

*The most irrelevant information is how their son or daughter compares with someone else's son or daughter*

The relevant question is "How is he or she doing compared to a year ago?" In wrapping up the conference, note the time at about 2 minutes prior to scheduled conclusion. Say to the parents, "We have 2 minutes left. Here are the issues I heard us talk about, what we discussed and what we'll do next." If it is necessary to continue at a different time... schedule it now.

# Build Rapport

Use the time to talk about all areas that affect learning. Discuss proper home study environments, the optimal brain food and homework, your discipline policy and the student's goals in school or life. This a golden opportunity to directly and positively affect the student through the parent. Take best advantage of it! Maintain your values, poise and integrity. Regardless of how frustrated a parent is, never promise to change anything that could violate your personal or professional standards. If you ever feel pressured or cornered by a parent, ask to take a fresh air break or say you'd like to think about it and schedule a follow up meeting or simply say you'll get back to the parent later. (And then do it!)

## Report Card Success Tips

Plan for it as an ongoing activity. Avoid last minute situations where you may be too rushed to do your best. Keep a file on each student (in primary), use a good gradebook at secondary. Make sure that you have created many different forms of assessment to make the report cards a chance for the student to show their strengths. You may want to include assessment in the seven intelligences such as: learning logs, drama, debates, music, role-play, models, mind maps, presentations, song, journals, have them create their own test questions, theater, etc.

Prepare parents for report cards. Make sure that the parents know how their child can succeed in each class. In the primary schools, take the opportunity to talk to them about the role of report cards. Encourage them to avoid any rewards or bribes for grades. Avoid "parent-shock." Make sure that they know well ahead of time if a student's grades have been dropping significantly. Talk to your students about your own grading policies. Have the policy written out and posted. Make it as clear and positive as you possibly can.

## Avoid Labels

Use positive language with parents when referring to their child. Remember, this child is their life! Avoid labels. Instead of saying a child is a trouble-maker, say "Susie often disrupts her classmates." Start each report card with a strength. Even if it is something a small as "Mary has such a great sense of humor." Refer to specific items, actions and classroom behaviors when at all possible.

## Distribution

If you pass out report cards in your classroom, do two things. First, talk to the students about what grades are for. Set it up as a positive experience by telling them that we all need feedback in life and this is some of the feedback on you. Secondly, pass them out at the end of class, naturally. Make sure that students know what to do if they feel they've been treated unfairly or have questions.

## Follow-up

If a parent contacts you about the report card and is unhappy, it's more important to be a good listener than a strong debater. Insuring future success with the child is important, so if the phone call is unsuccessful, meet in person.

## Your Health

Are you in your best health? You can be sure your students are getting subtle messages about your care for yourself (how you treat yourself and your overall self-esteem). Good teaching takes energy! Make sure you have an overall health and fitness program that includes stress reduction, relaxation, nutrition, cardio-vascular training, stretching and muscle toning. It sets a good example of participation, aliveness and self-esteem. Plus, you'll feel better, act better and teach better.

# Physical Messages

As you become increasingly convinced of your influence and suggestive learning impact on student behavior, your observations and distinctions will increase and with them, your results.

Posture is another powerful part of your presentation. Your posture gives an uninterrupted stream of messages about your joy, self-confidence and energy level. You may be pleased or surprised to know that you are not permanently stuck with your posture. There are qualified physical therapists and health practitioners who can do wonders with your back and shoulders.

A recent article in *Psychology Today* talked about the "mugger susceptibility" profile. It was discovered that persons whose posture was tentative, stooped and tired-looking invited attackers. In that same way, your room posture can often invite student attacks - whether physical, verbal or mental. This does not mean to walk as if there is a steel rod going up your back... it does mean to present yourself with pride, dignity and energy.

Avoid the "TGIF" and "Just try to make it through the day" attitude. Enjoy the *process* of teaching. Students will learn more from who you are as a person and how you deal with life than they will from what's in your lesson plan.

# Dress Standards

Your dress and grooming are the most visible and easily altered part of your presentation. John Malloy, author of *Dress For Success* and top nation-wide clothing consultant, used to be a teacher. As part of a research project, he did a study on the effects of clothing on learning in the classroom. The results are a powerful argument for the careful choice of clothing. Malloy summarized it this way:

> *"The outcome... proved that the clothing worn by the teachers substantially affected the work and attitude of pupils... a breakthrough in education! Clothing had a significant effect on discipline, work habits and attitudes in the room."*

Malloy claims that he has run surveys, experiments and tests which "would run several thousand pages" to find out the exact effects of clothing on people. In his experiments with teachers, he had two different teachers work with the same groups, then tested them separately. The teachers were matched for style, delivery and course content. The teacher who dressed more professionally and conservatively had students who out-produced the casually dressed teacher. His specifics include:

- Neatness counts - even dirt, spots or food marks on your clothing can be a source for an unwanted judgment.
- See yourself through your audiences' eyes. What looks great at 2-3 feet away may be quite ineffective at 10-20 feet away.
- Avoid strong bold patterns. They distract your audience - studies showed increased audience blink rates when exposed to loud patterns.

- Always be a contrast to your background. Make your outfit stand out just enough to be noticed easily.
- Keep your outfit quiet. Avoid things which jingle, crackle or scrape unless you're teaching preschool. Let your message be the noise.

Complete body hygiene is important. Check yourself for the following things. Are your clothes clean and pressed? Is your hair clean and combed? Are your shoes clean and shined? Are your face and hands clean and smelling good? Are your teeth brushed and breath smelling fresh? These all have the capacity to create or destroy that all-important rapport with your students.

# Your Self-Expression

Your language is a powerful medium of expression and the master teacher is very aware of it both in front of the room and in informal settings. As a role-model, it is inappropriate for teachers to use foul or abusive language, even when provoked. It is unprofessional (and not useful) to criticize (ever!) or make critical value judgments about your students. By the way, a judgment is different than an observation. Here's an example:

JUDGMENT:  "Johnnie is a real jerk-he doesn't want to learn."
**OBSERVATION: Johnnie is talking in a raised voice and is not completing his assignment.**

JUDGMENT:  "Susie is the brightest kid in the class"
**OBSERVATION: Susie has gotten the highest test score twice.**

JUDGMENT:  "That stupid assembly was a waste of my time."
**OBSERVATION: "I don't recognize any immediate value from the assembly."**

(Notice the shift from "it's out there" to "it's in my power")

# Affirm the Positive

At the beginning of reading, writing, math or other skill classes, it's common for students to say, "I'm awful at this." We hear ourselves when we affirm such thoughts and the effect of our words can be powerful. There is much truth to the self-fulfilling prophecy idea. Politely correct the statement made so the student would now say, "I used to do poorly in this," or "So far, my skills have not met my expectations." If that does not sound as if it is very different, or if the difference in the two phrases sounds trivial, please go back and re-read them. There is a universe of difference in saying, "I am..." versus "in the past I was...."

There's also a big difference between saying, "I'm awful at this" and "I'm not good at it." Your mind reacts strongest to the dominant influential words in the sentence. The mind hears "awful" in the first example and "good" in the second example. Which influencing words would you rather your students hear? Obviously the one that will build self-esteem.

This also applies to students. Never, ever call your students slow, rude, disrespectful, stupid, lazy or a pain in the neck. What you affirm you will reinforce. Affirm their goodness, their positive behaviors and what you like about them.

77

Instead of complaining about them by name-calling, simply tell them how it affects you. You're perfectly within your rights to say:

"I'm frustrated and irritated when you're late."
"I'm really disappointed when you let us both down."
"I'm hurt when you say that."

Learners need to know how they affect you. If you are embarrassed and hurt by their actions, tell them. However, you do not have a right to call them names. One mistake on your part can become a lifelong negative memory, polluting their school experience. Is it a double standard that they can call you names and you not able to do it back? Of course. No one ever said teaching was easy. It takes a thick skin and a heart of gold to teach. If you're unable to bite your tongue and keep negative comments to yourself, you have two choices: either work on your own negative behaviors or leave the profession. If you can't take criticism, find a job where you'll never be criticized. Your students deserve a fighting chance to make in this world. They need all the positives they can get.

# Take Acting Lessons

It's amazing how much "star" is bottled up inside every teacher. You have your own kind of charisma and electricity which is possible to bring out. Acting is a form of self-expression and one of the best things about acting classes is that they encourage the forms of self-expression which can ultimately serve you well in the room. For example, you can learn a simple facial expression which will create suspense, another which creates surprise, another which expresses appreciation and so on. From an acting class you have the opportunity to gain two important teaching tools:

1. You will be able to get your intended communication aligned with what actually "lands." Many teachers will say how much they care about their students, yet their body language shows otherwise. Or, a teacher may be really interested in the material and yet his presentation leaves the students bored to tears. This is one of the most common problems and a good acting coach can help you learn to get your communication across more effectively.
2. You will be able to utilize a wider range of expression in your presentation. Many teachers consider certain expressions and emotions taboo in the room. The only question to ask is, "How's your class?" If your class is terrific, you don't need much more flexibility. For most teachers, acting expands your choices and gives new possibilities for getting the results you want. If you have three ways to respond in class, you are likely to be less effective than someone who has ten ways. Behavioral flexibility is one of the biggest keys to room mastery and acting can bring it to you.

In a survey reported by Marilyn Ferguson in *Aquarian Conspiracy*, nation-wide leaders were asked to rate the most important instruments for social change. The one mentioned more than any other? Personal example.

# Set An Example

Teachers are observed, heard, felt and interacted with hour after hour. Every facet of a teacher's personality has an opportunity to surface and it usually does. Why pay attention to such detail about your personality? Because you, the teacher, are the single greatest determiner of your student's success. You are so much more important than the textbooks, the video, the room or the lesson plans. Because of that, the three most important keys to producing better students are:

> *Set an example*
> *Set an example*
> *Set an example*

In the late 60's, Marshall McLuhan popularized the expression, "The medium is the message." It may apply better to the teaching profession than any other. Although ultimately technology will augment or replace much of your impact, today you are the carrier of the room message. Because you have your own personality with attitudes, feelings and opinions, you will "package" your message uniquely. In short, there is no objective teacher. You are as much or more of a packager of information as a television set or videocassette player.

Because of this enormous influence, your own beliefs and values in education will filter and flavor your teaching. Take this as an opportunity to re-examine your "medium" more closely and make sure it represents you in the best possible way. In the moments before class begins, many details require your last-minute attention. These can make the difference between an average class and a great one. Top teachers take the time to make sure they have done their homework, just as they ask their students to do. For teachers, as with students, the payoff is enormous.

## Additional Resources for Further Study and Follow up

*Present Yourself* by Michael Gelb (Jalmar Press)*
*Awaken the Giant Within* by Anthony Robbins (Simon & Schuster)
*Unlimited Power* by Anthony Robbins (Simon & Schuster)
*The Skillful Teacher* by Saphier & Gower (Research for Better Teaching)

* These are available in the Appendix.

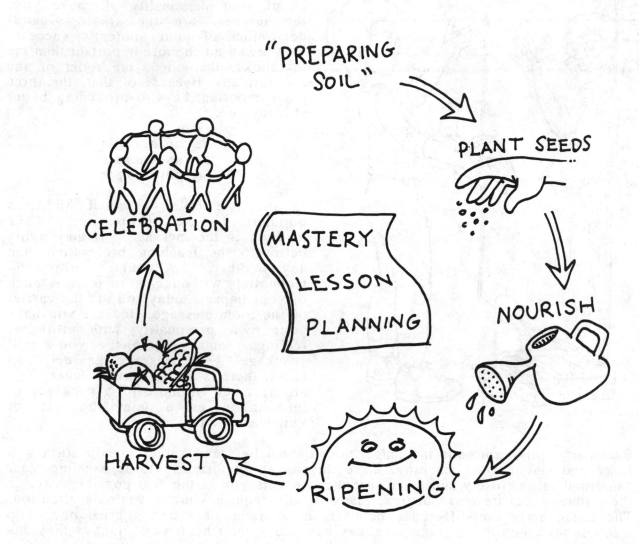

"PREPARING SOIL"

PLANT SEEDS

CELEBRATION

MASTERY LESSON PLANNING

NOURISH

HARVEST

RIPENING

# 7

## Lesson Planning

### Lesson vs. Learning Planning

Are you planning a lesson or planning learning? The old way was "Plan what there is to **teach**, then teach it." The new thinking is "What is there to **learn** and **how can it be learned** best?" After all, there are many, many "formats" suggested to teachers about the "right" way to teach. Where are the formats and plans that talk about how the learners will learn best? The shift in thinking for this chapter is a simple one: from lesson planning to learning planning.

**The Old Model:** From Teacher's Perspective,
Plan Content to Be Taught.

*Today's Model: From Learner's Point of View,
Plan How It Can Best Be Learned*

One of the first teachers to popularize the learner-centered approach was the popular therapist Dr. Carl Rogers. He called it "client-centered therapy." It focused on the needs of the customer, not the policies of a bureaucracy. It makes a lot of sense when applied to learning. Although the change seems subtle, it can end up being very powerful. Good lesson plans by themselves mean nothing. Some of the best designed lesson plans are guaranteed to fail unless the teacher has the resources with which to make them succeed. In fact, the more comprehensive, the more detailed the lesson plan is, and the greater the adherence to that plan, the greater your chances of failure. Why?

A great teacher navigates the course of learning. This means that you are ready, at every moment, to make changes, deletions or additions. Your students may respond in a way that prompts you to choose a totally different path. Draw mostly from your experience and the student's. Those are the only two things that count to them anyway. They will learn more from you than any textbook.

### Moving From "Covering the Content" to "Uncovering the Learning"

Our profession is NOT about filling up students with facts, but rather about opening up learners. Start with the premise that your students CAN learn and WILL learn. Avoid labels and make their genius your self-fulfilling prophecy. We're all in the business of creating environments in which exciting, fulfilling and empowering learning events can occur. We are in the service business and it is our job to make it work for the students. By recognizing that teaching is a service profession, we'll accomplish much more.

The course objectives are important, how you get there should allow for infinite possibilities. In summary, a good lesson plan will not make a poor teacher into a star. But a poor lesson plan CAN ruin even the best teacher's lesson. Contrary to a popular notion of "the better you are, the fewer notes you need," most highly competent teachers plan well. Creating the lesson plan provides clarity, and clarity leads to better classes. Masters can fail successfully, but the master always plans to succeed. "If I fail to plan, I am planning to fail."

## Benefits of Strong Learning Plans

- Allows you to stay focused on your outcome
- Gives you added confidence
- Allows for creative ideas to surface
- Gives you a place to make corrections and additions

In addition, strong learning plans can dramatically increase your chances:

1. To increase class structure and coherence
2. To have a concrete visual with which to "mentally walk through"
3. To experience satisfaction and a sense of completion
4. To create a permanent record of what's presented, when and how

The lesson plan is like the menu at a restaurant - it's a useful planning tool, but it's not the meal. In many ways, the process of planning is more important than the resulting physical piece of paper. The process insures you have thought out the salient points and how to present them. The lesson plan must get translated through you to the students. Translation and delivery are critical. The success of your lesson plans have more to do with the way you deliver them (the rapport, presentation skills and learning environment) than what's in them.

What master teachers have discovered is that there is always room for the spur of the moment story, activity, sharing, or inquiry if, and this is a big if... you have successfully taught your class all along. The structure is what makes the time and appropriateness for spontaneity. No one way of doing class is better than another, so your ability as a teacher to move flexibly with what is needed will create more time than it uses. A class could be both planned and spontaneous, for there is value which can come from each.

## Clarify Your Outcomes

The next part of learning planning is creating your intended results. This is often the easiest part for teachers since much training is directed in this area. Intended results are the behavioral objectives which should be specified in each area of the class or course. You need to have outcomes for your entire course, as well as for every one-to-one interaction, each activity and every talk. If you don't know what your goal is, how will you know when you've accomplished it?

A) **Does it have integrity?** Is the outcome you want consistent with the beliefs, values and attitudes that are necessary for the success of everyone? Is it consistent with the school policies? If the outcome has integrity, it's success is more likely.

B) **Does your outcome "dovetail" with learner goals?** Is it a "win-win?" Does it also include others in getting what they want? Have you included the wants and needs of the learners? If not, change it! This simple step dramatically increases the chances of achieving your outcome.

C) **Have you designated a time for completion?** Is your outcome for the next ten minutes or ten years? Is your short-term outcome consistent with your long-term one?

D) **Is your outcome stated in the positive?** Have you said what you **do** want to happen, not what you don't want?

E) **Do you have an evidence procedure?** How will you know when your outcome is reached? Do you have the resources to check it out? How would it look, sound or feel?

G) **Is the outcome of added value to your students?** Is it a new breakthrough, a challenge, a growing experience or a "stretch?"

Many of the previous outcomes are common for teachers. However, there are many additional outcomes you may want to consider. Some may not be so easily measured, yet could be of equal or greater value. For example, it may be useful if your students also got these items:

1. **Positive bias...** A good relationship with that subject, so that they have a continuing curiosity in it, know the relevancy of it and how it is related to their lives. A love of learning and an appreciation of that subject. Encouraging learning as a lifelong endeavor.

2. **HOW to learn it...** An understanding and awareness of, their own particular success strategies for that subject, and have some alternative ones for the future. In other words, do your students know how to learn it again? Are you teaching them the traditional WHAT to learn or the more useful HOW to learn it?

3. **The patterns of meaning...** Not just the disconnected information, but the larger patterns, models and themes.

To accomplish these, you must create a balance of the intellectual, emotional, physical, social, and aesthetic needs in your classroom. The easiest way to begin to include the above elements in your courses is through personal example and discussion. You must provide these. Your students will have no other place to get them in the classroom.

It is suggested that you create intended results for both a single class and the entire course. There is also the benefit of having clearly stated objectives by which to measure your progress. It is important to understand that the purpose of the course should have precedent over the intended results. In other words, if you feel you have to sacrifice a student's self-esteem in order to meet an objective, don't do it. The purpose is the very reason and intention of the entire course and the intended results are set up more for clarity and for providing a vehicle with which to measure progress.

The first step in creating the intended results is to identify the completed behavior. Using the sample guidelines above, we state an objective: "To be able to write the chemical formula accurately for photosynthesis." Notice that we said nothing about the teacher's opinions, interests, or judgments. We did not say, "To be able to understand photosynthesis well." This is because the last objective is stated in an individual teacher's terms... and what does "well" mean? To be able to write an article on it? Examples of clear and unclear objectives are below:

**UNCLEAR:** to learn the key parts of the class novel
**CLEAR:** for each student to role-play two characters, then submit a one paragraph summary conclusion on the experience by next Tuesday at 2pm - may be done in the form of a mind map, essay, audiotape, video or learner choice

**UNCLEAR:** to know the US. role in the Arab-Israeli war
**CLEAR:** learner to demonstrate 1) each major way the US aided Israel 2) theories on why they aided Israel 3) speculations about the future of that area 4) recommendations for success 5) demonstrate the relationships of this to other historic roles in history and 6) discuss the meaning in this for you, personally

# Three Major Learning Areas

Most commonly, the three major learning areas are cognitive (what we know), psychomotor (what we do) and affective (what we feel). There are many types of learners, so you need to insure each class has components which appeal to a broad base of them. Include a variety of these processes:

1. **Cognitive:** commonly known as what we know, but better defined as:
   A. Knowledge... being able to recall and define
   B. Comprehension... to translate into own words
   C. Application... using tools outside original context
   D. Analysis... to note strong and weak points
   E. Synthesis... to create from other parts
   F. Evaluation... to compare and contrast
2. **Psychomotor:** commonly known as physical skills, also:
   A. Accuracy... to be able to hit a target
   B. Coordination... to be able to move within parameters
   C. Manipulation... to create cause and effect
3. **Affective:** known as values, feelings and attitudes:
   A. Attending... participation and commitment
   B. Responding... intensity and quantity of response
   C. Valuing... importance and worth, biases
   D. Values expression... to be willing to share freely

# Accelerating the Learning

The book *Superlearning* by Ostrander and Schroeder first attracted attention to exciting new ways to learn. Published by Dell in 1979, it glamorized the global development of powerful teaching and learning disciplines. Accelerated Learning is actually the generic name for a field which embodies many separate but interrelated disciplines. One reason it is tough to define is that instead of it being a small fixed body of knowledge, it's a dynamic, growing and inclusive domain.

Brought to the Western world in the 1970's by Dr. Georgi Lozanov of Bulgaria, Accelerated Learning (different from the "Accelerated Schools project of Dr. Levin out of Stanford) is now gaining fast acceptance worldwide. The field is large because it includes other fields such as music, theater, storytelling, brain research, total physical response, cooperative learning, rituals, nonconscious learning, alpha states, suggestion, multiple intelligences and NLP.

Dr. Lozanov documented that by utilizing more of the potential of the human brain, we are able to accelerated the learning from 3-10X over the results of more traditional methods. No one in the Western world has duplicated those amazing results. However, many teachers and trainers have reported double the standard predictable gains and much greater student enthusiasm, a deeper understanding and greater long term value.

# Ingredients of Success

Exactly what is Accelerated Learning and how do you do it? First of all, it is the synergistic results of learning with positive, multi-modal joyful engagement. The primary medium is the teacher's artful use of positive suggestion. The accelerated learner becomes intrinsically motivated towards greater self-worth and mastery of content. It is an immersion environment in which the learner LOVES to learn and feels competent in the process of learning. Amazingly enough, much of the time, the learner is unaware of exactly how MUCH is going on. Only that a lot is going on and it is fun!

How do you know when a situation is accelerated learning versus simply good old fashioned teaching? Simple. There are seven ingredients to an accelerated learning environment. ALL SEVEN must be present for it to have the "magic" that gives it the well-deserved reputation that it has. Here they are:

**1. Sensory-rich immersion environment.** One full of sights, sounds and things to do. Affirmations on the wall like, "Your Success is Absolutely Assured." Possibly aromas from flowers, food or potpourri. Comfortable seating, with plenty of natural lighting if possible. Flood the senses with an interesting array of sensory-stimulating, fresh and new experiences. Put up large mind maps or memory maps of the upcoming content so that students can get a preview. Positive, uplifting music played. The purpose of this environment is both for enriching stimulation of the brain, to create novelty and to allow the learner to enter another world.

**2. Preparation and conditioning of the learner.** A traditional teacher hopes that students come to them motivated and ready to learn. An accelerated learning teacher assumes that students come with many barriers to learning and artfully plans an assault on those barriers. The barriers include:

- **Intuitive-emotional:** the fear of failure, embarrassment or even success... fear can be overcome by warm, positive teacher interactions and early successes in the subject area

- **Critical-logical:** the limiting decisions made by students who believe that they aren't smart enough, or it's not "in the family," or the subject is "too hard"... can be overcome by affirmation, significant successes, reframing or teams

• **Ethical-moral:** the values that hold that learning is "hard work" or that it's "no pain, no gain"... any limiting value originating from parents, the church, etc., can be overcome through cooperation and communication

• **Biological-medical:** poor learning because of inadequate nutrition, food additives, drugs... can be overcome through education, support and healthy alternatives

• **Cultural-Social:** these barriers include peer pressure, traditional folk culture, ethnic customs and learning styles... can be overcome by inclusion... insure the medium used to deliver the content is full of the participant's own cultural icons, myths, stories and meaning

• **Institutional-Physical:** these are triggered by the mere presence of a large bureaucracy or those suggested by television, radio or movies... barriers may be a dislike of authority, an irreverence towards school or approval of socially antagonistic behaviors

Think of all the student concerns and likely negative beliefs in your subject matter and make sure that you address each of those in your curriculum planning. Here's an example for math:

"I can't learn it"
"It's too hard"
"It is too boring"
"It is for geniuses or nerds"
"I'll never use it again"
"It goes in one ear and out the other"
"I'll forget it in no time"

Once you have identified the likely beliefs that are common underminers for your subject, plan to address each of them. For example, on the last belief listed above, set up some simple mnemonic device to insure that students remember each of the key points from the day's class. Put up posters or peripherals to help address those negative beliefs: "Math is easy" or "Math is a big part of my everyday life." Use positive suggestion in your language: "After you've successfully completed your group's fun project with those word problems, raise your hand, so I'll know you're all done."

**3. Diversity of learning styles, use of memory keys and multiple intelligences format.** This means presenting content in the following learning styles:
• visual, auditory, kinesthetic, olfactory and gustatory
• abstract, concrete, global and linear
• inductive, deductive, intuitive, match & mismatch
• field dependent, field independent
• past, present and future referenced

Use of memory keys means utilizing the five "natural" memory sources that we have (taxon is the one "unnatural" type). These easy-to-use memories are:

• musical... use of songs to learn (alphabet song)
• linguistic... use of humor, mnemonics, rhyme, puns, sequencing
• motor... use of body to learn (role-play, hands-on activities)

- contextual/spatial... based on location & circumstances
    (teach using various corners of the room, the outdoors, use
    desktops, costumes, vary lighting, sound, color, seating, etc.)
- sensory... use of intense visual, auditory, kinesthetic,
    olfactory and gustatory (use of intense aromas, food,
    specially-anchored sounds, costume, props, etc.)

Use of the multiple intelligences means creating the context where every student can succeed. There are many ways to be smart and the context determines the evidence. Dr. Howard Gardner of Harvard University says there are seven ways to learn:

- verbal-linguistic... lecture, tapes, sharing, reading
- interpersonal... groupwork, partners, cooperative
- bodily-kinesthetic... action, movement, simulations
- spatial... artwork, mindmaps, re-design of environment
- intrapersonal... self-assessment, intuition, metacognition
- mathematical-logical... problem-solving, math, prediction
- rhythmic-musical... patterns of music, sound and meaning

**4. Student-centered learning.** This means that students are involved in decision-making about the course, it's direction and methods. There are several reasons for this: 1) it develops responsibility in students 2) students are more motivated and participate more in decisions that they are involved in 3) the research shows achievement scores go up 4) students enjoy class more. Ways to do this are:

- ask for student input on content
- give students subject, and they create games with it
- give students choice about doing something now or later
- have a suggestion box and act on useful ideas
- allow students to teach, present and interact often
- students co-create rules, if appropriate
- use of teams, partners and formal classroom buddies
- empathic listening
- needs met for acknowledgment, privacy, acceptance
- cultural diversity encouraged and used for learning

**5. Strong use of suggestion & de-suggestion.** Everything we do reminds our brain of something. Lozanov said "Everything is suggestion." That means that the clothes you wear, the materials you use, the seating arrangements, the tonality of your voice, volume and tempo all give signals. The best ways to give positive suggestions to your students are the following:

- use of positive affirmation posters
- make the room friendly, greet at the door with a smile
- totally positive interactions
- music in a major key and with positive messages
- well-dressed, pleasing smile
- speak well of the possibilities of each student
- congruent gestures, tonality, volume, facial expressions
- use of stories with themes or myths that reach the nonconscious
- continual verbal, visual and kinesthetic affirmations

You'll also be countering the student's unproductive suggestions like "I'm a slow learner" or, "I hate school" or, "This is useless." Your counter suggestions or de-suggestions might be ones like, "I can learn quickly and easily," or "School is what I make it," or "This is an important part of my life."

**6. Emotions engaged with purposeful play and spontaneous celebrations.** This is one of the critical factors in learning acceleration for several reasons: 1) the emotions can only be engaged if the learner has been prepared for learning 2) the emotions are one of the keys to engaging long-term memory 3) the learning often becomes peripheral or secondary to the activity, hence perceived by the learner as less stressful and easier 4) emotions trigger the positive brain chemicals which may lead to a future love of learning. Examples of ways to engage emotions:

- simulations like cities, stores, restaurants
- re-do common games into academic games using cards, ball
    toss, puppets, commercials, school situations
- use of music, especially for rituals
- contests which are a win-win for the players
- theater, role-play and acting
- concert-readings (reading fiction or nonfiction to the interplay
    of music, usually from the classical or romantic period)
- celebrating milestones or end point successes
- fun rituals which open & close your class... like music, student
    drum rolls, "Oooohhhhs and aaaahhhhs" and cheers
- use of teams which interact strongly without competing

**7. Orchestrated learning through artful management of student states.** This is the one quality which, more than any other, leads to the "magic" in Accelerated Learning. After all, you can do a lot of things "mechanically correct" but unless you put your students into the appropriate states and read where they're at, you'll have a dead, boring class. In fact, some go so far as to say, "Managing states is your number one job." And they may be right. After all, all learning is state-dependent. And if you or your students are not in the appropriate states for learning, you're both wasting your time. It's that simple!

# Skills Model

1. **Create proper "state."** The teacher must evoke a personal peak physiological state of enthusiasm, excitement, flexibility, love and caring. Then the teacher must elicit from the students a state of interest, curiosity, confidence, attentiveness, joy and relaxation.

2. **Relationship developed.** The teacher establishes rapport with the students on both conscious level and non-conscious levels. Then the teacher creates a student-subject or skill relationship by making it global and relevant.

3. **Outcomes established.** They must be measurable, in directly observable behavioral terms. They must be beneficial and value-oriented so that the students know: "what's in it for me?" Outcomes must also be ecological and be in alignment with the students personal morals, ethics, emotions or personal history. Both the teacher and student must agree upon them.

4. **Give historical or literary metaphor.** Make sure that the students have internally accessed a model of the "parts" and the "whole" of what the skill is like when used, or some similar skill.

5. **Reality bridge established.** Create a "Future Party" to celebrate in advance, the successful mastery of the skills. Have the students get up and walk around the room as in a party atmosphere. Have them congruently congratulate others, with emotion, on their success in learning the new skill. This "bridge" activity allows students to begin to integrate the new skill with their personality and self-image.

6. **Demonstration.** Give an accurate demonstration after showing and telling the students what to look for first.

7. **Digitalization of the demonstration.** Next, re-do the activity in micro-steps so that each step is understood and repeated by the group. Elicit the steps from the students (have them SHOW you visually, TELL you auditorially, and DO it kinesthetically) to insure that they know each of the steps precisely.

8. **Instructions for the structured experience.** Tell and show the students how to practice the skill, whether it's with partners or in small groups. It is crucial that they do it with others to get the feedback, correction and reinforcement. The directions must be very specific and clear. Make them easy to understand, and present them in all three modes: visually, auditorially and kinesthetically.

9. **Closely supervised experience.** Make sure that you have adequate supervision to insure that the skills are learned. Discover the class leaders and have them help monitor others if you are unable to do it alone. Once you get the feedback that your presentation has been successful, it's time for closure. This means a teacher or student evaluation, time for questions, review, clarification and affirmation of what was learned. It's also useful to generalize the information to other areas, globalize its importance and review its relevancy.

10. **Check-in.** As soon as it's over, ask how it went, and ask for questions. Make sure that the entire experience is well understood and integrated. Also make sure that the students feel good about their experience of it and that their self-worth is intact. Then, make sure that the skill is generalized by the students and you to other areas of their lives. This gives relevancy and greater value to the exercise.

## Planning the Content Learning

Here is an example of a lesson plan format you can follow. If you have 45 minutes or 45 hours, it will work. You may want to use this as a guideline for your upcoming lessons. We'll start with the physical environment and the climate for learning.

What negative-suggestive factors could be eliminated from the learning environment? What positive ones can we build into it? The environment includes all wall posters, decorations, assignments, notices, etc., on the walls. It includes temperature, lighting, room neatness, circulation, setup, and the general impression created. It also includes the pre-lesson set - the clues and tools necessary to begin learning before class starts. Finally, the learning environment includes the personal, emotional and psychological readiness of the teacher, and his or her appearance.

## 1. Preparation

**Do as many of these as are appropriate:**
- Pre-expose learners to topic - (can be done hours, days and weeks in advance: this helps the brain build better conceptual maps)
- Offer learn-to-learn skills
- Teach brain nutrition and offer coping, self-esteem & life skills
- Create a strong immersion learning environment; make it interesting!
- Reinforce your own credibility and prestige
- Plan best time of day for learning each item based on brain cycles and rhythms
- Discover students' interests & background - they set their own goals
- Make sure your environment has many colorful peripherals posted
- Provide brain "wake-ups" (cross-laterals or relax-stretching)
- State strong positive expectations; allow learners to voice theirs also
- Create relationships, strong positive rapport
- Read audience states and make any adjustments before beginning

The teacher must first evoke from within an excited physiological state of flexibility, enthusiasm, care, positivism and love. Only in this state can a teacher have access to their own range of resources and only in this "electric" state can a teacher even hope to get the students excited over the class. Next, the teacher must elicit a resourceful learning state from the students themselves. Students must be accessing their best self for optimal learning. This means the teacher takes responsibility for putting the student "in state" before teaching anything.

Establish rapport with the students. It should be done on a conscious level by finding common ground and sharing the ways they are like their students. Also, and more importantly, rapport must be developed unconsciously with the use of artful matching and mirroring of your student's body language, gestures, and voice quality. In addition, the teacher must create a favorable relationship in the student's mind with the subject you are about to teach. In order for the student to want to learn it, they need to be curious and understand the relevancy and global nature of the subject.

Other preparation tools include: introducing the topic, exciting the students, making it relevant, clearing expectations, giving positive learning suggestions, imbedded commands, opening ritual, relaxation, early learning re-stimulation, selling the benefits of the material to the students, building teams, conveying interest in and care for, the students, physical stretching, building trust, establishing credibility, ground rules, etc. This is a good time for an "as if" frame where the students go into the future and congratulate themselves on learning so easily and using the learning confidently.

Put outcomes in measurable, behavioral terms. Make sure that they offer value and benefits to the students. Make sure that they are ethical, moral and emotionally comfortable for the students. Then, most importantly, secure student agreement on the outcomes. In some cases, it may be useful merely to secure a commitment to work towards the outcome, while with others it may be to have the students co-create them.

Start with the end in mind. Once in a while you might use the "As if" frame. They will "act as if" they have already mastered the material, and "act as if" they are at the end of your class. Describe it as a "future party" and have students get up and walk around and talk to other students. Have them brag to or congratulate others (with congruency and emotion) about the success they just had learning in your class. This role-playing insures that the students accept the new material as part of their self-image and become comfortable with it as well.

## 2. Globalization

**Do as many of these that are appropriate:**
- Provide the context for learning this topic and background (can be in the form of an overview first - this is the classic "big picture").
- Elicit from learners what possible value & relevance it has to them - learners have to feel connected to the topic before you begin. Let them express how they feel it's relevant, not just you telling them.
- The brain learns particularly well from concrete experiences first! Can you provide something real, physical or concrete?
- The optimum "hook" is one with novelty that meets strong personal learner needs and taps into curiosity and real life themes

This may also include puppets, flipcharts or other dramatic aids, such as slides, videos, special effect sounds, multi-media, plus anything else your creativity provides.

## 3. Initiation

**Do as many of these as are appropriate:**
- Immersion in the topic: Flood with content! Instead of the singular, lock-step, sequential, one-bite-at-a-time information, there's an initial virtual overload of ideas, details, themes and meanings. Allow a sense of temporary overwhelming in learners: it'll be followed by anticipation, curiosity, and a determination to discover meaning for oneself. Over time it all gets sorted out, by the learner, brilliantly. If that sounds like the real world of learning, outside the classroom, you're right.
- This can also be the time to provide concrete learning experiences. It can be problem-solving, a field trip, interviews or hands-on learning. Learners may have some choice in how to do this. Ideally it employs all the senses: visual, auditory, kinesthetic, olfactory and gustatory.
- It could be a group or team project to build, find, explore, or to physically design, etc.
- Learning is best when it's based on discovery, need and themes; allow them to discover something new they're interested in, help the learners make it important and needed, and make it thematic.
- Learners could attend theater, put on a skit, a commercial, or make a newspaper, etc.
- A well-designed computer program can work here, such as HOTS.

This step offers enough choice to engage many learning styles. It is *not* "go home and read chapters four and five." This step provides the source of discussion since it's experiential. The key here is that since all do it, all learners are on equal ground.

## 4. Elaboration

**Do as many of these as are appropriate:**
• Tie things together thematically, like a jigsaw puzzle making sense.
• Learners can write, ask or design questions, go into data bases.
• One option is for the learners to read up on the topic or watch a video.
• It's a good time to restate questions, write a test or hold peer discussions.
• Learners can sort, analyze or make mind-maps of the material.
• Learners can create a forum - use a large group or smaller teams.
• The teacher can answer student questions or elaborate on ideas.
• Students can play the teacher role - ask, interpret questions and ideas.

This is the processing stage. It requires genuine thinking. It may be an open-ended de-briefing of the previous activity. This is the time to make intellectual sense out of the learning.

## 5. Incubation

**Do as many of these as are appropriate:**
• This critical time is for unguided reflection, "down time"... The brain is most effective learning over time, not all at once.
• It is appropriate to have at least several hours, several days away from the topic. That way the brain gets time to subconsciously sort, process & connect ideas. Great for intrapersonal time.
• It could be a day off, a recess, silent time, journal writing time, relaxation time or simply a change of subjects.

Incubation can be either active or passive. Active review might include group unison oral recall, use of lap boards for visual recall or hand signals for kinesthetic recall. Passive review would mean an eyes-closed process with soft music in the background while you recount the key ideas. This could also be a relaxed re-delivery of the same material using music as a background. The purpose is to use it to "carry" the material in a relaxed way, while you add the content as a secondary backstage addition. In other words, focus the attention on the relaxation, so that the material becomes secondary - hence learned easier.

## 6. Verification

**Do as many of these as are appropriate:**
• The students create a presentation with teaching tools, using peer teaching.
• The student designs questions for a test, then the teacher interviews the student.
• Use both a written assessment and a verbal assessment.
• The student creates a project - a working model, a mind map, a video, a newsletter, etc.
• The student presents a role-play or lesson to the class.

This step is for the learner as much as the teacher. Using the ideas in this book on assessment, learners demonstrate what they know. Learning has to be made personally relevant. It occurs best when a model or metaphor is made by the learner about the new learning.

Make an ungraded quiz, self-corrected and uncollected. The students work together, usually in pairs, continually changing partners from one day to the next. This can also be one of several parts of the class which allows the students to integrate the content into the affective domain, the right hemisphere and the unconscious mind. For example if they learned your original material visually, now present it auditorally and kinesthetically. Especially use role-play, simulations, skits, etc.

This step could include group discussions, interviews, games, physical movements, a dance or a quiz show. Primary focus is on the activity, not the material. This is the time saved for review and wrap-up. Also, it's an excellent time to help students feel confident and competent with the material presented, to integrate it into the rest of what they know. To preview the next class, offer congruent congratulations and future pace them to using the material. This includes the closing ritual.

## 7. Celebration

**Do as many of these as are appropriate:**
- Students who use a rubric to evaluate their work can tell each other how they did. Celebration needs to engage emotions also; have a toast with juice!
- It's bragging time, it's time to peer share, it's time to show others a demonstration of your work. It's a time to share success & give acknowledgments to peers. Make it fun, light and joyful.
- Music, streamers, horns and compliments can be part of the celebration.
- It can be as simple as giving a classmate a "high-five", or as complex a designed activity as a class-designed and produced celebration party.
- In this step create the all-important love of learning. Never miss it!

This step provides for the all-important self-convincers. See chapter two for rationale. These are best provided primarily by peers, secondarily by a teacher. Reinforcement needs modality (V-A-K), frequency (repeat it) & duration (time).

You might start your close with a short relaxation exercise with the students in the form of "future pacing" their new skill. Have them go into the future in their imagination, then successfully use the skills. Make sure they see, hear and feel themselves use the skills and get reinforcement for it. Once the imaginary part is complete, have them get up and physically act out the same part in a "future party." Let the students tell others how much they have used their new skills, how good they are at them, and how easy they are to maintain. Have students shake hands, laugh, and have fun. Then, end the party, and congruently congratulate them for learning a new skill and wish them well.

# An Interdependent Approach:
# Thematic Learning Planning

The old way of teaching was to take a subject like math, science or history and divide it into smaller chunks called units. Then the teacher would sub-divide the units into daily and weekly lesson plans. Each day, the teacher would present a micro-chunk of the whole. It sounds logical. But it is not the way our brain is best designed to learn.

Imagine yourself as a three or four year-old once again. You get your first bicycle for your birthday. Now you're all excited and you want nothing more than to jump on it and go! But wait...you can't. Your parents have decided that you should learn to ride a bicycle the proper way in the right "order." They will teach you how to ride a bicycle by instructing you in the following units of content:

**A. History of the bicycle**
1. Original inventors
2. Purchase price & replacement costs
   i. New vs. used prices
   ii. Contingency plan for frame or mechanical damage
3. Transportation niche
   i. Advantages and disadvantages of usage
   ii. Comparisons with other modes
4. Mechanical & product specifications
   i. Materials used

**B. Safety**
1. Personal safety
   i. Proper strength
   ii. Defensive attitude
2. Neighborhood safety
   i. Possible hazards
   ii. Neighborhood culture
3. Sidewalk and Road safety
   i. Laws, customs and bicycle maintenance

**C. The Skills of Riding**
1. The mental approach
2. The first steps
3. Proper use of training wheels
4. Body positioning
5. Advanced riding skills

**D. Everyday Use**
1. Social advantages (visit with friends)
2. Value of exercise and fresh air
3. Storage of bicycle (locks, garage, etc.)
4. Permission (when, length of time, etc.)
5. Extras (Horn, basket, etc.)

Naturally, before your parents have completed teaching you just unit "A", you have lost interest and gone on to do something else. The brain is far more capable than the list above indicates. Obviously, a more typical child's approach is to get a few bits of important information, then hop on a bike and give it a try.

> *The brain learns best in real-life,*
> *immersion-style multi-path learning...*
> *fractured, piecemeal teaching can*
> *kill off the love of learning*

Amazingly enough, most kids learn to ride a bike just fine. But if you think about it, that's how you learned some of the most complex things in your life. Your native language, for example. Did you learn rules of grammar first? Did you get classes in it? Did you take tests in it? Of course not! You never formally were taught your native language. You "picked it up."

Is it possible that our brain can "pick up" other subjects? Is possible to learn science, history, geography, math, life skills, literature and the arts by just "picking them up?" Of course it is! That's the way our brain is designed to learn: multi-path, in order or out of order, many levels, many teachers, many contexts and many angles. We learn with themes, favorite subjects, issues, key points, questions, trial and error and application. That is exactly what thematic learning is all about.

> *Thematic learning is a process*
> *closer to the way the human brain*
> *is naturally designed best to learn*

The underlying principle is that our world is an integrated whole, and that one of the greatest gifts you can offer your students is the connectedness of classroom education to the real world. The thematic approach urges you to follow threads that weave throughout your student's world instead of a single subject or textbook. Textbooks are not only often out of date, but more importantly, they present a single viewpoint or approach which the authors have chosen. In this fast-moving information age, your preferred sources of information should be the student's real life experience, magazines, computers, videos, television, journals and libraries.

The theme approach was designed by master teacher Susan Kovalik and explained in *ITI: The Model*. You may want to purchase it. The basic components of it are as follows:

1. **Year-long Theme:** This is a year long, (or semester long), organizational structure consisting of a basic theme with a kid-grabbing title. If it's unknown by the kids, it's a poor cognitive organizer. Pick a topic that you can work with for a year.

   **Examples might be:** The Zoo (grade 1-2) "What Makes it Tick?" (3-5th grade) The Mississippi River (4-6th grade)

   Themes should have the following qualities: your excitement, student understanding and excitement, worthy of extensive time invested, plenty of materials and resources available for it, has application to student's real world, it has a clear pattern and the rationale is compelling for learners.

2. **Sub-Components:** The physical locations and the human issues. Use situations, events, contributions by students.

   **Examples from the themes above:** "The Zoo" (geography of the world's zoos, animals, systems to run a zoo, economics of a zoo, endangered species, colors of animals, foods eaten, the food chain, etc.)

   "What Makes It Tick?" (clocks of the past, the world as a clock, geologic time, famous clocks, making watches, timers, body clocks, calendars, mechanisms, computers, etc.)

   "The Mississippi River" (inhabitants, who is affected, geology, stores & businesses, the folklore, the uses of water, the name itself, fishing, changes in river paths, flooding, agriculture, weather, maps, etc.)

3. **Weekly Topics:** A specific aspect of the location or human issues will be studied, about one per week.

Suggestions: Use the newspapers, television, kid's examples and school issues to tie into each of the components.

4. **Relevant Key Points:** Concepts, skills, knowledge, attitudes, values, models and patterns.

Suggestions: Brainstorm the essential things you'd like students to learn. Identify your resources: physical locations, CD-ROM, library, school sites, guest speakers, computers, etc. Your goal is a real hands-on immersion. Study your districts scope and sequence of curriculum mandates. Integrate the child's points of curiosity; what are their "whys" and "wherefores?" You become a learner all over again and are-experience the joy of learning.

5. **Specific Inquiries:** These are the more precise applications of the key points. You may want to use the various levels of Bloom's Taxonomy and integrate the learning into Gardner's Multiple Intelligences.

**Examples:** The Zoo (*Knowledge:* list and describe all the animals in the zoo. *Comprehension:* group them in to categories and discuss why and how. *Application:* build a model lion enclosure that lions would like. *Analysis:* write and sing a rap about the daily life of animals... what is it like from their point of view? *Evaluation:* create a checklist of desirable enclosure qualities, visit your own zoo and evaluate ten animal's quality of life there. *Synthesis:* using what you've learned from ideal zoo environments, let's pretend visitors from another world came to earth and wanted to make a zoo full of humans. What do you think a zoo for humans would be like? Work in groups and draw it out on a huge piece of paper. Discuss and describe to the class).

## Thematic Learning in a Nutshell

To understand it conceptually, picture a spider web. The title is in the center (your year-long theme). If you have nine months, you'd have nine branches coming out from the center of the web, much like spokes of a wheel. Those are the monthly components. On each of the spokes, you'd have weekly topics, four of them. Certainly you can vary it as situations may arise to alter your plans. But this thematic style of teaching and learning has been demonstrated far more effective than the traditional unit, chunk, unit chunk, all unrelated and piecemeal.

The classroom becomes a living, learning laboratory. The learning is connected and the themes are relevant. Think of the classroom possibilities for discussion, projects, plays and writing! Give your students a list of at least ten addresses where students can write to for free information including US. Government agencies, the Chamber of Commerce as well as state agencies. Better yet, help them discover for themselves, how to locate addresses, phone numbers and contact persons for each unit. This is a terrific way for them to become a lifelong learner.

## Additional Resources for Further Study and Follow up

*The Mind Map Book* by Buzan
*Use Both Sides of Your Brain* by Buzan (Penguin)*
*Interdisciplinary Curriculum: Design & Implementation* by Jacobs ((ASCD)
*ITI: The Model (Integrated Thematic Instruction)* by Kovalik (Books for
    Educators)*
*Mapping Innerspace* by Margulies (Zephyr)*
*Mind Mapping & Memory* by Svantesson (Brain Books)
*Imagine That!* by Waas (Jalmar)*
*The Power of Color* by Walker (Avery Group)*
*Learning to Learn* by Ward & Daley (A & H Print Consultants)


* Items marked with an asterisk are available in the Appendix.

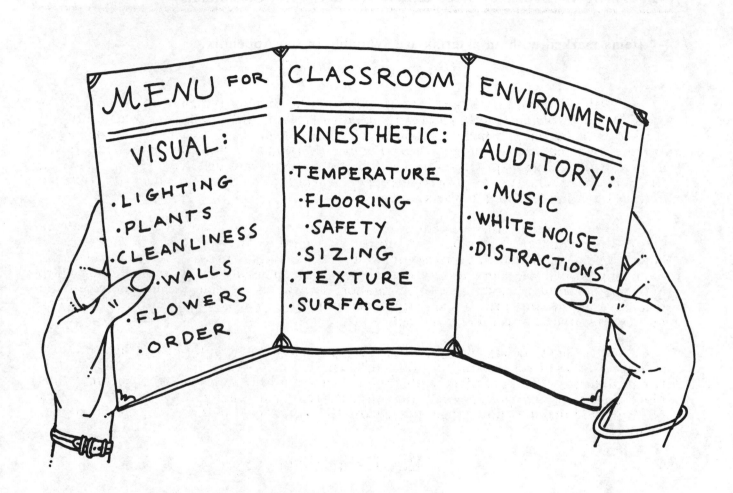

# 8

# *Learning Environment*

## Environments Can Teach

With all the hours spent in a classroom, the cumulative environmental effects on both students and teachers have tremendous impact. Many consider the traditional classroom a "prime obstacle" to learning. What can be done to change the negative associations that many students have about classrooms? A lot. An artfully designed and carefully planned positive-suggestive environment can do 25% of your teaching for you. Conversely, a poorly-designed learning environment can significantly detract from the learning process.

Every moment the student's eyes are not on you, they are taking in the classroom - sometimes in parts, sometimes as a whole. The environment they take in must reflect your end purposes or you risk results. A well-designed learning environment can do many things. At its best, it can create a favorable relationship between the student and the subject matter. It can also create rapport between the teacher and the student. It can stimulate thought, creativity and curiosity. It can build self-esteem, confidence and self worth.

At its best, it can inform, influence, persuade and excite. It can add to your student's level of responsibility, sense of justice and positive feelings about school. It can definitely do part of the job for you and much to make your classroom "the" place to be. When you change the environment you change the people. If this possibility intrigues you, then get ready for some big changes and even bigger results.

## Read This First

This chapter includes some generalities about classrooms. You, as a teacher, may be in the sciences, humanities, at elementary or college levels, in metaphysics, business or the arts. By their very nature, these teaching environments will be very different from one another. Make any distinctions, deletions, and modifications in order to make the information in this chapter useful for you. In spite of that, it's likely that you'll find this information to be extremely valuable. It's about how can you set up a classroom to improve the impact of what you are already doing.

Regardless of the room assigned, the possibility exists to make it work well. Teachers cannot always turn their classroom into a Better Homes and Gardens award winner or an Architectural Digest showcase, but it can be made bright, nurturing, expressive, useful, and humane.

To make a classroom look right, it usually takes some money. Much can be done for $50 or less. There are more ways to decorate a classroom for free than there are stores to shop in. There are major sources of paper, art objects, plants, and other classroom items that cost nothing or next-to-nothing. Most beautiful classroom environments are put together with a combination of donated, borrowed, budget-bought items and spontaneous creations. Having no or low classroom budgets cannot justify an ineffective classroom.

The research on the human brain in regards to enrichment is very persuasive. More challenge, novelty, engagement of emotions, color and feedback are ideal for the learning and growing of the human brain. This means an environment that is interactive, interesting, personalized and relevant. It also needs to be changed often, either by you or the learners.

*Research suggests that your learning environment*
*should be changed every 2-4 weeks to keep the*
*brain curious and your learners engaged*

Do your best to "unsettle the set" often and change the traditional associations that students have in the classroom. Make the classroom as different as possible every day. Change where you have the front of the room often at least once a week! Change where you have the back of the room. Have the students sit on the floor (yes, even secondary and college level students). Have them sit on tables, on the backs of chairs, on pillows, ANYTHING to keep changing the formalized lecture-theater style seating arrangement.

Everything that we have discovered about the brain in the last twenty years suggests that we need more stimulus, more change, more movement and more points of view in the classroom. The most unproductive arrangement possible is the standard, rigid sit-still format that is driving most students and hence teachers, crazy. Of course, whenever weather or finances permit, work with your students in the less traditional environments: take field trips, teach science in a nearby field and use the rest of the school or neighborhood as a place to learn.

# How to Get Help

To get help, be helpful. Help other teachers with their classes. Most teachers find themselves doing things that are actually the responsibility of others. The solution is to support those others in them doing their job more effectively, or be willing to do the jobs yourself, without resentment. Those last two words are important. The best way to do any job is with a song in your heart.

For example, if something is the responsibility of the custodian and it didn't get done, stop for a moment. Recall how many times last month you complimented or left a thank-you note for the janitor? Remember, too, that sometimes we must do what is necessary for the result we want, regardless of our job description! Winston Churchill said, "It is not enough that we do our best; sometimes we have to do what's required."

In an institutional classroom, the room is an on-going project and a system can be implemented where the students have their own team that rotates and is responsible for the looks of the room. They are allowed to create, give input and contribute the things which they are good at, whether it is drawing, painting, synthesizing, giving advice, or scavenging for useful items. In this spirit, it is possible to have a beautiful and functional classroom which is being constantly kept up by your own students. The appropriate time to set that up may not be right now, but something which is woven into the curriculum at a later time as the mastery within you expands. If you have to move from room to room, make up a "kit" to take with you that has your own "portable environment."

## Safety is First

Safety is a primary consideration for teachers, above all else. Each teacher should be familiar with how to prevent and deal with any type of physical emergency. Teachers must know where the fire extinguisher is and the nearest phone. In addition, you should have for easy access, a listing of doctor, police and fire numbers. In addition, make sure you know who to call in case of other emergencies such as a nervous breakdown, epilepsy, or psychiatric problems.

You should have a first aid kit on hand which includes plenty of gauze, tape and band-aids. Also have access to a broom for cleaning up glass, plus cloths and rags for spilled items. Know how to contact the building administrator or manager. Other necessary information includes knowing emergency procedures for fire escape, earthquakes, floods, hurricanes, windstorms, power failures, and blizzards. These are all part of the overall safety of your students and they are just as important as anything else a teacher does or knows about.

## Room Preparation

As part of your pre-class preparation, the physical room must be checked out quickly. Run through your check list to confirm all is ready:

1. Is the room neat and organized?
2. Is all the trash put away, chairs neat?
3. Are all chairs arranged the way they're needed?
4. Are all the books or handouts counted and readied?
5. Are the materials spot checked?
6. How's the room temperature, breeze, humidity?
7. Are your lesson plans out and ready?
8. What's on the chalkboard? There should be a greeting and any pre-class directions the students need.
9. How about the peripheral walls? Have you put up happy, thought-provoking posters? Have you rotated the ones you've had up for a while to keep the atmosphere fresh?

Many teachers have a mental or written checklist of their last-minute items. But many don't and most begin their classes in the same way they end: in chaos. It takes a distinct purposefulness to prepare your class in a way that includes all the necessary elements for super-results. When your class starts chaotically, students are put into a confused, disjointed state of mind and the learning effectiveness drops.

In the rear of the classroom, put a trash can by the exit. This increases the odds of trash going in the right place and saves clean-up work. If there is a clock in the room, the rear of the class is the best place. Of course, there should be a clear-cut policy about when the class is out - is it when the clock says so or the teacher says so? On the door at the rear of the classroom, there should be a note which tells visitors, intruders, messengers and observers exactly what to do before or upon entering.

## Temperature Is Critical

It is often overlooked and always important. The first thing a person will notice when they enter the room is the temperature of the room. Classrooms kept between 68 and 72 degrees Fahrenheit seem to feel most comfortable for the largest majority of students. Often a teacher becomes so engrossed in what they are doing that they are insensitive to the temperature. For this reason it is suggested that teachers leave their class after each break to get a sense of the outside temperatures. If at all possible, a teacher should find a way to provide good air circulation - windows are easiest if the weather and building design permits. Many teachers have found it helpful to attach a small indicator piece of cloth next to a window or air conditioner so that they can tell at a glance if the air is circulating.

For teachers who are interested and have access to them, ionizers and humidifiers have been found valuable for student and teacher comfort. About 20% of the population is affected adversely by atmospheric electrical charges. Many experience great discomfort when the weather turns super-dry and static electricity is everywhere. A negative ion generator can be useful in these cases.

## Use of Color

The walls of the classroom can be a real support to effects in your classroom. One of the ways the walls can add to the environment is in color. The shades, tones and hues on the walls are so important that entire businesses have been created to do color consulting for optimum working environments. If your walls are not a pastel blue, light green, or aqua, find out about the possibility of painting them. Some teachers have found certain yellows to work well also. Other colors create reactions, whether conscious or subconscious within many of the students. A wood paneling or brick-face can create a warm, home-like feeling in many cases, and the cost of paneling is reasonable.

## Power of Peripheral Stimuli

While the front of room is best kept aesthetic, simple and happy, the sides of the room are also important. How often do you see your student's eyes wandering around the room? In most cases, very often! In one study, it was found that while the recall of lecture material went down, the recall of peripherals was actually UP after two weeks! Put your most important instructional visual stimuli on the sides and up high. Then draw no attention to it - the students will find it and learn quite well from it, accidentally. In fact, the peripheral messages are often more powerful than the standard front-of-the-room approach. Be sure to make all of your messages positive and done with quality and simplicity.

The positioning of visuals on the wall can make a major difference in how they impact the student. The direction your eyes look indicates an access to a certain physiological mode such as visual, auditory or kinesthetic. If you want the item to evoke good feelings, put it below eye level for the students. When the eyes are looking down and to the right, the body can most easily access the kinesthetic mode. Items at this level would be past items of student work, and other things you want them to feel good about.

If you want students to talk about an item on the wall, put it at eye level, since your body accesses constructed or created sounds with the eyes looking to the left or the right. This area is for communications and upcoming events. If you want them to simply notice the information, just process it visually as in the form of review material, put it above eye level, because that puts the student in the visual mode for recalling the information. In the area of content, they can be used at least three valuable ways:

1. **As a communication board.** (Eye level for auditory mode) To post assignments, messages, lost and found, resources, and other pertinent bits of information. Things you want students to talk about go at eye level.

2. **As a results report.** (Shoulder-high or lower for kinesthetic) Found to be more useful to chart the progress of the class as a whole than to post individual test scores or well-written papers. Possibilities include putting up collective mind-maps of the week in review, group art projects, or presentations or even a large graph or thermometer showing the progress of the entire class as a team. Student work also goes at a lower level. Why? To access feelings of pride.

3. **As an inspirational area.** (High up for visual recall mode) An example is a large, bright colored poster saying, "Life Is Wonderful!"

In the class of a teacher of learning disabled students, the teacher (an excellent one in every other way!) had a poster with a nature scene and the message, "Things take time." What was coming across to the students might actually be the message "you learn slowly, so don't expect too much, too soon." In another classroom a poster was seen which said "School is something we sandwich between weekends." Here the message is that school "is something which gets in the way of things, and that weekends are what living is really for." Posters which inspire, challenge or enliven with joyous and supportive messages will add much to the class environment. A poster which says "You Can Do It" is much more useful than "Hang In There, Baby."

## Affirmations

Your room should be a fertile source of confidence, information and good feelings for your students. One of the best ways is to put 5-15 posterboards up, each a 16" X 20" up to 22" X 28" size. Use light colored boards such as white, natural, canary, pink, powder blue or light gray. Then in simple, easy-to-read letters, paint or print in reminders for your students. Put them in the first person so that the student reading them know that they apply directly. Put these signs up high, on the sides and back of the room. One above the door is especially potent. Change them often, and use them to refer to or repeat in class. These are useful, regardless of whether your students are four or forty. Here are some suggested affirmations:

*"I am a bright and capable learner"*
*"If you learned something new today, give me five!"*
*"Learning is fun, easy and creative"*
*"I do things simply, easily and playfully"*
*"I am healthy, happy and wise"*
*"I am the change I want to see"*
*"For things to change, I must change"*
*"I am a unique and precious being"*
*"I can do magic"*
*"I enjoy reading and using affirmations"*
*"For things to change, I must change"*
*"I love myself just the way I am"*
*"Every problem offers a gift"*
*"I am a resourceful learner of many choices"*

# How to Use Markers

Most teachers find it useful to have a chalkboard with colored chalk in addition to white. It allows for more choice of expression, in addition to being aesthetically pleasing and easier to recall. There is an extra-fat brand of chalk-stick gaining rapid acceptance. Many teachers wrap the base of the chalk with masking tape to prevent breakage and reduce chalk dust, while others use the metal chalk-holders.

The ceramic boards with the quick-dry markers are a great improvement if you can get them. One of the great benefits of using a flip-chart with large sheets of paper is that you can save what you write, and put them up on the walls. This is in contrast to the disappearing act that chalkboard material does each day. With the flip-chart, use several different colors of pens so that the visual impact is stronger. In making lists, alternate colors to increase visibility. Print legibly, keep the messages simple and useful. Then you'll have more interest in wanting to save the most useful ones. A newer item is called Static Magic - it's a plastic sheet that comes in pads like flip chart paper. It takes an erasable marker and shows color better. Ask for them at a stationery supply; they're made by Dennison.

# Lighting

Lighting is one of the most controversial areas in the discussion of classroom environment. It may be that each teacher has such different needs that it is difficult to obtain consensus. One point which most agree on is that indirect lighting or natural daylight is best. It is certain that some areas of the room have greater needs for light than others. The front of the room - both on you, the chalkboard and flip chart - is critical. Some have cited studies which indicate that full-spectrum lighting (natural or incandescent) is better than the fluorescent style. In many cases, you are not given much of a choice, so whether one kind of lighting is better than another is a moot issue. However, you can bring in inexpensive torchieres to augment your lighting scheme.

# Room Arrangement

Another area of physical environment is the arrangement of the room itself. Include unattached chairs and moveable desks for maximum comfort and flexibility. If possible have carpet all over or at least a throw rug at the front of the classroom. The room needs to meet the needs of the subject matter, the student and the teacher. To accomplish this, first notice what the course content demands are. They are obviously different in a woodworking class than in a speech class.

In general, position yourself at the front of the room in a way which puts the least depth from front to back with your students. In a rectangular-shaped room, be at the center of the longest side. It's far better to move from left to right across the stage than front to back. Decide what kinds of student-to-student interactions will be needed. Most teachers have carefully set the class to avoid exactly this. However, in the classroom of a master, student disruption and behavior problems are at a minimum. Students need teacher-student and student-student contact for the best learning. You will devise your plan depending on your situation. One of the most useful criteria for seating requires that the students do the following:

1. Be sure to sit more than one chair away (in any direction) from someone that you knew prior to the first class.
2. Be sure to sit next to a different person (on all sides) than who you sat next to in the last class.
3. Switch sides of the room and front to back in the room to freshen up your approach every half hour. Where you sit DOES change your perception.

# Open Space

Room size is also a critical factor for first impressions. For those teachers who have no other choice about room size, it is suggested that they use any resources available to create the illusion of the room being the size they want it. The apparent size of rooms can be altered by room arrangement and shrunk with dividers or enlarged with mirrors. In a standard classroom, students at desks need 10-15 square feet each and about 5-8 square feet without desks.

The chairs and desks that are used in most classrooms are an unfortunate compromise of price and quality. Most of the chairs used promote lethargy, back aches, poor breathing, neck pain and sore bottoms. Learn about anatomy so you can support the postures which are physically healthy. Here are three valuable suggestions:

1. Do keep the knees higher than the hips
2. Do support the arms and shoulders
3. Do get up and stretch often
4. If you HAVE to have desks - have a desk or table which is 3" or less from your belly button
5. Do have a chair with a seat from 16-22" from the floor, depending on your height.
6. Do make sure that your chair or a pillow provides lumbar (lower back) support.

# Seating for Success

The key for seating success is variety and appropriateness. It's important to maintain a lively and varied set of stimuli and seating is an excellent way to do that. Where a student sits in the class affects his or her learning experiences, so the solution may be to allow for some flexibility. There is some strong research by Dunn and Dunn that suggests that many students will learn substantially better when given a choice of sitting on the floor, standing or occasionally walking around. Forced "frozen" seating can impair learning!

This means you may want to allow students to choose a different seat each time they enter the room and make sure that they are in a different part of the room, too. Remind the students that the room looks different from each section and that they can gain additional insights and experiences by changing their viewing points. It's true in a sports situation and true in a room. The whole notion of switching seats helps students find fresh, unconditioned situations, leaving old fixed, limiting patterns behind. If at all possible, set up the seating so students can see and interact with each other. The novelty of it will wear off soon and the effectiveness will far outweigh any conversational distractions.

# The Sounds of Learning

The amount of stimulation that the human brain can accept and integrate is astonishing. The sounds of your room are just as important as the looks and feel of it. While your room may be visually attractive, 40% of your students learn best by sounds. Students love music and it can be used very effectively to enhance the classroom atmosphere by affecting attitudes. You can use music extensively in the classroom to create and evoke specific desirable mood changes.

For the set-up, keep it simple. Use stereo sound and position the two speakers as high as possible in the room and secure them to the walls or ceiling. Then be sure to mask the speaker wire so that it is invisible and out of reach. The tape cassette player should be cheap but dependable; keep it in a desk drawer which is either locked or off limits.

Begin playing your tape-deck music well before the start of class. The best way to decide which kind of music to put on is to observe the state of your incoming students. If they are lethargic or kinesthetic and you want them upbeat, put on faster-paced music such as exciting movie themes. If they are over-active and restless, put on slower-paced music with 40-60 beats per minute. For example, many teachers play lively classical music at the outset, slower music during moments of relaxation or test-taking and up-beat music during activities.

The music will set the stage and tone for the way you want to start class. It can put you in a great state as well as your learners. There are some specific suggestions in the chapter on presentation tools and more information in a later chapter on music.

# Ice-Breaking

Nobody has ever found a better way to start a class than by greeting students at the door. Some teachers reduce pre-stage jitters or nervousness by socializing with their students. If you do talk with them before a class starts, be on your best behavior. You may want to start parts of the course beforehand by planting seeds and suggestions about how much they'll enjoy it and how rewarding it will be. You could be preparing their mind with bits and pieces about how easy the subject will be. This is a good time to notice any prejudgments about the students, then just let them go. Be sure to make good eye contact, set them at ease and create positive expectations about the class. Pre-class mingling is also a good time to enjoy students and learn what common interests you have.

You may have noticed that the effective classroom is an affective one which appeals to all of the senses. It looks bright, playful and happy. It feels comfortable. It sounds joyous and enticing. It even smells great. When you maximize your environment, your teaching will be just that much easier because your students will be put into a more resourceful and receptive state for learning. And that's the whole point!

## Additional Resources for Further Study and Follow up

*Sitting on the Job* by Scott Donkin (Houghton-Mifflin)
*Present Yourself* by Michael Gelb *
*Brain-Based Learning & Teaching* by Jensen (Turning Point)*
*The Power of Color* by Morton Walker (Avery Publishing)
*Office Biology* by Weiner & Brown (Master Media Limited)

\* Items marked with an asterisk are available in the Appendix.

# *Presenting Skills*

## Presenting or Communicating?

We often call it presenting skills or platform skills. If you aren't communicating what you intend, you're wasting the audience's and your time. The "stand and deliver" method is dead. Communication is not like the proverbial arrow shot into the air, but more accurately the quality of understanding between two persons. The definition of communication? It's simple: "The transfer of meaning." Put more specifically,

*The meaning of your communication*
*is the response you get!*

If your room is burning down, and you yell "fire" and nobody gets up and leaves because they think you are kidding, you had better change your communication strategy. It's not enough that you do what works for most people most of the time. What's "enough" is determined by your resources and commitment to the outcome. If 90% of the students get your message about the fire and leave, are you committed to the outcome enough to insure the "safety" of the other 10%? In that same way, it is not enough that you teach a class in which 90% of the students get your message. The other 10% are getting "burned!"

*You are never the "main event"...*
*the real "show" is in your student's mind*

This does not mean that you will always get 100%, but it does mean that your commitment must be 100%. If you think about it, that's a drastically different message from what you grew up with. All our lives we are taught that if someone else didn't get the meaning of what we say, it's the other person's fault. There is a better way. Believe that the meaning of your communication is the response that you get. Your classroom results will go up dramatically.

## Three Part Communication

Your messages could be broken into three parts: content, delivery and context. ALL three are part of the process of communication. The effects of any of the three

can be destroyed or magnified by the other two. Any time the result of your communications is below expectations, ask yourself the questions on the checklist below:

- "Is it WHAT I am saying?"... I can change it!
- "Is it HOW I am saying it?"... I can change that, too!
- "Is it the circumstances?"... I can change them!

The focus of communication needs to be on the other party. In your classroom, focus on what's going on for the learner. Ask questions such as, "Could you re-phrase what I just said?" "What's not clear to you?" "How do you know you don't understand?" "What would it take for you to really understand this topic?" "When you say you're not sure, what parts are you sure about already?" Just by asking useful questions, you'll begin to understand how your students think, learn, and draw conclusions. Top teachers are curious learners, too. They are curious about what makes their students learn, how they learn and how they could learn better. Here are three areas of influence you have:

**1. Your content**....WHAT you are saying.

This, obviously, includes your subject matter. As or more importantly, it includes your ability to build relationships, add value, create motivation, elicit promises and prompt requests.

**2. Your delivery**.... HOW you are saying it.

This includes your posture, eye contact, positioning, expressions and gestures. It also includes the school's dress code, grooming and, especially, your voice qualities: tonality, volume, pitch, tempo and rhythm.

**3. The context**.... The CONDITIONS and CIRCUMSTANCES involved.

This area includes the class mood, the rules in effect, what's happened prior, etc. You have within you, at any time, in any place, both the ability and the responsibility to create the conditions and circumstances favorable to the learning process.

One last thought, which is perhaps the most important one: when you teach with an emphasis on people, rather than on curriculum, your communications are all student-based. This means that the focus is on the *effects* of the communication on your students, not the generation or creation of the communication. Communication is a two-way conversation with your students. The meaning of your communication is not what you intended, but rather the response you get. To succeed at the game of communication it takes the following:

1. Clear, well-defined outcomes for the interaction, presentation or conversation.
2. Well-developed perception and sensory acuity skills to be able to know what responses you are getting.
3. Enormous flexibility so you can keep changing what you are doing, if needed.
4. A personal commitment to the listener and your outcomes - you are willing to keep trying until you are successful.

Maybe the most important thing about your presentation is this: you need to bring all of you to it - your best self each time. Being mindful of your intention, caring and vision for your students, bring what is known as "purposeful presence" to your work. This means that you are awake, clear and "fully present." It means you are doing what you are supposed to be doing: listening, speaking, being "in the moment." Most of all, it means integrity, the embodiment of honesty, truthfulness and commitment to your values.

## General Guidelines

You have many kinds of learners in your audience and each has a lifetime of attitudes, beliefs, values and prejudices. Make your presentation a multi-media one, always. Use changes in your voice tonality, tempo, volume and pitch. Use visual aids. Use bright colored pens when writing. Write as much on flip charts ahead of time as possible. Write key ideas before talking about them to keep interest strong. Tell people to write key ideas down.

Take up a lot of space in the front of the room. Walk from side to side and front to back to include everyone. Use congruent and appropriate body language. Express yourself more than you think you need to. Make every day a challenge - stretch and try to grow to a new level. Be yourself and let your good qualities come through so that the audience can relate to you as a real human being, not a "teacher."

The super-teachers, master teachers who can teach nearly anything to anybody, need a vast array of specialized communication tools. When these tools are used as part of a presentation, the result is magic - a special kind of charisma. Yet, if you are willing to get beyond the "wow stage" of observing great super-teachers, you can discover the magic is actually many small things done well.

Charisma is great, but long-term results are what's really needed. This means taking the time to practice and learn many small things; maybe just one a week until they are all a part of you. Then believe in yourself as a good and worthy person and let that self-confidence come across. Be yourself, don't emulate another. Who you are is fine enough. Let that show through without any "acts."

## Planning and Organization

To plan your presentation, start with the learner in mind. That's right, the learner. For a moment forget about all the great and wonderful things you want to teach. What you are all about is learning, not teaching. Powerful presentation skills require asking the right questions before you even go into the classroom. What will the learner's mindset be? What does he or she already know? What does the learner bring to this topic? What are the biases, the beliefs and prejudices? What will the circumstances be? How can you alter them? What are the two or three things you definitely want to make sure are learned? What resources do you have at hand? How much time is allotted? The more questions you ask and the better the quality of questions you ask, the greater the likelihood you'll discover what you really need to know for success.

## Notes and Prompts

How can you present new material with a minimum of notes and prompts? You can't. It's no embarrassment to use notes. Many of the very best presenters in the business use them. Use three kinds of notes and prompts:

1. First, create a generalized outline or mind map of just the key parts of your presentation. See the chapter on lesson planning for ideas. This will be the one that you bring to class.

2. Write out a more detailed one for yourself. As you write it out, talk yourself through the lesson and visualize and feel yourself doing all the individual and specific things in your notes. This is the real planning for the lesson.

3. Optionally, write out your key points on a large sheet of flip chart or poster paper. Post them up on the back wall of the room. That way, you'll have all your key ideas right up in front of you for easy reference, without having to look down and lose eye contact.

## *OPENINGS:* Well Begun is Well Done

There is enormous potential for creating classroom magic during the first moments of class, when students are in a distinctive, first-time state of mind. The opening of a presentation has many purposes including: to orient the audience, preview material, motivate, inspire and gain rapport. Your students begin class with their own "mental set." Your job is to unsettle their existing mindset and create a new, more resourceful one. A carefully designed and artfully orchestrated introduction can make possible a significantly better class. Therefore, the purpose of an introduction or "set induction" as it is often called, is to maximize the effectiveness of the following presentation.

The length of an introduction, in general, is proportional to the entire presentation. For example, a ten minute speech might need only a one minute introduction. In a fifty-five minute class, the introduction might be five to eight minutes. In a two day workshop or seminar, the first one to two hours may be needed for the introduction.

## Keys to Introductions

The parts of a good introduction vary a great deal, depending on whether it's the first time you've ever been with this group of students, the length of the class, and a dozen other factors. However, these four keys are essential regardless of the circumstances:

**(1) Get attention**: If you don't have it, you are wasting your time. Usually this means you need to create a state-change to a more powerful psycho-physiological condition of excitement, and confidence in your audience. The best ways to get attention are to use curiosity, emotional or physical engagement and novelty.

**(2) Develop relationship, trust and rapport:** Create a connection with learners. With rapport, you can lead students almost anywhere.

**(3) Establish relevancy:** You can do this or the learners can do it. Answer the learner's question, "What's in it for me?" Provide essential information. Your students need to know what they can expect, what the rules are and how to operate in the situation you have set up.

**(4) Create a learning climate:** Establish a receptive learning environment. Reduce or eliminate stress, threat, anxiety and learner helplessness. Use a specific set of actions which will dramatically increase student response to class material.

# Start on Time

Always open the class and introduce yourself on time, even if you don't actually start any teaching. Do this whether everyone is there or not. Your time, as well as that of the other students is valuable and deserves to be respected. Fortunately, you can always have time for an introduction even if you are very rushed and have to say to your group, "I'll be with you in a moment... here's something you can begin with..." Starting on time is one of the ways you show that you respect the audience and their time. Being on time is also a way that you keep your agreements about when class starts and honor those who are on time and create a context of class as "worth being on time for." Here are some suggested openers:

1. **Situation:** Many students missing, first class, it's time to start.
   **Opening:** "Good morning and thank you for being here. I appreciate very much your being on time, and in the next couple of minutes, the remaining students who are looking for this room should arrive. We'll give them until five after, then start. Right now, let's learn a couple of things about your neighbor."
2. **Situation:** Many students missing, time to start, not the first class.
   **Opening:** "Good morning and thank you for being on time. Obviously some students are not here, but it's time to start. Today we'll..."
3. **Situation:** Time to start, everyone on time.
   **Opening:** "Good morning and thanks for being on time! Give your classmates a hand! Today we'll be..."

# Tools for Openings

Be generous with your eye contact. Enjoy "taking in" all of your students for a moment, so they know you have personally seen them and acknowledged their presence. Let them know by your facial expressions and body language that you are happy to have them in class and that you are excited about the upcoming lesson. Make sure your posture and positioning say you are open to your students. Avoid starting out behind a desk or table. This softer, gentler manner "invites" student attention instead of other more direct ways which "scream" for attention or "insist" upon it. Try the "invitation" first.

# Non-verbal Attention Getters

Bring a boom box or CD and play exciting upbeat music such as a movie theme from a big hit. If a movie production company has already spent millions creating a favorable impression on the public, you may as well take advantage of it! Make eye contact and do any of the following: begin clapping... raise your hand... hold up an interesting object... motion towards the clock... stand fully straight and attentive... open your mouth and pause... have a student get the attention of others for you... move to the center of the room... stand in a designated spot... or be in an unusual spot, look anxious and ready to start.

There are, of course, countless ways to get attention. You have to find the ones you like and that work for you. Other methods include to: hold up your finger to your lips vertically... have an event occur which signifies that class is ready to start... play an instrument, a drum... put on a special hat... pass out a book, handout, or class item... use noisemakers... do charades or mimes... do magic tricks... say "my next statement will affect your grade"... give coded messages... use puppets, finger plays... announce good news... hold up an unusual object or picture... have a science experiment set up... use unusual lighting.

## Positive Greetings

The first few words can be a greeting, a story, a question or an event. You are the best judge of what's appropriate. Each of these must be presented with your own style and flavor.

Whatever the greeting, put energy into it! It could be "Good morning", "Hello, boys and girls(ladies and gentlemen)!" or "Hi, and welcome to...." Congruence is critical at this time. Make sure your verbal message is also conveyed by your body language and gestures. Project your voice and make sure you are talking to each and every student. After you have greeted your audience, you might give a direct call to action. This can be appropriate at times.

The most common kinds of greetings are those which ask for attention, or to start a process. Possibilities include:

"Please turn to the person sitting nearest you and welcome them"
"Everybody take a deep breath, please"
"Please say hello to three others"
"Eyes and ears up front, please"
"You sssshhhh-ould find this class very interesting today"
"Please find the best colored pen you can from the tray in the back"

Any request is best started with a tone of respect, support and expectancy that it will be followed.

## *SUCCESS TOOLS:* Develop Rapport

Rapport is thought of as a mysterious "chemistry" that tells you if your students are "with you." More technically, it is a distinct physiological state of positive responsiveness. With rapport, you can lead your students nearly anywhere. Without it, you're likely to be ineffective and frustrated. As a teacher, it's critical to have your audience continually responding to you. Only then can you insure your students will get the appropriate learning experiences. Your students do not need to like you for you to have rapport with them. Rapport equals responsiveness, not affection. As a teacher, you can do just fine if others dislike you - but you must have responsiveness.

The relationship you develop with your students will be the single most important thing you do to encourage learning. Rapport gives you the continual responsiveness based on your relating to each other instead of using threats or promises of better grades. Your effectiveness in using power, control or threats on students will continually decrease over time. And your ability to use the positive favorable relationship you have developed with your students only increases.

Many times you have established rapport unconsciously. As a professional educator, a teacher must be able to develop rapport with nearly anyone almost anytime! In a way, rapport is the ability to enter a student's world to see things the way he or she does, to hear what he or she hears and to feel what he or she feels. A class with good rapport consists of students who feel validated and important.

# Work the Group

*Influencing With Integrity* by LaBorde is an excellent book on this subject. Good rapport building also includes the flexibility to respond appropriately. If any one strategy is not successful, do another and keep changing strategies until you succeed. There is a difference between building relationships with individuals and with groups. After a certain size (10-15), it is not your group. It becomes over time, as Michael Grinder says, *the "group's group."*

In other words, the group has it's own energy and culture separate from you. Learn to understand the group's culture as quickly as you can. If it's your class, and it's the first day, and they are all from diverse backgrounds (they have not been together before as a group) you can strongly influence the norms of the group. But you'll never completely control the group, nor would you want to. A resentful group can be quite a nightmare!

Here are some things you can do to develop relationships within the group. Be interested in your students instead of trying to be an interesting teacher. Greet them at the door with a smile, handshake or hug, whichever is appropriate. Give warm, sincere and authentic greetings that convey real caring and interest in every student. Repeat the dose daily throughout the year. More than anything else you can do, being a caring and genuine teacher will build relationships.

# Respect Gradient

Be sure to respect the emotional, physical, psychological, and spiritual mood of the students. Be sure to respect the beliefs, opinions, prejudices, attitudes and experiences of the audience. The way to do this best is to meet and match them at the start and slowly "pace" and "lead" them to the place you want them to go. If you want to do anything which is out of the group's experience or simply new and risky, build up to it slowly. Do intermediate steps, set an example and prepare them for it gradually. Be sure to ask permission of the group for anything you need that requires the trust of the group.

# Provide Key Information

Each student comes into your class with many questions. Some of them seem trivial, some are obviously more critical. "What's coming up?" or "What do I do if this happens?" or the most common one, "What's in it for me?" "Will this be on the test?" "Will I be embarrassed, threatened or pressured today?" You must answer these questions soon, so that learners will be able to focus on the learning.

# Student Fears Addressed

The three biggest fears of students are that the class will be boring, that they won't learn anything, and that they won't be treated fairly. Let's take a closer look at these fears and what to do about them:

1. **Are you interesting?** One of the biggest fears of students is boredom. Regardless of the value of the course, students want to know right up front

if you are interesting, fun, and can make class go quickly. Every student has had the misfortune of suffering through a slow and boring class and the last thing they want is another slow, boring class. Assure them either verbally (you can say, "What I've found is that students learn more when they enjoy what they are doing. This class will be a lot of fun."); or non-verbally by using plenty of expressions and showing lots of life.

2. **Are you competent?** Maybe the second greatest fear is that they won't learn anything. It's important to establish credibility and professionalism so students have confidence in your ability. Here are some possible ways to state your competence:

*A new teacher:* "My name's Eric Jensen and I've been interested in science for over six years. I did successful graduate work in environmental science with an emphasis in systems thinking. You'll find I know my subject well, I teach it in a fun and new way, and I love sharing as well as learning with you."

*A veteran or tenured teacher:* "My name's Eric Jensen and I'm pleased to have you in class. I've worked successfully with over 10,000 students in the last 15 years and am confident you'll do well, too. Because of the new way this class is set up, you'll not only learn a lot, but have fun doing it.

3. **Are you fair and trustworthy?** This question is prompted by the thought of being evaluated and the fear of failure or, just as bad, not getting what is deserved. It's important for a teacher to give the students some assurances or a sense of fairness. A possibility is: "In the past, other students have found me easy to talk to, my evaluation methods to be fair, and I'm sure you will too."

# Preview Coming Attractions

Have you ever noticed the catchy headlines of the publication *The National Enquirer?* They are "Five Ways to Improve Your Marriage," or Why Single People Are Less Lonely," or "New Diet Amazes Even Scientists!" and others. As much as tabloids are criticized, people buy them! In the same way, you can preview your class material to your students:

**Biology Class:** "Today we'll be learning about DNA. We'll find out how nature has put enough information in your genes to fill 10,000 volumes of *Encyclopedia Britannica.*"

**Ancient history:** "How would you like to have 20 slaves working for you, for 20 years? What would you have them do? Today we're going to talk about a civilization that had 20 slaves per citizen."

**Health class:** "In a few moments we'll learn why you can't catch a cold at the North Pole during the winter."

**Geography:** "Next we'll discover how there are pieces of matter on our earth that are older than the earth itself." Or, "We'll discover which country has sand dunes as high as a 35-story building."

**Literature:** "One of the things we'll find out today is what author wrote a 6,000 word poem when he was twelve years old."

# Guidelines for Success

Make sure you give the all-important information on how to succeed. It will vary from group to group, but it may be as simple and general as:

1. Participate
2. Take notes
3. Review notes 2X/week
4. Follow directions
5. Set goals
6. Ask questions

The important thing for students to know is that they have choice in how the course will turn out. These choices include learning responsibility, commitment and clarity. Ideally, every part of your course will add value to your life and the lives of your students.

## Oral Contracts

In addition to students sharing expectations, you need to share yours. They should know what you expect them to learn, by when and in what form they will be required to demonstrate competency. Share your expectations and get agreement with your learners. In other words, give them your evidence procedure for determining if they have met your evaluation criteria. If it's appropriate, be sure to put the expectations in writing if they affect the evaluation process. Once in writing, the students may refer to them later, giving certainty, peace of mind and predictability.

## State the Rules

Students also need to know the ground rules. Can they talk in class, move around, go to the bathroom or sleep? What happens if they're late, chew gum, eat in class or disrupt? In an adult class, can they smoke? What about listening to pocket stereos? Is there a dress standard? Any area which is the least bit uncertain needs to be taken care of in the introduction. Each student brings expectations into a learning situation and the more you handle ahead of time, the fewer problems you'll have later.

## Logistics

Students need to know the location of the pencil sharpener, the bathroom, the trash can, the resources, the drinking fountain and the clock. They also want to know when time breaks are, where they are allowed to go on breaks, what they are allowed to bring back into the classroom and what time to return from a break. Make sure students know what forms to turn in, where to put them, and the deadline. Usually there are a dozen bits of data that students need to know the first time they are in your classroom. Having logistical information allows students to relax and become involved with the process of learning.

## Elicit Needs, Provide Solution

What's more powerful, you telling the students the relevancy of the course and you setting the goals... OR... the students determining the relevancy and the students setting their own goals? You know the answer. Learner-generated needs and goals are far more powerful than teacher-imposed ones.

Students need to know the benefits of taking your class. What will a student "get" by being in your class? Benefits are especially attractive to someone who has needs, so spend a few moments learning about student needs. The more a student perceives need for your material, the greater the motivation. Build on student needs to "sell" your course! Here is a sample interaction for a teacher who is going to introduce study skills:

1. To help establish needs ask one of these:
   "How many of you think your studying takes too long?"
   "How many of you fall asleep sometimes while doing your reading?"
   "How many of you have had the experience of studying for a test, thinking that you know it, then blowing it at test time?

2. Suggest possible benefits to your audience:
   "Who would like to know three ways to cut study time in half?"
   "Is there anyone who'd like to be better at _____?"
   "How many would like to have a choice of colleges to go to?"
   "Who in here would like to learn more ways to earn a living?"

Now, ask them for what *they* might get out of learning better study skills. This quick activity creates immediate recognition of students' needs and offers benefits for taking your class. It can also create a feeling of commonalty among students. By hearing responses to these questions, students get a sense of the needs of their classmates. They know that others are in the same "boat" and this can lessen fears of "looking stupid."

## Certainty Affirmations

A similar tool that can work, depending on your audience, is the certainty affirmation. Tell your students, with certainty and congruency, that they will learn and remember the subject you teach. It might be something as simple as: "I've taught this course many times and my students always get it. I am certain that each of you will master this subject." It's easy for them to feel like they'll succeed in the midst of certainty.

The possibility of failure should never deter your confidence. If you communicate uncertainty and hesitancy in learning ability to your students, guaranteed, it will impact their own ability to learn. In short, any doubts on your part become a self-fulfilling prophecy. As a professional, you can't afford a negative thought.

The research is compelling; what you think about a student affects his or her chances for success. You have a moral and ethical obligation to believe in the ability and positive chances for success in every single student. If you don't believe that they can succeed in your class, you may want to: (1) have the student transferred to another class with another teacher (2) learn the teaching skills to help them succeed (3) consider whether teaching is right for you.

## Congruency is a Key

Super-teachers are powerful because their gestures are congruent with their message. When your non-verbal message is the same as your verbal message, your effectiveness is multiplied. While the content of your verbal message is usually weighted at about 10% of the total impact of your presentation, that leaves 90% of the impact to your non-content areas such as gestures, positioning, expressions, voice range, tempo, pitch and volume.

The best ways for you to discover your own level of congruency are: (1) tape record your class and listen to the audio tape (2) video-tape your class and watch it (3) get some feedback from students and other teachers (4) put a mirror in the back of your class for a day. Take acting lessons from a local junior college or university. In addition, voice training is excellent if you can find a good coach. A third option is dance, mime or movement workshops. Each of these has the capacity to bring you out, allow you to express yourself and to use much more of the space in the front of the room which better aids communication.

# Different Types of Voices

As a presenter, you'll want to use several distinctly different types of voices. Each has a different body physiology and each creates a different result. Michael Grinder calls two of these the "credible" and the "approachable" voices. The first is for sending, the second is for feedback. These are very culturally dependent. Culture can mean gender, nationality, geography, circumstances, etc. Traditionally in male circles, in sports and the military, you'll hear much more of the "credibility" voice. Among women, you'll traditionally find more use of the "approachable" voice. Both have important roles in the classroom. Learn the culture of your audience and use the one that's appropriate for the group. If you consistently use the same one, you limit your own choices and the ability of the audience to respond to you differently?

The decision, regarding which voice pattern to use, is easy to make. Ask yourself what you want. Am I sending information or do I want to receive information? Do I want to make an impression with my agenda, or do I want to discover another's agenda? Do I want my audience to laugh, to be introspective or be impacted? It doesn't matter as long as you're purposeful about it. Michael Grinder says it best:

> *"The systematic use of nonverbals is the basis for successful communication"*

The credible voice has less variance, less inflection and ends the sentence on a lower note, with the chin down. The credibility comes from the fact that your statements end with the finality and authority which says, "This is a fact - and don't dispute it!" The pattern is like the famous four musical bars from Beethoven's Fifth, "Da-Da-Da---Dah!" Use this voice when you are telling it like it is, giving commands, facts, calls for action and strong opinions. With this voice, you're giving your agenda and you want to maintain position, power and credibility. There are many legitimate times to use this voice, and the larger the group, the more you're likely to need it. It is the voice of control.

The "approachable" voice is used for the times when either the group is smaller (15 or less) or when you want feedback from a larger group. This voice of yours is higher, has more variance and regardless of where the tonality starts out, it ends up higher at the end. You have more of a bobbing, up-and-down head movement. It's the voice that you use when someone has just given you an amazing or astonishing or surprising bit of information and you respond by saying "Really?" Your voice goes up, and the other person is expected and invited to respond. To be successful as a presenter, you need both voices, the credible one and the approachable one.

There is a definite time and place for both. And by the way, you'll have other personalities and voices than those two. How can you or your audience distinguish between the different voices? It's easy.

# Dramatize Your Point

Many teachers use special costumes on certain days to make a point more real. Some teachers have the students dress up like the subject they are studying. Others bring in special objects, posters, recordings, props or guests. Could your students dress up like Aristotle, Queen Elizabeth, Booker T. Washington, Einstein, a Medieval peasant, a slave, Mark Twain, Florence Nightingale, an Aborigine, Churchill, or Newton? If so, it might be a good way to dramatize a particular point some time. Even in your own presentation, you can dramatize a point with greater theatrics, gusto and aliveness. To dramatize is to make bigger-than-life, to parade, and to be bold and flashy about a subject. Bring objects to class for students to feel, investigate and ask questions about. Rent and watch "Dead Poet's Society" again.

# Keep Sentences Brief

If you can say a paragraph in a sentence, do it. If you can say a sentence in a word, do it. It is usually more powerful to say a shorter phrase than a longer one. Say it, then pause... let it settle for a moment, and continue on. Long-winded sentences lose audiences. If you have a list of items to read off, make sure that you read only a few items at a time before stopping. Then break the pattern and continue. Here's a great way of delivering lists - interrupt yourself to remind the audience to focus. Say: "You need to know there's A, B, C,... wow, get this! D, E, F,... everyone focus... G, H, I, J..." This keeps the audience from simply "checking out" because they know a long list is coming up. Here's an abrasive slogan from the advertising business regarding the attitude of the consumer towards information: "Tell me quick, tell me true, or else my love to heck with you!"

# Positive Wording

A common pattern of ineffective teachers is the use of negation - they spend more time telling their students what *not* to do, than what *to* do. The best teachers put most of what they say in the positive form. Negation exists only in our language, not in our experience. If you say, "Don't do that!", it doesn't tell the person what *to* do, it only says what to avoid. Therefore it creates no action, involvement or empowerment.

If someone says, "Don't think of the color purple, think of any color as long as it's not purple", you have to think of purple to know what not to think of! In the same way, if you say to your students, "Don't be late", they have to think of what lateness is like in order to understand the sentence. Why would you want to remind them of what lateness is like if what you really want to do is remind them of "on-time-ness?" It makes more sense to say, "Be sure to be on time." Simply word your sentences so that student knows what you want.

Old way: "Don't forget, I said 'don't turn in your papers late!'"
**New way:** "Please remember to turn in your papers on time."

There's an exception to the rule of negation. There are times that a negation can serve you and your student. If a student needs correction, it's better to use the negation to soften the message.

Old way: "This paper is sloppy, incoherent and illegible."
**New way:** "This paper will score better when it's neater, tightly-worded and uses shorter words."

## Let's Get Physical

Students need and want physical movement to be at their best. They love to get up and move around: "the mind can only absorb what the seat can endure." Part of the reason many students don't participate is that they sit slouched over, with poor breathing, and limited circulation in a stuffy room. Be responsive to your students! Watch them closely to see what they need. After a few minutes or at most, a half hour, the best thing to give them may be a 60 second stretch break. Movement is best; have them walk around the room or do a "moving" assignment. Be sure to refer to the chapter on energizers; it has over 100 ways to get up and oxygenate!

## *CLOSINGS:* Parting is Such Sweet Sorrow

What's the best way to end a class? For some, the bell does the job, for others, class is over when they run out of material. One of the best opportunities for learning can take place during the last few minutes of class. If you create your class with sufficient planning and attention you'll look forward to those last few moments feeling complete and satisfied. Following are some ideas, tools and thoughts that can help give the entire class a sense of wholeness about your subject and, ideally, an inner sense of accomplishment.

*Think of closure as important - it's worth about*
*ten percent of the entire session or class*

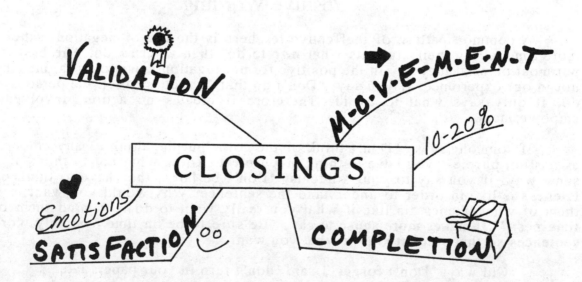

Class closures belong in the category of completing unfinished business. A well-taught class needs an ending to tie pieces together and relate the parts to the whole. This simple act insures that the value students receive remains intact. Even if you are rushed and running out of time, closures are well worth taking the time to do them. If you are doing a ten minute class, do a closure during the last couple minutes. In a 50 minute class, do a closure in the last five to eight minutes. In an all-day course, take 30-45 minutes for a closure. Closure is not part of the presentation, but allows the presentation to have an impact, to "settle in." Closure is the last word, the final thought, the ribbon around the package!

## Advantages of Powerful Closures

Closures offer time for students to integrate the course material in a way that truly adds to their resources. It can afford an opportunity to ask some important questions: What was the point? Did I learn anything? Have I enhanced my sense of myself? How can I grow from this experience? The closure will allow the student to make useful conclusions about what was just taught. Your job, as the master teacher, is to insure that the experiences in your class become an "added value" to your students. At the close of class, are your students in the process of leaving? Leaving can be physical or mental. Most teachers feel as if the clock is like a burning fuse on a stick of dynamite during the last few minutes of class. Students seem compelled to be clock-watchers! Make it your personal challenge to create a kind of closure that will capture the attention and imagination of your students well enough to make it a memorable experience.

## Five Keys

A successful close to a class includes five things: 1) a sense that something was accomplished - movement occurred; 2) that it was worthwhile both internally and externally - validation; 3) that it was understood and believed; 4) that they know the next step to take; and 5) that it is complete at least for now - wholeness.

Learners like to know progress was made and that they came a long way. This feeling can come from many sources including a review or test. It can come from the student's own discoveries during the class. Invite introspection and self-discovery. Ask students to ask themselves "what happened today, what did I learn, how does it affect me or how do I feel about it?" This is a great time for you to get some closing feedback on the effects or value of the class.

Students like validation, meaning that what occurred has been accepted and approved by the students as affirming, enhancing and real. It gets the stamp of approval and is labeled as worthwhile and beneficial to the students. This often takes the form of generalizing the experience to other areas of a student's life. It validates that each is a good person and enhances self-esteem. This can come from either you or the students or both.

A good closure offers a sense of completion. Students like to know that a section or part of something is done. They need to feel everything has been taken care of, in their internal experience and in the external course material. Students need to have their questions answered, their upsets handled or excitement shared. Completion also means that you have led students into the future with the information ("future-pace") - how will they use it and when? Additionally, make sure you give students congruent congratulations for their attention and presence. The closure may also need to provide information for the student such as scheduling, announcements or assignments. Finally, students should leave your class with an excitement and curiosity to learn more.

A good closure is not something added on to your class if you have time. It deserves equal time, if not top billing, with the presentation and introduction. You must make the commitment (being willing to do whatever it takes to make it happen) to use a closure each and every time you teach a class.

The closure handles such questions as "Does anyone else feel the same way I do?" "Was this worth while for me?" "What do I do with what I've learned?" "What's next?" "How can I continue to learn more on this subject?" "Do I understand and remember what I got?" "How does this fit in with everything else I know?" "What if I can't use any of this information?" "What's coming up next?" Questions of these kind are on the minds of students as your course nears closing, and having answers adds to students' sense of wholeness and completion.

The actual strategies for closure are straightforward and simple. Try all of these ideas and decide which you can use to close your class skillfully.

## Discover the Conclusions

There's a saying that goes something like this: "It's not what happens, it's what you do about what happens." A variation is: "It's not what you learn, it's the conclusions you draw about yourself that make the difference." Another possibility for closure is to respond to your students' sharings in such a way as to ensure positive conclusions have been formed. If a student has come to a potentially damaging conclusion about a just-completed activity, you'll want to lead him or her to a more resourceful one.

An example is in the quote, "I don't work well with others." Here's a person who has come up with a potentially disabling conclusion. If left alone, this could hamper progress in your class as well as events in the rest of the student's life. In this case, ask some clarifying questions:

"I appreciate your sharing that. What do you think, specifically, causes you to not work well with others?"

"Thanks for letting me know. When you say others, I wondered if anyone, specifically, comes to mind?"

"I respect you for letting me know. Could you imagine what it would take for you to be able to work well with others?"

"It's great you shared that with us, thanks. I was thinking, if you were to solve that how would you go about it?"

With each question you ask politely and respectfully, you are helping that student reach inside themselves to discover resources they didn't know were there. You also have an obligation, as a learning coach, to make sure that any conclusions drawn are useful for the student's life. This intervention is not only preferred, it's the reason that you are in the classroom - to shape beliefs, attitudes and values.

# Review Time

One of the fun pieces of the closure process is the open oral recall drill. It can generate much energy and confidence within each student. To start an open review, begin with a sentence such as, "Today we started with the concept of _____ and how it affects the _____. Then we learned another form called _____." As you ask the question, the students answer orally in unison.

*There are no failures in the classroom...*
*There are, however, often unrecognized gifts*

As you can tell, this kind of review requires mostly simple recall skills. Ask for items you are confident students know. The oral recall drill reinforces that they know the material, and they have a lot fun doing it together. Most of this review is structured as a sentence completion. Make sure the answer is clear, singular and something that was discussed in class. For example, "There are three kinds of class closure we've mentioned so far. The first one is sharing, the second one is visualization and the third one is the _____."(open review)

# Using Mind-Mapping

Mind mapping is an organizing tool used for note-taking and recall. Mind-maps can be used as a fabulous classroom tool during the closure process to review and test. Students have fun doing these in groups of 2-4. Have them create, as a team, one large mind map of the class's lesson. They will need to recall, organize, plan and think about the material once again and this process alone is worth the effort. In addition, students arrange the material in such a way, using visuals so their recall will be even greater. Usually a group can put together a quality mind-map in ten minutes or less. Teams can also plan and work on a mind map of the entire course or year of school. That can take one to two weeks. Put completed mindmaps on display around the room so each group's work can be admired.

# Discussion

A common and useful form of closure can be discussion. Subjects that are excellent for the discussion are part of the evaluation process: relationship, strategies and course material. Discussion also works well if you break the class up into small groups and have each group work with group leaders whom you have previously trained to lead discussions. Open the discussion with questions such as:

"How do you feel about this subject today compared to before?"
"What was the best way for you to learn this?"
"What points interested you the most?"
"What did you learn about yourself today?"
"How could what you learned, and how you learned it, affect your life?"
"Why do you think this was taught today?"

# Feedback to You

Even if you have just three minutes, you can get reasonably accurate and useful feedback on how they and you are doing. Try several different kinds of questions until you get the information you need for superior teaching. You can get oral feedback by asking for information. You can get kinesthetic feedback through questions asked and hand raised or foot stomped or standing to "vote" on things. Or, you can get visual feedback in the form of a quick evaluation. These quick ones can be very useful if you teach your learners what you want and how to make it speciifc.

---

## Class Evaluation

Date:

Directions: No name, please. After each thought, please comment.

1. What I enjoyed or was most valuable about class was:

2. What I disliked about class was:

3. What would have made class better was:

4. What I discovered about myself today is:

5. Any attitudes changed, or new perspectives:

6. I describe my attitude now toward this subject as:

7. What I'd like to know next on this topic is:

8. Other comments:

---

One of the most important parts of the student's evaluation process is that you must read and do something about them! Look for areas you need to improve, notice the feelings and moods of your students. If a student is exceptionally troubled, you might mention at the end of the next class that "some of you expressed some concern over how things are going, and I'd like to invite you to meet with me for a moment after class."

## Reconnect the Learning

Make sure that you continually reconnect what you are doing with what the audience has come for or planned to get. You can do this by:

1. Checking in with an oral contract you made
2. Verifying results from a checklist
3. Posting a list on the wall and having students check off completed items
4. Self-assessment; using team or individual checklists
5. Participant sharing or presentation on connections made or value received

# Preview Coming Attractions

One of the more important parts of a closure is the advertisement. Tantalize your students with interesting tidbits of learning coming next. Figure out what would be interesting to your students and turn it into a commercial for the next class. Use the form of a question, challenge or a muse. In a study skills class, you could say, "Next class we'll be learning how to reduce study time and increase reading comprehension. Anyone interested...? Great! See you next time!" Or, in other classes, it might be:

"Next class we'll learn ten new words in Spanish that could help you out of a jam."

"When we meet again, we'll find out how learning about rock formation has made millions of dollars for some enterprising people."

"At our next meeting, we'll learn to use a power tool that can save you dozens of hours of valuable time."

"Next time, we'll discover who was the only president in our history to never marry and why."

# Congratulate & Celebrate

The close of class is the perfect time to acknowledge and appreciate your students for their participation. For every single class, regardless of what was taught or how well the students learned, find something that you can sincerely appreciate or acknowledge. Make sure that your student congratulations are sincere and you demonstrate that sincerity with congruent posture, voice, words, tonality and gestures. Learners especially remember the openings and closings... make the closing memorable! After students have done some kind of review, here's what else they can do to complete the class:

- Complete their learning logs
- Put a learning thermometer on wall to jump up to & touch
- Each does their own self-assessment & shares complete teacher feedback
- Post up a hand print above door, "If you learned something new, high five!"
- Walk around the environment with a partner explaining new learning to them
- Do peer teaching
- Play partner word association
- Your students create self-test questions
- Everyone can quiz partners during a stand-up review
- Put on celebration music - use streamers and party poppers
- All members complete team charts or individual charts
- Add some kind of celebration - if it's worth learning, it's worth celebrating!

# A Closing Ritual

Every teacher could add to their effectiveness by establishing a closing ritual to integrate the conscious content with the unconscious part of students' experiences. Some are:

1. Everybody repeats the class theme (it could be any one that you select, maybe the thought of the week such as "it's in every one of us")
2. Everyone sings a class song
3. Students give all the others a standing ovation
4. A simple closed-eye thought for the day
5. The use of a class mascot as a theme reminder
6. A student shares/the class philosopher
7. Clapping/a tai chi clap/dancing
8. Simply standing up and taking in a deep breath of energy
9. Pointing out or noticing the class accomplishments
10. A class cheer

Whatever the closing ritual, get class permission first or simply wait until the mood of the class is such that permission is already granted. Introduce the ritual with energy and enthusiasm. Be consistent and have fun with it. Some students may be slow to join in, be patient, they'll learn to enjoy the routine. The closing ritual is the final experience students have in your class so make it fun and upbeat!

## Additional Resources for Further Study and Follow up

*Present Yourself* by Michael Gelb*
*Envoy* by Michael Grinder

* Available in the Appendix.

CHECK OUT WHAT YOU PUT OUT

# 10

## Powerful Listening Skills

### Two Ears, One Mouth

Should we be listening more than we are speaking? In the best classrooms, you'll find teachers who do just that. Regardless of the effectiveness of your presentation or teaching skills, you may be ineffective as a teacher unless you have strong listening skills. Potentially, listening inspires others, compliments them and has the capacity to enrich and nurture a relationship. The dictionary defines listening as "to hear with thoughtful attention." It also means "fully present with the intention to get the intended meaning of the communication."

### Worst Listening Mistakes

There are many more ways to listen poorly than to listen well. What often occurs in a conversation is one or more of the following:

1.  Trying to figure out a way of leaving the conversation
2.  Wanting to impress the other person
3.  Trying to find flaws in the other person's argument
4.  Forming judgments about them
5.  Preparing your next statement
6.  Trying to avoid or prevent rejection
7.  Figuring out how to make the other person wrong
8.  Trying to buy time until you have a clever response
9.  Checking your watch or the scenery
10. Pacifying the speaker
11. Thinking of what advice to give, then giving it
12. Drifting off and daydreaming
13. Listening only to what applies to you
14. Pretending you know what the other person is thinking
15. Continually changing the subject or controlling it

It's surprising how many ways there are to NOT listen. But if you think about it, most people talk AT each other. There is very little genuine listening. In fact there's a whole movement going on now (out of the Boston area) called the Dialog Group. They are encouraging people to learn to really listen and really talk in a way that generates honest communication. After all, we've all heard plenty of listening mistakes. The list we started above is continued below:

16. Rebutting, arguing, and debating with the speaker
17. Constantly bringing your own story into it
18. Agreeing with the listener when you really don't agree
19. Asking inappropriate questions that interrupt often
20. Providing solutions before the speaker feels heard
21. Preparing to "top this" with a comment about how you did something better, cheaper, easier, smarter, etc.
22. Over-identification..."Oh, you know the same thing happened to me, except....." Then you switch the attention to you.
23. Giving advice (most of the time, the speaker doesn't want it)
24. Lecturing to them on how they never learn, on why they let that problem happen to them, etc.
25. Asking trivial questions that interrupt the essence of the speaker, like the "20 questions" game of "...What color did you say the car was?"
26. Constant reassurance that everything will be fine, whether it will or not
27. Ignore them non-verbally while still pretending to listen
28. Listening as if you have to defend or justify your own position

On the flip side, the only task you have while listening is to understand the speaker's world from his point of view. Receive, understand and appreciate the communication, then acknowledge that fact by providing feedback to the speaker.

## Listening is a Learned Skill

Effective listening is a skill you must practice if you are to master speaking and presenting. Listening is a commitment to understand another's reality. It often requires detachment so you can hear without becoming personally engaged.

Unfortunately, our society offers few role models for effective listening. Actively question media's communication models. For an evening, listen to several television sitcoms. Notice how often the listener communicates with a put-down, then the canned laughter begins. Put-downs are a poor source of humor and should be banned from your classroom. Show a videotape of a typical program and ask your students for an analysis of the communication skills used. Each time a put-down is used, ask the questions:

1. What was the put-down?
2. Who laughed?
3. How did the listener feel?
4. How would you feel?
5. Does the put-down add to another's life?
6. Eventually, how might the listener feel about him or herself?
7. Could the speaker have said something funny and still be fair and respectful to the listener?

# Use a Listening Voice

Some voices are termed heavy and authoritarian. Other voices are labeled "easy to listen to and more approachable." When you want to be listened to, or to listen to others, use your "approachable listening" voice. This voice of yours has more variance and regardless of where the tonality starts out, it ends up higher at the end. You have more of a bobbing, up-and-down head movement. It's the voice that you use when someone has just said something and you respond by saying "Really?" Your voice goes up, and the other person is expected and invited to respond. To be listened to and to be good at listening, listen to your own voice and ask yourself, "Am I ending the sentences on an 'up' tonality or a 'down' tonality?" The 'up' one invites uncertainty, responses and doubt. The 'down' one says "This is how it is."

# Learn What the Speaker Needs

A good listener knows that when the speaker is talking, the subject matter is often of secondary importance. Speaking is an act of personal disclosure and sharing. To the speaker, what's important is himself: needs, feelings, attitudes, observations and opinions. The topic of the conversation is simply a vehicle. Few speakers feel genuinely listened to and as a result, it is a rare honor for them when you are a good listener. To be listened to is to be validated. It says your thoughts, feelings, observations and needs are important to me. As a result, most of the time the speaker simply needs to know that his communication has been fairly and empathically heard. One's actual response is secondary.

# Many Ways to Listen

Surprisingly, there are many kinds of listening styles. This means that people develop a filter through which messages are processed. Here are six different kinds of listening styles.

1. The **leisure** listener has an acute ear for what pleases him or her, listens for the non-verbal messages, enjoys the stories, is present in body but often not mind, is seldom intense and listens as if it's a ride at an amusement park.
2. The **inclusive** listener has a wide listening band of interests, relies heavily on the key idea, is widely accepting, at times even gullible, and notices non-verbal messages well.
3. The **stylistic** listener evaluates the message by the medium, is fully tuned to the physical presentation of the speaker, watches for non-verbal messages, evaluates speakers for credentials, listens for style and flair, or gets bored.
4. The **technical** listener listens to those who have a track record or who are qualified to use up precious listening time. He is interested mostly in how and why something works, has a narrow listening band and is often a detached and unemotional listener.
5. The **empathic** listener listens for the emotional state of the talker, detects voice fluctuations, tempo, tonality, etc., is sensitive to physical touch, and often becomes part of the drama of the conversations.
6. The **non-conforming** listener is most attentive to information which directly affects him, has a narrow band of listening interests, is excellent at sniffing our the story behind the story

Did you identify yourself with a particular style? If so, you are "receiving" on only one "band" of a radio station. To be more effective, you'll need to learn which is your own style, then learn how to become a better listener by using the style that is most appropriate to the situation.

# How to Listen Successfully

Quite simply, there are two important listening styles for teachers. One of them is empathic listening which is a response to **emotionally-laden speaking** and the other is precision listening, which is a response to **content-oriented speaking**.

In both of them your outcome is discovery... you need to allow the speaker to become more visible with empathic listening and to have the content become more clear in the precision listening mode. What works consistently is knowing which one to use and using it effectively.

# How to Create a Listening Environment

The pre-requisite for any tape of effective listening is the fostering of a safe listening environment in your classroom. The first condition is trust. Only after you have demonstrated consistently that your students can trust your responses and openness, will they feel safe and willing to take risks in seeking. To increase class trust among students, teach "respond with respect". More than teaching it, embody it. Never, ever put a student down, EVEN AS A JOKE. Never, ever be sarcastic to a student or belittle a remark. You must set the tone of love, safety and respect in the classroom.

If one of your students makes a habit of responding with "put-downs", use a nonverbal signal as an alert. It may be some theatrical sign such as a line drawn across the throat with the wave of the finger. This signals an inappropriate response and requires a respectful one. With increased feedback, the quality of classroom communication will improve.

In addition, each person must agree that active listening requires commitment to the "work" of listening. This means more than silently pointing eyes and ears toward the speaker. To fully receive another's communication, give your fullest attention to the speaker. Actively hear all of what is being said. Be willing to ask questions if anything's unclear.

Your own mood is important to monitor as a way of preparing the listening environment. Before you put yourself in the position of listening, ask "What am I feeling right now?" If there's an unexpressed emotion inside you, it may create a distorting filter for the message. As an angry person, you hear differently than if you just won the lottery. Find a way to set aside your feelings so you can go about listening without the added filter.

Listening also requires a certain amount of clarity of intention. Do you need to be in a closer place to hear better? Are you willing to say, "I'm sorry, I didn't get that. Would you repeat it, please?" Being ready to listen means that you are in a receptive state, committed to listening, and clear that you are ready to discover, not preach. The first of the two listening types is the empathic style.

# Empathic Listening

This may be the most important listening style. It's for those moments when a student uses emotionally loaded speaking. Whenever you detect any emotion out of the ordinary from a speaking student, use this style. It is for the following circumstances:

## When a student is:

1. Angry, frustrated or upset
2. Hurt, saddened or worried
3. Jealous, bitter or sarcastic
4. Excited, happy or enthused
5. Hopeful, uncertain or tense

Empathic listening engages the listener very little in terms of auditory responses. It does engage the listener non-verbally. You'll want to be in the shoes of the speaker. It's a way of listening that asks the listener to simply "be there" in partnership as a best friend. It is appropriate to listen this way when another would like to speak about something emotional. For example, "I am so sad... my best friend was hurt and is in the hospital." Your response would be "Oh... I'm so sorry... (or maybe: "It sounds like it's painful for you, too.")

This style of listening goes after the speaker and tries to **make the speaker more visible, not the content.** Notice the listener did not say, "Which hospital" or "when are visiting hours?" For empathic listening, here is the way to approach it with success:

1. Listen for the feelings behind the message
2. Let the speaker know you are listening and care
3. Avoid interruptions or lengthy comments
4. Listen for the relationships in the speaker's world
5. Be an "invisible" listener-make the speaker visible

Listen in silence with full attention on the speaker. Listen with an ear for the relationship of what they say **to their own lives,** not yours. Most listeners are so "into" their own world, they rarely experience the speaker's world. Untrained communicators have only one mode of communication, that of relating the message in terms of their own lives. Resist that temptation and listen to the speaker as if you were in his or her shoes living the experience yourself. Only then can you truly be empathic.

Live the expression "To walk a mile in another's moccasins." It is difficult to over-emphasize the importance of learning to get the message from the speaker's point of view - his or her experiences, feelings and meaning. Yes, you may have your own point of view which filters the message, but to the extent that you can let it go and enter what's actually going on in the other's life at the time, you can better understand the message.

Listen with respect. Every person who communicates has a message to give you. They do not always know what their message is, and they do not always communicate their message well to you. However, their communication to you is their way of including you in their world. In some way, the fact that you are there at the moment is a real blessing to both of you.

135

Listen to what's not being said. Various percentages are bandied about from 50-90%, regarding the amount of communication which is non-verbal. As a listener, you can be assured that it is the majority of the message. The non-verbal is often the best clue to the full message-it will reveal things about the speaker that the voice will not.

Listen for feelings and voice changes. As valuable as the content of the message may be, learn to tune into the feelings of the sender. Often feelings are a more accurate clue to the meaning than the words. Emotions are not easily hidden and there are many ways to spot them. One of the clues that ranges from very subtle to very obvious in detecting emotions is voice. As children, we became very in tune with the differences in our parents' voices. There are obvious ranges of volume, but the most useful ones in listening for emotions are the cracking of the voice, the drop in energy level, and changing in tone - of each speaker, which may be a signal that an emotion has been triggered in the speaker.

## Here's The Real Skill

Many times, you'll want to recover the generalization and deletion. What isn't said can be as important as what is said. Three ways to listen for what isn't said are generalization, deletion, and distortion. Speakers often generalize: this statement itself is a generalization. A typical generalization is making a blanket statement based upon a single incident. For example, after one upsetting incident at school, a student says, "School is stupid". A deletion is information left out so you get an inaccurate picture. Let's say that a student was doing well in a class until his last exam. Upon receiving a lower than normal grade, he might say: "I'm doing lousy in this class." The deletion was that all other times he was successful. In addition, he deleted his observations, needs and feelings.

Distortion is a change in the meaning of the information. For example, let's say a student is doing well in a class and the teacher makes a supportive comment. The student's distortion might be: "You are just saying that to be nice. I'll bet you say that to everyone." The student took the message and distorted the meaning to have it fit the meaning he wanted.

Listen for other messages. If we listen carefully, we can find that a speaker often has a strong bias in one direction or another. For example, if a speaker is continually saying what an awful job another teacher is doing, you may suspect some ulterior motives. If you hear a teacher complain about a fellow teacher, you may want to reply with, "I'm sorry to hear you're not happy with him (or her)."

## Avoid These Listening Mistakes

A common listener reaction is to divert attention from the speaker or topic. This is frustrating to the speaker because it prevents him from truly being heard. The three most common mistakes of poor listeners are offering similar stories, solutions or taking the message personally.

In similar stories you hear what is being said just long enough to think of a similar experience which happened to you, to tell back. If the speaker is sharing his troubles, DON'T jump in and try to make him feel better by telling about your own troubles. This tactic shifts the attention from the speaker to you, the listener. It doesn't allow the speaker to feel heard and understood.

Most people don't like to "be fixed." This means there's no need to start a "Dear Abby" in your mind where you are trying to fix, advise or correct the supposed ills of the speaker. If the speaker wants to know about your troubles, wait until you have given justice to his sharing. Just relax and be an empathic and caring listener, giving the other the same attention and respect you'd like when you are speaking.

"Solution listening" means that you and I listen just long enough to discover the "problem" and then give advice on how to solve it. The mistake is in shifting the attention from the speaker to the problem. When a speaker shares his troubles, just listen. Do not offer solutions unless you are asked. Why? Offering a solution shifts the attention from the speaker to the issue and at this stage of the conversation, the focus should be on the speaker.

The third mistake is engagement, taking a message personally. Receive the communication with disengagement. It is a rare speaker who can deliver a message from a perspective other than his own. Each message is colored by a lifetime of values, perceptions and personal experiences. For example, a student may say to you, "I don't like this class. You like the other students more than me." In fact, the student is really saying, "I don't experience feeling special, having self-worth or well-being in this class. I feel inadequate to other students and would at least like some more attention and recognition in class." The only way to find out for sure is to ask. But the important thing is to detach yourself from the meaning and effect on yourself and focus on the meaning of the message to the speaker.

Listen with easiness. This skill is contrasted to "listening on edge," where the listener is constantly ready to respond, either verbally or mentally. To listen with ease means to give the speaker "permission" to simply speak. It means that you don't need to placate the speaker by constantly saying, "I know what you mean... you're right as always." It does mean you can respond appropriately... "Hmmm. Yes... You bet..." To listen with ease also means to accept what the speaker is saying without making judgments.

Your objective is usually to make the speaker more "visible," more complete in his sharing. Since much of a speaker's world is often masked, this tools serves to recover lost or deleted information. It is your role as listener to use the clarifying tools only as they are necessary to complete the communication.

To be a good listener means to stay out of the boxing ring and courtroom. The boxing ring occurs when the listener is constantly sparring with the speaker, either verbally or mentally. You may have met a person who constantly interrupts or argues with you, continually missing the meaning of the communication. Your comment might be: "Whew, it's hot. It must be over 90 today!" So the 'boxer' jumps in and says "Yeah? I heard it was only 86 at noontime!" That's an example of a chronic "communication boxer" who has no intention or commitment to get the meaning of the communication, but rather simply wants to fight.

## Listen to the Person First

Suppose a student says "I didn't do my homework because there's no place to study in my house." You could listen with the reaction of "That's just an excuse," or "Why don't you create a better place to study?" But to actually enter the student's reality would be to listen carefully to find out more of what's going on. And know that the student is making the best decision for the choices available to him at the moment. In other words, if the student avoids doing homework, it's not because the student is lazy or stupid. This doesn't mean that the act is justifiable, just that students are only going to do what they feel their best choice is, not what your best choice is for them.

For example, a student may say: "I feel like everyone in class is doing better than I." If you jump in and say, "No, that's not true. You did better than a third of the class on the last test," you have missed their communication. What the speaker is saying is that he is dissatisfied with his academic performance. He wants to be heard. Other conclusions you might draw from his statement are all your own opinions and should be checked out with the speaker.

# Reading Non-Verbals

Pay attention to body language and calibrate it! It's common to read gross generalizations about the meaning of body language. For example, "when your legs are uncrossed while sitting, you indicate openness." But, many times legs are crossed merely to rest one leg or foot. Below are some of the common gestures and the most commonly given explanations for them. You may feel discomfort knowing, after consulting several experts in the field of communication, that the explanations which emerged were often contradictory:

- Legs uncrossed - openness/receptiveness/macho/cool
- Scratch head - puzzled/nervous/impatient
- Tug on the ear - ready to interrupt/lending an ear
- Touch their nose or jawbone - doubt/contemplation
- Open extended palms - to explain a generous offer/openness/ disbelief
- Hands on lips - impatience/silence/deep thought
- Hands on knees or leaning forward - readiness/stretching/ attention
- Clenched fist - power/anger/control
- Hands in pockets - hiding meaning/relaxed/cold atmosphere
- Shrugged shoulders - uncertainty/negative/tight neck
- Hands clasped behind back - authority/humility/service
- Looking downward, deep in thought/bored/feeling emotions
- Steepled fingers - confidence/boredom/scheming/a barrier
- Holding up objects - reaching out/hostility/distance
- Closed palms on the chest - struck by a thought/honesty/ defensive
- Clasp both hands - grief/anticipation/confidence
- Eye contact - interest/anger/boredom/distrust

Use all of your sensory acuity skills to listen. Pick up on a flush in the face or the neck, or a dilation of pupils. It could be the texture of the skin changes, as in getting "goosebumps." The ear, nose, throat, hands or legs may twitch as a response to an emotion filling the body. An obvious visual clue is tears, which could be signaling sadness, anger, relief, frustration, or joy.

The eyes may have an increased blink rate or twitch when the speaker moves into either highly emotional messages or they are reliving an experience, or even lying about it. The eyes may also squint when the intensity of the message goes up. The mouth gives excellent messages because it is also delivering the content. Watch for tightened lips, narrowed jaws, frowns, smiles, held-back laughs or lifted lips. An astute observer will also notice the breathing rate of the speaker. As the breathing rate quickens, you may guess the speaker is experiencing some anxiety, excitement, or other stimulating emotion.

The key to reading body language anytime is calibration. Observe, then check it out. Avoid assumptions, find out with questions. Avoid rules about what certain gestures or physiologies mean. Try something, check it out. Calibrate, calibrate, calibrate.

# Precision Listening

This is for information gathering. It engages the listener fully into the conversation. The listener asks questions such as "how specifically" or "who specifically" or "exactly when did you plan to do that?" It's a style of listening that goes after the content of the material to make the subject content more exposed and visible. It makes the content more real by engaging the speaker in defining the content and eliciting promises regarding what to do about what was said. For example: "Boy, am I in trouble; I'm flunking geometry." The listener would ask, "You mean you did poorly on the last test or you are likely to get an F in the class?" Then, once more information was elicited, the listener might ask questions such as "Well, what do you plan to do about it? When will you start?"

It is for the time when the emotions are calm and the content is the most important matter at hand. In this case, it's important to make the content more visible so that misunderstandings are reduced. Precision listening is really listening with a commitment to understand "and resolve" what the speaker is saying. It means that you become actively engaged in drawing out the details of the content in a way that insures you understand what the speaker is saying. The steps to follow are:

1. Listen fully without interrupting
2. Give feedback to the speaker on what was said
3. Ask for relevant details
4. Clarify, challenge, appreciate and respect elicit requests and promises, retrieve deleted information
5. Ask if there's a next step to do

To make precision listening work, assist the speaker when necessary. Many speakers haven't the slightest idea what they really want to say - they talk around the subject, but not directly to it. They mask or exaggerate their fears and often present to you an image of who they think you want to hear. For you to read through all of their distortions, deletions, and generalizations takes a real desire to get the intention and a willingness to respectfully question the obvious. Many speakers omit the obvious and it's your job to get the message as best as you can. Give speakers as much opportunity as possible to deliver the meaning without putting words in their mouth.

While precision listening is an active, challenging role, keep this in mind: It is unfair to others and is counterproductive to constantly monitor or challenge another's communications. If you do feel puzzled, unclear, or something doesn't sound right then ask for a clarification, but always with respect and politeness. You are doing both yourself and the other a real favor when you use these tools politely, as they are intended.

Understanding is important, so paraphrase if necessary. Restate in your own words what you think someone just said. It is not repeating the exact same words like a pet shop parrot, but rather what you translate them into. Listen carefully to what has been said, then use the words and phrases you are comfortable with and restate as best you can the same statement. When you paraphrase correctly, you show that you really understood what was said and the speaker gets the real sense that you were 'with' him. Here's an example of paraphrasing:

    Speaker - "This has been one of the longest weeks I've ever had in school."
    Listener - "Sounds like you've been through the wars, David."

This upcoming example is called parroting. It's a case of the listener being a tape recorder instead of a compassionate and empathic human being. It's an example of how NOT to paraphrase:

    Speaker - "I'm real happy with the score I just got on my test."
    Listener - "So you're real happy with the score you just got on your test, Huh?"

Complete communication provides the listener with "whole" information. It includes feelings, needs, thoughts and observations. When the listener gets incomplete communications, the mind has a tendency to "fill in" the missing information. That can lead to inaccurate conclusions. Here's an example:

    Speaker - "My notebook was stolen - I can't believe someone would do that!" (included an observation and a thought; it lacked a feeling and a need)
    Listener - "Sounds like you're really upset...I'm sorry it happened. Do you need some help with your notes?" (listener tries to fill in missing items; the feeling and the need).
    Speaker - "I'm so sad." (feeling expressed, what's missing is thoughts, needs and observation)
    Listener - "I can tell it's really brought you down. Tell me what else has been going on...."(listener asks for deleted information)

If you would like to encourage trust, safety and student rapport, make sure that you always acknowledge and appreciate the speaker for sharing. Say with sincerity, "Thank you for sharing that with me...." Or, "I really appreciate you being willing to share that with me - I feel honored and privileged." Or, in another example, you might say, "Thank you for letting me know that; it must have taken a lot of courage to share it with me." Notice that in each of the examples above the listener always acknowledges that he received the communication before addressing any of the issues.

One other thing: you may want to add something that lets the speaker know that you understood the essence of what was said. For example, "It sounds as if you've had a rough day. I sure hope things get better for you. Thanks for sharing that with me." There was a re-statement of what was understood as well as an acknowledgment.

Clarify if unclear. Most of what is understood is different from what is sent and we have become accustomed to living with the chaotic results. In order to communicate more successfully, you must train yourself to become more precise and insist on reciprocal clarity from the speaker. As you might guess, some tact is required to do it successfully. When you ask for clarification, first acknowledge the speaker.

How do you clarify foggy conversations? By asking the right questions! Ask such questions as: Who specifically, what specifically, and how specifically. Clarify statements by asking, compared to what?, all?, every?, none?, never?, always? You can also ask, what would happen if...? or would it be possible to...? Since not everyone is ecstatic about having their communications dissected, you may want to soften up some of your clarifiers. Use phrases such as... "I'm wondering what specifically you mean by...." Or, "I'm curious whether...." "Here's an idea, tell me what you think...." In each of the examples below, you'll note a student comment and a way for the teacher to clarify the question and stay in rapport with him or her.

# Clarifications

Student - "I don't understand this."
Teacher - "I'm sorry I wasn't more clear for you. What specifically don't you understand?"

Student - "I don't want to do it."
Teacher - "I appreciate your telling me. Exactly what is it you don't want to do?"

Student - "I'll bring it by later."
Teacher - "Thanks for the offer. What time were you thinking of?

# Generalizations Corrected

Student - "Geography is a pain in the neck."
Teacher - "I'm sorry it's not more fun for you. Specifically which part of it is tough?"

Student - "Teachers are really supportive here."
Teacher - "I appreciate your telling me. Which ones come to mind?"

Student - "Everybody knows it's a big waste."
Teacher - "Thanks for sharing that with me. Whom are you referring to specifically? What do you mean by a waste?"

# Unspecified Nouns, Pronouns and Verbs Exposed

Student - "I'm ecstatic."
Teacher - "That's great; tell me more."

Student - "He ripped me off."
Teacher - "What a bummer! Exactly what happened?"

Student - "I feel scared."
Teacher - "I appreciate your sharing that. What is it that you feel scared about?"

# Limits Clarified and Exposed

Student - "I couldn't tell you that."
Teacher - "I appreciate your honesty. Have you thought about what would happen if you did?"

Student - "I can't do this."
Teacher - "Sounds like something's in the way. Could you imagine what would happen if you did?"

Student - "I have to be this way."
Teacher - "I respect your choice. You must have had a good reason for saying that. I was wondering what would happen if you changed it?"

## Absolutes Exposed

Student - "I can never do anything right."
Teacher - "Thanks for telling me. What you said is possible, but can you think of a time when you did do one thing right?"

Student - "Nothing good ever happens to me."
Teacher - "Sounds like you're pretty down right now. Can you think of something good that you'd like to have happen today?"

## Imposed Values Made Evident

Student - "Assignments are a waste."
Teacher - "I'm sorry. Is there any way I could make them more meaningful for you?"

## Lost Performatives Retrieved

Student - "It's not good to keep us late."
Teacher - "I appreciate you keeping track of it. Whom do you think it's not good for?"

Student - "It's rude to say that."
Teacher - "I appreciate your sharing your thoughts. It's rude to say what, according to whom?"

Student - "That's a waste of time."
Teacher - "Sounds like you are frustrated or bummed. Anything you can do to make it worth your time?"

## Distortions Challenged

Student - "I know you won't accept this paper."
Teacher - "You sound hesitant to turn it in ...could I ask why?"

Student - "He should know better than to say that to me."
Teacher - "I respect your opinion. How would you guess he'd know?"

## Distortions Clarified

Teacher - "You drive me crazy!"
Student - "I'm sorry. What specifically have I done, that you chose to get irritated about?"

Student - "If David hadn't had to go early, I would have had my assignment."

Teacher - "It sounds like you felt things were out of your control. How, specifically, did you put yourself in a position where David had control over your assignment?"

Next, discover if there are any additional steps to take. Most of the time, the listener is sharing more about himself than the issue or topic of the conversation. As soon as the sharing and disclosure is complete, the speaker usually is satisfied. Sometimes, he just had something to "get off his chest." In other cases, there's a legitimate interest in the topic. As a listener, you must check it out. The most appropriate action for the listener is to ask the speaker if there is anything that can be done. If, and only if, the speaker gives you permission, should you shift from being a listener of a real human being to a problem-solver.

Finally, acknowledge the communication and the speaker. The speaker deserves to know if you understand what is being said and if you can empathize with the sharing. There are two issues for the speaker: the primary one is self. He wants to feel listened to and to be worth paying attention to. The secondary issue is whether or not the meaning was understood.

Student - "I can't do anything right."

Teacher - "I appreciate your point of view, and it must be frustrating for you. I'd love for you to succeed. Would you like some additional choices?"

Student - "Geography" is a pain in the neck."

Teacher - "Thanks for letting me know. I wish it was easier for you. You are important to me... can I help on anything in particular?"

Student - "I didn't get the assignment.'

Teacher - "I'm glad you checked with me - it shows me you care about how you are doing. This assignment is important, here it is...."

The key to empowering your speaker is simple: meet the speaker where he is "at." Accept his reality as true for him (it is!), then allow him to see, hear or feel his own inner beauty. Find a gift in every problem, a jewel in every situation and appreciate something sincerely about that person, regardless of what was discussed. You will excite, inspire and motivate your students and they will love it, too. Can you imagine how much more willing your students would be to communicate if you responded this way? Your students will feel so appreciated and noticed that their interest and motivation will go up dramatically. Wouldn't it be worth it to try?

---

| *Additional Resources for Further Study and Follow up* |
| --- |

*Frogs into Princes* by Bandler & Grinder (Real People Press)
*Envoy* by Michael Grinder (Grinder & Associates)
*Righting the Educational Conveyor Belt* by Michael Grinder (Metamorphous)*
*Influencing With Integrity* by LaBorde (Science & Behavior Books)
*Messages* by Matthew McKay
*Making Contact* by Virginia Satir

* Items marked with an asterisk are available in the Appendix.

# 11

# Successful Interactions

## It's All About People

A critical part of a your job, and the part for which you are often the least trained is interactions. Specifically, the moments when the you, the teacher is talking one-on-one with a student. Those times could include: when a student asks questions, when the teacher asks questions, inquiries, discussions, when ideas and feelings are expressed and even during pre- and post-class encounters. All of these times can have a major impact on students' lives and often have more impact than the actual class.

It may not surprise you to know that classroom interactions can be some of the primary events in a person's life. Many students have made paralyzing or resourceful life decisions as a conclusion about and in the aftermath of, classroom interactions. Many students will say things such as, "Oh, I could never do that. I don't have the talent." (Maybe in fourth grade a teacher said as much to them.) Or, "I was thinking about becoming an attorney." (Her tenth grade teacher may have said she had an aptitude for business, legal and communication work).

When was the last time you heard a student talk about a lecture heard a year ago? They don't talk about lectures - or even classroom activities as much as they do about those moments of one-to-one interactions. Does each and every single interaction matter? Poet Hugh Prather says, "Are there any wholly useless encounters? I know this: there are no insignificant people...."

Momentary interactions, some of them merely seconds long, are a critical part of the class. It's been said that "we are all therapists, whether we know it or not." In other words, with each and every interaction, there is an opportunity to heal or damage. There is no middle ground - you cannot leave your students feeling neutral after an interaction because it's human nature to draw conclusions. Every interaction is initiated with the intention of accomplishing a result and of reaching an outcome. The outcome is important, but so is the vehicle for that outcome. When a student asks a question, he or she will either feel good for asking it or he or she will not.

## The Key to Interactions Is the Process

For example, if you say, "Who knows the answer to that question?" An erroneous assumption is that the answer is the most important part of the interaction. There are two items as important as the answer to the question: the process and the context. Process means how the student arrived at the answer, the way in which the

145

question is asked and the way in which the teacher responds or acknowledges. Context means the circumstances surrounding the asking of the question. If you ask the question with an intention to empower and support, you will come across in a different way than if you ask the question to determine who has the correct answer.

# Are They Just Common Sense?

Unfortunately the meaning of the phrase 'common sense' is very different depending on who you talk to about it. Interactions that leave students and teachers feeling better, more knowledgeable and more resourceful are the result of being wide awake and clear on your outcomes as well as the result of having behavioral flexibility and sensory acuity. You've got to know what you want, know how to get it and know when you have achieved it.

# Three Key Qualities

Successful interactions have three qualities. First, each person feels respected and treated fairly. Second, both people must get the outcome desired from the interaction. Third, they must each experience a sense of completion and closure. Successful interactions are not accidents. They are a result of your creation of classroom conditions which make it safe and worthwhile for students to interact openly with their teachers.

If your students don't participate, share, or ask questions, you can be sure that it's not that they have nothing to say. Classes naturally generate lots of questions and responses. Expression is a natural human trait and it is the unnatural circumstance which suppresses it. Here's how a classroom atmosphere can be created that encourages interaction and at the same time, structures it into appropriate formats:

1. **Class agreements**... for interactions such as these, others must remain quiet while a person is speaking. Encourage students to share from their own experiences or creations instead of telling others how "the world is." This allows students to learn to validate, honor and respect themselves as well as their thoughts and feelings because the teacher is placing a priority on what the student says, not what some textbook says. Of course this also means that an answer that the student came up with, or figured out is perfect for sharing, too.
2. **Time**... be sure to allow sufficient time for interactions, for they are a key part of the learning process. Class allotments may vary from as little as 10% of class time to as much as 80%, depending on the nature and circumstances of the course. If the teacher rushes interactions, students will withdraw from contributing.
3. **Role modeling**... have students share their own attitudes and thoughts about interactions. For example, students might be told that questions are appreciated and that it's safe to ask them. Tell them that you always support them, and you will not use interactions as a way to make them wrong or to pick on them. Let your students know that their questions don't have to be the "question of the year" to be worthy to ask, and that it's better to ask it than to let it go unanswered. You also can open up sharing by self-disclosure.

You may not need to do this formally, though it's likely that some kind of initial discussion about class interactions would be useful. You are the one who creates the openness and the circumstances which can make successful interactions possible. It's not the students, the administration, or the outside world. You have the power and the ability to make your classroom perfectly safe and at the same time, a powerful learning experience.

First of all, develop a systematic procedure for scanning the room for raised hands, whether it's going row by row or section by section. One of the most frustrating experiences for students is to have something well up inside of such importance that they are willing to risk sharing it with the group, only to have a teacher miss their hand up in the air. Again, it's easy to blame the student who doesn't raise his or her hand high enough or wave it around, but the blaming doesn't serve you as a master teacher.

Look, listen, feel, see, notice, scour, perceive and search the room constantly for cues that a student is ready to share something. Your students will give you non-verbal clues more readily than the verbal ones. You have got to begin to notice the raised eyebrow, the shift in posture or breathing. For some students, it's very invalidating not to be recognized. In addition, to make it easier, you may want to set up some simple courtesy guidelines for listener behavior such as eyes on the Speaker.

## Use the Non-Verbals

The next step to take is to move further from the person who is ready to ask the question. This makes him or her speak up and it includes the rest of the students in the interaction. Make eye contact, and before you indicate that it is time for them to speak, check your physiology. When you have students raising hands, ready to be recognized, it's a signal for you to shift your whole physiology into another role. You have a presenter role in which your body language, your tone, tempo and physiology is strong - you are putting out a lot of energy. The moment that a student wants to contribute, share, or ask, you must make a shift internally from a visual mode to an auditory or kinesthetic mode. It's a softer, more receptive and open internal state.

Is it possible that you look bored, hostile, aggressive or close-minded? The proper physiology is the one that gives the message to the student, "I'm interested in you, your question, your well-being, and I respect you." This means an erect but not rigid posture, full face-to-face attention, with shoulders facing the student. It means both hands are at your side or clasped behind you. Your physiology will be your key to effective communications. Anytime your communications seem to be off, check your physiology.

When you want to invite participation, nod your head and end your comments or questions on an 'up' voice tonality. Then, indicate with a nod of the head or eye contact or with a motion of your hand that it is time for the student to speak. Instead of pointing, gesture towards the student with an open hand, palm up. This is usually accepted by questioners as less intimidating or confrontational. Hence, they feel their comments are more likely to be welcomed in the future.

## Questioning Strategies

So far, we have mentioned several pre-speaking steps for you to take: (1) keep your eyes open for signs of a question or comment (2) check your physiology before you recognize the speaker (3) indicate with an outstretched arm and open palm gesture that it's appropriate to speak.

147

Next, make sure the speaker has the attention of the class before beginning. If not, have him wait a moment until the rest of the class is ready. Be sure each person has heard the question. If necessary, have it repeated. Be sure you ask in a tone that lets the class know that the question is worth hearing. For example, "John, that question is important, and I want everyone to hear it. Will you please repeat it?" Avoid blaming the class. Rapport is lost by stating, "The class was being rude, please ask the question again, John."

At this point, you might use your body to continue to regulate the volume of the question-asker. Be sure you move to the opposite side of the room to listen. This encourages them to speak up so others can hear and it puts enough space between you and them to include the rest of the audience. Also, make sure the speaker faces most of the class. If the speaker is up front, have him face the class. If he is on the side of the room, adjust the speaker's direction so he reaches the other students.

Or, you might use your hands as a movie director, raising them from a low to a high point to indicate that you wish the speaker to raise the volume. Of course, you can also cup your ear or lean towards the speaker to indicate your need for greater volume. Stay in rapport with the speaker, being ready to match tonality, tempo, volume, gestures, posture and breathing.

If you need responses such as to a question, outstretch your arms with open palms up and wait. If someone is talking, asking or sharing, be sure to thank and acknowledge them every single time. It's a way of creating more student respect and reinforcing the contribution.

# Should You Interrupt?

Surprisingly, there are three instances during which you might interrupt. Ordinarily you'd let the response remain intact without corrections, changes or interruptions. The three exceptions are: (1) if it is extremely unclear, or dragging on when the attention of the class has disappeared; (2) if the question contains an initial premise which, as stated, makes the rest of the question invalid or inappropriate to answer; or (3) if the comment contains any damaging, profane, critical or hostile parts which you cannot, in good conscience, leave uncorrected. If you need to interrupt, do so respectfully, let the speaker know why and then have him continue.

*Your students are more interested
in how much you care
than how much you know*

While the question is being asked, quiet your mind. There's a tendency to do one of two things, neither of which is useful. First, one might "check out", daydreaming in another world, not at all tuned into the question. Second, the opposite may occur. You might be overly engaged and reactive to the question so that while it is being asked, you are thinking of the answer, how to win, be right, dominate, or get control of the person. Let the student complete the question without being corrected for errors that don't affect the essence of the question. If the student asks a question to which your response is anger, pause for a moment, allow yourself to relax and get centered before answering.

# Personal Preparation

It's important to give the framework in which you are able to answer or not answer. Here are some choices to make before you actually respond to the question:

1. Let the rest of the class know if the question is extra-important or critical to their success. It can serve as an attention getter.
2. Let the speaker know if you do not know the answer. Don't make it up, instead, let the person know how to get the answer, when you will have the answer or how you both might come up with the answer.
3. If it's appropriate to not answer, there are several choices: invite the person to "stay with" the question and explore the nature of the question instead of giving a pat answer. Another possibility is that it's not the time to answer the question. In which case, you should acknowledge the speaker for asking it and let him or her know that you can answer more fully at a later time.

# Your Actual Responses

First, acknowledge the student. Students risk being thought of as wrong, stupid or inadequate for asking a question. One of the biggest reasons students don't ask more questions in class is most have been embarrassed at one time or another. Reinforce the student by giving acknowledgment for asking the question or for asking a certain type of question. You might say, "Thanks for asking, Joe...", "The answer is...", or "I'm glad you brought that up, Joe..." You may simply answer the question, thanking the student for asking. Once you've acknowledged the speaker, you have additional options. You might ask the speaker if he knows the answer to his own question. For example:

Student: "What's the real cause of a recession?"
Teacher: "I like your question, thanks for asking it. Some say it's related to interest rates, employment rates and the overseas value of the dollar. Would you agree or disagree, and why?"

Notice that you have opened up the possibility that the student may already know the answer. It's a form of acknowledging the awareness and reservoir of information we all have. Another possibility is to turn to the group and ask, "Who would like to offer some possible answers to that question?" Here you'd be using the question as a way to empower others.

Here are a few additional suggestions for answering questions. Respect the student and the question. This means avoid jokes about it or making light of either the question or the student. Those can be trauma-inducing actions and thus dangerous. Stay with the sincerity and intent of the question. Avoid judgments about what the students should have known and studied, or about the quality of the question. Use the student's name when responding. For example, "Good quality question, Jenny. I like questions that deal with central core issues."

An excellent way to encourage future questions is to make sure that the answer you give is brief. First, give the big picture overview, then the specifics. Students get turned off by long-winded answers. They're often boring and it takes the focus off the question putting attention on the teacher's answer. That's not the way to build rapport with students, nor is it a useful strategy for recognition of the student's contribution.

## Think Before You Ask

Also, be sure to respect the thinking style of your asker. The way some students learn is by mixing and contrasting. If you ask, "Why is the ocean blue?", you may have a student who says, "All oceans are not blue. What about the Red Sea?" Respect each person's style of thinking. The way some students learn best is to find exceptions to the rule. They are not being negative or sarcastic. Others, of course, will do the opposite. If you ask, "How are these cars different?", you may have a student who says, "They're not, they're practically the same." It's quite possible that a student learns best by matching and comparing. As you discover the thinking style of others, you stay in rapport with them and reach your outcome easier.

Finally, make sure that you create and continue the element of rapport in the conversation. Match predicates, adjectives and adverbs if mentioned in the conversation. It gains rapport and creates better communication. For example, a student might say, "I see what you're saying, but I have what I think is a good question...", To match it, use the same key words: "Johnny, you're right, that is a good question. Notice that the answer can be clearly seen from the perspective of..." (matching the descriptive words good and good, plus matching the visually-oriented words see with "notice, seen and clearly").

## Hostile Questions

One of the primary jobs of a teacher is to maintain constant rapport with your students. When you get a hostile question, it is because the rapport has been broken. The moment you hear a hostile question, relax, center yourself, and re-establish rapport. Then discover the student's needs and do whatever is necessary to re-create a new alliance.

150

One easy way to gain rapport is with non-verbal matching of physiology. If students are sitting, lower your eye level by leaning against a desk or sitting on it momentarily.

For verbal matching, listen to the content of the student's comments. Ask yourself what is going on in the student's world to cause such action. What does the student believe in order to ask that particular question? Place yourself in the student's shoes to understand it from his or her point of view. Listen for predicates such as "I feel that..." or "I hear that..." or "The way I see it..." Match the predicate in your answer. Match the tonality, tempo, and volume. If a student is aggressive, your response could be aggressive at first, leading to a softer more receptive way of speaking.

Open your response with one of these three rapport-builders, "I appreciate..." or "I agree..." or "I respect..." Complete the sentence as you and the student move towards co-creating a mutually satisfying solution. As an example:

STUDENT: "You don't know what you are talking about. This is really stupid!
TEACHER: "Maybe you could help me out a little. What doesn't make any sense to you and what are some things we could do about it?

Listen, empathize and respect their point of view. Repeat back to them what you think their point is, so they know they have been understood. Always handle an irritated participant completely so that the rest of the group can relax and move on with the day. Even if you need more time with them later, ask for an appointment with the upset person from the front of the room so that they know you care and are willing to work things out. Never leave someone upset, hurt or brooding in your audience. Never, ever make fun of anyone except yourself from the front of the room. Never embarrass others or you risk shutting down the rest of the group and reducing their likely contributions.

# Asking Content Questions

Check your intention when you ask questions of others. There are lots of reasons, purposes and potential outcomes and it's critical to have clarity on your intended outcome. An optimal outcome for each question that you ask is to empower the student who answers it.

Make sure that your questions are asked with compassion. There must be no intention to "win" or "make another wrong" by asking a question that cannot be easily answered. You must have the intention for students to be successful and feel greater self-worth. Eliminate trick questions unless used in the separate context as a learning tool. Ask the question with full expectancy of getting an answer and engaging the entire class.

**Old way:** "Is there anyone who can answer the question of how the US could decrease unemployment?"

**New way:** "Everyone get ready to answer this question: What are some of the ways that the US could decrease unemployment?"

The new way engages the whole class in the learning and encourages the student to contribute, participating more than ever before. It's an old idea and a simple one. Involved students are more successful.

# Whom To Call On?

The answer is difficult. How you decide depends on what you want to occur in the classroom. What's the outcome you want? Do you want everyone kept on their toes? Do you want to work with a few students who need extra help? There's no "pat" answer. Successful teachers use many procedures. Try these suggestions:

1. Call on a volunteer. As you continue to create a more open class atmosphere, more and more hands will go up automatically. It's easier for the students this way, but there's always the possibility that the same ones may volunteer each time.
2. Call on students you feel could use the biggest boost in self-confidence. Of course, you must have the interest and skills to insure their success.
3. Call on the student you have selected as a class consultant for the day. Every student has some special or unique knowledge or talent. Make it your job to bring out the best in each.

**Old way:** "Today we'll be discussing history, so open your books to page twenty... Now, who has something they'd like to share about what they've learned?"

**New Way:** "Kevin, you know much about guns. Since weapons played a big part in history, I'd like you to be a class consultant in that area today. Just signal me when you have something you'd like to add."

# Before You Ask Questions

This is often of little importance to the teacher in the moment it's happening, but it is often VERY important to the learner in the moment. Use any of the following strategies:

*Provide a "mistakes OK" safe climate for Q & As*
*Assert that there may be multiple answers to your question*
*Check in with audience before asking Qs to insure readiness*
*Everyone may get a partner or learning buddy to serve as consultant*
*Utilize response cards, signals, cues*
*Utilize 3 boxes of understanding before asking*
*Give a multiple choice menu with the question*
*Ask who is ready and has the answer*
*Provide more wait time - respect learning styles*
*Use selective calling... only call on those that know it*
*Utilize team and group cooperative responses*
*Use a signal to let you know they're ready*
*Role reversal, have participant check your work*
*Do a drawing for names in a fishbowl or a hat*
*Tell & show them at the stars all the Qs to be asked*
*Do Jeopardy turnaround - they have answer, ask you the Q*

# Types of Questions

There are many types of questions that may be useful for you to ask in the classroom. Educator Arthur Costa identifies and makes distinctions for three types of questions. The recall question is intended to elicit stored data from prior knowledge or experiences. The best description is that it's close to a stimulus response mechanism. The recall question draws from students the kind of information that a card file or computer might. Here are some examples of recall questions:

Identifying: "Which is your favorite book on teaching?"
Completing: "This chapter is on successful classroom _____."
Matching: "What other books are similar to this one?"
Listing: "Name all of the important chapters in this book."
Observing: "What subtitles do you see on this page?"
Reciting: "Earlier I said there are how many types of questions?"
Describing: "Describe the cover of this book."
Defining: "What's the definition of a successful interaction?"
(Also included are questions which require counting, enumerating and selecting.)

The second type of classroom question requires processing. It is one designed to process information acquired and is usually associated with analyzing or cause and effect. It uses different skills than the recall question and requires more exact, detailed information. Some examples are:

Comparing: "What do you and your students have in common?"
Sequencing: "In what order should you call on your students?"
Inferring: "What can you infer from the first sentence on this page?"
Classifying: "How would you rate this book so far?"
Contrasting: "In what ways is this book different from the last one you read?"
Analyzing: "What could you say about that answer?"
Organizing: "How could you arrange this information better?"
(Also: Questions which require distinguishing, grouping, explaining and experimenting are considered processing)

The third category is the application question. The student is asked to move out of the immediate information to come up with new or hypothetical information. It's a creative state of make believe, construction, fantasy and invention. Examples are:

Applying: "What would happen if you learned all the tools in this book?"
Generalizing: "Now that you're a better teacher, what can you say about your self-esteem?"
Speculating: "What would happen if every teacher knew what you now know?"
Modifying: "How quickly can you adapt this book to your own classroom?"
Forecasting: "Based on last year's growth, how good will you be next year?"
Distorting: "After you teach one great class, are you the best teacher ever?"
Deleting: "What is it you want to ignore about this book?"
Inventing: "I wonder how many ways you could tell others about this book?"
(Also: questions which require theorizing, examples, judging, imagining and extrapolating)

## When You Get the Answer You Like

Use the opportunity to follow up. You might say to the student, "Can you tie the answer into what others have said?" Can you ask them to expand on what was given? Remember to always acknowledge and thank them for the contribution.

# What if the Answer Is Wrong?

Many teachers and educators become dogmatic about the importance of the right answer, rewarding the students who know it and penalizing those who don't. The major argument suggested is that "either you know it or you don't-there's no in-between ground." In this age of computers and easily accessible mass storage, ask yourself, "What's more useful, to teach students information or to teach them strategies to learn or create new information?" In other words, how your students came up with the answer provides the information necessary to become successful in modern life.

It's permissible for your students to fail momentarily with a wrong answer as long as they are using or learning a process that will eventually allow them to succeed. Failure is encouraged in the larger context of being successful, and in fact, failure is the information needed to become successful. Failure means you discovered that the content was not correct, and you had an opportunity to discover the process. Was your strategy useful? Would you use it again? If not, what's an alternative strategy? In that framework, could you ever call a wrong answer a failure?

# Handling "Wrong" Answers

Some research says that our handling of wrong answers had led to an artificially low ceiling on performance. In a direct, single-answer recall situation, the student who offers the wrong answer may actually be using a higher order, more successful strategy for learning than the student who comes up with the correct answer. Many students read more ambiguity into a question than is usually intended, leading them to wrong answers.

Yet the strategy for most teachers is to encourage the simplest or most efficient path to the answer rather than stressing that there are many paths. The real problem is that you'll end up with inflexible learners. Powell says that "teachers listen for the expected answer rather than to the answer they get... and the student who cannot frame his ideas the way the teacher does quickly learns to be a failure." Increase awareness of multiple learning strategies and you'll discover that your students may show dramatic gains in test scores, enthusiasm and even IQ!

Given that wrong answers can be more useful than correct ones, what's the actual response to a student who has an "incorrect" answer? Here are some possibilities:

*Prompt them for a better answer...Do the "hotter & colder" game*
*Ask them to say more about their answer to clarify what they mean*
*Ask for repeat performance in 5 min... check back*
*Give more non-verbal or verbal clues to coax them*
*Walk them through the steps of learning or logic to get a better answer*
*Say your answer is a " good contribution" or "good effort" & move on*
*Change the question to make the problem more understandable*
*Put the answer on hold & ask if others would like to add or comment*
*Change your question to make their answer right*
*Give the correct answer indirectly within 30 seconds after attention is switched*
*Express humor at the situation... but never, never, never at the student*
*Use confirmatory phrases such as "so your answer is... so that means..."*

*Do a "break state" to shift the attention away from student*
*Course rule: all answers are temporary until we validate them*
*Give credit for saying "I don't know" or suggesting a possible answer*
*Have them find two others who agree with the answer & add to it*
*Re-assign the problem again, change one variable*
*Give partial credit for giving the process of how they got the answer*
*Always acknowledge and thank them for the contribution*

Make sure to use your senses to find out if the student feels complete with the interaction. Does he or she feel good about what was contributed or learned? You can tell by the physiology, posture, expressions and voice. If you were successful, the physiology will be confident and beaming self-worth. If the eyes are dropped, shoulders are slumped and voice is lowered, you can be sure the interaction did not achieve the intended result of empowering the student. If you are the least bit unsure, check with the student: "Jane, now that we've talked about this for a moment, what are you feeling, or what conclusion is on your mind?"

## Student Sharing

Sharing is just as important for tenth graders or college students as it is for second graders. It's valuable for many reasons. One is that everyone is on equal footing. If this activity is handled properly, it can be an opportunity for students in several ways: (1) to learn about other students by listening and watching others (2) to gain confidence through speaking to a group (1) to gain acceptance for being themselves (4) to learn and discover something about themselves (5) to gain self-worth.

Simple rules for sharing are that: (1) you must speak from your own experience (2) you be considerate and respectful - no put-downs, profanity or pre-judgments and (3) you are respectful of the time available.

The moment of sharing time can, for each student, be a fabulous opportunity for acceptance of themselves and others. Therefore, be sure that students can hear and see one another well. If you notice others are losing attention while one is sharing, you may need to refocus the class and encourage the speaker to include classmates in the sharing process. You may also remind students that what's being shared might relate to them.

## How to Respond

The teacher's primary role during student sharing is to stay "in relationship." Be sure you provide eye contact and create rapport through either nodding or matching some of the gestures. The way to respond is to put yourself in the student's shoes for a moment, suspend judgment and join his or her reality without being caught up or paralyzed by it. When a student shares something, simply respond with comments such as, "I appreciate your sharing, thank you." Or, "I enjoyed what you had to say, thank you." Or, "Thank you very much for sharing yourself." Or, "Great, thank you." Or, "I respect what you have to say, thanks." In that way, the student knows he or she is appreciated, heard and respected.

# Validate Student Contributions

By validating student contributions you can foster an increase in classroom thinking skills. There are several ways to allow the students a chance to experience feelings of confidence and self-worth through a question-answer interaction. First, acknowledge the contribution. This can be easily done with the simple statement as above in item 1. Second, you can refer to a student's comment at a later time in class. For example, "As Johnny said earlier...." It is a major boost for a student to be quoted by the teacher! Another tool for validation is to write student comments on a flip chart or the chalkboard, saving it for the whole class to see.

# Responding to Creativity

Imagine a student coming saying, "I made up a new theory on why the Civil War happened." Or another student saying to the English teacher, "I have a new kind of poetry." Or a math student saying, "I am making up a new way to find square roots." While some teachers would respond receptively, others might raise eyebrows skeptically and ask for proof. If your outcome is to foster self-esteem and creativity in the thought process, you'll respond with enthusiasm and support. Say to that student, "That's terrific. Tell me more." These brief moments can make a big difference in a student's life. Be ready for them.

# Discussion and Inquiry

Teacher-led discussions have the capacity to enliven, inform, inspire and perhaps most importantly, allow students to understand how others think. If done poorly, students will be resentful and unwilling to participate in the future. If you plan to have a discussion or inquiry process, first get clarity on your intended outcome. If your outcome is to pursue the truth, you are in trouble! After all, whose truth are you after, yours or a student's?

Nobel prize-winning physicists David Bohm, Niels Bohr and Albert Einstein have all said that there is "no fixed reality." It's all decided from the point of view of the observer. We each participate in the momentary creation of our own experiences, our truths and subsequently, our universe. Therefore each of us has a different, yet equally valid truth. The quest for a single "truth" in the classroom is not useful. It is useful to evaluate the relative merits of a point of view or a suggestion. Be open to ideas.

# Pre- and Post-Class Dialogues

One-on-one contact is important for both the teacher and the student. If it's a positive sharing, just listen. If there's a problem, be extra alert. When a student talks to the teacher about something, you can be sure it is important to him or her. What you do or don't do in these moments is very important. Often when a student comes to you, he's feeling unresourceful and helpless. Your outcome must be to empower the student to add to his resourcefulness so at the completion of your interaction, he will be stronger and more able than before. These times are prime opportunities for assisting the student to think! In other words, your interaction must add to the student's sense of his own ability, not further his sense of dependency and helplessness.

If the student's head is hung low, you've got two choices. One of them is to change his physiological state. Politely ask him to move his head more upright to eye level. This will immediately pull him out of the "victim", or "poor me" physiology and get him into another state, probably auditory or visual instead of kinesthetic. Another possibility is to match the posture momentarily so the student feels a commonalty with you. Assume a posture that is similar, pace your voice tempo with him and match breathing, if possible. Immediately begin to match predicates, match the same state he is in, then lead him to a more resourceful one. Here's an example of a dialogue:

## Do You Make This Mistake?

*Student:* "Look, I'm doing awful in this class. I don't see how I can get my grades up, and I just flashed on the final next week."
*Teacher:* "You sound really concerned. Thanks for talking to me about it, maybe you're right, our last class was an earful."
*Student:* "Well, that's not exactly it..."
(Notice that in the first sentence, the student used visual words: look, see, flashed. The teacher responded with mis-matched auditory words: sound, talking and earful. That *does not* create rapport!)

## Here's a Winner!

*Student:* "Get a load of this. I keep a stiff upper lip when studying, but it all boils down to the same old thing: I'm knee-deep in trouble."
*Teacher:* "Thanks for touching base with me. There's a couple of things that'll help you come to grips with this if you can just hang in there while we build a strong foundation."
*Student:* "Good idea, I can handle that."
(In the first sentence, the student used the kinesthetic mode: get a load, stiff upper lip, boils down to, knee-deep. The teacher matched the information modality and ended up with being able to offer some strong support. Find words in the teacher's response which show they were able to gain rapport.)

The first thing you might say to a student who comes up to you is to acknowledge him. For example, "I appreciate you coming up to talk to me - you are important to me." The next step is to listen. Listen quietly, nodding and staying in rapport. Listen without judging, or trying to solve the problem for that person. Allow that student to be able to be himself without your additions or subtractions of advice or ideas. Allow any silence if it arises. Now, keep in mind what your intended outcome was - added resourcefulness and completion.

The next step is to help the student identify resources which are already there and could be of assistance. Do not offer advice, especially if the conversation is personal. For example:

*Student:* "I need some help... I just don't feel motivated to do my homework."
*Teacher:* "Thanks for coming to me, I'll do the best I can to help you handle it. As far as your homework situation, what do you feel is going on?"
*Student:* "Well, I'm not sure, I'm just not motivated."
*Teacher:* "What other possibilities are there?"
*Student:* "I guess I could (student names choices)."
*Teacher:* "Which of those choices do you feel best about?"

157

*Student:* "I like the one that (student names a choice)."
*Teacher:* "Good, I'll do what I can to help you make it work. In fact, how about if you check with me in a week? However, I want you to know you did great at coming up with some solutions; you're pretty resourceful. As you continue to feel more confident, you'll find that you'll be able to easily come up with even more solutions in the future.
*Student:* "I hadn't really thought I knew my own answer."
*Teacher:* "Take a deep breath... how do you feel now? Is everything OK or is there anything else you'd like to talk about,"
*Student:* "Actually, I feel pretty good."
*Teacher:* "Good... thanks for stopping by and good luck."

# What If You Fail At It?

What would you do if a student asked for help, then you in turn, asked if they could come up with some solutions and they couldn't? Here's an example of two ways to draw out information:

1. If the student says "I don't know the answer." You might respond with "I appreciate you sharing that, but I wonder, if you actually did know the answer, what would you say it is?"

2. You could say, "Do you know anyone in this class who might know the answer...? How do you think that he or she might answer that question? Just guess..."

One of the most useful ways to help students cut through problems is to help them cut through the vagueness to get at the core of the problem. Ask specific questions when needed and you'll get better quality answers.

| Statements | Your Response |
|---|---|
| Something is "too much, too many, or too expensive" | compared to what? |
| nouns, pronouns (he, she, they, it, who specifically?) | who or what? |
| verbs (moved, asked, wrote, tried, hurt, inspired, etc.) | how specifically? |
| shouldn't, couldn't, can't do it | what causes or prevents? |
| must, have to, got to | what would happen? |
| all, every, never, always, only | repeat, "every one it always?" |

*Student:* "This doesn't make any sense to me."
*Teacher:* "What specifically doesn't make sense?"
*Student:* "I've always disliked math."
*Teacher:* "Always? What about when you were in pre-school?"
*Student:* "I can't go through with this."
*Teacher:* "What would happen if you did?"
("What prevents you from following through?")
*Student:* "They don't let me ask questions."
*Teacher:* "Who specifically, won't let you ask questions?"
*Student:* "This is much too hard."
*Teacher:* "Compared to what?"

You can add "softeners" in front of your questions to insure that the student receives your questions gently and respectfully. Before your question, add the phrases, "I'm wondering... (what specifically...)? Or you can say, "I'm curious. What prevents you from following through?" And, "Would you possibly be able to tell me how specifically...?" These can make sure you get the outcome of clarity while still staying in rapport with the person. Once again, the secret is to use sensory acuity to determine the student's reaction to your questions.

*It's not what happens*
*that counts... it's how I respond*
*to what happens that counts*

In this chapter we've explored classroom interactions such as the student question, the teacher question, sharing, discussion and personal meetings. The importance of clarity on your intended outcome is tantamount to success. With every interaction, reach for the goal of greater self-worth, greater resourcefulness and completion within the student. (Interactions are not the main course of the meal, but they are what holds it together). Good interactions make the class go better and ineffective ones can poison it. Using these tools to create better interactions, you may notice some surprising changes in your students, and all of them good!

---

## *Additional Resources for Further Study and Follow up*

*Envoy* by Michael Grinder (Grinder & Associates)
*Righting the Educational Conveyor Belt* by Michael Grinder (Metamorphous Press)*
*Effective Secondary Teaching* by Quina (Harper & Row)
*Metaphors for Metamorphous* by Rooney (L.E.A.D. Consultants)
*The Skillful Teacher* by Saphier & Gower (Research for Better Teaching)
*Making Contact* by Satir (Celestial Arts)

* These are available in the Appendix.

12

# Activities for All Ages

## We Know Better Now

Early classrooms were primarily intellectually oriented. The goal was to train the cognitive mind, and the lecture format was most common. In the early 1960's, the experiential format emerged and with it the whole genre of humanistic psychology was applied to the classroom. In the early 70's research substantiated and validated the importance of teaching with far greater variety of strategies such as the use of humor, music, play, games, puzzles, plays and cooperative learning. This wider "band" of teaching came to be known as "whole-brain" learning. Good teachers have known this all along and eschew lecture when at all possible. The result is a new wave of classroom activities which make learning fast, fun and effective.

Do you want validation for using games and activities? Read Harvard professor Howard Gardner's book *Frames of Mind: The Theory of Multiple Intelligences*. It has provided a framework for understanding not only how learners can be intelligent many ways, but how to nurture those seven areas. Gardner says your learners may learn best using bodily-kinesthetic, spatial, verbal-linguistic, intrapersonal, musical-rhythmic, interpersonal and mathematical-logical activities. A traditional classroom lecture provides only verbal-linguistic. This means many learners would be starved for learning in other areas.

In addition, recent discoveries in brain research have validated the use of many types of games which were previously dismissed as "play." These three primary discoveries involve the role of emotions, the library of mind-body states and the importance of low threat, high challenge exercise to the brain. Engaging the emotions helps activate the mid-brain area. That helps us understand it, believe it and remember our learning. Our body has a library of memories that are activated in each physiological state. Using role-plays and other learning games creates a "body-memory" that allows us to learn with our muscles as well as our mind. Physical activity promotes better oxygen flow throughout the body and brain which makes better thinking possible.

Activities require that the teacher create them properly, monitor them closely and complete them judiciously. When activities are well-run, there may be no "down time" at all. In general, activities require as much or more time than a presentation.

161

Activities can produce tremendous value if there's a real commitment from the teacher to be fully present and alert throughout the entire activity. An "absent" teacher is one who is not able to be gathering information and providing feedback or support - two key roles for teachers.

Are activities a low priority? What about the possibility of changing your priorities? It is possible that one or more of the following is occurring: too much or too detailed information is being given. The material could be worded more concisely. Your lecture material could also be covered by activities.

## Advantages of Experiential and Cooperative Learning

The group process may be the best means of promoting low-stress learning in or out of the classroom. As a child, your most fruitful learning came as a result of actually "doing", either alone or in a group process, and by being with your family. With all the age diversity, you still managed to relate to and learn from everyone. You may have learned much from a grandmother or uncle and naturally passed on to a sibling all that you learned. The lecture format precludes student cooperation and team play. As a result, many students have learned to keep to themselves. Years of structured class discipline have made the whole notion of cooperation foreign to them. Cooperative class activities can break up unproductive cliques and can create new learning opportunities. It offers other important things to students:

- *Strategy:* The style of working together as a team means that students are offered information in different formats than a lecture. It often makes the difference between a student being successful in your subject or doing poorly in it.
- *State:* The casual relaxed format means that the physiological and emotional state of the student is often more conducive to learning. For many students, it's simply more fun.
- *Closeness:* The sense of "family" where you are supported, listened to and trusted. It can create a sense of belonging and reduce the psychological and emotional distance between classmates.
- *Influence:* The opportunity for sharing, persuading and self-disclosure on a regular basis. In a class of thirty, many students are not comfortable with contributing to the class. But in a group of three or four, it's quite safe.
- *Creativity:* A classroom activity is an opportunity to bring out the best in your students; the most fresh, valuable and useful ideas. It's an opportunity to break through stereotypes and self-limiting ideas about what can and cannot be done. It also can encourage critical thinking and problem-solving.
- *Excitement and Curiosity about Learning:* Activities re-capture those qualities that creative children express so well; a heightened sensitivity, a value of discovery, spontaneous behavior, wonderment, and strong desire to understand and learn. The adult world is a dull gray compared to the child's world of 3-D technicolor with sounds, smells and touch.
- *Opens Up the Learning Process:* There's an unlimited variety of ways to describe learners. You may have heard learners described as analytical or relational, left or right-brained, visual, tactile, or auditory. Canadian educator Gregorac has identified four types: the concrete sequential, abstract sequential, the abstract random and concrete random. John Geier identifies the dominant, steadfast, compliant and the influencer. Which one is the correct way of labeling a learner? Is there a single, right and correct way? Highly unlikely. That's the beauty of a variety of classroom activities: they provide alternative ways for students to learn how they learn and succeed.

- *Whole-course Content:* Activities which are chosen, planned, run and completed well have the capacity to encapsulate large bodies of knowledge and experience. They can give students a holographic sense of the entire course, thereby accomplishing something a lecture could not.
- *Tests and Evaluations:* Well-run activities can serve as vehicles for the teacher to gather information about who needs help, who's on schedule, and what needs to be done next. Sometimes evaluative information will surface that would never have surfaced otherwise.
- *Lightness:* For many students and teachers, activities provide a break that doesn't occur in other classroom methods. Students, as well as the teacher, appreciate a break from the routine.
- *Self-worth and Validation:* A successful activity can provide students with numerous opportunities to succeed as well as simply feel good about themselves.
- *Integration:* It's an opportunity for the student to become competent with and familiar with the material in the physical sense while the unconscious mind is integrating the experiences into the whole life-learning of that student.

If you have problems with discipline during lectures, you may experience the same problems during activities-but then again, you may not. Often your students just need a change. The moving around, the talking, and freer schedule that goes with activities can give your students the classtime 'break' that leads to better concentration even during lecture. One of the most important things for your students to have is casual relaxed conversation about the subject matter. This casual interaction time is what shapes the perceptions, attitudes and memories of that subject in your student's mind. Activities can provide a unique open atmosphere of discussion and unstructured learning. In short, "down time" can become valuable time.

# Four Key Steps

There are four parts to successful classroom activities: (1) selection and planning, (2) set up and introduction, (3) operation and maintenance, and (4) debrief and closure. Each of the parts are important and require careful attentiveness to achieve your desired result.

# Selection and Planning

First thing to develop are criteria with which to evaluate activities. The key is to know the limitations and the possibilities of each so you can make an intelligent choice. Here are seven criteria for choosing activities.

1. **Intended Outcome.** What is the activity designed to do? What are the intended results? Are those the results you want?
2. **Numbers.** How many people is the activity designed for? Does it require groups or pairs? How will you divide students for maximum benefit?
3. **Interest.** Is the activity interesting? Is it new or thought-provoking? Is it relevant to the topic at hand? Can your students make the connection to the content in your course? How will you create curiosity and interest?
4. **Manageability.** Is it an activity that can be easily monitored? Can you set up others to act as monitors? Do you need training or a prior experience to run the activity successfully?
5. **Time and cost.** Can the activity be run successfully within the time frame you have available? Is there sufficient time for the introduction and

the closure? Can you afford the activity? Are you distinguishing between the actual cost of the activity and the real value to your students?

6. *Simplicity.* Is it an activity that can be easily understood by your students? Is the intellectual level of the game appropriate for your students?

7. *Completion.* Do you know how to complete the activity with the students? Do you have the tools and abilities to confidently lead the closure and completion process to insure that the students get maximum value?

Next, handle the complete logistical preparation. There are physical pieces which need to come into play for the activity to be successful. For example, will your activity create any noise? Do nearby rooms or groups need to be notified? Can your activity be interrupted? If not, make some 'Do Not Disturb' signs and post them nearby. Is the room set up properly for the activity? If not, either enlist some support from other students, a set-up crew, a janitor. Do you have out all the materials for the activity? Have you made a head count and matched numbers to be sure that you have enough? Do you have extras or spares of everything needed? Is it in stacks or groups for easy dispersal?

# Set-Up & Introduction

It's critical to allow students to reach into their own experiences and discover what your proposed activity could mean to them, based on their past. An easy way to do that is simply through asking questions. "How many of you remember learning how to ride a bicycle by reading a book?" "How many of you learn better by actually doing something?" "How many of you would rather go to the beach than read about it?" "Who gets more enjoyment out of actually doing something than thinking about it?" "How many of you would like a break from our usual lecture routine?" As you continue to elicit a show of hands, you'll be allowing the students to create the value in themselves in the activity you are about to initiate.

**Get the Students Physically Active!** The opening of the activity is also an excellent time to get the students up to stretch and move around a bit. The brain weighs about three percent of the total body weight, but it consumes 20% of its oxygen. In order for your students to perform at their best give them oxygen! Create times for a few deep breaths or some stretching to awaken the body's senses and send extra oxygen to the brain. The more of those the better-you could have a oxygen break every 15 minutes.

**Know the Outcome.** Next, students need to know what, specifically, is the objective of the activity. The objective is very different from the purpose. The purpose is usually some open-ended statement such as "To expand..." "To increase..." But the objective, also known as the intended result or the outcome is a clearly defined goal that can be measured and described in sensory terms. For example, "The objective is to circle the gameboard with your gamepiece as many times as you can during the 20 minute game time while following the rules exactly." Once you have told the students the intended outcome, post it. Put it up on flip chart paper or on the chalkboard so students can refer to it easily.

**Make the Directions Extra-Clear.** One of the easiest ways to ruin a potentially successful activity is with poor directions. Most directions are C.I.P.U. This means, "Clear only if previously understood." With directions, avoid nominalizations such as "be fair, be responsible, stay honest, etc." Those are not specific enough to elicit equal behavior from all students. Describe the directions in clear specific language by continually asking for questions. "In this game, fairness means that you'll...." Wait until you have given directions verbally, visually, and often, kinesthetically (have students actually try them out). Then write out the 3-5 basic steps and post them, pass them out or write them on the chalkboard. It's much more clear to use colors rather than numbers and terms such as "above" and "below" rather than "left" and "right."

**Also include clear time references.** If it's a timed activity, let the students know whether you are using your watch or the wall clock (advantages to each). Let them know what to do if they finish early or run out of anything-time, materials, people, etc. Explain to the students your policies on things such as noise (how much is OK?) and trash (what's messy and what's not?). Make sure students know what your role will be and if it will change throughout the activity. Also make sure they know what to do if they get lost, confused or need help.

# Group Selection

Use a sociogram to aid in the selection process. First, have each student fill out a 3 X 5 card with their name at the top, underlined. Then have them add the names of five others they feel they can work with effectively. Next, decide how many groups you'll need to have: 4-6 students per group for elementary, three students for 6-12th grade. For example if your high school class has 36 students, you'll need 12 groups, if your elementary class has 24 students, you could have 4- 6 groups.

Collect the cards and sort them using your best-behaved class leaders as the nucleus for each group. Then add one student to each group who needs support for more appropriate behavior. With your "best" and "worst" behaved students as a core, add additional students to each group keeping in mind both the male/female and the student's preferences for group members. This sorting process can be done in less than an hour and can easily be done by one of your more responsible students. Plan on changing groups throughout the school year.

How else can you select groups, pairs or teams for activities? The first thing to do is to ask yourself what is the outcome you want. Do you want each person to have a personal breakthrough or solo experience? Do you want to open up any particular student? Do you want to break up any unproductive cliques or support any unresourceful students? The next question is what processes will go on as a result of the activity? Are any likely to cause a problem for some of your students? If so, you may need to arrange them differently.

Can your students change groups, teams or partners during the activity? What will you do if you see a pair or team that is not working well together? What's your strategy? All of these questions need to be addressed in your mind before the activity even starts because something as simple as the pairings can make a difference between success and failure of the activity. Here are some possibilities for choosing groups:

1. Teacher subjectively selects. In this case, the teacher would say, "You go with him, you go with her, and you two go over here..."
2. Students subjectively select. Allow the students to get into groups on their own. Give them 60 seconds to break up into groups by finding their own team members or partners. If there are any who are left at the end who don't have partners, have them raise their hands, then let the extras pair up with each other.

3. Counting process. Have the students count off by ones, twos and threes (or whatever group size you want) then just say all the ones go over there, etc. This can, of course, be done with A-B-A-B.

4. Arbitrary differences. In this process, the teacher simply uses arbitrary criteria to determine groups. For example, "You and the person sitting next to you are partners, the one with the shortest hair is an 'A' and the one with the longer hair is a 'B.' Or, you could pick groups by birthdays, last names, street names, astrological signs, room location, clothing worn, etc.

5. Gaming process. This sets up a completely different context, depending on what you want. Bob McKim invented a game called 'barnyard' and it goes like this: have students count off A-B-C-D-E, in maybe five or ten groups, so that everyone has a letter. Then assign an animal to each letter such as all As are sheep, all Bs are pigs and all Cs are chickens, etc. Then make sure the students are all in the center of a large space, with the chairs cleared out. Then everyone closes their eyes and makes the sound of the animal that was assigned to them. Naturally, you'll have a room full of clucks, moos, baaahs, grunts, etc. The goal of the game is to find all the other members in your group by the sounds alone. Once they are all in clusters, the students can open their eyes and the game is over. It's a great way to break down some barriers, choose groups and have fun at the same time.

Anytime you create teams, you have a special dynamic going on. Here are some suggestions:

1. Allow time for team members to create rapport with each other through sharing personal information such as family background, key influences, behavior patterns or highs and lows.

2. Allow the group to create its own identity using a group name, a leader, a logo or a group cheer.

3. Make sure that each team as a whole and each individual team member has a vested interest in contributing. Create a win-win game with friendly competition or group cooperation games.

4. When the activity is over, make sure that each team is acknowledged- a different award to each team works well. Have the team members congratulate each other and give strokes to them yourself.

# Operation & Maintenance

During the activities, it's important to monitor your own profile as well as the students. First, be sensitive to "group energy." Is the activity as a whole slow and boring? Then either do one of two things: quickly change the rules to enliven it or cut it short and keep your losses to a minimum. If the activity appears to be too lively ask yourself if the aliveness is creating a problem. Lots of noise and movement and fun is not a problem unless it's creating damage or students are being disrespectful of persons or property. Again, if the aliveness of the activity is a problem, you have the same two choices as above: change the rules or stop the activity.

Next, be extra sensitive to any individual situation developing such as detachment, hostility, anger or depression. This means that you must have your sensory acuity turned up to insure you catch things early and deal with it on the spot.

Another thing to be sensitive about is the ongoing process of the activity itself. Listen, watch and feel using your best sensory acuity to make sure the activity is meeting your goals. Use this time as a time to make personal contact with students who may need an extra smile, an encouraging word, a pep talk, or just a touch on the shoulder. In addition, be conscious of the time elapsed and make sure you give time signals so students are aware of the time. Also be sure to have allowed time for the completion process at the end of the activity. In a 50-minute activity hour, you might spend 10 minutes to set it up, 25 minutes to run it and I 5 minutes for the closure.

# De-brief & Closure

The closure is a time to let students surface with their joys, frustrations, conclusions, insights and expressions. But before they do that, be sure to clear off the tables or put all the materials to the side so the focus of the next few moments can be on the speaker, not any physical objects.

Often neglected, the closure is the most important part of the activity process. It's not what happens in life that counts, it's what you conclude and do about what happened that counts. During this time you are to assist the student in coming up with conclusions which will allow him to have more choices in the future. Herein lies the real value of the classroom activities.

During the completion or processing of the activity, stay focused on your intended outcome. Your intention is to have the students become more resourceful than ever before and to have greater self esteem. Ideally, the results and conclusions drawn by the student reflect an increased sense of power, confidence and well-being. This is the time for students to report or share the results of the activity just completed. You may either call on them or ask if anyone has anything they'd like to share about the just-completed activity. The kinds of responses useful to have expressed are the following:

1. What actually happened during the activity? What events happened in your group or team?
2. What went on for you, specifically? (describe your feelings, thoughts, judgments)
3. What did you learn, see, hear, do; about yourself, and the entire activity?
4. What conclusions can you draw about yourself and similar activities?
5. What other conclusions can you draw, true or not, that would add to your resourcefulness for the future?
6. What is it that you'd now do differently, given the same situation again?
7. How does this relate to your life?

After any of those questions, the reaction the student gives will be the most important part. Your goal in the closure process is to find a way to make sure that your students are able to leave the class with greater resources than they came in with. You'll need to listen carefully, giving full attention to each person who shares an experience of the activity. Make sure that your body is turned toward the speaker, with all your antenna out for maximum sensory acuity. Be sure to respond with an appreciative comment such, as one of these:

"Thanks very much for sharing a part of yourself."
"You've been great, thanks a lot."
"I appreciate what you said and want to acknowledge you for sharing."
"I respect what you've said, thank you."
"Thank you for sharing yourself."

167

Notice that each of the responses are designed to acknowledge the student for simply contributing. At times, your response may say nothing about what was said. Simply acknowledge the student for sharing and participating. In addition, be sure to follow through each of the comments shared so that the student feels validated and more resourceful. It's also important to give students a holistic and global sense of what: the activity was for and what it accomplished. When that occurs, your classroom activity will have accomplished all that you hoped it would.

# Types of Activities:
# Grouped by Multiple Intelligences

**Note:** Every activity will use more than one of these multiple intelligences. They are grouped in these categories to be a reminder that the greater diversity of the intelligences you use, the wider range of your audience you'll reach. Your learners will be happier, learn more and express more of what they know.

**Verbal-Linguistic Activities:** Use of presentations, speeches, role-play, dialog, interactive games, writing, group work, doing reports, discussion, listening to tapes and reading - especially books with dialogue. Includes the Hollywood-quiz show, Secret word, The Word in Between, The Word on Your Back, Whisper game, Question & Answer, Missing Vowels, Sale of the Century, Whiz-Kid games and others designed to make learning fun and competitive.

They include interviews of famous stars, simulated TV shows, skits, telephone games, or people's court. Includes classroom, discussions, guest speakers. In classroom discussions, conflict and controversy were found to be significant learning promoters when applied in a cooperative environment. Students learned more and remembered more with healthy conflict, concluded David Johnson, a University of Minnesota researcher.

**Intrapersonal Activities:** Independent activities. These are the solo ones; designed to encourage independence and stronger thinking skills. They include thinking, communication processes, creativity games, language games, self-processing, discovery processes, reading, creating tests, problem-solving, personal assessments and mind-mapping. Use of solo thinking strategies, imagery, journal writing, relaxation, learning about one's self, focusing and concentration exercises, self-assessment, metacognition practice, reflection and time to be alone and process.

**Musical-Rhythmic Activities:** Use rhythm games, hand and knee clap, foot stomp, give them a musical instrument or let them make one, making fun sounds, learning with music, use a Kazoo, use background or environmental music, write music, singing, piano, musical performances, take a common song (Happy Birthday, A-B-C, Farmer in the Dell, Row, Row Your Boat, Rock-Around the Clock, etc.) and re-write lyrics, using key words from the content you're working within the lesson.

**Logical-Mathematical Activities:** Use of computer time, writing applications, programs, objects to sort, classifying, gadgets to take apart or fix, magnets, math, science, reading, discussion, exploring, solving mysteries, word problems, breaking codes, dominos, bingo, museum trips, riddles, analyzing information, outlining, grouping and calculation activities.

Learning teams are groups which have a specific project such as to solve a riddle or class problem. Memory games have students use memory devices to memorize class material in a fun way; often under time pressure, in a games-like way. Debates can work when prepared well on topics students choose. Drills can be direct-recall unison drills for review, vocabulary, facts, lists, etc.

**Spatial Activities:** Mind-mapping can be done in groups: get a poster-sized sheet of paper, give it to groups of 2-4, then let them mind-map a previous class, guest speaker or text material as a review or new learning. Then either hang up the mindmap or have the group share it. Here the teacher, a guest or a tape uses a closed-eye process to create specific results. It includes visual imagery, early memory restimulation, trance induction and psycho-kinesthetics.

Use of art, building, design, changing locations, stacking objects, putting pieces together, sports, large pieces of paper, trying things from a different angle, movement, likes mind-mapping, basketball, video, ice-skating, films, skateboarding, map making, charts, snowboarding, theater, wind-surfing, sculpture, surfing, rollerblading, drawing & painting.

**Interpersonal Activities:** Use of friendships, competition, interactive games, teams, pair up with partner, one-on-one discussion, peer teaching, group work, collaboration & empathy. Synergy games (team problem solving) are valuable for creating cooperation and team play. Also includes cooperative learning, simulations, learning teams, memory games, debates, synergy games, drills and mind-mapping.

**Bodily-Kinesthetic Activities:** This is the area of self-expression a la "Sesame Street." It includes plays, acts, mime key points, pantomime stories, puppet shows, magic acts, dances, talent show, skits, songs, poems and role-playing. It also includes ball-toss, New Games, hand-clapping, mime and learning games. Use of stretching, role play, classroom demonstrations everyone can do, hands-on practice, field trips, multi-media computers, classroom experiments, mechanical instruction and building models, Simon Sez games, demonstrations, changing seating, drama, exercise, body sculpture, crafts & hobbies, dancing, games & sporting events.

The seven most critical qualities for games are: 1) have a compelling purpose, but make your games fun 2) make learning the by-product, not the focus 3) provide learners with choice & control in playing the game 4) keep novelty and challenge in the games and 5) keep them simple 6) make them a win-win, so no one loses and 7) rehearse it thoroughly before doing it.

This chapter features structured activities for all ages and all types of intelligences. You may want to get even more ideas on this important topic. If so, refer to the chapter on energizers and sponges.

---

## Additional Resources for Further Study and Follow up

*Energize!* Carol Apacki (Quest Books)
*Beginnings & Endings* by Baca & Cobb (HRD Press)
*Rhythms of Learning* by Brewer & Campbell (Zephyr)*
*Brain Gym* by Dennison (Edu-Kinesthetics)*
*Energizers* by Jones & Bearley
*Turning Learning Inside Out* by Leff & Nevin (Zephyr)
*Playful Perception* by Leff (Waterfront Books)
*More New Games* by New Games Foundation
*The New Games Book* by New Games Foundation
*Silver Bullet* by Karl Rohnke

\* These are available in the Appendix.

MANY
WAYS
TO
LEARN!

# 13

## Learning Strategies

### Keep Track of Yourself

One of the most valuable habits you can have as a presenter is this: Keep a blank legal pad or 3-ring binder up front, so you can write down what works, or great ideas or lessons you learned, in the moment. Keep the notebook there every single class. After over two decades in teaching, I still take notes while I teach. I learn from myself, from my students and I generate ideas for future presentations. Never trust that you'll remember the idea later. The memory is rarely as faithful as the enthusiasm of the moment. A great way to use more of these proven learning strategies is to put them on an index card, one per card. Each week, pull out a card and use that strategy. Over a period of a year, you'll be using many highly effective tools to boost learning and recall.

When you are introducing a new idea or process, keep your stress low. Instead of following your front-of-class written notes and keeping your eyes on the content, write out all the key ideas on a piece of poster paper. Post the "cheat sheet" or flip chart against the back wall. You can teach, with hands free, and eyes out towards the group. The students will have an extra peripheral to learn, so they can master the content. Most importantly, you'll have a way to present with confidence and keep your eyes and attention on your students.

### Introduce Pre-Exposure

Does prior exposure to information speed up the learning? Researchers say "yes." The brain may have a way of putting information and ideas into a "buffer zone" or "cognitive waiting room" for rapid access. If the information is not utilized over time, it simply lays unconnected and random. But if the other parts of the puzzle are offered, the understanding and extraction of meaning is rapid. Learning and recall increased when a pattern was provided prior to exposure to the learning material. He also found that providing "post-organizing clues" was useful. The clues related to past learning and provided a framework for recall. Make sure that you pre-expose your learners to the material starting months to weeks in advance. Examples include:

1. Course description mailed out prior to attending
2. Talking to other past participants
3. Reading one of my books
4. Watching a video on the course
5. The colorful peripherals in the courseroom

6. The transparencies that re previewed in the first few minutes
7. The workbook given that they browse through
8. My own specific "previews of coming attractions"

Would it help if you put up poster-sized graphic organizers, mind maps or webbing? Yes. It worked in 135 studies of the effects on learning of advance stimulation and organizers where some form of "advanced organizers" were consistently positive. Mapping our ideas gives learners a way to conceptualize ideas, shape thinking and understand better what they know. But most importantly, it solidifies the learning to them as "mine."

*When it comes to learning, limit the surprises...*
*constant and varied pre-exposure will encourage quicker*
*and deeper learning far better than any surprise value*

Use pre-exposure with positive visual suggestion by color-coding key items. Five hundred subjects showed much greater recall than subjects who did not get the color-coded material. By preparing the mind, it learned on its own clock, in its own way. It's the essence of "ownership."

Many students who seem like slow learners may simply need pre-exposure to lay the foundation for better comprehension and recall. Pre-expose learners to your topic before officially starting it. Visually, you can prepare them with a note before the course begins, then posted mind-maps two weeks before beginning the topic or with preview texts and handouts. You can also get them ready with oral previews, examples and metaphors. Kinesthetically, you can offer role plays with similar experiences, simulations or games.

# Use Visualization

Visualization can be an excellent tool for learning. Everyone visualizes, even those who are dominantly auditory, kinesthetic or have lost their sight. If a learners say, "I can't get a picture in my mind," help them learn how they do it. Ask them to use a book as the layout for their own house or bedroom. Ask them to decide where the front door would be to get oriented. Then, ask them to point to where the window is, where they keep their clothes or where there is a book in the room. These simple acts, of pointing to the layout, remind them that they do have stored pictures in their brain, that they draw upon, as a blueprint for the answers you've asked for. In fact, they *have to* visualize to get the information! Here are seven keys to visualizations and guided relaxations.

**1. Read your audience**
Most of the time you'll need to prepare them for it. Remember gradient, gradient, gradient. Get them into the state first, then start slowly.

**2. Be well prepared**
Have a pretty good idea what you want to say, your key words and get the music ready well ahead of time.

**3. Know your outcome**
Have a clear idea of what you want to use the exercise for. Uses can be to access certain states, pre-exposure, metaphors for resourcefulness, to connect with a particular person, idea or emotion, etc.

### 4. Keep it low-threat, low pressure

You may start by pacing the breathing, adjusting the physiology, changing your tonality, using music and building "Yes" sets. Then, you may simply ask or invite them to close their eyes to relax even more.

### 5. Use multi-sensory terms

A wide range of words like, "listen, sounds, hear" or the visual ones of "see, appear, pictures" or the kinesthetic ones like "feel, get a grasp of, or handle this." Match your tonality to the rate of those three...visual is fastest, then auditory and kinesthetic is slowest. Remember 20% cannot visualize at all, so provide several ways to participate in the exercise.

### 6. Keep reading the responses

Keep reading what you are getting. Watch for sighs, tapping, weight shifts, fidgeting and opened eyes. If you're off course, give them some "if, then..." commands to re-gain rapport. "If you're feeling ready to move on, then take in a deep breath and relax your arms and hands even more."

### 7. Take your audience out of it gently

Give them a gentle warning 3 seconds before you're done. Invite them to come back to the room slowly, when they're ready. Ask them to move their eyes to each of the four corners of the room to get re-oriented. You might even want them to discuss what they saw, heard & felt with a partner.

# Use Analogy

Analogy is one of the most useful of all communication tools. It can be the perfect vehicle by which your students understand in 10 seconds something which might ordinarily take 60 seconds or even 60 minutes. Good analogies say a lot without having to say a lot: "Like trying to sneak a sunrise past a rooster", or "Like taking candy from a baby." It causes a feeling of "Ahh-Ha!" not "Huh?"

Einstein had a great analogy: "When you sit with a nice girl for two hours, it seems like two minutes; if you sat on a hot stove for two seconds, it'd seem like two hours."

# Discover Learner's Prior Knowledge

When prior learning is activated, the brain makes many more connections. Learning, comprehension and meaning increase. The research reveals that the importance of discovering and relating to previously learned material is much greater than earlier thought.

Many learners who should do well in a subject actually underperform because the new material seems irrelevant. Unless connections are made to their prior learning, comprehension and meaning may be dramatically lessened. Before starting a new topic, ask the students to either discuss, do role plays or skits, or make mind maps of what they already know.

# Goal-Setting

There are many types of goals that you may have for your students. Some are directed by an external agency (state standards for outcome-based learning, as an example). Others may be your own goals ("I want them to develop a real love of learning"). But student-generated goals are certainly the most critical. Even better are student-generated goals which are continually increased as the challenge of the work increases.

Make sure the target has to be at an optimal level of difficulty - "challenging, but attainable." Then the goal-pursuing process will only be effective if the learners have: 1) ample feedback to make corrections; 2) capability beliefs to sustain pursuit in the face of negative feedback; 3) the actual skills needed to complete the task; 4) an environment conducive to success.

Avoid giving goals too much attention, or they may become counter-productive. Learners report that they feel self-conscious, make simple mistakes, and sometimes experience test anxiety and "choke" on material, forgetting things they should have known.

**Goals are best when they are:**
*1) created by the learner*
*2) concrete & specific*
*3) due on a specific date*
*4) self-assessed often*
*5) re-adjusted periodically*

Let students generate their own goals. Have them discover whether their own beliefs can support them. Ask them about the learning environment. Is it supportive to achieving the goals? Do they have the resources to reach their goals? Most learners who want to succeed are capable of succeeding, though they often lack the beliefs to do so. Ask learners to set their own goals for today's class. Make sure the goals are positive, specific and obtainable by the end of class. For example, a goal could be as simple as wanting to learn two new interesting things. You then need to provide the resources and learning climate to help your learners reach their goals. Then hold them accountable. Check back later to assess results and celebrate, if appropriate.

## Mental Practice Boosts Learning

Research found that thinking before a learning activity improved learning. Elementary school children were asked to practice visualization, imagery and make believe. Then their performance was measured. The group that did the visualization first, then learned, scored higher than the other group who didn't.

Before you went to your last job interview, chances are you rehearsed the interview in your mind many times over. This kind of practicing accesses the information, rehearses it and, in a sense, "pre-exposes" your mind to it.

In some cases, your learners may not be unmotivated, they may just need mental warm-ups. A few minutes invested early in the class could produce a big payoff later. Create a daily routine for your students. Before you start, have them do both physical stretching and mental warm-ups, such as mentally rehearsing a role-play, asking questions, visualizing, solving problems or brainstorming.

## Chunk Up or Chunk Down

A "chunk" is a computer term which means bundles of information. To "chunk up" is to find the next larger bundle of a similar kind. To "chunk down," you break the same bundle into smaller units. This process enables you to communicate better with your students by putting your information into the language they can understand better. This can open up learning channels because sometimes information is too generalized or too specific to work with. Here's an example: a student says "I don't understand math." In this case, chunk down - say, "I'm pretty sure you understand addition, so what specific part of math do you not understand?"

Here's another example: a student says, "I've got to do all this work on a term paper for just 20 lousy points? It's not worth it." In this case, you could chunk up from the level of the assignment to the benefits in life it could bring. Say, "You're right, that is a lot of work for 20 points. Yet, doing it can bring you pride in yourself and better grades. Then, when you get accepted at a good university for your extra effort, you'll be glad you did it." In your classes, any time a student does not understand something, chunk it - either up or down until the desired outcome results.

## Relaxation Boosts Learning

Many studies have shown that stress can lower your learner's intelligence. In one study, increased stress lowered IQ scores by fourteen points! Chronic stress robs ones' ability to think. You may have seen this over and over. The more the stress, the more students tighten up and underperform. In other words, a relaxed nervous system is best for learning.

Take the time, before beginning each and every class, to relax your students. Here are some of the best ways to relax them: 1) slow stretching 2) laughter and humor 3) music 4) games and activities 5) unstructured discussion and sharing 6) low-stress rituals 7) visualization.

## Isolate Key Points

In your teaching, figure out what are the two or three key points for the lesson, the unit or month. Keep referring to those, post them, weave them into your discussion every chance you get. Those keys will become like the center of a spider web to attract other information and create meaning.

## Board Skills

For many good reasons, traditional chalkboards are fast disappearing around the world. Surprisingly, it's one of the most difficult tools to use well. On one hand, it can enliven an otherwise difficult-to-understand lecture, and on the other hand, it can put students to sleep. When using a chalkboard, make sure you have an excellent eraser - one that's quiet, large, and effective. Make sure that you have colored chalk. At the minimum have white and yellow. If possible, get some of the other bright colors such as orange, pink, or bright blue or green. Make sure that all of your students can see well from every corner of the room.

Make sure that you stay out of the way when you write on it. Use big letters, and print. Put less on, but put more important information on it. Ensure that your words are legible, and face the group when you talk. Tell your students first what you are going to put on the board, then write as simply and succinctly as possible. Finally, be sure to show relationships between items if there are any (use arrows and circles). Leave lots of blank space around each item you put up.

Use symbols, arrows, faces and cartoons...they increase understanding and recall. Before you erase, ask if anyone needs more time to jot down what's been done. Use it only to clarify, or reinforce; at its best, it can simplify the difficult. Put your material on it when students are engaged in something else so that they don't have to wait for you. Keep the board clean and well-erased when not in use.

## Modeling the Learning

If you are stating that a topic is interesting, be interested in it. Bring things from home, talk about with gusto and animation. Your learners will learn more about the topic by how you do it than what you say about it. If you're talking about the use of non-verbals, prepare your own so that you are showing what you're telling. If you're talking about the importance of spelling and vocabulary, share with your students a new word YOU learned today. If you're talking about how important history is, share what you've read, heard or a historical place you've visited lately.

## The Flip Chart/Overhead Alternative

A flip chart consists of a white drawing pad or newsprint attached to an easel-like stand. The flip chart's advantages are that you can use more colors, brighter ones, and that the message can be stored easily. It's often very useful to put major points (each one in different colors) on the paper, tear it off, then post it up on the walls for easy review and reference. They can serve as unconscious reminders for your students and also serve as a conscious reinforcement of the quality and quantity of material which has been covered. Again, as with chalkboards, print legibly, use colors, and keep it simple.

For more reasons than just ecological ones, transparencies are making a comeback. Using erasables, they can be re-used much better than paper from a flip chart. They are not lasting, since once they're out of sight, they're out of mind. The good things is that their size allows you to make a big impact with them. Make sure you are using color on them always. Either use a color printer for the transparencies or color them by hand. Use permanent markers for the best color, since the water-based ones hold color poorly and smear.

## Use Colors Well

There's a great deal of research out now on the effects of color on our attitudes and non-conscious reactions. When making murals, posters, signs or writing simple messages on the flip chart, be aware of the impact of how you use colors. Here are the results of the research and some suggestions with how to use each color:

*Red* - urgent, present time oriented, feelings, heart, important
        (limited usage keeps impact high)
*Blue* - strong, past-oriented, tradition, factual, cold, impersonal
        (use when presenting controversial information)
*Green* - soothing, future-oriented, relaxing, growth, positive
        (has widespread uses)
*Orange* - active, playful, communications, assertive
        (could be used much more often)
*Black* - dominant, dying, serious, intrusive, cold
        (limit usage as much as possible)

# Presentation Cards

Many successful teachers are using presentation cards, or p-cards as they are known. These are cardboard-backed visuals on 8 1/2" X 11" paper which illustrate key lecture points. A teacher might have a whole stack of them with a kind of associated questions on the back. That way, you can hold up these 'cue-cards' and ask the students what they represent. It's a good, quick and fun way to make visual associations with the information about the topic. For example, you could hold up a math problem, and ask what theorem it represents (question and answer on the back). You could hold up the cover of a book and ask what else that author wrote. You could hold up a symbol from your lecture and ask what concept it represents. All of these are ways to increase audience participation, while at the same time, increasing the actual learning going on.

# Discussion Cards

A favorite tool of many are discussion cards. Put your students in groups or teams. Write up key phrases, then put a question at the bottom of the card (which might be a paragraph done on the top half of a standard sized paper). Give a group ten minutes (or whatever's needed) to read and discuss the cards. Then the team leader reports on the nature of the discussions to the whole group.

# Peripherals: Posters, Signs and Banners

Your students are going to spend many hours in your classroom. It's unrealistic to think that their eyes will be on you every single moment. Since their eyes will wander around the room, take advantage of that. Make every part of the room a learning experience for them and a reminder of the principles you are teaching. Use large signs made on poster board which have simple and powerful messages on them. If the eyes of a student look above me, they may find a message such as "If you can dream it, you can become it", "Learning is fun, Easy and Creative", or "Miracles as Usual." Add "I learn quickly, easily and playfully", or "You Can do Magic." It doesn't matter whether you actually refer to the signs or not. The ideas will affect your students positively - especially over time.

# Multi-Modal, Multi-Media Sources

When is the best time to use a CD-ROM, a slideshow, a video, a film or computer? Only you can know. Each one of them has the potential, when used with the appropriate audience at the right time, to create a powerful learning experience not available through ordinary lecturing. There's no need to balance your teachings so that you have a certain number of hours which are for lecture, and a certain number that are for multi-media presentations. Your question should be "What's most powerful?" Or, "What's the ideal for this time?" Then do whatever works! One of my favorites is to double input to students by lecturing to them on topic at the same time as showing a film or video. This way, the students not only have a choice, but usually end up by understanding both of them. It simply turns into a game and their concentration is better than ever!

## Use Guest Speakers

One of the best and the worst experiences for students is to have a guest speaker take over the class. When it is the worst experience for the students, it is usually because the classroom teacher: (1) did not actually observe and pre-select the guest in a teaching situation first (2) did not prepare the guest properly for the audience (3) did not prepare the audience properly for the guest (4) the subject matter was inappropriate (5) does not have sufficient criteria by which to pick guest. It is very important to make sure that the guest can add something that you cannot add to the audience. Students become familiar with and attached to a teacher quickly and can resent outsiders.

When it works well, it can be magic. Some of the important steps are: (1) go over with the guest what he or she wants to say (2) go over with the guest what you'd like them to say and get an agreement on what will be said (3) tell them about the audience and their needs (4) prepare the audience be giving the guest a gracious introduction (5) tell the audience how to respond to the guest, both during and at the end of the presentation. Do they ask questions, applaud, or stand up? Make sure that you have anticipated many possible scenarios and planned your responses. Good preparation can make things run smoothly and insure that it provides the value you wanted.

# Better Notetaking

To encourage more and better note-taking, teach your students mind-mapping or other forms of creative note-taking. Make available a box of colored pens for your students. Buy the ones with a nylon or felt tip that are thinner than a magic marker, but fatter than a pencil. The first thing that happens is that the students open up to a more playful learning mood. There's some kind of magic in colored pens that lightens up a group of students and gets them to take creative, expressive and functional notes. Then constantly remind them to write it down. It helps them understand and recall better.

There is strong evidence to suggest that colored pens make information easier to recall than what's recorded by a standard thin-line ball-point pen or pencil. Tested and proven with thousands of students over many years, they do work. The ways that they can be used in class as a form of participation are simple. After each point that you make, ask the students for a quick and simple symbol that they can use to represent it on their own mind-maps. This unleashes creativity and builds recall and understanding.

# Add Music

Yes, music does belong in today's learning environments. Not just if you're a music teacher, but if you teach anything! Music is an exciting and useful addition to the classroom. It takes time, creativity, flexibility and patience to bring out the full potential of it. Start small, then work your way up. With practice, you'll be using it just as easily as your own voice! There's a whole chapter on the use of music. When you're ready for it, dig in!

# Why Engage Emotions?

Why engage emotions in learning? There are many good reasons. It's useful to know them in case you are asked or you need to explain why you do what you do in your classes or workshops.

1. **It builds long-term memory.** The more intensely that you engage the emotions, the longer you'll recall what you have learned. In fact, what you remember most from your childhood is your lowest lows and your highest highs.
2. **Functionality.** It meets the needs, partially, of those learners who are kinesthetic, internal feeling-type learners. This is a great way to reach those learners who are most in touch with how they feel.
3. **Love.** It helps instill a love of learning. The only way that your participants will develop a real deep love and passion for a topic is to access emotions with in the process of learning about it. That's how the brain creates that love of learning.
4. **Fun!** It's much, much more fun to learn when emotions are being engaged. It gets the blood flowing, action up and makes it memorable. Is that enough of a good reason to do it?

*Engage emotions on a consistent, positive level*
*and you'll have smarter & happier learners*

5. **New Research.** Top neuroscientist Damasio says that emotions are a key part of the logic and reasoning process. The brain makes better quality decisions when it engages some emotion, he says. The design of the brain is such that it is biologically prefers integrating emotions into thinking. He cautions that too

much emotions can impair clear thinking. But he also makes a case for the validity of emotions, too.

## How To Engage Emotions

**1. Role Model.** Teacher or presenter simply role models the love of learning and enthusiasm about their job.
*Example: Bring something with great excitement to class. Build suspense, smile, show off a new CD, book, clothing item, animal, etc.*

**2. Through the use of celebrations...** also acknowledgments, parties, hi-fives, food, music played and fun! The celebration can show off student work.
*Example: When students are done mindmapping something, I'll often have the get up and show off their poster-sized mindmap to 8 other pairs. The goal is to find at least 2 things you like about it. They carry around their mindmap, point out things, and get things pointed out. The celebration music is on and everyone has a good time.*

**3. Using theater, role play and drama.** The bigger the production, the higher the stakes, the more the emotions engaged.
*Example: Your group volunteers to put on a school-wide play. You have: rehearsals, stress, fun, anxiety, anticipation, suspense, excitement and relief.*

**4. By setting up controversy...** could be a debate, dialog, argument, convincing time, real or artificial. Any time you've got two sides, a vested interest and the means to express opinions, you'll get action!
*Example: Play tug of war...everyone gets a partner and picks a topic from the list that all have been learning each person has their own topic and their goals to convince their partner in an argument why their topic is more important... after the verbal it has to be settled physically with a giant tug of war, all partners are on opposite sides...*

**5. Through the purposeful use of rituals.** You may use from 2-25 rituals in your class that can instantly engage learners. These rituals could include how to arrive, how to leave, how to celebrate, and how to get started on a project.
*Examples: You start class with an activity where everyone pairs up answers three questions...they go for a short walk while answering them... the questions are: 1) what am I most grateful in my life right now, 2) what am I most passionate about and 3) what could I genuinely get excited about it if reached my goals I set for myself today?*

**6. Teams interplay.** It can create plenty of engagement and emotion by how they work, react and connect as a team.
*Example: Each time teams complete their tasks, they could give a team cheer. Or they all have a special cheer for each member upon arrival.*

**7. The arts.** Through the use of music, games, activities and energizers that get everyone going. See the chapter on energizers for dozens of ideas.
*Example: Class or teams put on a play, teams create fun rituals to celebrate like a cheer, a dance or a shout.*

## The Self-Convincer State

All learning is state dependent. If you're in a state called "leave me alone," you'll learn very little. If you're in a state called "curiosity," you'll learn much more. The better you are at reading and managing states, the better you'll be at eliciting the best states for learning. The ideal starter state for learning is called motivation. You can bring that out in your students through arousing curiosity, challenging activities, creating anticipation or even confusion. Once the learner is ready, you'll want the state of acquisition. That's the moment where the learner is inputting the data and linking it up with relevant associations to create meaning out of it.

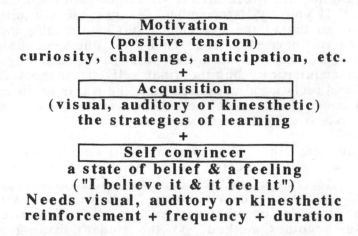

```
┌─────────────────────────────────────┐
│            Motivation                │
└─────────────────────────────────────┘
           (positive tension)
  curiosity, challenge, anticipation, etc.
                    +
┌─────────────────────────────────────┐
│            Acquisition               │
└─────────────────────────────────────┘
      (visual, auditory or kinesthetic)
         the strategies of learning
                    +
┌─────────────────────────────────────┐
│           Self convincer             │
└─────────────────────────────────────┘
      a state of belief & a feeling
      ("I believe it & it feel it")
   Needs visual, auditory or kinesthetic
   reinforcement + frequency + duration
```

The next step is the most critical. This is the self-convincer state. He must now FEEL THE FEELINGS of pride and accomplishment after the reinforcement. This final state is critical. It's called "Now I know that I know and I feel good about it." That's the key piece that creates the motivation to loop back up to the original motivating state of wanting to learn.

This state is triggered by three variables: modality, frequency and duration. Modality means either visual, auditory or kinesthetic. Frequency means the number of times that it is experienced after the initial learning. Duration means the length of time of reinforcement. Here's an example: A student comes up to you and says, "How do you think I did on my research project?" You say, "I'm real happy with it. It's your best effort yet." The students thanks you and walks away. Ten minutes later the same student comes up again. He asks a similar question about the project. This time you give new feedback. At one point, his eyes light up, and he is visibly pleased. He got what he really wanted: that self-convincer state. That's the state called, "I know I know it and I feel it."

Remember the movie "Home Alone?" In the movie, the 10-year old boy Kevin (played by Macauly Caulken) is left alone home while burglars try to break in. He frustrates and foils their break-in attempts. His celebration state, his self-convincer is demonstrated by the physical motion of clenching his fist and drawing it towards himself while saying, "Yes!" That his way of saying, "I did it and it feels good!"

Most teachers or trainers remember to reinforce a student who has just learned something. There's nothing wrong with that, it's just incomplete. The incompleteness is that unless the experience is coded INSIDE (with a feeling), it's always dependent on an external reinforcement, which is rarely available.

In other words, how will the student know he knows it unless he tags each learning experience with an internal feeling, a self-convincer that he can bring with him everywhere he goes? Have you ever been on a word processor or typewriter or writing a letter and spelled a word, then realized it was wrong, but you weren't sure

181

how to spell it correctly? That's because you have no internal tag for the correct spelling. You have to go to the dictionary. You needed the self-convincer state.

## How We Get Self-Convinced

It's the same thing if you leave the house, then halfway down the road you think to yourself, "Oh no, did I turn off the stereo, or turn on my answering machine or leave the iron on?" If you don't remember, it's because you either didn't do it or you did but attached no tag to the experience, no emotional good feeling that you could re-access when you needed it later. That's the one key, the one tip that keeps kids into learning. Yes, the million-dollar part of the learning cycle is not the motivation, not the acquisition, but the final self-convincer state. When the kid knows he knows it and feels good about learning, he wants to do more. This is not a reinforcement, that comes from you. The self-convincer comes from inside the kid. You can certainly evoke it with the right activities.

How do you get the all-important self-convincer? One, from your reinforcement. If you give sincere reinforcement, in the student's preferred modality, he'll often feel good and self-convince. That means you ought to learn what ways, visual, auditory or kinesthetic that each of your students like reinforcement. If he doesn't for whatever reasons, (low self-esteem, inappropriate modality, etc.,) use the other method: ask the student leading questions such as "How to you feel about doing so well? Or, "How would you feel if you did as well a you wanted to do?" "How did you feel the last time you did well?"

Can you hear that all of these are feeling questions that elicit emotions, not a yes or no answer? What you are after are signs that he has internalized the reinforcement you gave him... hence became self-convinced. The signals are usually a nodding head, a smile, a deep breath, eyes which go down indicating a feeling state, a weight change, change in posture, skin color change or any combination of those items. The key signal that a student has accessed feeling is *eyes going down* for a second.

You can tell that what you are trying to get at is to have the student attach a feeling to the acquisition so he has an internal way of knowing he's learned it. There's something else going on. Every positive experience that you can have students attach to the classroom will create the associations you want for the love of learning.

## What To Do About It

Remember the key to self-convincer states are simple: offer a variety of modalities, do it more than once and do it for more than just a few seconds. Have students celebrate with neighbors or partners every time they do well. Set up more opportunities for acknowledgment and celebration. End your session on a high... use a special class gesture, a sound or a high-five. Make sure students have emotion in it so it'll give the desired effect you want. Even if they have to fake it at the beginning, their brain will get used to it and soon crave it like a drug. Acknowledgment and approval can be just as addicting, but in a positive way!

That completes the cycle: motivation, acquisition and the all-important self-convincer state. So what causes students to get hooked into a better or worse loop of poor achievement? It's simple. Remember, I said that all learning is a matter of states. The states that a student OUGHT TO go through are motivation, acquisition and self-convincer. But it doesn't always work out that way. What happens is that many students get motivated, but don't acquire the material because it's not presented in their preferred learning style, so they'll most likely go into one of two other states. It will be either a positive state, such as curiosity ("How could I get this?), challenge ("This isn't going to get ME down!"), anticipation ("I can't wait 'til I get this.") or confusion ("This puzzles me, I've got to find a solution.")

Or, the student could go into a negative state such as frustration ("I hate it when this happens!"), irritation ("This teacher is getting on my nerves.") or anger ("Somebody's gonna get it!"). These states direct the student OUT of the learning process instead of creating more motivation to get it correct. So the brain makes a critical state change when acquisition fails to occur. And the state change makes all the difference whether we eventually label the kid as a genius or not. Geniuses are simply learners who get motivated, challenged and curious from failures. So he or she gives up, while the genius keeps trying to figure it out. Remember it was Edison, the man who holds more U.S. patents for significant original inventions than any other human being who said that genius is 99% perspiration and 1% inspiration. Now that saying makes sense, doesn't it?

So, let's put all this in practical terms. What you'll want to do to create motivated students who have a love of learning is the following three things:

1) **Start a policy** that every time a student doesn't learn something the first time, he changes his state into a resourceful one. Make it a fun class thing, so it can be popular.
2) **Set an example,** by you trying to do something in front of the class, failing, then going into a resourceful state, then solving it. You say that's not your style? Guess where kids get their behaviors? 99% of it is from modeling adults - non-conscious learning. You need to model how to handle failures gracefully and with fun an excitement. You need to plan them, set them up and repeat different variations of them so your students can learn.
3) **Interruption.** Make sure that you do a "state interrupt" anytime any of those negative states start happening. Do it by a physiology change. Tell students to stand up, stretch, circle the room, play a game, listen to music anything!). It's fun and easy. Remember, you can motivate your students and you can give them a lifelong love of learning if you pay attention to states and manage them carefully to get the effect you want.

In this chapter we've revealed dozens of effective learning strategies. The key to making them a part of what you do is simple. Add one per day or just one per week. Takes notes on how and when you used it. Write down how you would change it for next time.

---

| Additional Resources for Further Study & Follow up |

*Energize!* by Apacki
*Decartes' Error* by Damasio
*Brain-Based Learning & Teaching* by Jensen (Turning Point) *
*The Skillful Teacher* by Saphier & Gower

* These are available in the Appendix.

# *14*

## Rituals and Affirmations

### Rituals Enrich Our Lives

Everyone has rituals. The point of this chapter is that your rituals can inspire, inform and energize and instead of create boredom. First, let's define a ritual. A ritual is an activity which is consistently triggered by an event. In other words, when A occurs, B always occurs.

As an example, if you do a roll call for attendance every time you start up class, that's a ritual. If you do several things in a row, every time, that's a routine. A routine is a group of rituals clustered together. Most of us have a morning routine for getting ready to go to work.

If you chew gum often, but not at any particular time of the day or day of the week, that's not a ritual. A ritual is predictable. That's what makes them so valuable. In today's world, with so much change and a new global map coming out every 12 months, it's very reassuring and comfortable for learners to know that some rituals will happen every day. It can lower stress. Following are classroom and workshop rituals that may be useful. Believe me, there are many, many more. These are the tried-and true ones.

### Seasonal rituals

These could be an annual play, or any of the local state, regional or national holidays. They could be specialy festivals. One city has an annual carrot festival. It could be sports; every spring is the "March madness" for college basketball. It might be an intellectual contest like a college bowl.

### Morning Rituals

**Greeting at the door...** Say each person's name and greet with a smile. Say something positive about that person, or say what a great day it'll be. I check them for supplies, homework and materials. If they don't have them, ask what they can do about it... I use the same song as a ritual to "call" them in... I change the song after about two to four weeks they can get tired of it after that long. There's something up on the flip charts or board that is positive and encouraging... When it's time to start, I always start on time. I say to the group, "If you've made it here on time, raise your hand & say yes!" Next (within 2 seconds), I say, please turn to the person sitting

185

next to you and say, "Good morning, glad you're here!" Daily, I ask them to check on their neighbor to find out if their neighbor has something to write with... it's just a ritual of accountability.

**Attendance Rituals...** if you do this task, reinvent the task so that it becomes a positive ritual that gets students ready to learn. For example, have students answer with their name and a review word from yesterday, sing their name, stand up, say the previous person's name, use another language, or each person has a number and they just count off. Do anything but have a boring roll call! That's a big waste of time and gets students disinterested from the start.

**Globalization Rituals...** means I give a daily global overview of the material to be learned that day. I use music and it's a lot like movie previews of coming attractions. It's fun and inspiring to hear!

**Stretching...** I ask all students to stand up and take a minute or so and join their team in a circle facing each other about 10 feet apart, hands to side. Then the team leader leads the rest of the team in a slow stretch to wake up their body or slow it down, whatever's needed. All do slow deep breathing to oxygenate the body. Use verbal suggestions. They get about 30-60 seconds each of stretching time as they lead the rest of the group, then rotate to the next leader... until everyone has been a leader.

**Morning walk...** In workshops, I often ask participants to pick a partner and go outside for 10 minutes on a walk. They can use the walk to get fresh air, meet someone new and to answer 3 questions... what am I grateful for, what have I learned in the last day and what is my promise to myself today? By doing those three questions, it puts their attention on the present, the past and the future. And they usually enjoy the walk.

**Mind Mapping...** is a daily ritual in my workshops... every day the participants get out paper and make a mind map of yesterday from memory. They are allowed to talk to the people near them to refresh their memory. They get about 10 min. for it... it builds recall, confidence and learning.

**Teaching a Partner...** is a ritual that follows up the mindmap. Each day, after the mind-map, everyone goes at least 15 ft. away from their seat to find a new partner. Then, while standing, they teach their partner what's on their mind map. Naturally, the other teaches, too. Each usually learns something new, gets a quick review and discovers that they had questions that needed to be answered. So I always follow up this teaching with a ritual called... Morning refresh, question and review...this is the ritual: Everyone asks questions from the previous day's material... it's usually brief because they've just had a partner teach them about it.

**Break or recess rituals...** before I send participants out to break or recess, there's a simple ritual I do. It's designed to do several things. First, it puts closure on what we just finished learning. Second, it affirms something about it or yourself. Third, it nonconsciously helps integrate the just learned material into what they already know. It's called the "yes" clap. Participants stand facing their partner, hands out to the side, palms up. I say, "In your left hand, put all of your previous knowledge, whatever you brought with you today. In your right hand, put all you have learned today. Now, when I say ready, bring them together in a simple clap, by saying the most powerful word in the English language, 'yes!'" After the big clap, they're all energized and ready for something new... I immediately have music ready to fill up the deadness void after the noisy clap. The music is hip, upbeat and always fits the mood.

**Music rituals...** When I start up a workshop, in the 5-10 minutes before I start, I always play two songs... one is to develop the mood of the audience, to get it inspired, excited, curious and ready to get started. That's an instrumental with lots of hip keyboards and drums. Then I always play the song designated as the call-in song.

**The call-in song ritual...** In either a course or a class one song becomes the designated (by me) "call-in" song. That's the one that I put on 2-3 minutes before the scheduled start up time so that when the song's over, I startup. I like to use upbeat songs that have a clear, decisive ending, that most people know. Examples include: Pretty Woman, Splish-Splash, Rock Around the Clock, La Bamba, Great Balls of Fire, etc. I usually use certain songs as a ritual because they have the words that are appropriate for what I'd like the participants to hear. For example, I might use the song "New Attitude" by Patty LaBelle for a song about changing behaviors or "Hot Together" by Pointer Sisters for teamwork.

**Lunch time rituals...** At my workshops, when we come back from lunch, for the first few minutes, the ritual is always joke time. I always read one, just to liven up the group, then I open it up to others. Naturally we want to avoid racist, sexist or other inappropriate jokes.

**Learning rituals...** If we are about to start something new, or if we have all just learned a skill, it's good to emphasize it with a ritual. Here's a simple one: if each person is sitting outside of a team or partner (on their own), ask them to turn the person nearest you and say, "It's easy!"... If they are sitting in a team, and you just gave them all a project with a deadline, then to get started, tell the class to turn to their team leader and say, "Let's do it!"... Once the class is done with a project, topic or area... I always have a transition ritual... like "take in a deep breath"... or "turn to the person nearest you and say, 'You're a genius!'" Or, something on that topic, such as "I like your learning style!"

**Afternoon Closing rituals (Passive Review)...** Each day, near the end, I have everyone stand up, then raise the shoulders, tighten their fists and then relax them back down again... Then I ask them to relaxe and allow their eyes to close. While they are still standing relaxed, I walk through the entire day's content and processes. I take about two minutes, so it's a very condensed review. I have relaxing music on in the background.

**Teams Self-Assess Rituals (Charts)...** In my workshops, I often have team charts made up by the teams to track progress and to self-score the charts (see special report on team-building for the chart information).

The team leader report is an accountability and hype ritual. I like it because I ask the leader of each team, after scoring their own charts, to tell the whole group how their day went or how their team is doing overall. If you're doing a good job of managing them, you'll get lots of positive feedback. It builds up a nice collective agreement about learning, affirmation and celebration.

**Closing Song...** At the end of the day, the song is always "Wonderful World" by Louis Armstrong. It's so soothing, positive and sweet... When that's over the tape has a pause, then it plays "Happy Trails" by Roy Rogers.

**Final Messages...** at the end of the day I usually give previews of coming attractions for tomorrow... I make it fun and curiosity-building.

**Final "Yes!" clap...** Participants stand facing their nearest partner, hands out to the side, palms up. I say, "In your left hand, put all of your previous knowledge, whatever you brought with you today. In your right hand, put all you have learned today. Now, when I say "ready", bring them together in a simple clap, by saying the most powerful word in the English language, 'yes!'" All clap.

# Affirmations

Our world is full of affirmations. We say, "Have a great day," or "Happy Holidays," or "Be careful," or "Have a safe trip." Why do we affirm? We like to wish the best for others. Affirmations "make firm" that which you want. It's a suggestion, a prediction, a blessing and well-wishing. The more you affirm goodness in others, the likely you are to find goodness.

Conversely, you can also affirm negatives. If you say to another, "You are such a pain in the neck," you are simply "firming up" your impression of the person or encouraging them to "firm up" their opinion of themselves. To get the best out of our learners, it's important to affirm the positives and let the negatives go. This does not mean to adopt an "I don't care" attitude. It means you do care enough to affirm the goodness in your learners. When negatives occur, deal with the problem more than the person. The chapter in this book on discipline will give you some ideas.

Many think of affirmations as something said to another. There's more to it. The affirmations you use can be visual, auditory or kinesthetic. You can encourage what is seen, heard or felt in many ways. Here are some examples.

# Visual Affirmations

**1.** You offer a smile, a positive gesture, an affirming written note, a special comment on paper, a positive grade or score.

**2.** You could also create room displays for your learners: posters, signs, projects, pictures or student work.

**3.** You could ask your students to mentally rehearse upcoming actions. They could practice doing them successfully, over and over until they're ready to do them in real life.

# Auditory Affirmations

**1.** What and how you say affirmations to your learners depends on many things. It might be the relationship you have with them, their age, culture and even the state they're in at the moment. You could say to the student: "I'm pleased with your work. It was much more detailed than what was required, more interesting and creative than I expected and that meant a lot to me." Or, you could simply say, "Great enthusiasm, I love it!"

**2.** One of the most under-used types of affirmations are student to student. Your learners often value what their peers say and do as much or more than what you say. That's why it may make sense to ask your students, at appropriate moments, to turn to their neighbor and say, "Good morning, glad to see you!" After an activity, you might say, "Turn to your partner and say, great job!" Or, at the end of the day, you might finish up with, "Turn to the person nearest you and say, "Thanks for a great day!" Some criticize this as "hype" and phony, but there are three reasons for these types of affirmations.

What seems phony and contrived initially can become genuine over time. When you were three years old, your parents may have forced you to say "Thank you" each time a gift or favor was given. As a child, "thank you" felt phony and contrived. Over time, you learned the value behind gratitude. As an adult, it's well worth while to learn the value of affirmation, too. It also teaches your students a powerful habit of affirming others instead of criticizing them. Last, there's much research about the positive value of engaging emotions for the best recall.

**3.** One of the best affirmations is one a student gives to him or herself. This is the all-important self-talk. Positive self-talk is one of the characteristics of learners with strong self-esteem. You can't make a learner say to him or herself, "I'm a terrific learner!" However, you can encourage it, make it easy to say, and role model it in front of others so it's more likely to happen.

## Kinesthetic Affirmations

**1.** The most common type of physical affirmation is the celebration type found particularly in sports. They are the student hi-fives, hugs, handshakes and back-pats. These are great to build into a class ritual so that learning is constantly being celebrated. That affirming attitude helps reinforce the joy of learning and "win" in it for all.

**2.** Another under-used type of kinesthetic affirmation is called, "voting with your body." This is the teacher-to-student, "if, then" action request. "If you are this, then, please do that," says the affirming teacher. "If you're ready for a break, please stand up." Or, "If you learned something new, raise your hand and say, yes!" Or, "If you're ready to try out something new, please move to your right." If it's used sparingly and non-manipulatively, it can be quite useful.

**3.** The third type is a student's internal kinesthetic affirmation. It can be learner-generated, or teacher-generated, by asking questions that elicit positive feelings. Let's say a student does well on a project. You approach individually, and lower yourself to eye level or even kneel a bit lower (that brings their eyes down to look at you, in a more kinesthetic angle). Ask a question about their work that includes feeling words such as, "How do you feel about how your project turned out?" The answer forces the learner to access feelings two ways: 1) your physical position invites feelings, and 2) the content of the question invites feelings.

## What to Put On the Walls:

There are many types of useful posters to use. You might divide them into the following categories:

1. **Student Work**
   Consists of team charts, self-assessments, artwork, samples of excellent work
2. **Symbolic learning**
   Consists of icons, logos, pictures and drawings. Powerful use of symbolism to give messages to the non-conscious. Can be effective using

anything that has it's long-established meaning: teams working together, sunrise, sunset, peace sign, mountain top and celebrations.

3. **Preaching**
These are the type of slogans and didactic messages that would be best left unsaid, but can be powerful as a peripheral. Learners often turn off to most verbal "preaching" messages. Examples include, "If it's to be, it's up to me."

4. **Content Messages**
Post up a summary of the course. Preview coming attractions. Put up key elements in graphic patterns, like mind maps. Post them well in advance of the course (2 weeks) and leave them up after the course is over.

5. **Affirmations**
These affirm the good in your learners. You may use the words "You, I, my and me." It is also effective to make it generic, non-specific to any names

# Sample Affirmations Peripherals:

- Learning is Fun, Easy & Creative
- The future belongs to those with serious dreams
- Act as if it were impossible to fail
- The more you learn, the easier it gets
- Luck is often disguised as hard work
- All unhappiness is caused by comparison
- You can't vote to make things the way they are, you already did
- If life gives you lemons, make lemonade
- If you think you can or think you can't, you're right
- Success is a journey, not a destination
- Inch by inch, it's a cinch
- Failure is a success if you learn from it
- Get an education in school and you'll have it for life
- If you play victim, you give up your power to change
- You can have anything you want, if you give up the belief that you can't have it
- You're as happy as you make up your mind to be
- If your rug is pulled out from under you, learn to dance on a shifting carpet
- Your greatest advantage is your ability to learn
- Nothing can hurt you unless you give it the power to do so
- Others can stop you temporarily, only you can stop you permanently
- Before you can break out of prison, you must first realize you're locked up
- The biggest risk in life is not risking
- The mind is like a parachute. It works best when open
- No on can make you feel inferior without your permission
- Focus, Breathe, Listen
- I Choose to Respond Positively, NOT React
- If you don't live it, you don't believe it
- If it's worth learning, it's worth celebrating
- Breakthroughs Occur When I Commit Myself to
  Something I Don't Know How To Do Yet
- Get In - Get It Done - Get Out
- The Difference Between 99% and 100% is 100%
- Live Your Vision With Passion
- Communicate to the Person Who Can Do Something About It
- Learning is a Big Part of My Life
- Be Bigger Than Your Problems

- The First Step In Life is Getting What You Want
  and the Other 99% is Wanting What You Get
- Who I am Makes a Difference
- If You Continue to Do What You've Always Done,
  You'll Get What You've Always Gotten
- I am Greater than My Highest Thought
- Get a Life - Get a Degree!
- Compliments and Criticisms Have Little to Do With the Listener -
  They More Likely Reflect the Values & Beliefs of the Speaker.
- My Success Is Absolutely Assured
- I Succeed By Asking Questions
- Reaching Goals Feels Good
- The Difference between Ordinary & Extraordinary is that little "Extra"
- I Rejoice in My Choice
- I Am Unique and Special in All the Universe
- A Smile is My Style
- It is Safe For Me To Express Myself
- The More I Enjoy, The More I Learn
- I Absorb & Retain With Ease & Joy
- Don't Wait For Your Ship to Come In... Swim Out to It
- You Get in Life Exactly What You Put Up With
- For Things to Change... I Must Change
- To Raise Yourself, Praise Yourself
- I Study Smarter Every Day
- If It's To Be, It's Up To Me
- There's No Such Thing as Failure, Only Feedback
- Carpe Diem (Seize the Day!)
- Fear is: False Evidence Appearing Real
- It's Not IF I Can, It's Only a Matter of How
- I Can Succeed. I Will. I Do. It's Now Done.

You create the weather, the climate and the long-range forecast in your room. Affirmations and peripherals are part of the climate. If you want a positive climate, don't hope it will happen. Be proactive and make it happen.

Two suggestions about using peripherals and affirmations. First, ask students to brainstorm and create their own for at least part of the wall space available. Second, rotate them monthly so that you'll have novelty for the brain's attention. With positive affirmations, you'll create a "can-do" climate that will make your job easier and boost learning like crazy!

## Additional Resources for Further Study and Follow up

*Think* by Robert Anthony (Berkeley)
*Think Again* by Robert Anthony (Berkeley)
*Think On* by Robert Anthony (Berkeley)
*The Rubicon Dictionary of Positive, Motivational, Life-Affirming & Inspiration Quotations* by John Cook (Rubicon Press)
*Healing Words* by Dossey (Harper Collins)
*Teacher's Inspiration* (Great Quotations, Inc)
*Motivational Quotes* (Great Quotations, Inc)
*Begin it Now* by Hayward (InTune Books)
*A Bag of Jewels* by Hayward & Cohen (InTune Books)

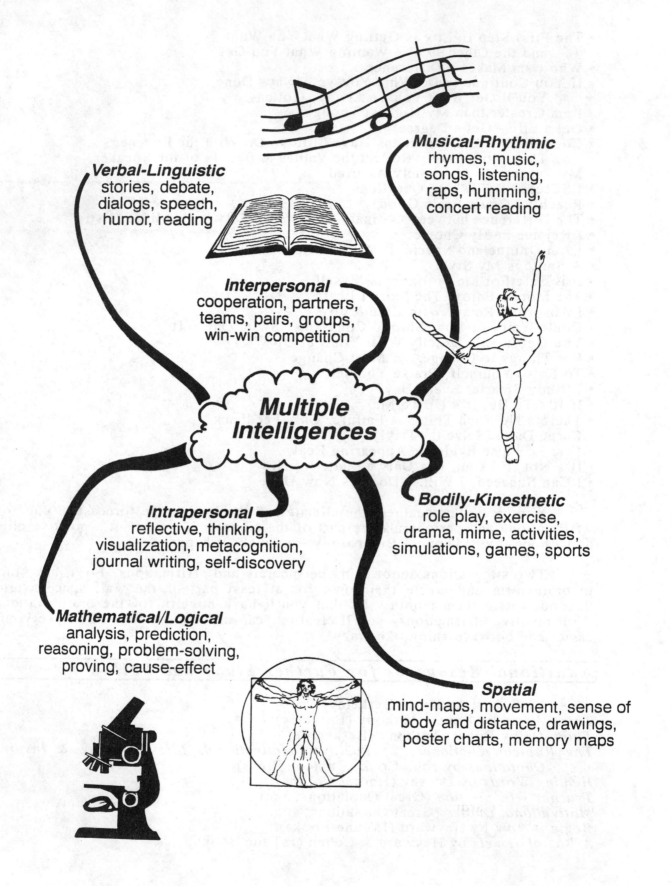

**Musical-Rhythmic**
rhymes, music,
songs, listening,
raps, humming,
concert reading

**Verbal-Linguistic**
stories, debate,
dialogs, speech,
humor, reading

**Interpersonal**
cooperation, partners,
teams, pairs, groups,
win-win competition

*Multiple
Intelligences*

**Bodily-Kinesthetic**
role play, exercise,
drama, mime, activities,
simulations, games, sports

**Intrapersonal**
reflective, thinking,
visualization, metacognition,
journal writing, self-discovery

**Mathematical/Logical**
analysis, prediction,
reasoning, problem-solving,
proving, cause-effect

**Spatial**
mind-maps, movement, sense of
body and distance, drawings,
poster charts, memory maps

# 15

## Multiple Intelligences

### Teaching Content or Discovering Intelligence?

In order to boost learning and intelligence, it's useful to know what it is. Dr. Robert Sternberg says, "Intelligence boils down to your ability to know your own strengths and weaknesses and to capitalize on the strengths while compensating for the weaknesses." He says that when we think of intelligence, we are really talking about our ability to react intuitively, creatively and constructively to a wide range of experiences. In other words, being "street smart" is just as, or more important than, being "book smart."

For years, the official way to measure intelligence was the IQ test, the Stanford-Binet or the Weschler. Using the tests, individuals would be rated at various levels. Yet researchers and educators have long suspected that something is amiss in this assessment. Often students who were assessed as "smart" or "genius" had very ordinary, if not miserable lives. And often students who were assessed as "ordinary" or "average" had very successful and extraordinary lives. After all, the IQ test was developed decades ago as a screening process for immigrants and for sorting wartime recruits. Could it be that the IQ form of assessment is inaccurate or incomplete?

### Intelligent People

Read this list: Ella Fitzgerald, Carl Sagan, John Williams, Martha Graham, Bill Gates, Helen Gurley Brown, Quincy Jones, Albert Einstein, Shaquille O'Neill, Indira Ghandi, Margaret Thatcher and Steven Segal. Which one was or is more intelligent? You guessed it! All are intelligent, in their own way! Did you know that every single one of them was labeled by their teachers as having some kind of learning problem?

Fortunately, In the late 70's and early 80's, things began to change. With support from the VanLeer and MacArthur Foundations a project was headed up by Dr. Howard Gardner, professor of graduate education at Harvard University. The project purpose was to discover the nature of intelligence and consider alternative ways of thinking about it. Because the researchers wanted to start with no prior assumptions about intelligence, it was named Project Zero.

# Defining Intelligence

Dr. Gardner first had to define intelligence in order to research it. He used two criteria: 1) one demonstrated the ability to use a skill, fashion an artifact or solve a problem 2) one did that in a way that is valued by the particular culture where one ordinarily lives. In other words, an Australian Aborigine may not be able to measure up as highly intelligent in downtown Tokyo, New York or London. But he or she may be quite intelligent in the outback of Australia. The same could be said in reverse for a banker or stockbroker who succeeds in the world of global finance but, of course, would likely die in three days in the remote outback.

# Who Is Intelligent?

Gardner's research led him to find many different ways of being intelligent around the world. These ways included skills such as those used by a Pacific Islander who can sail from island to island at night with no formal navigation system and an equally talented choreographer of Broadway musicals. Certainly these people were succeeding in the eyes of their own culture. But there was no apparent link to formal schooling. Gardner grouped the array of human intelligences into just seven categories. He purposely included what some refer to as "abilities" because he wanted them to get the respect they deserve. Instead of having one single figure or mark that assesses our intelligence, he says that each of us has our own unique combination of these intelligences and that they can and do change over a lifetime. Here are the two models; the old and the new. Gardner said that there may actually be hundreds of different types of intelligences but he grouped them into seven manageable categories.

The seven intelligences are: Logical-mathematical, interpersonal, spatial, musical-rhythmic, intrapersonal, bodily-kinesthetic and verbal-linguistic. Gardner first presented these ideas publicly in 1983 at the Tarrytown conference in New York. We'll introduce each of them, talk about how to identify them, and what you can do with each of them.

# Logical-Mathematical

**Description:**
It's the ability to discern logical or numerical patterns. Those with the ability to solve mathematical or life's daily problems; one who asks many "why" or "how" questions; one who likes reasons for doing things; one who wants to sort, classify and understand information; one who wants to predict, analyze, theorize, fix things, offer advice, work in the physical and theoretical sciences or simply make sense out of their world. It's the ability to pursue extended reasoning and detailed analysis. Occupations could include teachers, bankers, astronauts, buyers, computer programmers, accountants, inventors, engineers, mathematicians, scientists, or an appliance repair person. <u>Famous</u>: Astronomer Carl Sagan, Plato, Bill Gates, district attorney Marcia Clark, Johnny Cochran, TV analysts Lehrer-McNeill or Ted Koppel.

**In the classroom:**
This student is an effective problem-solver. He or she likes things in place and in order; and dislikes chaos and confusion. Repetitive seatwork bores this student the most. Catch this student with questions like: "How would you solve this?" "What would an expert say about this?" Reach the student with challenges, problems and projects.

**You could develop this more by:**
Outlining the material, doing statistical analysis, solving problems, creating puzzles and solving them, finding patterns, comparing and contrasting the material, classifying ideas or objects, exploring new material, finding locations, making calculations, computing averages, creating time sequences, using a calculator, predicting the future, creating a problem-solving guide for your subject, solving ecological problems, finding examples of how it all relates to something else. These students like computers, tangrams, inventor's fairs and the HOTS program.

# Interpersonal

**Description:**
Those with the ability to influence others, to negotiate, to listen, to handle conflict resolution, to persuade, to get along with others, to influence, to form teams.
This student works well with diverse groups of people and enjoys the company of others. Occupations can include teachers, customer service representatives, therapists, politicians, beauty queens, religious leaders, actresses and actors, managers, social workers, telephone operators, salespersons and waitresses.
Famous: Talk show hosts Oprah Winfrey, Sally Jessey Raphael, Montel Williams or Mike Donahue.

**In the classroom:**
This student prefers to work with others. Small groups and workstations attract attention. They like student council, peer counseling and service-learning projects. Working alone is distasteful. Reach this student with strong communication activities. Attract his or her attention with words like "We can do this next..." or "What did we learn today?"

**You could develop this more by:**
Doing more role-play and practicing empathy, using cooperative learning groups, giving feedback to others, using peer assessment, getting feedback, creating teams to solve problems, working with just a single partner, doing subject matter drills with a partner, quizzing each other, reading around or singing around in a group, using peer coaching.

# Spatial

**Description:**
One who has the ability to judge and use the position of themselves or other objects in relation to other persons or objects. Dr. Gardner emphasizes that spatial intelligence is different from visual. Spatial is more the three-dimensional relational sense. It is not the ability to see anything, but rather the ability to see things in relationship to others. A person could be legally blind and still have strong spatial intelligence.

This includes the ability to parallel park a car, fill a dishwasher, pack luggage, design or decorate a room. One with high spatial intelligence can find a particular piece of paper even on a very messy desk. Occupations may include architects, athletes in a team sport, landscapers, jugglers, airline pilots, chorus line dancers, sculptors, muralists, painters, navigators, organizers, logistics people, flight deck workers on an aircraft carrier, heavy machinery construction workers or movie directors. Famous: Outdoor muralist Wyland, skaters Peggy Fleming, Brain Boitano, Nancy Kerrigan, quarterbacks Warren Moon, Dan Marino, Steve Young or John Elway.

**In the classroom:**
It's the perceptions of the world around us in their physical relationships to each other. This student often fidgets and doodles. He or she loves a picture-rich environment full of posters, mobiles and art. Reach this student with activities that allow kids to paint, arrange, do origami, make mazes, create geo-block designs, build and draw. Catch with questions that ask them to "imagine or picture something."

**You could develop this more by:**
Mind-mapping, organizing, color coordinating, drawing, sculpting, rearranging the room to suit the subject, making wall displays, using guided imagery, re-setting the chairs, changing teaching locations, designing graphics, logos and flyers; by having students line up according to height - birthdays - alphabetical name order (or other combination), playing ball-toss games, circle or line dancing and human sculpture.

# Musical-Rhythmic

**Description:**
One who has the ability to translate the sounds of nature or those created in the head into patterns of music. This includes the ability to tap dance, clap in unison, dance, compose music, play music, create rhythm games and songs. Musical-rhythimic intelligence does not have anything to do with the talent for singing. Occupations include many pre-school or elementary school teachers, cheerleaders, tribal cultures that use music for ritual and entertainment or communication, musicians, jingle-writers, choir leaders, theater directors and composers. <u>Famous</u>: Composers Quincy Jones, Rogers and Hammerstein, John Williams, Lerner & Lowe, Paul Simon.

**In the classroom:**
This learner is sensitive to sounds and has the ability to respond to them. Reach this student by creating time for dancing, singing, listening, rapping, jingles and using instruments. This student is distracted by teacher talking too much, repetitive tasks, scattered noise and sitting too long. Catch with questions like: "How does this sound?" Use sounds or special effects to open a class.

**You could develop this more by:**
Using concert readings, making class affirmations, doing "clap and slap" memory games, team cheering, having musical performances, putting information to rhythms, creating a jingle, rapping, playing instruments, making up sounds for the subject you are studying, having environmental music in background, practicing humming patterns for memory or mood changes, turning an essay, short story or movie into a musical, listen for natural sounds and using them in learning. This student likes presentations using a musical score to highlight key parts.

# Intrapersonal

**Description:**
This student has the ability to think about thinking. He or she likes self-assessment, reflection, planning, enjoys tasks in solitude, uses intuition often, is a daytime dreamer, may enjoy journal-writing, meditation, focusing, self-discovery, knows their strengths and weaknesses, is likely to enjoy solitude and asking the big questions of life such as "Why are we here?" "What happens when we die?" "Is there a God?" Occupations include authors, fishermen, philosophers, sailors, artists,

farmers, spiritualists, backpackers and hermits. <u>Famous</u>: Simone DeBeauvoir, Microsoft Chairman Bill Gates, James Michener, Socrates, Eleanor Roosevelt and Thoreau.

**In the classroom:**
This student likes to be alone & reflect. He or she thrives on self-reliance and individual work. This student wants to manage his or her own work. This learner is annoyed by too many teacher-directed activities, too much structure, rules and textbook teaching. Use phrases like "What would you do if this were you?" or "How would you feel if...?"

**You could develop this more by:**
Giving more silent reflection time to think about what has been learned, having students think about HOW they arrived at their solution, writing an essay on "What I have learned from life," putting yourself in the situation of a play and imagining what you'd do, asking how you could apply what you learned, doing guided imagery, writing in a diary or journal, meditating, doing self-assessment on personal or course goals, practicing methods for self-control (temper, breathing, focus, etc.), and figuring out how to go about solving a problem, labeling yourself by a type of personality, learning style or favorite intelligences, teaching decision-making with steps to take for better thinking.

# Bodily-Kinesthetic

**Description:**
The ability to control body motions and manipulate objects. One who uses his or her body to accomplish a task, entertain or express one self. Examples might include: dancers, actors & actresses, rock climbers, martial artists, new games leaders, gardeners, athletes, mimes, bicycle messengers, clowns, triatheletes, astronauts, coachs, sheep shearers, Olympians, construction workers, frisbee players, inventors, dog trainers, bowlers, farmers or custodians. <u>Famous</u>: Michael Jordan, Martina Navaratilova, Arnold Schwartzenegger, Madonna or Olympians Carl Lewis and Jackie Joyner-Kersey; actors like Meryl Streep, Steven Segal, Robert DeNiro, Denzel Washington or Dustin Hoffman.

**In the classroom:**
This student enjoys role-play, sports, field trips and manipulatives. He or she dislikes having to sit too long. Instead, he or she prefers to be able to get up, (on their own schedule) and stand, walk around or stretch. Catch this student's attention by asking questions like "How does this grab you?" or ask, "How would you respond to this?"

**You could develop this more by:**
Stretching, changing seats, creating a play, playing Simon Sez, using the body to learn, creating simulations, role-playing, making sporting events, using theater, changing positions in the room, dancing, rearranging the room, haiving the students stand up while you lecture, making the students go to different parts of the room to discuss a subject with a partner, creating a drama to learn a concept, forming his- or herself into shapes, playing charades or Pictionary™ and other games, shaking hands, using sign languages, re-enacting great moments from history, learning each topic with a physical gesture attached, allowing students to build with Legos, weave, work with wood, perform in plays and do class jobs.

# Verbal-Linguistic

**Description:**
This learner has a good command of the language, the ability to form thoughts, likes to talk, tell stories, argue, debate, tell jokes, shape arguments, read, discuss, interpret and re-think. Possible occupations include: attorneys, writers, judges, editors, public speakers, translators, negotiators, comics, talk show hosts, poets, secretaries, authors, elected representatives or teachers. <u>Famous</u>: Robin Williams, Martin Luther-King, Connie Chung, William F. Buckley, Malcolm X, Lily Tomlin, Arsenio Hall and Garrison Keeler.

**In the classroom:**
This student prefers busy graphics, posters and slogans in the environment. He or she is very sensitive to language, and sarcasm or belittling is an extra turn-off. Provide opportunities for this student to read, dialog, use affirmations, peer teach or be involved in discussions. Use expressions like, "What's your opinion?" or "Tell me, please, why would you say that?"

**You could develop this more by:**
Lecturing, listening to guest speakers, writing or giving speeches, reading, listening to tapes, creating a dialogue with partners or within teams, writing and playing parts in a play, learning vocabulary, writing up steps to an experiment, giving instructions, creative writing, talking out a problem to solve, making up puns, creating crossword puzzles on the subject, being an announcer or sports caster for a classroom event, impromptu speaking, using humor, joking, diary or journal writing.

# Additional Key Considerations

Each of us has some of each of the intelligences. We have our own unique combination of them. But the degree of expertise in each varies widely. For example you may be able to play "Mary Had a Little Lamb" on a piano, but that's very different from composing an opera. You can jog or walk, but not play professional sports.

The amount of talent you have in each of your seven intelligences does not correlate to success in society. For example, you may be the most talented basketball player in the world, but if you are unwilling to work hard, get along with your teammates and be at practice every day, you'll never become a star. On the other hand, you could be low in most areas, but have just enough interpersonal intelligence to be the best customer service representative in your company.

Your specific intelligence areas will change over time. For example, a college athlete may excel in three sports at age 21 and yet by age fifty, be very low in bodily kinesthetic intelligence. Yes, the body will remember many of the moves, but it won't be able to perform the same.

Intelligences are cultivated more than they are inherited. And different cultures tend to reinforce certain intelligences. There are tribes in Africa in which everyone is taught how to sing and play music. As a result, all are strong at the musical-rhythmic intelligence. A Samoan or Fijian islander learns early in life that celestial navigation can save his life. Hence, he grows that particular spatial skill at an early age. Urban street kids usually find that verbal-linguistic and bodily-kinesthetic intelligences provide critical survival value in daily threatening situations.

The better your own intrapersonal intelligence, the better you'll be at rating yourself. In other words, to even talk about your own intelligences, you'd have to have some intuition or skill at self-assessment.

You can "grow" intelligences. Most three year-olds are low in all the seven intelligences. Years of life, interaction, work and school boost various ones. The good news is that we have no "fixed" intelligence. The bad news is that the brain does have developmental stages in which each of the intelligences are more easily nurtured. The critical stage for developing foundational musical-rhythmic, spatial and verbal-linguistic is from ages 3-6. Bodily-kinesthetic intelligence seems to be able to be developed from as early as age three up to age seventy. For developing interpersonal, mathematical-logical and intrapersonal intelligences, there seems to be no age limit.

Do what you are good at and usually contentment will follow. In general, the happiest and most successful people have purposely developed areas that they were at one time, weak at originally.

## Your Action Steps

Now that you know the basics about multiple intelligences, what do you actually do about it? There are two primary strategies, instructional design and assessment.

In the area of instructional design, the ideal is to provide learning opportunities for students to be able to succeed regardless of their particular strength.

That means variety. It also means that some students may not succeed easily at everything. Some may be a bit uncomfortable. But the good news is, that over the length of the course, you'll reach your students better and reach more of them. You'll also reach them on a deeper, more profound and meaningful level.

Here's the difference between an average teacher and a great teacher. An average teacher teaches so that at any given time, they are reaching 60-80% of the learners. A great teacher teaches so that at any given time, they are reaching 60-80% of the learners. So, what's the difference? With the average teacher, it's the same 60-80% all term long. With the great teacher, they rotate and use variety so that they are reaching a different 60-80% every day, and ALL of them over any given week.

## How to Reach Everyone

Design your classes, workshops or trainings so that they include at least three or four of the following sub-components from each of the seven groups. You already know the basic order and the format for organizing your lesson. You may be using a model that includes: creating a certain physical environment, an introduction, the initial activation of learning, elaboration of the learning, evaluation and celebration.

## How to Nurture
## The Multiple Intelligences

Make sure that you tap into every one of the seven multiple intelligences in your work. You can design lessons that use all seven within each hour, but it's a lot of work. If you teach elementary, you'll easily reach all seven at least once a day, probably a half a dozen times. Bruce Campbell, a third grade teacher in Washington State, has set up seven "learning stations" around his classroom.

Each station offers his students a way to learn the subject. He divides up his class into seven groups and they get time on each one, then he rotates them to the next. Bruce says that when he starts at the beginning of the year, students usually like one station. By mid-year, they like three or four of them and by the end of the year, they usually like most or all of them. Now there's a teacher that's growing dendrites in his students!

At the secondary and college level, you may reach three or four in one class and all seven within a week. Never, ever let a week go by without reaching all seven or you run the risk of students getting bored or frustrated.

## Integrating Across The Curriculum

The most commonly used system for implementing MI is webbing a lesson. Put the topic or unit in the center of a piece of paper and circle it. Then make seven spokes, like a wheel, coming out from the center. At the end of each spoke, list one of the seven MI. Then take a few moments before you begin a unit, and list some of the ways that you could use each of the particular MI on the topic you have.

**Here's an example:** Let's say it's a science topic, like severe weather.

**For verbal linguistic:** You could read an opening dramatic sequence to the class or have them read to each other. They could write out their own dramatic opening using the omen of bad weather.
**For musical rhythmic:** They can write a catchy jingle to warn others about a dangerous storm on the way. They could bring in music to play which refers to weather.
**For logical mathematical:** They could analyze data, predict, organize information make graphs or solve logistical problems relating to a severe weather evacuation.
**For spatial:** Students visualize the impact of the severe weather on their own neighborhood or design a logo for the weatherperson. They could design a weather magazine, a mobile or TV show format.
**For bodily - kinesthetic:** They act out the formation, event and dissipation of a severe storm. They could create & perform a play.
**For intrapersonal:** Students could read about it, write down in a journal how they would feel about it roaring through their neighborhood. They could critique the unit and their own reactions to it. How might they improve on it for next time?
**For Interpersonal:** They can work in cooperative learning groups to jigsaw what they have learned. They could also create a play to communicate what they have learned.

Relax and have fun. Do some experimenting. What is new and a bit intimidating for you today may become comfortable, like an "old hat" by next month.

## Assessing Multiple Intelligences

There are dozens of ways to evaluate students who are learning using the multiple intelligences model. Keep student's work in a large process-folio for convenient safekeeping. The old portfolio method meant keeping just samples of the student's best work to date. A Process-folio keeps the interim stages stored, too. It is important, Gardner says, so that you can better assess progress. Here are some of the possible ways to assess students. Which one of the following would you be willing to use in addition to the ones you use now?

- Students create jingles or songs about a unit
- **Give students a choice on the type of assessment**
- Journal or diary with reflections and personal growth
- **Get credit for community or business work**
- Create a song and sing or perform it
- **Produce a videotape(or audio tape)**
- Peer assessment (with your established criteria)
- **Build working models that demonstrate knowledge**
- Interviews with you
- **Make a chart of progress in the course**
- Write a story or article
- **Perform a play, musical or dance**
- Create artwork, a painting
- **Graphic organizers like Venn diagrams**
- Make an advertising flyer for the course/subject
- **Re-do the lyrics to a song with the new key words**
- Produce a large mindmap
- **Self-assessment using personal or course goals**

The greater the variety of assessment methods, the higher the percentage of students will succeed. Why? All of your students have several intelligences and are smart and gifted- in some way or another. You may want to make sure that you use alternative approaches to identify and assess your students.

David Lazear recommends these approaches in observing and listening:

1. **Observe the type of intelligence used the most.** Students tend to do what they like or are most successful in. Find out who are the questioners, the hummers, the doodlers, the active learners, the talkers, the loners, etc.
2. **Provide students with a choice of games to play.** Discover which ones they pick: Pictionary, Monopoly, crossword puzzles, manipulative puzzles, charades, music recognition, etc. Then observe what they do during that game.
3. **Reflection on play, movie or musical.** After students watch one of those, ask which parts struck them most and were really memorable. Was it the music, the action, the relationships, etc.?
4. **Problem-solving.** Give students a problem to solve which can be solved many different ways. For example, the one about the man and the woman starting out walking from the same place. The man takes two steps for every three the woman takes. They start out together, and immediately lose synchronization. After how many steps will they be back in synch again? That problem can be solved using just about every one of the seven intelligences. But which one is chosen by the students?
5. **Inventions & model-building.** This option allows learners to focus on the types of intelligences that they are strongest at. This more authentic assessment insures that students will have a way to be recognized for their abilities, sharing their talents and knowledge. And when all students succeed, everyone succeeds.

# What Are Other Key Implications?

The primary contribution is nothing less than a paradigm shift. The old way of talking about learning was that some will do it better than others. The old way of talking about intelligence is that there's an IQ average of 100 for everybody, and you are either above average, average or below average. The old way says there are some learners who are deficient in intelligences. But Gardner's theory says differently.

The real impact of multiple intelligences will not be felt for years. But today it says to us several things: First, that learner may do it differently than another, but they are no more or less intelligent. One learner may solve a problem by visualizing it, another by talking it over and another my reading about it, then putting a pencil to a paper. Secondly, that no one is below average, since we no longer compare learners, except to him or herself. It also means that if we express our intelligences differently, we may want to teach and assess our learners differently.

There are tremendous implications to this in the classroom. No longer can a teacher talk about "high" and "low" kids. No longer can a teacher talk about "my high achievers, my gifted kids." Why?

*We all are gifted...*
*some just haven't opened their gifts*

The old adage that one is smarter than another is different now. We ask more useful questions such as: In what ways am I smart?

# Where Do Gifted and Talented Programs Fit In?

With multiple intelligences, there is no ability grouping. Are there ever any special education students at a multiple intelligences school? Yes, but very few. Here's why: the only way you could ability group is to first compare students; and a comparison of two students is one of the most irrelevant activities an institution can perform. How Karen does compared to Diane is absolutely immaterial. Karen's brain may be as much as three years ahead or behind Diane's in development. Karen has an entirely different multiple intelligences profile than Diane. Either of them may have a miserable and unacceptable home environment which provides constant stress and dramatic undernutrition. The only relevant bit of data about Karen is "How is Karen doing today compared to Karen's performance of a week ago or a year ago?" Now that's useful data!

The Key School is a public elementary school in Indianapolis, Indiana. When is switched over to using the multiple intelligences model several years ago, the school policy became "Every student is gifted." And they have proved it. Ordinary children act and perform like those in the special schools for the gifted. The difference? Two things: 1) an attitude that everyone is gifted 2) the use of multiple intelligences by skilled teachers.

Howard Gardner says the following:

*"In my view, the purpose of schools should be to develop intelligences and to help people reach vocational and avocational goals that are appropriate to their spectrum of intelligences. People who are helped to do so, I believe, feel more engaged and competent, and therefore more*

*inclined to serve society in a constructive way." My belief in the importance--indeed necessity--of individual-centered education derives from two separate but interlocking propositions.*

*First of all, it has now been established quite convincingly that individuals have quite different minds from one another. Education ought to be so sculpted that it remains responsive to these differences.*

*Instead of ignoring them, and pretending that all individuals have (or ought to have) the same kinds of minds, we should instead try to insure that everyone receives an education that maximizes his or her own intellectual potential.*

*The second proposition is equally compelling. It may once have been true that a dedicated individual could master the world's extant knowledge or at least some significant part of it. So long as this was a tenable goal, it made some sense to offer a uniform curriculum. Now, however, no individual can master even a single body of knowledge completely, let alone the range of disciplines and competencies."*

When regular teachers are trained in multiple intelligence strategies, their students learn more effectively and efficiently. More of their students learn better and they retain the learning longer. Self-confidence is up and so is love of learning. This means you'll have fewer problems, fewer students who need special attention or special skills from a pullout program.

*It's now time for educators and parents*
*to quit asking the old question, "How smart are you?"...*
*the new question is, "How are you smart?"*

## Additional Resources for Further Study and Follow Up

*Seven Kinds of Smart* by Thomas Armstrong
*Multiple Intelligences Handbook* by Bruce Campbell
*If the Shoe Fits* by Carolyn Chapman (Skylight)*
*Multiple Assessments for Multiple Intelligences* by Chapman & Bellanca (Skylight)*
*Multiple Intelligences: Theory in Practice* by Howard Gardner
*Multiple Intelligences in Action* by David Lazear (Skylight)
*Seven Ways of Knowing* by David Lazear (Skylight)
*Seven Ways of Teaching* by David Lazear (Skylight)*
*Seven Windows to a Child's World* by O'Connor & Callahan-Young


* Items marked with an asterisk are available in the Appendix.

# 16

# Music in Learning

## The Sweet Sound of Learning

Nature has provided us with such a rich array of sounds on our planet earth, it was only natural for humanity to copy them and use them. Most of our musical instruments are, of course, variations of animal or other natural sounds. So, the use of music as a learning aid is an old and quite ancient idea. Primitive man used it in many ways.

More recently, research has been done by Manfred Clives of Australia, Georgi Lozanov of Bulgaria, Don Campbell of Texas, Steven Halpern of California, Don Schuster of Iowa, as well as by others, to measure the effects of music on the nervous system. Results show that music affects the emotions, the respiratory system, the heart rate, the posture and mental images of the listener. These effects can dramatically alter the composite mood, state, and physiology of a person. Here's the key: when you change the state of the listener, you get direct access to state changes. This means music can change the behavior of your students. The effects are documented in many books including the *Brain-Based Learning & Teaching, The Learning Brain, Musical Brain, The Healing Powers of Music, SuperLearning* and in Journals of the Society for Accelerative Learning and Teaching.

Why use music in an educational environment? Quite simply, it can work marvelously to energize, align groups, induce relaxation, restimulate prior experiences, develop rapport with another, set the theme or the tone of the day, preach, be sheer fun, appreciate and inspire.

## The Role of Music in Learning

Does music belong in a classroom where the subject is not music? Absolutely yes! There are many ways to use it. Chances are, you learned the letters of the alphabet with a song. You probably learned many words and phrases through folk songs. You learned rituals, manners and social skills with childhood songs. As you get older, you have associated many situations, feelings and people with special songs. Listening and playing music is a powerful way to learn. Consider some of the following advantages to using music:

- Embeds the learning faster, on a deeper level like the "alphabet song"
- Relaxing after stress or after getting discouraged
- Collects and brings whole groups together

205

- Motivates the group to get up and get going
- Use as a rapport builder with certain members or the entire group.
- Energizes and brings new life to the group
- Appeals to the particular cultural values of the group
- Comforts the soul during hurting times
- Something to have fun with when you need a change of mind set
- Boosts achievement by activating the thinking portion of the brain
- Harmonizes situations when the group seems on edge or calms down hyper students

Music can also stimulate the right hemisphere to increase better attentiveness, build concentration and focus creativity. It can activate more of the brain, it can take the pressure off you as a presenter, it can help create sound curtains to isolate classes or groups and can bring forth qualities of the music that reside within each of your listeners. It can help create bonding and closeness, too.

For most students, school is a hostile and alien environment. They're being told what to do, in cold, uncarpeted rooms that someone else decorated. The one thing kids relate to the most, besides their friends, is music... and it's missing from most classrooms. The first thing most kids (and many adults) do when they get in a car or arrive home is turn on music. Why, you ask? To relax, to energize, to change moods, to feel good.... So, why a taboo against it in schools? It's just out-dated thinking. We decorate the walls visually, why not appeal to and utilize, the other senses such as auditory and kinesthetic? You can make your learning environment much more user-friendly, build rapport with kids and enhance the learning process with music. Do you need any other reasons to use music in education?

## Two Great Reasons

If so, here are two more: it's likely your students will love it, they'll perform better and feel better. Plus, you will too. One of the great side benefits of using music in the classroom is that it affects you, too. It will make your work more fun, keep you activated, interested and creating more in the moment than ever before.

Although it certainly helps to be a musicologist, you can still get great results with knowing just the fundamentals about music. The tapes and books recommended in this chapter are a good start. You may find a renewed interest in taking a music class and I suggest that very much. Here are the key things to know.

First and foremost, all music has some sort of pace with which to measure beats per minute. The single most important question to ask about classroom music is, what's the tempo, the pacing or the beat of the music? Meaning, is it slow, medium or fast? The beat of the music affects both heart rate and breathing - the two most important determiners of mood, feelings and state. So remember, the beat is the distinction you need to be able to make. In general, your selections will be instrumental. The exceptions will include some popular music, but then only for breaks or special effects, outside the lecture time.

## Getting Started is Easy

Learning to use music is an on-going process. Plan to invest some time and money to make a quality presentation package. Expect to pay from $60 - 150 for a new, low-cost portable classroom music system. Get a medium quality stereo tape player with separate detachable speakers.

As a starter kit, expect to pay about $75 - $100 for your first 6-tape starter kit and tape cassette holder box. Include 2 Baroque, 2 new-age relaxation tapes and 2 more popular upbeat ones. Use them for awhile to become comfortable experimenting with when, what and how to use them. When you are ready, you can expand your tape collection. A more complete and advanced tape collection might have 24 tapes in it. My suggestion is to include:

- 6 Baroque tapes (2 of them from the later romantic time)
- 2 jazz tapes
- 6 special effects tapes including comedy, fanfare stretch music, TV tunes and others
- 3 focused slower tapes
- 2 upbeat
- 2 popular rock n' roll
- 2 custom-tailored to your audience

Some of the music you may want is unavailable by ordinary means. The special effects ones are an example. If you need to get recordings of them, ask a student to do it for you, do it yourself or find someone who has already pre-recorded all the sounds you need.

Before you take your tapes to class, make sure that you have tested them and labeled them according to the situation in which they might be most useful. Try color-coding them with multi-colored peel-off dots to make for quicker in-class identification. The dots might signify classical, popular, new age or special effects. Set up your tape player in the front of the room and lay out all your cued tapes.

Think about what's being taught so you know what kinds of specific music can be used and when. Prepare ahead with several tape options so you can make sure that you are totally ready. Use music as a partner, an aid in the learning process. Always be sensitive to the existing mood in the classroom and respect it. If a sensitive, troubling or emotional process just took place, avoid music or use low-volume, low-key music that matches the mood. If a high-energy activity just took place, be ready with up-beat, high-energy music to match it. Music should serenade, romance and invite the audience - and maybe provide an occasional nudge. Obviously, it should never intrude. In short, use music to lead and entice.

First, cue up all your tapes by either rewinding them or fast-forwarding them to the spots where the music of your specific choice begins. Secondly, get all of the tapes out of their boxes or cases and have them easily accessible for quick usage. Thirdly, place them either in the order of projected usage or by category. You might label the categories as follows:

**1. Classical Music** - (this is best for the active lecture presentation) include Beethoven, Mozart and Rossini. Have available music from other classical eras for dramatics, special imaging and storytelling such as Mozart, Satie and Rachmaninoff. This can be used as a low background, almost a "white noise"... or IF the teacher is trained in concert readings using the music as a carrier of dual-plane suggestion.

**2. Slower Music** - (this is for Imagery and Relaxation) include New Age artists such as Steven Halpern, Georgia Kelly, Adam Geiger, Daniel Kobialka, Zamfir, Ron Dexter, George Winston, and the long-time classic canon in D by Johann Pachelbel. This catagory includes nature music and environmental sounds.

**3. Popular Music** - (this is for break time or high activity) include a variety of upbeat popular music that has both an active, fun beat to it and has positive lyrics. You'll really need to be selective, picking the music more by individual case, than by an artist. Examples of upbeat positive music for adults include "I'm So Excited" by Pointer Sisters or "We are Family" by Sister Sledge. There's hundreds of these selections from Elvis to Nat King Cole. For an older group you can play older music and the audience will still relate to it.

Remember that if you're teaching adolescents, none of your audience was born BEFORE 1980, so be careful of the age of your music selections. Music from the 60's, 70's and early 80's may be thought of as outdated unless a particular song is a classic.

**4. For Background Music** - Use primarily baroque, (naturally, this include Bach, Corelli, Tartini, Vivaldi, Alinoni, Handel, Fausch and Pachelbel). Use "Four Seasons" by Vivaldi, "Brandenburg Concertos" and "Water Music" by Handel. When selecting these (often found in the "bargain bins"), make sure most of the compositions are played in the major (upbeat) key and done by a full orchestra (not two violins).

**5. Upbeat Popular Instrumentals** -these are for Stretch Breaks or even a welcome back to the room - Use exciting, fun or adventurous tunes such as movie themes (if you do, tailor them to your audience's age) or TV show themes. For a college audience, try the "Top Gun" anthem and "Beverly Hills Cop Theme Axel F" by Harold Faltermeyer. Try "Miami Vice" theme by Jan Hammer, the "Love Theme" from St. Elmo's Fire by David Foster and "Somebody's Watching Me" by Rockwell. For younger students, ask them what is popular. For your older audience, try themes from "Star Wars," "Raiders of the Lost Ark" by John Williams, "O-Bla-Di-O-Bla-Da" by the Beatles and "Hooked on Classics."

**6. Special Effects** - Use these for those moments when you need a song that says it all. Try the themes from "Twilight Zone," "Mission Impossible," "Rocky" by Bill Conti, TV Cartoon themes, "Chariots of Fire" by Vangelis, "Eye of the Tiger" by Survivor, "Break on Through" by the Doors, "Mickey's Monkey" by Smokey Robinson & the Miracles, "The Curly Shuffle" by Jump'n Saddle. You can set the tone of hurry up, slow down, have fun, get confident, etc. You can also use the more standard special effects such as trumpet fanfare, applause and others.

What and when you tell your audience that you use music as a part of your presentation depends on the length of time with your audience and extent of the relationship you have with them. In general, and especially for shorter presentations, let the audience know right away why you are using music. With more long-term audiences, you can tell them as their curiosity grows.

# Gentle and Delicate

Be careful of the gradient of expectations in your audience. With some audiences, you might be able to start off very strong. With other more sensitive groups, start slower and build up. In other words, do some research on your audience ahead of time. And above all, whatever you start out with, be congruent and positive about it.

In general, turn up volume slowly and turn it down slowly when you use it. This makes it easier on the ear - it's just like the eye's sensitivity to lighting - do it gradually. The exception is after a final good-bye or "let it go" when there's been no music on beforehand, start the music volume up high because it matches the high volume of the group's vocal completion crescendo.

## Be Flexible

In general, your audience will love music. Experiment, try recording you own. You are a pioneer in this field. Use music with purpose. Allow for quiet times for your students to breath …avoid saturation…the effects of music are far more powerful when the freshness and newness of it is retained. Avoid rigidity with it. Be flexible, listen to your students. For example, many folk tunes and jazz pieces make a perfect compliment to the classroom.

If students want to bring their own tapes, make two requirements. First, that you can preview the tape to insure that it fits in with the messages and values that are consistent with your course. Secondly, that you decide the timing of when and how to use it. In general, avoid heavy metal music - but appreciate the contributor and ask for other choices. Sometimes they'll have a second choice. The key is to stay in relationship with your students - use music as a bridge, not as a way to emphasize differences in taste. And finally, have fun with it. Music is a real joy, make sure that you are saying that with all your self-expression as well as having it be in the music you play.

## Music Player Options

Right now, you have three choices. Each has their advantages and disadvantages. Here are some of each:

> **CD player with standard discs**
> clarity of sound/remote control option
> more music storage in less space, recordable discs
> more expensive/less portable
> **2) Audiocassette player**
> ease in creating your own recordings
> lower costs/tapes that break & mangle
> greater availability
> **CD ROM with computer keyboard**
> ultimate in convenience
> lack of available music
> more expensive/less portable

## Suggestions Before Purchasing

**CD Player purchases:**
If you can afford it, get one that can take several discs at a time. Get a remote control. Get only the features you actually need. Think small for the player. Detachable speakers are ideal or at least good quality ones. Otherwise you defeat the purpose of getting the great quality of CD sound. The new decks let you record music on to a blank CD.

**Cassette Tape Player Purchases:**
Get a dual deck player. It gives you much more flexibility during your trainings. The "high speed dubbing" and "quick cue" are both important. Detachable speakers are ideal or at least good quality ones. Turn them up high in the store and listen carefully to them before purchasing.

**CD ROM w/ Computer Keyboard Purchases:** Make sure you buy it for the other things besides just the music. Get the one with the most power you can afford. Check the used market--you may find a great bargain. Ask around among "Tekkies" (those who are in the know about computers and ROM music) before you purchase so that you become an educated consumer.

## Duplication for Audiotapes

For most of your music, use 10 minute to 30 minute custom-bought tapes. These are tough to find at a regular music store or department store. Radio Shack has the 30 minute ones, but these are of low-grade quality. Look in your local yellow pages under the category of "Tape duplicating," "Recording" or "Music Production." There are usually several companies in town which do tape cassette duplicating for their business. You make duplicates of every tape and keep your originals at home. Buy a box of cassette labels from either a duplication place or from a good office supply. Print or type on each label the exact content. Label the general type of music on the tape. Color code them so they are easy for you to find in a hurry. For example, you might do it this way:

*Green label* tapes are for relaxing... new age, slow Baroque, etc.
*Red label* means fast, upbeat, movement... popular songs, upbeat jazz, etc.
*Blue label* means background... Baroque in Adagio, ocean waves, etc.
*Yellow label* for specialty music... special effect, trumpet, dance, clock, etc.

In addition to color-coding, I also will draw a simple symbol or tape a picture from a magazine to the cassette so that I can identify that particular tape from several feet or even yards away. In a hurry, I often need to locate a certain piece of music very quickly and having a "right-brain" visual, draws attention to the tape quicker. Label each of them with your name, phone number and address, as well.

## People Suggestions

Set the rules about who touches your music system and your tapes or CDs. Be persistent in your rules, your selection of music and others will respect your choices. **If someone complains:** Your volume may be too high, so turn it down. The complainer may be an auditory learner. You'll need to change their seat position in the room farther away from the tape player. Be respectful to the entire audience.

They may simply need time to adjust (3-10 exposures to the music over a few days.)It's possible you'll get complaints about the volume of the music. If you do, then (while that person is watching) go over to the music and turn it down just a bit. Thank them for their input. This is your cue to do a couple of things. First, make sure that you explain, sometime soon, more about music - why you use it and how it can assist learning. Then, make sure you have everyone switch seats soon, too. The complainer may have been sitting too close to it or may be especially sensitive.

Or, they may not understand the reasoning behind using music or even that particular piece. Do you know the logic? Have you explained it to your audience? How is your rapport with the group? If your rapport is low, you'll get more complaints. If your rapport is great, you'll get fewer complaints. Sounds like building rapport is pretty important, isn't it?

Remember that when someone complains, they may simply be a chronic complainer so that no matter what you or anyone else does, they'll complain. Just start right in on them, too. Build rapport every minute you have. I've worked on that and never had a serious problem with using music. In other words, everyone who has complained to me in my workshops has eventually dropped the complaint.

## Strategies for Playing Music

Research by musicologist Don Campbell says that the right ear is better for more logical information and the left ear is more for feelings, emotions and pleasure. That means that the ideal in your teaching or training is to situate yourself to talk more often on the left side (seen as you face the audience) for your talking and play music on the right side of the audience. Now that can create a dilemma: how do you attend to your music system if it's on the opposite side of the room?

One possibility is to have detachable speakers and have the actual system with you on the student's right side... but the speakers on the other side. Or, use a remote control with a CD player. Or, plan your musical selections far ahead so that you have a few seconds of lead time to walk to the other side of the room. Or, you can simply relax about the whole thing and do it the way you want to do it.

The first time you have a chance, you might find it beneficial to educate your audience to why you use music. I usually am very brief and say something like, "You've all noticed that music is a part of this learning experience. Both my experience and research says that it helps concentration, enjoyment and learning. We'll talk more about it later on."

Be positive and receptive of other's concerns. The music has to work for both you and the audience or it isn't working at all. Allow for diversity of music for all from the choices listed below. Use primarily your choices, remembering your favorite type of music may not be the audience's favorite. Respect your audience values as well as your own. Think of visual, auditory, kinesthetic and multi-cultures in your music selections.

## Making the Right Music Choices

Your primary decision about which music to use is answered by asking this question: "What is the 'state' of the learner I wish to evoke?" Since music affects the state of the audience you should always be asking the critical teaching question: "What is my target state for the audience and what state are they in now?" Music can be the gap-bridger.

How it can be done might be with lyrics, but you will primarily be evoking the state you want through *type of music, volume and beats per minute* (BPM.) Type of music means Classical, Jazz, Marches, Rock-n-Roll, Baroque, New Age, Romantic, Big Band, etc. Volume is important because the same composition can either be low-key background or pulse-quickening lead music. The beats per minute provide the pacing:

> **Low beats per minute = 40-60 (Relaxation)**
> **Moderate = 60-70 (Alert)**
> **High = 70-120 (Active)**

Choose music carefully based on the state you want to achieve among your participants.

211

## Tape Tips
dual-deck
duplicates
duplicates
10-30min.
students help
preview 1st
cue during activities

## User Tips
educate 1st
sound sensitive
firm rules
stay in rapport
ask insider
be patient
write out words

**MUSIC**

## Choices for Selection
Baroque (1600-1750)
Classical (1750-1820)
Romantic (1820-1900)
Traditional/New Amer. (1900-30)
Swing/Big band (1930-50)
Jazz (1920+)
Show tunes & movie themes (1930+)
Rock'nRoll (1955+)
Pop music (1965+)
Relaxation-New Age (1975+)
Special Effects

## Learn about
beats per minute
40-55 = Slow
  adagio, largo
55-70 = Moderate
  adante
70-140 = Fast
  allegro
Moods are critical:
  major=upbeat
  minor=somber
Symphony=4 mvmnts
Concerto= 3 mvmnts
Overture= 1 mvmnt

# Types of Music to Use:

**Pre-Renaissance (before 1600 A.D.)**
This era ranges from the early Christian music and through the middle ages, Romanesque and Gothic up to the Renaissance. The bulk of this music was either minstrels with very few instruments (usually flutes, tambourines, percussion, bells) or Gregorian chants. For centuries, African and Asian tribal music was made with a variety of percussion, bells and wind instruments.

This music is available in the specialty section of some of the more complete music stores. Several teachers have reported successful uses of chants as a calming tool for elementary children.

**Baroque (Composed 1600-1750)**
Composers include: Vivaldi, Bach, Handel, Telemann and Correlli. Music of this era was simple, ornamental and regal. Best used for background, harmony & restful alertness. It is characterized by balance, unity and counterpoint. The music was all written by "house musicians," those who were permanently employed by a church, court, council or opera house. These composers wrote for specific occasions and the music usually glorified God, the king or the particular event.

**Classical (Composed 1750-1820)**
Composers include: Mozart, Hayden, Rossini and Beethoven. The music of this era was full of energy, surprises and contrast. Classical music hatched the modern orchestra, the symphony, themes and motives, the sonata, the concerto and the overture. It's great for creativity background, storytelling and lectures. The composers were usually supported by a patron who financed them in exchange for the publicity, ego gratification and primary access to the compositions.

**Romantic (Composed 1820-1900)**
Composers include: Shubert, Tchaikovsky, Chopin, Wagner, Verdi, Dvorak, Rimsky-Korsakov, Debussy and Brahms. Music of this era is characterized by passion, suspense, wonder, impulse, ecstasy and depth. Expect it to evoke a sense of freedom with connotations of the fictitious, far off, legendary, fantastic or surreal. You've heard a great deal of Romantic music as the background for movie themes and Disney animations. The music can set the stage for emotions, clear out anger, arouse interest and curiosity. It can announce an arrival, help us to fall in love, evoke rage, depression or backdrop a chase scene. Truly a flexible and powerful choice for the learner. Experiment a lot and you'll find gems.

**Post-Romantic & Early American (1890-1920)**
Composers include: John Phillips Sousa, George Gershwin, Maurice Ravel, Scott Joplin, Strauss. These composers stood on the shoulders of the giants of the past to create whole new music forms. The great marches, ragtime and sweeping waltzes all came out of this explosive era for music. These selections can be some of the most useful for teaching and learning. The music evokes grandeur, emotion, humor and excitement.

**Big Band (Composed 1930-1955)**
Composers include: Glen Miller, Dave Brubeck, Les Brown, Stan Kenton. The music was written for live audience performances as dance music for the "swing" dance step. It's fun, upbeat and happy. It can be used with groups as break or recess music, or for background during team projects.

**Traditional Jazz (Composed 1920-1960)**
Composers include: Dizzy Gillespie, Count Basie, Claude Bolling and Louis Armstrong. The innovator who transitioned jazz from the older style to the newer was the legendary Miles Davis. Jazz, like other forms of music, was written as both a personal statement and a story to tell. Early jazz could be danced to or listened to at clubs, which became the most popular. Use for upbeat movement, activity and teamwork.

**Modern/Popular Jazz (Composed 1960-present)**
Composers include: George Benson, David Sanborn, Miles Davis, Oscar Peterson, Wynston Marsallis, Kenny G, Richard Elliot, Grover Washington, Tom Scott, Chick Corea, Joe Sample, Spyro Gyra. Written as artists creative expression. Written primarily to listen to (vs. dance music)

**Modern Popular Music (1955-present)**
The Nashville sound, The Philadelphia beat, the California sound, Country-Western, Motown, New Wave, Pop Rock, Soft rock, (I'll omit heavy metal), Gospel and Rap. Good music to use from this era are the ones used for popular movie soundtracks.

**New Age/Earth-Environmental Music (1975-present)**
Composers include: George Winston, Paul Lanz, Dave Grusin, John Klemmer, Steve Halpern, Ray Lynch, Paul Winter, Vangelis, Kitaro, etc. Best for relaxation, uplifting, creativity, meditation, concentration or focus.

**Special Effects (1950-present)**
Disney soundtracks, Olympics, Movie, TV and Cartoon themes. These are best for fun, activity, suspense and celebration. Use the Turning Point special effects tape for these effects or build your own library of off-the-wall sounds.

# When To Use Music

Use music **30% or less** of your total class time to avoid saturation. Use in the following situations:

**Background music during presentation** (low volume)
*Four Seasons* by Vivaldi, *Water Music* by Handel, *Brandenberg Concertos* by Bach

**Brainstorming, creative problem-solving mind-set**
*Piano Concerto #5* by Beethoven, *Etudes* by Chopin, *Claire de Lune* by Debussy, *Piano Concerto #26 & 27* Mozart, *Swan Lake* by Tchaikovsky

**Calming Music (see also relaxation music)**
*Amazing Grace* (traditional spiritual song) Classical guitar composers, piano music, *Claire de Lune* by Debussy, *Trois Gymnopedies* by Eric Satie

**Celebration of something positive, successes, wins**
*Celebrate* by Three Dog Night, *Celebrate* by Madonna, *Grand March* from *Aida* by Verdi, *The Creation & The Seasons* by Haydn, *Celebration* by Kool & the Gang, *Halellujah Chorus* from *"Messiah"* by Handel

**Closing ritual song (for a positive ending each day)**
*What A Wonderful World* by Louis Armstrong, *Happy Days* theme on Vol. #3 of *TV Themes* by Steven Gottleib, *Happy Trails* by Roy Rogers on Vol. #1 of *TV Themes* by Steven Gottleib

**Special introduction of a student, guest speaker**
*Fanfare for the Common Man* by Arron Copeland, *Rocky Theme* by Bill Conti, *Olympics Theme-1984 Summer Games, Star Wars & Raiders of Lost Ark* on *Best of John Williams, We Will Rock You ("We are the Champions")* by Queen

**Mindset for thinking of new ideas, units, subjects**
*Thus Sprake Zarathrustra* (2001 Theme), *Blue Danube* by Strauss, *Fantasia* by Disney, *Suites for Orchestra* by Bach, *Toy Symphonies* by Haydn, *Musical Joke* by Mozart, *Desert Vision & Natural States* by Lanz & Speer, *Silk Road* by Kitaro

**Group singing, games, pop songs, traditionals**
*Snow White, Songs of the South, Bambi, Dumbo, Winnie the Pooh, Mary Poppins* on *Disney Soundtracks* (Vol.#1,2,3) Hap Palmer Songs

**Start, openings - everyday psych-up, beginnings**
Epic Movie Soundtracks: *Chariots of Fire, Superman, E.T., Rocky, Lawerence of Arabia, Born Free, Dr. Zhivago.* "Oh! What a Beautiful Morning" from *Oklahoma.* All of the *James Bond 007* soundtracks, the theme from *The Mission*, Ravel's *Bolero, Well-Tempered Clavier, Prelude in D Major* by Bach, "Amanda Panda" song from *Saving the Wildlife* by Mannheim Steamroller or the *Hungarian Dances* by Brahms. Most tracks by Yanni.

**Specialty situations, Special Effects for danger, fear, fun, laughter**
*Jaws, Mission Impossible*, Comedians (Wright, Leno), Clocks, Bells, Drum Roll, Screams, *Twilight Zone, Flintstones*, Hi-Ho, "Zip-a-dee-do-dah..." create your own, buy a special effects tape from Turning Point or have students in class be responsible for different sounds and you call on them.

**Storytelling, concert readings & metaphors**
Classical artists: Beethoven, Mozart, Haydn, *Neverland* by Suzanne Cianni
Romantic music...Wagner, Dvorak, Rimsky-Korsakov

**Slow Stretching, deep breathing, relaxation**
*Summer, Autumn, Spring & Winter* by George Winston, *Silk Road* by Kitaro, *Barefoot Ballet* by John Klemmer, Michael Jones on Piano

**Test-time & quizzes/create alert, low-stress state**
Use same Baroque music used during original presentation of content or soft piano or violin concertos (with orchestras, not a solo)

**Transition Time or "mass movement"**
(activities like stretch breaks, cross-laterals, energy-builders, switch seats, etc.)
*Hooked on Classics* by Philadelphia Harmonics, *1812 Overture* by Tchaikovsky, *William Tell Overture* by Rossini, Theme from *Rawhide, Peanuts Theme* by Giraldi or Benoit

**Visualization, Relaxation & Imagery**
All recordings by Daniel Kobialka, *SeaPeace* by Georgia Kelly, most by the artist Kitaro. *Summer, Autumn, Spring & Winter* by George Winston, Steven Halpern's music

**Writing, pre-writing, get ideas, emotions flowing**
Theme from *Exodus* by Handel, *Nocturnes* by Chopin, *Peter & the Wolf* by Prokofiev, *The Egmont Overture* by Beethoven, Environmental Music: birds, flute, waterfalls

# Concert Readings

What are concert readings? A concert reading is the purposeful use of music in teaching or training, with planned content interplay creating an effect like a sound track for a movie, play or an opera. Why do they work? Lozanov found that well-delivered concerts can open gateways to learning, reach the subconscious, create better understanding of subject matter, activate long-term memory and reduce overall learning time. How? There are three types of concert readings in accelerated learning:

**A. Decoding:** the initial globalization. Short, light & fun, using intriguing, attention-getting music... can also be done as a chorus, parable, chant, or poem. It builds confidence and anticipation. These are done at the beginning of a new session when a fresh topic is introduced...length 3-7 minutes... use dramatic, light or bizarre music to inspire

**B. Active Concerts:** detailed material, dramatic presentation, using classical or romantic selectionssuch as Beethoven or Haydn; eyes open, places new material in context, metaphors... could be reading of plays, scripts, dialogue or text... can be used in the middle or next to last part of session... generally once every 5-10 hours of learning time... these are done for 5-15 minutes... let music play for 10-30 seconds first...never compete with the music... "sound surfing" means you use the musical pauses - go silent during the louder, more active parts, then pick up pace again

**C. Passive Review:** the low-key review of key points... it may use the exact material used for an active concert... but using baroque selections in a relaxed way, students are relaxed, with eyes closed... these are done for 5-8 minutes at the end of a session

## Presenting the Active Concert

**1. Content.** Make sure that you know your content well and are comfortable with the meaning of it. Tell the students what you'll be covering; give them a short preview of the material verbally. Do this even when you are using handouts of the material.

**2. Music.** Make sure that you have listened to your music many times so that you know it well. How long does the introductory movement last? When does it go up and back down again in volume? How about the pacing and tempo? Know your music well.

**3. Create the environment.** You may want to change the lighting a bit. Have the learners stand and stretch, do some deep breathing. Give positive suggestions of expectancy. Allow students to sit comfortably.

**4. Credibility.** Stand with authority. Announce the name of the musical selection; the composer and specific piece. This will prevent some listeners from being distracted during your reading trying to figure out which composer and selection it is.

**5. Volume.** Make the volume loud enough to fill in the non-speaking parts and quiet enough so that you can talk during the "down" times.

**6. Pause.** Get the attention of the audience. Create anticipation. Wait until the introductory movement of the selection is over before you begin (usually it's from 5-35 seconds into the piece).

**7. Be Dramatic.** Make large movements and gesture to emphasize key points. Think of yourself as a Shakespearean performer and enjoy making a show. Finish with a dramatic statement or final closing remark.

**Experiment!** Doing concert readings is a great way to have fun, be creative and embed some powerful learning. Repetition is the secret to comfort. And with comfort, you get confidence and competency.

# How to Get Started

Start with just one tape or music selection. I recommend a Baroque selection, maybe Handel's *Water Music* or Vivaldi's *Four Seasons*. Get used to using it. Make your mistakes on it. Have your successes with it. Learn when to use it. Just one tape will keep your stress levels low.

When you're comfortable and competent with that one tape, add another. Use that for awhile until you're comfortable with it, too. Over time, you'll be able to build up your selections until you can bring many of them to your place of work. I typically bring 24 tapes (over 200 selections) for a workshop. Over time, you'll get used to using all of them and have a really great time. And your students will, too! Take risks and have fun!

---

| *Additional Resources for Further Study and Follow Up* |
|---|

*Brain-Based Learning & Teaching* by Jensen *
*Special Effects for the Classrom* by Jensen *
*The Lind Lists* by Lind Institute of San Francisco
*Accelerated Learning with Music: The Trainers Manual* by Webb and Webb*
*Six Concerts: Music to Learn* (audio tapes) by Terry and Doug Webb*


* These are available in the Appendix.

# 17

## Teams & Cooperative Groups

### Learning Can Be Noisy

The old way of teaching was simple. The teacher stands in front of the room and teaches. The students sat in rows, lined up, quiet and obedient. Those days are gone in classrooms where learning is really going on. Today's classroom is busy, interactive, flexible and the learners may be up front as much as the teacher. Why the change? Two reasons: first, we now know more about the brain and learning, so we know the advantages of interactive learning. The old model of stand and deliver is dead. Second, we now use a greater diversity of learning styles and intelligences to reach a wider range of cultures. More people learn that way.

Teams and cooperative learning are two different things. A cooperative group can have common characteristics with a team. A team can also work cooperatively. Still, they are definitively different and should be used for different purposes.

### What is Cooperative Learning?

Let's define each of the two options more explicitly. Cooperative learning is an active learning process in which academic and social skills are fostered through face-to-face student interaction, individual accountability and positive interdependence.

It is very different from the other two types of group structure; competitive and individual. The most common group structure that teachers use is competitive. Nothing's wrong with it - it's a competitive world. But use it for 10-20% of your time, not more. This is where a teacher says, "We are having team competition for the class best." This structure is clearly win/lose. Basically, it's a system or structure built on scarcity of goods. "There's only so many A's, so many prizes, so many goodies, and if you're the best, you get it." The other, individual structure, is a case where there may be no scarcity of goodies, but you are on your own, sink or swim. No one helps each other out or shares knowledge and skills.

There is a big difference between cooperative learning and teamwork. Cooperative groups may work as a team. And teams may cooperate. But in cooperative learning, part of the explicit team experience is to learn collaborative skills, whereas usually a team is designed to produce an event or artifact.

219

**Who it is for:** It can be used and is being used at all grade levels from K-12 through college. It also works with all ability levels. In the past, it seemed to make the most sense for kids in grades 3-6, because of the particular stage of social development they are at while in those grades. Now, there are so many creative derivations of it that many teachers are finding it powerful for grades 7-12 as well.

**When to use it:** It is ideal to use when introducing skills which are challenging, have more than one right answer, are intrinsically rewarding, allow all students to contribute and involve many senses. Examples include research, spelling, writing, math problems, literature, language, science, reading discussion or special projects, etc.

**Why use it?:** The benefits include higher student achievement, mainstreaming special education students, improved social skills, increased cultural awareness and peer acceptance, a greater sense of belonging, a boost of self-esteem and greater responsibility. It's tough to find a disadvantage to it!

# Key Background

It's MUCH more than just "group work." The following 5 components need to be present for it to work its "magic." Make sure you use all of them.

1) **Positive interdependence...** kids have to depend on each other in order to succeed. A good way to do this is through a limited supply of materials, one "set" per team.

2) **Face-to-face interaction...** kids have to see each other and be facing each other close up to have the social accountability to make it work...put kids in groups of three and have chairs face each other.

3) **Individual accountability...** the best way to do it is to give students roles and responsibilities... have a recorder who takes down the actions of the group, an encourager who supports and makes encouraging statements, a timekeeper who has either a sweep-second or digital watch and a checker who makes sure that everyone is on task and handles the supplies - getting and putting the materials back.

4) **Use of collaborative skills...** these are the backbone of cooperative learning and there are different ones you'd want the kids to work on depending on whether they are in lower or upper grades and how their incoming collaborative skills are.

> **Grades K-5:**
> Stay in seat, use names, encourage, look at others, share feelings, keep things calm, keep voices low, say "please" and "thank you", repeat what has been said, stay on task, ask questions, give ideas

> **Grades 6-12:**
> Paraphrase, listen for feelings, listen to learn, show appreciation, direct eye contact, share feelings, disagree in positive way, check for other's understanding of the work, give and hear opinions, evaluate

**5) Group processing**... this skill is the understanding and true learning experience of the day. At the end of each lesson, students will make consensus statements on "What I learned... and how I felt..."

**Preparation:**
A.  First do a lesson plan with clear objectives...make sure you know what you want to get out of it - what you want to see, hear and experience.
B.  Carefully engineer the appropriate groups - make them heterogeneous... group with a diversity of ability, gender and any other differences. Also, if you have any kids who you know will fight, separate them initially. As your groups mature, later on in the year you can put them together to heal the wounds.
C.  Begin small - use easy/familiar/non-content chunks... make your collaborative objective simple and create some early "wins."

---
### The Ten-Step Process:
---

1)  Context: state objectives clearly for the lesson...create an anticipatory set.
2)  Task Explanation: tell them exactly how to do the task that you are requiring them to do... give simple, clear instructions, both auditory and visual, (kinesthetic if needed).
3)  The "Moment": check for questions...get them thinking...ask them..."If you did have a question, what might it be...?"
4)  Introduce Collaborative Focus: introduce social skills to be learned or reinforced. Be sure to model them...what does it look like, sound like, have kids practice for a few seconds with their group... go multi-sensory for review... also be sure to set up the rules and roles in the group... who is the recorder, the encourager, etc.? Answer any last minute questions.
5)  Students Begin Work: set it all in motion with minimal intervention on your part... just positive strokes.
6)  Group Processes Statements: formulate statements within the group for creating and sharing of both academic and social skills.
7)  Students Share Academic and Social skills: the statements you want them to share start with "I felt..." and "I learned...."
8)  Teacher Shares Academic and Collaborative Observations... tell the kids what you saw, felt and heard.
9)  Closure and Completion: sharing and check for group and individual accountability... who participated, who did their assigned job, etc?
10) Celebration: student celebration... have them go around and give high fives or other acknowledgments with fanfare. Make it like a party, lots of fun for one-half to one minute. Then, have them set new goals for next time.

# How To Create & Manage
# High Performance Teams

If it's not right for you to use cooperative learning (especially good for K-6), it may be right for you to use teams. Here's how to make teams work like magic. Before you start with the notion of building teams, we're going to presuppose that you already assessed the need and the cooperation level of the appropriate audience and it is, indeed, appropriate to continue.

In general, teams are used differently than cooperative learning groups. Teams are good for about 4-6 weeks. It takes about 1-2 weeks to learn to work as a team, then by the last week, they get bored with each other. The best time of the year to use teams are:

- Weeks 2-6 of the school term... it helps establish cooperation and reinforce the other values that you create
- When there is a particular project that demands teamwork and high productivity
- The last 2-4 weeks of the year when you want tighter focus and cohesion There are 10 steps to doing them right, so let's get started.

## #1. Engineer the team composition carefully.

There are many choices on how to select teams: randomly (count off, names in a hat, etc.), by learning style (go for diversity such as mixing visuals, auditories, etc.), by months of the year (creates an astrological mix), by participants picking their favorite other team players, by age (diversity is key), by past performance levels (careful!), by common themes at work or school (all interested in this topic), by games (close eyes, make barnyard sound and find like animals), etc.

There's no right or wrong way to do this one, so you'll have to take in this information and make some judgment calls. If you have a specific "relationship" problem to solve or a "problem person" that you are trying to "fix" by grouping in teams, be willing to accept whatever happens. That person could figure out what you're doing and get resentful and become a saboteur. Team size is ideal at 5, either 4-6 can work well. Never have a team of over 7--break into sub-groups.

## #2. Allow team members to know each other better

Teams are not a team until the bonding and magic of synergy occurs. Otherwise, they're simply a grouping of people. Getting to know each other is critical. Some allow this process to happen naturally over time, as it does in some schools or businesses. Personally, I never trust the intimacy process to occur naturally. People have too many things to do and rarely share the things that truly matter with another person unless you formalize the process and give them time.

Here are some simple activities you can do in a team to insure that they all know each other. Before you start any of these, make sure that the group has a timekeeper and knows the signals to give to the rest of colleagues. Make sure that you have coached other team members on how to be a good listener and the appropriate body language to give the speaker. Tell them that there are no questions allowed or comments during the sharing process time. It's just for the speaker.

After everyone is done, they can ask other questions and quiz each other or share war stories. Questions for your team members to share the answers with are the following: 90" biography ( no work-related information, only family, school, hobbies, taste, etc.); what are the most important things that have been going on in your life during the last 7 days; who was the most influential person in you life and why and how is your life different; what is it that you are most excited, happy or committed about; or, what is it that if you knew it would help you understand better why I am the way I am? There are a lot more possibilities, but the point is to get members to talk about something that creates some closeness, that requires some moderate risk without making it too uncomfortable? You know your audience, so use your judgment.

222

### #3. Get team leaders

The team leader is always self-chosen, never appointed. The question to put out to the group before choosing is "who is willing to be most committed to the success of the team?" then let each person go around the circle, and share why they do or don't want to be the team leader, with no prompting from others. If two people want to be a team leader, rotate. One does it for one month, and one does it for the next month or whatever. If no one wants to be the leader, tell the teams more of what is involved in being a leader and how it's an opportunity to grow, demonstrate leadership, impact others, make a difference, etc. Usually, there's no problem.

### #4. Develop team spirit

Team spirit can be developed lots of ways. You'll want to choose the ways that are most appropriate for your group's age and context. With any or all of these ideas, give the teams a time limit for each. Ask the team to pick a team name (90"), Have them create a wild cheer (4 min.). Have them come up with a choreographed skit with the cheer (6 min.). Have them create a special gesture and saying for their team (3 min.). Have them do up a logo or coat of arms (12 min.). Have the team read a poem together or solve a problem together or lean an activity together. Use your imagination for even more ideas. It's critical to allow and encourage wild celebrations and noise. If you suppress it at the start, it'll disappear fast.

### #5. Identify team goals

Teams need a way to know if they are doing an effective job as a team. Ask them to set goals for the time that you'll have them in teams. Goals need to be positive, specific, measurable and ones that the whole team can get excited about. Then have the leader announce the goals to the rest of the larger group so their teams can be inspired and challenged. Make sure the goals are specific, positive and measurable. After they are announced, make them public.

### #6. Establish relationships

The relationships on the team largely determine the likelihood of success. Make sure that each of the team members verbally and specifically tell the team leader that they are willing to be led by the leader and the leader must tell the members that he or she is willing to serve as leader and that he or she is committed to the success of the team, no matter what. A big key to relationships is that every person on the team feel listened to and feel encouraged to participate. If just a couple of members are dominating the team, resentment will eventually set in and the team effectiveness will diminish. Also make sure that you develop a positive relationship with the team leaders since they are the ones you'll meet with the most often. They are your leverage, your ticket to managing the teams.

### #7. Create a management system

The management system I prefer most is a self-assessment, a team scorecard. A sample team scorecard is included below...one for students and one for adults. Use a scale of 1-10 for measuring most of the things on the chart. Ten minutes before the end of the session, allow the teams to meet and let the team leader collect feedback on their performance. Some items will be obvious like attendance - what % of the team was here for this week? Others like "contribution to group" are subjective - on a scale of 1-10 if 1 is sleeping and 10 is so many contributions that the teacher or trainer has to ask them to restrain themselves, what level were we at? I discourage 10s because there's no room to grow and a 10 is supposed to be the ultimate achievement. But, obviously, they can have a ten if they feel they deserve it.

223

What kinds of things do you put on a chart for teams to use in assessing themselves? It depends on the grade-level. For K-3, use from 3-5 items. Suggestions include: on time, enthusiasm? courtesy, safety or new things learned. Your categories would change for older students. With high school-age learners, I use criteria like: contributions to group, participation on team, team spirit, goals reached, on time, participation or respect. List your team's self-assessment criteria in rows, from top to bottom. Off to the right, label each column, from left to right, with a date. Once a week, teams can have a short meeting and assess themselves. The charts are good for about 4-6 assessments, then it's time to take a break from them.

## Team Name:

|  | Week #1 | Week #2 | Week #3 | Week #4 |
|---|---|---|---|---|
| Team Spirit |  |  |  |  |
| Contributions to Class |  |  |  |  |
| On Time |  |  |  |  |
| Participation on Team |  |  |  |  |
| Task Completion |  |  |  |  |
| Creativity |  |  |  |  |
| Goals Reached |  |  |  |  |
| Cooperation & Respect |  |  |  |  |
| Average Score |  |  |  |  |

**#8. Discover personal or hidden agendas (elicit promises & requests)**
These are the actions that make the team move along, getting things done. Examples are promises of attendance, contribution, participation, support, etc. Requests are in the form of asking others for support such as, "I haven't been on time lately, could you notify me 30 minutes before our meeting?" The team leader will want to keep track of who is asking for what and who is promising what.

### #9. Create a public scorecard

Scorecards keep teams accountable and increase positive peer pressure. Even though each team has its own management system and scorecard for itself, you'll want a way to list all of the other teams on one major scorecard. At the bottom of each individual team chart is a place for a team average. That's the number that you'll put up on the composite chart of all teams. It's easy to see if the team is improving if it's numbers are going up. However, make sure that the items that you are measuring are the ones that accurately reflect the feelings and empirical evidence that the team is, indeed, being successful. Otherwise, the team will discount the growth and treat the scores like a joke.

Each time you measure the composite of all teams, you'll come up with an average of all the team averages. Let's say each team is measuring 9 items. Let's say their average score was 8.5. Then collect all the other team's scores, too. You may get a 7.4, a 6.8, a 9.3 and etc. Get an average so you can tell the whole group how all the teams are doing as well as chart the progress of each individual team. Peer pressure will keep scores honest.

Creating the scoring system is only useful if you're going to allow announcements by the team leaders of how they are doing, and the team cheers. Turn the scoring into a big celebration circus. If you downplay the scoring and remove the celebration process, you'll regret it and the teams will cease to perform up to par. Keep the energy high, use sound effects and enlist the other teams into wild cheering support at each team announcement. I promise you, the wild, unbridled energy you can create and sustain is the fundamental key to teams working on a long term basis. Any team can last for the short-term, the long-term requires emotions!

### #10. Relax and play together

Make sure that you allow your teams time, either structured or unstructured to relax and play together. Let them do a skit, juggle, play a game, a sport, go to an event, sing, go out to eat, to drink, to be on the same team, to do new games, etc. This allows the team a chance to lower their guard and really get to know each other better. Generally the more each of your team members know each other, the more they accept each other and will work together to succeed.

---

## *Additional Resources for Further Study and Follow up*

---

Call the Cooperative Learning Center (612) 373-5829
Read magazines like *Learning '90, Teacher, Creative Teacher*
Materials and Books: *Circles of Learning* by Johnson and Johnson
*Learning Together & Alone* by Johnson & Johnson (Prentice-Hall)
*Structuring Cooperative Learning* by Johnson and Johnson
*Cooperative Learning* by Slavin. (Prentice-Hall)

* These are available in the Appendix.

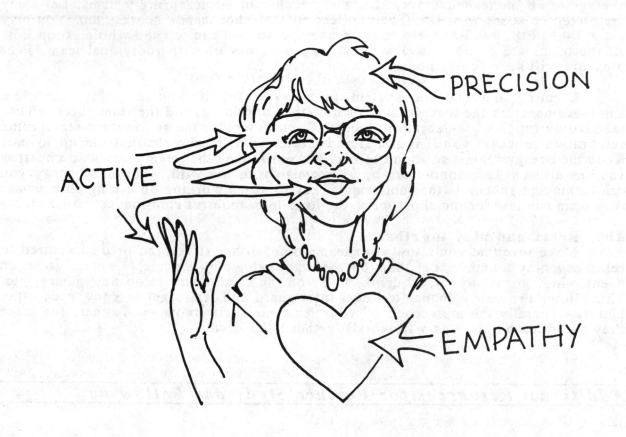

# 18

## Thinking & Intelligence

### Do You Create Intelligence?

We have all heard others describe certain learners as "sharp, advanced, smart, gifted or high." We've also heard other learners described as "unmotivated, low, dull, slow, disadvantaged or special education" kids. Is it really that easy? Is it really fair to slap on a classroom label because the learner doesn't perform a certain way? In order to talk about learning and intelligence, it's useful to know what it is. Dr. Robert Sternberg says, "Intelligence boils down to your ability to know your own strengths and weaknesses and to capitalize on the strengths while compensating for the weaknesses." He says that when we think of intelligence, we are really talking about our ability to react intuitively, creatively and constructively to a wide range of experiences. In other words, being "street smart" is just as, or more important than, being "book smart."

### What Role Do You Play in Learner Intelligence?

You play a vital role in the kind of intelligence your learners develop. How? First, existing intelligence can be nourished and brought out of hiding. Second, new intelligences, not previously demonstrated can be developed. Last, new attitudes about intelligence can encourage greater growth by the students. In short, you play a part in your learner's lifelong intelligence.

The old notion of a fixed intelligence is out of date. In fact, it's often done a great deal of damage to the learner - not just to their self-esteem, but to their entire life. If you believe you're intellectually inferior, you make limiting choices. Soon, your beliefs become a self-fulfilling prophecy. Do you think this sounds far-fetched? In 1971, Harvard professor Robert Rosenthal described experiments in which teachers expectations of student intelligence actually raised their IQ scores! How many times have we heard it? Plenty! The results from his landmark book, *Pygmalion in the Classroom* bear repeating:

1. Forming expectations is natural and unavoidable
2. Once formed, expectations tend to be self-sustaining; we communicate those expectations with subtle and powerful cues
3. We are more comfortable with people who meet our expectations and less comfortable with those who don't meet our expectations

Specifically, let's apply it to learning:

4. High expectations lead to higher performance
5. Better performance leads us to like the learner more
6. We treat those whom we like better and they learn more

You might be thinking, "I don't do those things, but I'm sure others do." Are you thinking you're too experienced or too sharp to avoid doing this? Think again. Every teacher communicates expectations in some way or another. Let's say there are two groups of learners in your class, those about whom you might develop low expectations and those about whom you might develop high expectations. We'll call them the "L" group and the "H" group, respectively. Which of the following do you do?

- Interrupt Ls more often than the Hs
- Give Ls less specific and less frequent feedback than Hs
- Praise Ls for marginal or poor responses
- Criticize Ls more frequently for poor behavior
- Give less wait time to Ls for responses
- Provide Ls with less academic support time than Hs
- Seat Hs closer to you, Ls further away
- Give Ls less challenging work

Where do all these low and high expectations about the learners come from? You'd be surprised. Most teachers think that they come from other teachers, class records, parents, socioeconomic background or observations. Nothing could be further from the truth! Teacher expectations come from within. The potential you perceive about your learners is directly proportional to your belief in yourself. How much do you believe that you can positively influence your learners? In short, the successful teachers, the ones with consistently higher expectations and results, did not get those expectations from outside. They generated those expectations based on their own skill and experience levels in bringing out the potential of their students.

*The secret to classroom success with all your learners is to treat every student as "gifted and talented"*

Why treat everyone as gifted? Howard Gardner, Harvard Graduate Professor of Education, concluded that there is not just one way to be smart, there are over 200 ways! Gardner researched the nature of intelligence and defined it as the ability to: 1) use a skill, 2) fashion an artifact, or 3) solve a problem in a way that is valued by the particular culture of that individual. In other words, a Wall Street stockbroker and an Australian Aborigine can both be considered highly intelligent... in their own culture. If they switched roles with each other, both would have a difficult time surviving (although I suspect the Aborigine might last longer).

Gardner grouped the array of human intelligences into just seven categories. He purposely included what some refer to as "abilities" because he wanted them to get the respect they deserve. Instead of having one single figure or mark that assesses our intelligence, he says that each of us has our own unique combination of these intelligences and that they can and do change over a lifetime.

# Multiple Intelligences

**Verbal-Linguistic** *Recognize by:* use of core operations of language. The learner is sensitive to the meaning, sound, inflection and order of words; loves language, reading and talking; has a good memory for dates & names; likes to tell stories, to listen to stories, and likes a variety of voices; remembers jokes and enjoys reading. *Ways to reach:* presentations, speeches, role-play, dialog, interactive games, writing, group work, reports, discussion, tapes and reading aloud - especially books with dialog.

**Intrapersonal** *Recognize by:* a student who enjoys solitude; likes thinking; is happy to work alone; has a good understanding of strengths and weaknesses and is good at goal-setting. The learner has the ability to develop successful working models of themselves and the ability to learn and develop new behaviors based on self-knowledge. *Ways to reach:* thinking strategies, imagery, journal writing, relaxation, self- discovery exercises, focus/concentration exercises, self-assessment, metacognition practice, reflection and time to be alone and process.

**Musical-Rhythmic** *Recognize by:* an appreciation of sounds; sensitivity to rhythm, pitch, timbre; making music or rhythm. The learner is constantly humming, tapping and singing. *Ways to reach:* allow for rhythm, give them a musical instrument (Kazoo, etc.) or let them make one, make fun sounds, learn with music, use background or environmental music, singing, piano and musical performances.

**Logical-Mathematical** *Recognize by:* strength in math & problem-solving skills. The learner has ability to discern logical or numerical patterns; ability to pursue extended lines of logic and reasoning; asks "why" and "how" questions, wants to reason things out, wants to know "what's coming up next" - sequential thinking. *Ways to reach:* computer time, writing applications, programs, objects to sort, classifying, gadgets to take apart or fix, magnets, math, science, reading, discussion, exploring, solving mysteries, word problems, breaking codes, museum trips, riddles, analyzing information, outlining, grouping and calculation activities.

**Spatial** *Recognize by:* a strong and active imagination; likes to design, draw, read graphics and posters; needs pictures to understand; likes puzzles, mazes; organizes space, objects and areas. This learner has the ability to mentally manipulate forms, objects or people in space or transfer them to other locations or into other elements. It's the capacity to recognize forms/shapes and how they relate and interact with another. It is also sensitivity to the balance and composition of shapes. *Ways to reach:* art, design, changing locations, stacking objects, putting pieces together, sports, large pieces of paper, trying things from a different angle, movement, mind-mapping, basketball, video, ice-skating, films, skateboarding, map making, charts, snowboarding, theater, wind-surfing, sculpture, surfing, rollerblading, drawing & painting.

**Interpersonal** *Recognize by:* strong people skills. The student has the ability to make distinctions among others in moods, feelings, biases, thoughts and values. It's the ability to act appropriately using knowledge of others. This learner loves to talk and influence, usually a group leader, or organizer; communicates well; good at conflict resolution, listening, negotiating & persuasion. *Ways to reach:* friendships, competition, interactive games, teams, pair up with partner, one-on-one discussion, peer teaching, group work, collaboration & empathy.

**Bodily-Kinesthetic** *Recognize by:* an ability to handle objects skillfully, either fine or gross motor movements; also the ability to control your own movements for function or expression; the desire to move; constant movement or commitment to comfort. The student wants to get up, move around, tap, touch, fiddle with and do things. *Ways to reach:* stretching, role play, Simon Sez games, new games, building models, demonstrations, changing seating, drama, exercise, body sculpture, crafts & hobbies, dancing, games & sporting events.

You can teach and assess in a whole new paradigm. Instead of the deficiency model "Is he or she smart or dumb?" You'll use the empowerment model: "In what ways is he or she smart?" It is more difficult to assess students using multiple intelligences, but much more rewarding and accurate. A student's profile can and will change; especially over the next ten years. Over an entire lifetime, there may be many changes in a person's intelligence profile, though probably none as dramatic as from ages 2-20.

Two areas of multiple intelligences for your immediate action are presentations and assessment. Use all seven intelligences in your instructional design. For assessment, make sure that your learners have choices on how to express their knowledge through varied assessments.

In a mathematics class, a learner who is average in mathematical-logical intelligence, but low in interpersonal or verbal-linguistic skills, may be poor at explaining or expressing what they know. Yet if they are strong in intrapersonal skills, they may be able to assess their own progress and troubleshoot for mistakes. If they are strong in spatial, they may be able to make a graphic of what they knows. And if they are strong in musical-rhythmic, they could express ideas with sound. Each of your students has a unique combination of intelligences and having one is unrelated to another. You could be high interpersonal and high intrapersonal, too. The power of this model is that the questions have now changed:

*"How smart are you?" is now irrelevant...*
*a more powerful new question is,*
*"HOW are you smart?"*

If you have decided you are going to test, it makes sense to test in ways that reflect the real learning going on. The old, out-dated notion of testing and intelligence is like a thermometer. In the old model, you were either smart and high up on the thermometer, or in the middle (average) or low (below average intelligence). In the old model, you were tested for primarily written and speaking (verbal-linguistic) or problem-solving ability (mathematical-logical). Many intelligent learners have been labeled stupid, average or slow because: 1) the presentation style of the teacher did not tap into all seven intelligences; or 2) the assessment was so narrow that it never allowed the learner to demonstrate what they really knew.

We now know that is a tremendous loss of talent and ability. We must teach and assess in the seven intelligences to reach all learners, not just give lip service to the concept of equality. In the chapter on presentation, you'll find many ways to use the seven multiple intelligences in your teaching. The chapter on assessment will give you many assessment strategies that fit the multiple intelligences model. With practice, it'll become automatic.

David Lazear, one of the pioneers in translating Gardner's Theory of Multiple Intelligences, talks about four levels in developing use of them. He's authored many helpful books on the subject including *Seven Ways of Teaching* and *Seven Pathways of Learning*. Each level, he says, takes Multiple Intelligences a step further and insures that they will become a productive part of the learning process.

**Level 1:** **Tacit Intelligence** ("I've always used the seven intelligences, I just never called them by that name."")

**Level 2:** **Aware Intelligence** ("Now that I have a name for them, I'm more conscious of when & how I use them.")

**Level 3:** **Strategic Intelligence** ("I know when and how to use each of them.")

**Level 4:** **Reflective Intelligence** ("They are an integrated part of my daily personal life, as well.")

You'll get what you develop. If you have so-called slow learners who find your content a bore, look in the mirror. Ask yourself, "How could I make this come alive with excitement, curiosity and challenge? How can I provide more feedback in a low stress, supportive environment?"

Other researchers such as Moore, Anderson and Wenger have verified that one of the best ways to boost thinking and intelligence is by describing your own perceptions and recording your own observations onto audio tape or CD. This examination of one's own thinking, sensing and organizing language, provides a powerful vehicle for the brain's development as a problem-solver and thinker. Intelligence is often the ability to bring together many diverse bits of information to create new thinking, to maximize potential and provoke solutions. The brain needs a large number of circuits and connections to make the best possible decisions. By providing more consistent, better quality feedback and tying it all together, the brain integrates the information into higher quality relationships and patterns.

Here are ways to increase the frequency and value of feedback. 1) Greet students at the door. 2) Comment about the previous learning. 3) Allow them to peer teach daily or weekly reviews. 4) Have them talk themselves through their thinking, out loud. 5) Learners keep score charts for their team and post the results. 6) Encourage the use of a journal. 7) Have them make up and take "mock tests" that don't count. 8) Have them pair up with other learners and prep for a test. 9) They correct their own homework, quizzes, tests. 10) Learners present to the group and get oral or written feedback.

# How To Understand Your Student's Thinking

When you or I say "I am thinking," what we are really saying is, "I'm trying to manipulate internal symbols in a meaningful way." Thinking is composed of accessing prior or creating new modal representations. All representations fall into these categories:

1. **Visual.** These include pictures, symbols, words or "internal movies."
2. **Sounds.** This includes voices, music, nature or technology.
3. **Feelings.** How you feel about something is part of the thinking and decision-making process; especially if you're a kinesthetic learner.
4. **Others:** It's certainly possible to think using other senses. Since they comprise such a small percentage of our thinking, we'll set them aside for the moment.

As we learned earlier, our mind, body and feelings are all an integral part of learning and processing. There is no separation. As a result of this, it will come as no surprise that HOW you are thinking can often be discerned by observations of your body. When we are tense or happy, we can say nothing and another can pick up all the needed clues. And, just like our body, our eyes provide some of the best thinking clues.

# Use Eye Movements For Thinking Clues

Our brain is designed so that our thinking style can often be determined by particular shifts in eye movements. Where your eyes are positioned better enables the brain to access certain senses. There are seven basic eye movements that related to thinking. These are useful for 90% of right-handed learners, and reversed for many (but not all) left-handers.

The best way to determine the particular eye (and thinking) pattern for a learner is to observe that person in a "real-life" no stress situation. The relationship between eye movements and cognitive functioning has been well documented. Cognitive activity occurring in one hemisphere *does* trigger eye movements in the opposite hemisphere. The information below is a useful generalization, but remember, each student is unique.

**1. Visual thinking of stored picture memories.** Looking up and to the left allows you to access stored pictures (visual recall). Questions you can use to verify are: "What car was parked next to yours in the parking lot?" "Describe your bedroom." "Walk me through the clothes in your closet."

**2. Visual thinking of created new pictures.** Looking up and to the right is where your eyes usually go to create new images. Questions you can use to verify are: "How would you look with a radically different haircut?" "What would you do to rearrange your living room?" "What would a dog look like with cat's legs?"

**3. Auditory thinking, recalling sounds.** Eyes go to the left; that's the usual way we accesses stored sounds (what was said or heard). Questions you can use to verify are: "What did the other person say, right at the end, of your last phone conversation?" "What's the 9th word of the 'Happy Birthday' song?" "When you were a kid, how did your mother call you when she was mad at you?"

**4. Auditory thinking, creating new sounds.** Eyes go off to the right, creating new sounds. Questions you can use to verify are: "How would a dog sound if it has a voice like a pig?" "What sound would you get if you heard a siren and a rooster at the same time?"

**5. Internal dialogue (talking to yourself).** Eye direction most common is looking down and to the left. When you see another walking down the street talking to him or herself, notice where their eyes are.

**6. Experiencing feelings.** This is down and to the right. If you know another person failed to complete a task, you can ask them, "Did you complete the task?" In many cases, before answering, their eyes will go down (meaning "I feel badly about it"), then go back up to continue the conversation.

**7. Digital, for memorized information.** Eyes will go straight ahead for this interaction. You are asked, "How are you?" Your polite answer is, "Fine, thank you." You probably kept your eyes straight ahead the whole time because you did not need to search for or rehearse the answer.

**Visual Mode
Creating Pictures**

**Visual Mode
Recalling Pictures**

**Auditory Mode
Creating Words**

**Auditory Mode
Remembering Words**

**Kinesthetic Mode
Experiencing Feelings**

**Auditory Mode
Talking to Yourself**

# How to Use Eye Accessing Cues
## To Promote Better Learning

You cannot use this information about eye accessing cues to determine if another person is telling the truth or lying. Experienced liars will rehearse their answer so much that they can say it without having to access or create the information on the spot. But you can use this information to help understand why many students underperform.

As an example, a student whose eyes are roving at test time may actually be searching within his or her brain for the answers. Eyes to the side mean he or she is trying to recall or construct sounds. Eyes up and to the side mean he or she trying to recall stored images (maybe a text, computer, chart, etc.) or is creating new images (assembling thoughts). It takes eye movement to get the internal information.

Students who have trouble spelling are very likely unaware of the value of putting their eyes in the appropriate positions. Here's an example of many possible success strategies:

1.  Start with their eyes looking down to access feelings
    Student should access a positive, prior feeling to start
2.  Eyes up and to the right to create a new image
    See the new word, in full or chunked down
    If learner is auditory, say the letters by looking to right
    If learner is kinesthetic, trace the letters with finger
3.  Eyes closed, looking to the left
    recall the stored image... if correct, then
4.  Eyes on paper, write out the correct spelling
    check your work, looking up to left
5.  If correct, look down and feel good, then celebrate
    if incorrect, chunk down the word, repeat correctly

Useful Ideas: The implications of the brain's eye accessing patterns are enormous. When students create posters, art projects or murals, the best placement is shoulder high or above for best recall. When you put student work up on the wall, put it low if you want them to access feelings, head high for discussion and overhead for storing the pictures.

When you present new material, stand to your learner's right (on the right side of the classroom from their point of view). When you review, stand on the left side (from their point of view). This simple strategy allows your learners to learn the information easier.

At test time, let students move their eyes around. A student who is constantly told... "Keep your eyes on your own paper," may actually be moving his eyes to get a picture or sound in his brain. It's bad to say to him or her "Keep your eyes on your own paper!" Usually, that accesses the "Bad dog" feelings, the eyes go down and they forget what they were thinking of. Ask students to spread out their desks so they have greater personal space at test time. This lowers your own stress about the possibility of cheating.

# The Importance of Thinking

Biologically, the brain learns to solve problems to advance survival chances. The best thing we can do, from the point of view of the brain and learning, is to teach our learners how to think. Thinking takes many, many, forms. These forms include:

- learning to gather information
- flexibility in form and style
- asking better quality questions
- the ability to weigh evidence
- understanding & creating metaphors and models
- strategies to conceptualize
- the ability to deal with novelty

What makes learning to think and thinking to learn complex is that there are so many different forms of thinking. Additional ones include:

- generating possible strategies
- discussion and brainstorming skills
- being effective at finding mistakes, discrepancies and illogic
- generating alternative approaches outside your usual domain
- strategies to test hypotheses
- generalizations: what can be said that is "in common" with all the parts
- thinking of new meanings for things

We don't know how easily or quickly thinking can be taught. We do know it is valuable and it can be taught. For example, you might want to offer these thinking skills:

- the ability to identify and organize information, values and events
- learning about something and learning to describe it objectively
- sequencing: figure out the logical or natural order of events
- problem-solution: assessing the apparent problems and potential solutions
- thematic/concepts maps: grouping, thematic information based on defining characteristics such as age, location, function, culture, value, etc.
- thinking for creativity: a twist, a turn or a new approach
- the ability to step outside your role or culture
- composing or creating new thinking

Sometimes the best way to teach thinking is to do thinking. That is, walk through your own thinking steps out loud so your learners can learn from you. You might want to teach the following steps:

- learning to "reframe" the problem so that it is not a problem
- learning to discover the source of the problem to prevent reoccurrence
- finding ways to deal with life's difficulties
- process/cause: discovering the flow/process and speculating on causes
- thinking about thinking (metacognition)
- altering your own styles of thinking
- applying your thinking skills to add value & joy to your own life
- application of thinking to enhance others lives

Creativity, life skills and problem-solving are the primary skills in the teaching of thinking. Can all types of thinking be taught? Absolutely yes. It not only can be taught, it should be a significant part of any school curriculum. It's part of *the* essential skills package needed for survival in today's world.

*Being especially good at problem-solving*
*does not guarantee success in life...*
*But being poor at it does guarantee failure*

What is the best way to teach problem-solving, creativity and thinking? In brain-based learning, it is with real world problems, with real people under real conditions. Put the brain under the conditions of relevant, challenging "survival" (real or imagined, but with positive stress) and it will excel in learning. The brain loves to think and learn. For children, games are all about inventing new ways of thinking. For adolescents, school survival requires thinking skills. Adults need thinking skills to deal with their daily challenges.

# How To Help Your Learners
# Learn to Think Better

How do you get your learners to "grow" their learning skills? There are many ways to learn thinking skills. Since thinking is obviously internal, the trick in teaching and learning it is to make it external so that others can discover and "coach" the process. Here are some of the best ways to teach others to think better:

Useful Ideas:
1. Use examples or stories imbued with personal meaning
   Give relevant examples of how others solved problems
2. Create team projects, so all feel safe to use metacognitive options
   Let your learners have time to think about thinking and discuss it
3. Role model - you "walk" your students through the process
   A well-guided facilitation or use of a checklist of ideas & questions
   You and your students can solve a problem together, out loud
4. Learning through debate, meaningful dialogue or discussion
   Set up a coach, a listener and a thinker to learn the process
5. It can be developed through introspection, reflection & feedback
   Journal-writing, partner feedback and steps to follow can help
6. By using large challenging projects with deadlines for public display
   Here's where the learners are forced to learn, to "survive"
7. The use of mapping or graphic organizers to visually "see" the
   models of thinking, the patterns, the sequences, the extent of detail

Today's forward thinking learning catalysts now talk about how to turn *any topic or situation into a creative-growth learning experience.* Today's teachers are providing all subjects, topics and experiences with the parallel thinking and learning processes, strategies and insights are built-in to the lesson. There is no need for a special course on thinking. Gardner and Sternberg both believe that this ability, the skills to relate learning to our lives is one of the keys to intelligence. They also suggest that dealing with moderate novelty provides learners with critical and valuable life skills. Too much novelty and you are testing only creativity and too little and you're not testing problem-solving enough. You may want to vary the amount of novelty you offer until you feel you have the right blend for your learners.

# Orderly Learning

Should all learning and thinking be sequential and orderly? No. Researchers say the learner climate of suspense, surprise, disequilibrium, uncertainty and disorder can lead to a richer understanding of the content. Some say the brain is designed for chaos. In fact, these researchers say that the behaviorist, reward-punishment, super-ordered systems attempted in most learning contexts are actually the least likely to produce the desired results. Why? The most effective learning is either real-life or patterned after real-life, and real life can be suspenseful, surprising, uncertain and disorderly.

*Some researchers postulate that*
*learning only occurs at "impasses"*

Most of the time, we simply repeat stored "programs." That's not learning, that's replication of a habit. The brain runs programs and patterns all day. Only when we are stopped in our tracks by a problem or situation and forced to rethink it is there the possibility of new learning. Naturally, many times, learners, even at an impasse, will choose a prior "tried and true" path and no learning occurs. But the point here is this: the experience of chaos and confusion may be one of the few ways to naturally trigger new learning. Does this mean that excess chaos is good? Hardly.

The more routine and ritual you provide for the learners, the more chaos they can handle. Teachers who have sloppy lessons, with scattered thinking and poor preparation will find that their students may begin to reflect the excess chaos. Learners with teachers who over structure, manipulate and control the learning may find that learners resist by creating disruptions or detachment.

The optimal is an orchestrated learning environment reinforced by the structure of positive rituals and infused with choice, novelty, chaos and challenge. We should encourage a sort of "orchestrated disequilibrium" much more often. Utilize learner-generated role-playing, simulations, theater, songs, experiments, field trips, extemporaneous speaking and meaningful project work in which chaos can occur. Allow the activity to run its natural course when possible. Minimize intervention.

# Spelling Success Strategy

To the untrained teacher, students are simply "thinking." Actually, you could break down what they are doing into many kinds of thinking processes. The two most dominant might be recall and creation; that is, you either already know it and are remembering it or you are constructing it in your mind. When we process information internally, we do it with any of our five senses: sight, sound, touch smell or hearing. The founders of neurolinguistic programming, Richard Bandler and John Grinder, have observed that most people (especially right-handed ones) give clues through their eye movements as to which of the sensory modes they use.

The value of this information is enormous. If you know what mode a person uses you can better understand and communicate with them. For example, if a student's eyes are down and to the right, he may be experiencing some feelings. It's a cue for you to know that you may want to respect those sensations for a moment before you talk to him. Or, you may want to get him out of those feelings by asking him to look up. This will cause him to access the visual mode thus changing the kinesthetic sensations. Here's the specific breakdown and how to access the cues:

V.r... (up and to the left for normal right-handed persons) Visual Remembered: seeing images of the past. Simply ask a question such as, "What color is your living room rug?"

V.c... (up and to the right) Visual construct: seeing newly created images. Simply ask, "What would your brother look like if he dyed his hair green?"

A.r... (looking to the left) Auditory remembered: recalling sound heard in the past. Simply ask, "What was the last thing I said?"

A.c... (looking to the right) Auditory construct: creating new sounds in your mind. Simply ask, "What would your name sound like spelled backwards?"

A.i... (looking down to your left) Auditory internal: talking to yourself. Simply ask person to sing happy birthday to himself.

K.i... (looking down to your right) Kinesthetic: feelings and emotions. Simply ask, "How would you feel if you were sad?"

K.e... Kinesthetic external... touching and feeling anything real from the outside world, from the feel of clothes to the feeling of clapping your hands.

What are the implications in teaching? They're infinite! Let's just take a couple of examples. When your students are taking a test, what would assist them in recalling prior visual information (what was on a handout, picture, drawing or in a text)? The answer is that they could recall it best by looking up and to the left. In order to construct an image of how something would look (such as if they were composing, writing, etc.), they would look up and to the right to have the best access to that information. If a student wanted to recall what you said, he'd look to his left side. If he's composing and wants to "hear" how something sounds, his eyes would go to his right.

Let's assume that a student is trying to do his or her best on an exam and is accessing information. The student's eyes would need to move around a lot! What do most teachers tell students to do? "Keep your eyes on your paper!" Guess what that does? By having to put the eyes down, it puts the student into either the kinesthetic mode (feelings of anxiety, fear, etc.) or in his auditory internal which means that he will be talking to himself about it (maybe telling himself how hard the test is). Many teachers inadvertently keep students from scoring well on tests because of where they tell their students to look while taking it.

How do you use accessing cues in conversations with students? If the eyes are down and to the right (student's right), it's likely that they are strongly into their feelings. If you want to communicate with them, you have some new choices: (1) gain rapport by matching their experience. Say, "You must be feeling low, David." This creates an immediate sense of rapport between you and the student. Or, (2) break the state by switching the state. Say, "David, just for a moment, could you please look up at this..."

This will pull the student out of his feelings and make it easier to present something that is visual. (3) Pace, then lead. You would also talk about feelings and begin to lead him out by slowly having him access sounds or visuals. The possibilities are endless and you'll be discovering more of them every day.

# Spelling/Math Strategy Outline

A good speller (or a student recalling math formulas) uses a primarily visual strategy while a poor speller uses either an auditory (sounds the words or letters out) or kinesthetic (spells by how the word or letters feel) strategy. Here's an example of a primarily visual strategy:

1. For spelling: prepare a list of words to be learned or use the ones on a student's list.
2. Use the eye-accessing chart to determine the direction of the student's gaze while recalling visual-remembered material. For example, "What color are the curtains in your living room?"
3. Explain to the student that it is more useful to recall what something looks like when his or her eyes are pointed in the visual direction.
4. Ask the student what his or her favorite color is. Explain that it is easier to remember words in color.
5. Show the student the first word or formula on the list. Have the students glance at it, as if taking a snapshot.
6. Have the student look up to his or her best recalling direction and visualize a picture of that word in full color.
7. Ask the student, while looking at the word in his or her mind's eye, to read the letters backward to you. (This insures that the picture is in his or her mind). Make sure that the eyes stay up in the recall direction.
8. Next, ask the student to spell the word or formula forwards. Once again, make sure that the eyes stay up in the recalling mode.
9. Tell the student, "from now on, you will simply remember this picture in your mind and be able to recall it perfectly."
10. Repeat steps 5-9 for any new words, formulas or equations.

Note: "Chunk down" longer words into 3-letter units. Make sure that this method is practiced until it becomes automatic. Make sure the student visualizes as directed. Make sure that each of the steps are followed explicitly and that the eyes are pointed in the correct direction at the proper time. If a student has difficulty, have them create an imaginary TV set. Either way, this is a very powerful strategy when done properly.

# Are Questions Better Than Answers?

The better the quality of the questions asked, the more the brain is challenged to think. The Socratic Method may have more than history going for it; it may be best for our brains. In study after study, learner performance scores improved when the questions asked of the learners improved in depth.

Useful Ideas: Instead of asking students questions which require a statement of fact or a "yes" or "no" answer, ask more thought-provoking ones. Instead of: "What is it called when things keep falling back towards the earth?" ask, "What theories are there about gravity, which ones do you think are true, and why?" And, as mentioned earlier, the HOTS computer program succeeds precisely because it is NOT a quickie, or "math facts" type of shallow thinking. It succeeds because it asks questions that stimulate thinking and discussion. This shapes lifelong patterns of meaning-making, and eventually, character.

## Learn to Re-phrase Questions

The best way to help learners solve a problem may be to restate the problem. When re-thinking training was provided for 200 students in two separate studies, it was found that flexible thinking was significantly more useful in problem-solving. Let's say, students are asked to design a clock with no moving parts and no face. By visualizing, they may get stuck and come up with no answer. By re-framing the problem and asking new questions, however, they may come up with other solutions, such as a talking clock.

Restating questions can lead to creativity and self-confidence. It can be very empowering to reformat questions. Typically, a teacher asks a question like "What was the Berlin Wall?" or "What brought it down?" A more empowering question would be to ask learners "What interesting questions could we ask about the Berlin Wall?" Get learners involved in being a part of the solution by asking the question in different ways. If students say a class is boring, ask them, "In what ways could we make it interesting?" Of those ways, "Which ones can be done legally, on no budget, within school rules, that everyone can agree with?" Have your learners make up the test questions instead of only answering them. Let students do all of the lower-level quizzing of each other on simple-answer questions.

## Listen to the Type of Answer

By analyzing a learner's "wrong" answers, we can discover meaningful information. Often the wrong answers fit a pattern or reveal something important about the type and style of the learner's processing. Because teachers often listen for the expected answer, they miss out on the more interpretive and qualitative possibilities. Profoundly informed people generally read more ambiguity into a question than was intended.

As an example, a student completes a multiple choice test. Wrong answers usually get a zero and are 100% wrong. Yet the student may have a more profound understanding of the topic than the single answer possibility indicates. What if the student made the same type of mistake 10-15 times? Does your feedback indicate that? The learner would love to know if they are just one or 15 answers off!

A physics teacher has a test question: "Using a barometer, how can you tell the height of this building?" The "proper" answer is to say, "Measure the air pressure at the bottom of the building and then compare it with the air pressure at the top of the building. Then use a prescribed formula to compute the difference in feet or meters." Unfortunately, a student who got the answer right was marked wrong because he found other, more creative, ways to calculate the right answer.

After all, you could: 1) Tie a string onto the barometer and throw it out the top of the building. Then when it lands, measure the length of the string needed. 2) On a sunny day, use the shadow cast by the barometer and the building as a comparison and compute the ratio. 3) Go to the stairwell of the building. Using the barometer as a ruler, count how many times you need to flip it end over end to get to the top.

Multiply that number by the length of the barometer. 4) Take the barometer to the building inspector, engineer or architect. Offer to trade the barometer to that person in exchange for the exact height of the building... etc.

**Useful Ideas:** Allow learners to work in groups to self-assess their tests. Let them formulate rules for the patterning and understanding of the experiences and information. Have them share and shape their discoveries instead of being evaluated by a "superior" who tells them what is right and what is wrong.

---

## *Additional Resources for Further Study and Follow up*

*Changing & Rearranging* by Anderson (Metamorphous)
*Lateral Thinking* by deBono (Harper & Row)
*How to Become an Expert* by Gibbons (Zephyr)
*In Search of Understanding: The Case for the Constructivist Classroom* by Grennon (ACSD)
*Turning Learning Inside Out* by Neff & Nevin (Zephyr)
*A Different Kind of Classroom* by Marzano (ASCD)Thinking,
*The Know It All* by Peterson (Zephyr)
*The Private Eye* by Ruef (Zephyr)
*Beyond Teaching & Learning* by Wenger (Project Renaissance)
*Pumping Ions* by Wujec (Doubleday)

\* These are available in the Appendix.

# Memory

**Old Way**
Use of
Semantic,
Taxon, list-
oriented, facts,
texts, names, etc.
memorized

**Better Way:**
Use of location cues
Circumstances
Body learning
Musical
Linguistic
Embedded in Context
Sensory

# 19

## Memory & Recall

### Learning To Remember

One of the common teacher and student frustrations is that, after learning, much of it seems forgotten. Is it the student's job to figure out how to learn and memorize and recall? Or is the teacher's job to help learners memorize and recall better? The answer is both: it's your job to introduce them to the learn-to-learn skills that help them memorize better. But once they have the skills, your job is to simply allow them time to use the skills and support the process.

*Asking students to learn and memorize material*
*without providing them with the skills to do it*
*is rude, unprofessional and unrealistic*

How do your students store and recall their learning? It is becoming increasingly clear that multiple memory systems may be a fundamental part of the design of the brain. In other words, the more ways that you engage your learners, the more ways it is stored. Research shows that different kinds of learning may require different ways to store and recall them. In one study, learners were asked to use either rote or elaborate strategies to memorize words. Those using the rote method had higher forgetfulness ratios and a lower recall performance. The rote method involved simple repetition, also called "semantic" memory or "list-related" memorization. While this method is slow, requires review and often boring, it can be fairly accurate in isolated cases. But it's not very effective or efficient for the 90% of learning that needs to happen.

*If something is worth learning,*
*it's probably worth remembering*

We know that learners tend to remember much more when there is a field trip, a musical, a disaster, a guest speaker or a novel study location. Why? Multiple memory systems are activated. Learners often seem to forget a great deal of what is taught, but the problem may be a reliance on singular memory system.

Activate multiple memory systems with a variety of teaching activities, such as reading, listening to a lecture and seeing a video. Then follow up with projects, role-playing, at-home assignments, music, discussion, field trips, games, simulations or drama. Why? Researchers discovered a critical biologically-based difference between the two ways we deal with new information:

### Our brain sorts and stores information
### based on whether it is embedded
### in context or in content

The difference between the two can be described quite simply: Information embedded in context ("episodic" memory) means it is stored in relationship with a particular location or circumstance. Information embedded in content is usually found in a book, computer, list or other information storage device. Our spatial or contextual memory can be described as primarily based on *location and circumstances,* or context. Research discovered that it has unlimited capacity, forms quickly, is easily updated, requires no practice, is effortless and is used naturally by everyone (e.g., "What did you have for dinner last night?"). This natural memory is only context-dependent; it may be based on your movement, music, intense sensory experiences, sounds, puns, relationships and position in space and time.

### Reduce the amount of rote memory used
### Increase the amount of contextual, natural memory

The formation of this natural memory is motivated by curiosity, novelty and expectations. It's enhanced by intensified sensory input (sights, sounds, smells, taste, touch). The information can also be stored in a fabric or weave of "mental space," which is a thematic map of the intellectual landscape, where learning occurs as a result of changes in location or circumstances, or the use of thematic teaching, storytelling, visualization and metaphors.

Information embedded in content is usually learned (or attempted to be learned, through rote and by following lists. "Semantic" is the type of list-oriented, sometimes rote, unnatural memory which requires rehearsal, is resistant to change, isolated from context, has strict limits, lacks meaning and is linked to extrinsic motivation. (e.g., she asks, "Remember that article you were reading last night? What was the name of the author?" He replies, "Gee, I don't remember. Why do you want to know?") This type of memory is unnatural and requires practice and constant rehearsal to keep fresh. That's why most people have the experience of "forgetting" so much trivia. The brain is simply not designed to recall that type of information.

### Semantic memory is NOT natural...
### in fact, it's a very unnatural way
### to learn and remember things

This type of information gathering and memory of content without a context is difficult for the brain. This type of learning is typified by seated school work and homework ("Study for Friday's test by reviewing chapter six."). Information learned with the semantic method:

- is usually out of "real life" context, isolated and meaningless
- is harder to update, change and revise
- often requires extrinsic motivation

A trip to a local science museum would provide our brain with heavy "embedding" in context. Millions of information bits, all in context, would be remembered for years. A two-week study session in science using a textbook is heavily embedded in content. And it all may be forgotten a day after the "big" test. Granted, the textbook is cheaper. But with some imagination, many teachers create much more "context" for the learning. It can be done with dress, language, food, environment and visitors.

244

Should we throw out "book learning?" No. Just because the brain is generally very poor at learning that way, we shouldn't discard the source. Semantic learning does have its place. When you ask for directions, for example, you want the shortest route from A to B. You don't want to drive all over the city to figure it out (although that would create a stronger "contextual map"). On the other hand, if you ask others what of significance they have learned in the last year, 90% of what they tell you will probably be contextually embedded information (vs. "rote" or "book learning").

## Attention and Memory

Increased student attention might feel reassuring to the teacher. But you do not want attention all the time. In fact, that's a sure way to hurt the learning. Our mental "gates" allow information to either be taken in (from the outside world) or processed for meaning (internally), but never both at the same time. This has tremendous implications for classroom learning:

*You get either your learner's attention*
*or they can be making meaning of it...*
*but you cannot get both at the same time*

Get attention, then allow for meaning-making. Be sure emotions are engaged, for best memory. When rats are injected with adrenaline, they remember longer and better. Emotion and arousal causes your body's internal "chemical cocktails" to spritz out, flooding the system with norepinephrine, adrenaline, enkephalin, vasopressin, ACTH. Researchers think these chemicals are "memory fixatives." They signal the brain, "This is important, keep this!" In fact, the rats injected with adrenaline remembered far longer than those who weren't injected.

What you probably remember most from your teaching career was your lowest "lows" and your highest "highs." This applies across all areas of your life: the best and worst vacations, meals, dates, jobs, weather and so on.

The philosophy used to be: "Keep things under control. Don't let the students get out of hand. Suppress emotions!" The new philosophy, based on the way the brain learns and remembers best, may well be: "Purposely and productively engage the emotions; make the learning personally compelling, deeply felt and real."

Make a purposeful strategy to engage positive emotions within the learner. Without it, the learner may not code the material learned as important. Long, continuous lectures and predictable lessons are the least likely to be remembered. Utilize the following: enthusiasm, drama, role-plays, quiz shows, music, debates, larger projects, guest speakers, creative controversy, adventures, impactful rituals and celebrations.

## The BEM Principle

Research has verified that an easy way to remember something is to make it new and different. That's because our brains have a high attentional bias towards something which does not fit the pattern (novelty). Once you have gone past the first item in a list or an experience, the novelty effect of it has eroded. You'll generally remember the first and last moments of a learning experience more than the middle. Psychologists refer to this as the BEM principal, (Beginning, End and Middle), the order in which you are most likely to recall something. There is a distinctly different mental set at the beginning of an experience (anticipation, suspense, novelty, challenge, etc.) than the middle (continuation, more of the same, boredom, stability). The ending mental set is much different, too (new anticipations, emotions, etc.).

Your students may be able to remember much more of what happens if you provide more novelty (let them do much of it) and more beginnings and ends (and less middles). Introduce short modules of learning instead of long ones. Break up long sessions into several shorter ones. Have your students provide surprise introductions to new topics.

# Memories Change
# Because We Change

Did you know our memory is changing all the time with new information and changes in beliefs and circumstances? Because we change, our perceptions of the event's circumstances change in relationship to our lives. Ordinarily (unless there is trauma), memory requires "repeated rehearsal in different contexts." It requires updating and new categorical input, as well as associations. This updating engages our creativity and thinking skills.

# Summary: How to Insure
# Greater Memory & Recall

There are many, many ways for your students to remember what they've learned. Some of them you can do "to them." Others are best learned by the students so they can use them on themselves. Here are some of the best ways to help them recall learned material:

| |
|---|
| • Attach a strong emotion to it with a purposely designed intense activity |
| • Repeat it within 10 minutes afterwards, then 48 hours and then 7 days |
| • Give students or let them make a concrete reminder, like a token or artifact |
| • Act it out in a skit or do a fun, but engaging role play |
| • Use acrostics (first letter of each key word forms new word) |
| • Put it on a large, colorful picture or poster |
| • Chunk into groups of 7 or less to make each group of data easy |

✔**Pause, please and go back over the list above and put a mark next to the idea that you haven't used, but would like to start using more.**

| |
|---|
| • Students identify key qualities & patterns of new information |
| • Personalize the lesson by using student names, neighborhoods, etc. |
| • Both you and the learners summarize on paper and words |
| • Use a link system to link one idea to the next with action, absurdity |
| • Put it in greater context with trips, reading, discussion |
| • Use acronyms; the space agency in America is NASA |
| • Add more "What's in it for me?" to it increase the incentive for learner |

✔**Pause, please and go back over the list above and put a mark next to the idea that you haven't used, but would like to start using more.**

- Review in all five of our different senses; sight, sound, touch, etc.
- Implement the learning in some way, add it to your own personal life
- Use storyboards (like oversized comic strip panels) of key ideas
- Make a video or audio tape; the more complex the better
- Transfer it to your computer and use it often
- Use pegwords to link numbers or pictures to an idea for easy recall
- Create or re-do a song; re-write the lyrics of an old favorite, make a rap

✔ **Pause, please and go back over the list above and put a mark next to the idea that you haven't used, but would like to start using more.**

- Make up or use a childhood story with the info, then tell it
- Start with something exotic, then familiar, then unusual again
- Increase accountability: have a review check-up at regular intervals
- Real situation practice; go to the place where the learning occurs
- Hold unguided discussion on material; at least 5-15 minutes can work
- Make it more relevant & important by engaging more personal life
- Follow up with journal writing; give enough time for reflection

✔ **Pause, please and go back over the list above and put a mark next to the idea that you haven't used, but would like to start using more.**

- Build a working model that embodies the key elements of the idea
- Create or support learner study support groups
- Better nutrition: in several studies, the lecithin from wheat germ helped
- Create a positive association with the material; emotions are best!
- Partner to partner summary; make sure learners have choice
- Use dramatic concert readings; read key points with music backdrop
- Learners mindmap it, share their mindmaps, then re-do later in week
- Learners teach it to small groups of peers, or adults
- Do a month later follow-up & through with video, writing, talk
- Learn contextually in different places so each location is a key clue

✔ **Pause, please and go back over the list above and put a mark next to the idea that you haven't used, but would like to start using more.**

Now that you see what a wide variety of strategies there are for memorizing the learning, you can rotate them on a daily basis. By using both a variety of methods and empowering your learners, you'll make the learning more effective and more fun. And a terrific side benefit is that the confidence levels in the learners will soar. So take the time to help students develop a terrific memory and recall system. The value will come back to repay you a hundredfold!

---

## *Additional Resources for Further Study and Follow up*

*Use Both Sides of the Brain* by Buzan (Penguin)*
*Quantum Learning* by DePorter (Dell)*
*The Learning Revolution* by Dryden & Vos (Jalmar)*
*SuperMemory* by Ostrander & Schroeder (Carroll & Graf)

* These are available in the Appendix.

# 20

# Energizers & Sponges

## Activate the Learning!

The purpose of energizers are primarily to "wake-up," energize, activate and stimulate the mind and body of your learners. Although activities of this type are often used just to break up the boredom or "move the body around, that's underestimates their potential impact. "Sponges" are usually more mental activities that can engage learners for just a few moments. Originally they were to soak up time, the way a dry sponge soaks up water. But today's teachers know that classroom and learning time is much too valuable to waste with time fillers. Teachers want the learning to be deepened, widened and made more enjoyable for the learner.

*Teaching well is a high-risk career,*
*if you're not risking, you're not growing*
*and if you're not growing, neither are your students...*

Are all these energizers and sponge activities useless? It depends on how you do them. Recent brain research tells us that 1) physical stimulations boosts mental stimulation 2) learning done with the body is generally more effective than with the mind only, because we use of **two** types of memory: declarative/semantic and procedural, and 3) the engagement of emotions increases the impact and recall of the learning experiences. That's pretty compelling evidence in favor of using these types of activities.

## Energizers are Appropriate for For K-12 & Adult Grade Levels

That's right, all grade levels can use energizers. The activities listed below are the tried and true classics plus a few new ones. Every single game was invented by someone, and can be adapted or changed by someone (like you!). Won't older students think the games are silly or stupid? They will, if you do. Can you play "musical chairs" with adults? Of course, I and others, have done it successfully. It's all in the attitude you have.

There are hundreds, if not thousands of energizer activities for your class or group. Each of these can be altered or improved upon to generate another 99 games. Use your creativity and courage to innovate. Since you may have very specific needs, browse the list first, then come up with the perfect ones that exactly fit your group!

For every sponge and energizer that is done "content-free," there's a hundred variations you could add to make it doubly powerful. As an example: You could either do the game "simon says" as just an ordinary stretch break, or you could turn it into a half dozen fun learning activities. These are listed alphabetically, so you can find them easier.

With all the activities, be sure to let the audience know all the directions clearly, chunked down into simple steps. Tell them the activity will be safe and fun. You may get better results if you first ask your group to take in a deep breath and stand up. Then, in that state they're more likely to want to participate.

**Ad-ons...** It's a fun way to review a topic. Invite one person to come up to the front of the room and act out or posture something that they have learned from the course... another comes up and joins the impromptu living sculpture... another comes up, one at a time, adding on until you have one giant human scenario that represents what they've been learning.

**Around the World...** All stand up. You or students ask a question. If they know the answer, they can take steps around the room. Each question is worth a certain number of steps depending on it's degree of difficulty. The student's goal is to move completely around the room by answering questions. Great for spatial-kinesthetic learners.

**Ball toss...** 5-7 students stand in a circle about 10feet apart, facing each other. One has a ball or bean bag. He tosses it to a person to start the game. Content could be "Q & A", or just to continue a story, give a compliment, word association, math facts, states & capitols, etc. Keep the game fast and light. Give students control & set clear rules.

**Barnyard...** It's a fun way to form groups. Assign a number to everyone up to the number of groups you want (6 groups, everyone gets a number from 1-6). Or, if you want six groups, simply go by birthdate months. Everyone from January and February are in this group, etc. Assign a noisy animal from the barnyard to all groups. For example the 1s are all dogs, the 2s are all cats, all 3s are sheep, all 4s are goats, all 5s are chickens and all 6s are horses. Then, have all of them stand up, and mix around for 30 seconds. Next, they all close their eyes and make the appropriate sounds. Each groups tries to form by trying to find all similar animals by sound. Can be a riot of fun!

**Birthday line walls...** All stand up, then get into a single file line. Everyone stands in a line, in order of their birthdays from January 1-Dec 31...Variations? Of course! They have to do it within either a time limit or without speaking, or once they are all in line, then you go do "Circle run-ons" game.

**Body-brain-gym & cross laterals...** The purpose is to activate the brain through movement. Especially use cross-overs, from right to left or opposite. touch hands to opposite knees, give yourself a pat on the back on opposite side, touch opposite heels, air swimming - one arm in one direction of freestyle and the other arm swimming in the other direction, touch nose and hold opposite ear then switch, do "lazy 8s" in front of you by tracing the pattern of the number eight with your thumb ups sign...start your 8 at the center, arms length, going up and to the right, do big loops on both     sides and switch sides.

**Body machines...** Role play how a machine works: stand up, pair up, as a duo, create and play-act like a car, truck, computer, bar code reader, etc.

**Body pass...** whole class lays down, in line, like fallen dominos... all lay on their backs and pass another person's body, along above them, over and over, the last one, keeps starting up the new person. It moves along like a bicycle chain.

**Circle "run-ons"...** All stand up in their own groups or teams, facing the group leader. The audience is given a topic for review. The group leader starts a sentence on the topic and leaves it hanging... (such as "Energizers are best for..."). The person to his or her left (or right, or whomever's chosen), continues the "run-on" sentence, but again, leaves it hanging for the next person. The goal is to keep the sentence going for as long as you can.

**Clapping games...** You start a clap or rhythm, students    pass it around the room. Then the first student starts a clapping rhythm and others follow suit. Use a pattern, they listen and repeat the pattern. Good for memory & music skills.

**Commercial breaks...** A great way to review. Each team is assigned a topic or they choose one. Throughout the class, different teams offer an impromptu TV commercial break. Only, the point of the commercial is to review the content. Although it works well with teams, it can be, depending on the group, be done with individuals or partners. Each person could come up in front of the room with a partner... they get do a 30" commercial, using the material that they've been learning... they make it fun, bizarre, cute, etc.

**Creative Handshakes...** All stand up. Go introduce yourself to others and find a new way to shake 5 different peoples' hands. This builds creativity.

**Creating teams** Team deciders or dividers might be: birthday months or seasons born in, male-female/boy-girl, barnyard--animal sounds, new/experienced favorite desserts, brand of toothpaste, favorite autos, color of eyes, etc. Or, Use "Psychic handshake" method...All stand up. Great for forming teams. Everyone gets a number from one to six...(or whatever the number of teams you want). It's all done non-verbally. Each person goes around shaking hands and meeting new people. You shake their hands the number of times that your number is...when you get a matching handshake, they are on your team.

**Expert Interviews...** All stand up. All get *new identities*... half the audience becomes an expert in the topic you're teaching and half are the famous reporters doing the interviewing... take 2 min. to get the story, reverse roles with another party. Make it dramatic with music

**Follow the Leader...** used as a memory game, perception practice, skills practice. A team or group leader takes the rest of their group with them. They act or say, others follow along and repeat.

**Frisbee review...** who ever catches Frisbee, says one thing that they've learned in the last couple of minutes or hours... or they say implications of what they've learned.

**Get to know me charades...** stand, pick a partner, tell that partner 3 things about yourself using no words, only charades, then they tell you 3 things... Or, they could demonstrate 3 things about your school, your company, an idea....

**Gordian knot...** Teams of 6 or 8 stand in a circle, facing each other, 2 feet apart. One reaches across with one hand and clasps the hand of another. Each person clasps the hand of the opposite person, so both hands are full. You now have everyone holding the opposite person's hand. Now, they have to untie themselves from this giant knot while still keeping hands clasped.

**"Hot seat" activity...** Team sits in a circle. One person is "it." Everyone else gets 60 seconds to say acknowledgments to the person in the hot seat. The listener has to remain silent or say only "Thank you." After each, rotate to the next person.

**Humor break...** everyone stand up, close your eyes, if you can think of a recent or old joke, raise your hand. Open your eyes, everyone with their hands still down cluster around someone who raised their hand who knows a joke. They tell the joke, round of applause, switch groups and joke tellers.

**I did it my way...** It's the use of music & song activities in a fun way. Write out the lyrics to a song and pass it out. Students revise and re-write lyrics using key things learned. Or, re-contextualize the use of song. The audience can write brand new words to sing or act out and everyone participates.

**Instant replay...** Stand, pick partners, one acts it out, the other replays it. You might add time restraints, add sounds, then words.

**"I went shopping & I bought"...** Storytelling is good for alphabetical ordering and memory. Tell a story of one item you bought, they recall, then keep adding items on to the list, one at a time.

**Lap sit...** Good for your whole group... all stand in a circle, facing the back of the person in front of you, just six inches behind the person in front, hold on to their waist and all gently sit down on person's lap behind you... at the same time... it's fun!

**Laughter is good...** Team joke-telling time... team or group gets 3-4 minutes to share, among themselves, their favorite or the latest joke with each other. Then at your request, have them point to the person whose joke they'd like shared with the whole group. They ask the joke teller if he or she would share it with whole group. Rotate groups, round of applause.

**Learn a magic act...** They are cheap and fun to do. A local magic shop can help you learn disappearing coin games or others. Use magic to make a point or let the audience do it.

**Line dancing...** Or square dancing with new vocabulary words to learn. Get a dance leader to make it fun.......invent your own versions for your own content.

**Massage a team...** for age appropriate groups only. Everyone stand up in their teams, put their left shoulders to the center, raise their hands above their heads, you put on music, then each lowers their hands on to the person in front of you and gives a gentle massage.

**Matching faces/matching sounds:** Group stands in a large circle. You or some student starts with a face or sound, then "passes" it. That means the person to their left repeats it and "passes it" again to their left...and so on...until all have done it and a new person starts up the cycle with a new face or sound. Variations...pass a face in one direction, a sound in the other direction...pass a "body movement," face and sound from several key points in the circle.

**Movement of the Masses...** Have students stand up & walk fast or run around the entire ground floor of the building just to get their circulation up. As a review, they are to tell ten others what they think has been the key word from the last half hour. They most Set a few rules first: safety, time, courtesy, noise, etc.

**Musical chairs...** Everyone in a circle, on chairs, except you, who stand outside the circle, managing the music. There are only enough chairs for each person. Once the game starts, you quickly remove one of the chairs, pulling it outside the circle and setting it away. To start the game, you ask all to stand up and walk around giving positive affirmations to other participants, while playing fun, loud music. When the music stops, everyone grabs a chair. The one left standing, continues the game. They ask everyone to stand up and gives them all a new assignment. Here are some examples they might give:

**My friend...** Great to meet new people. All pick a partner. Take 5 minutes and talk to each other. Introduce others in front of class or around room. Builds language, creativity, speaking and memory skills.

1. Get to know you activity... introduce yourself to as many people as you can in 30 seconds. Or, find someone with a birthday in your same month or year.
2. Measure... find three people taller, three people shorter or the find the person closest to your exact height.
3. Music-related... find out where and when and how you first heard the song being played.
4. Do partial or selective groups... "Anyone who is not left-handed, stand up. Now, find a seat quickly!" You get the idea... any game, musical chairs or not, has a hundred variations!

**New Seats...** Everybody stand, find and introduce yourself to three others you don't know very well, then everyone switch seats to another part of room... new seat must be at least 10ft. from old one.

**New York City Night Sounds...** One team at a time assigns individual or team sounds that might be heard in New York. They begin to make their sounds, then you add another team's sounds, until you have the sound of a full city. Then a round of applause.

**Opposites attract...** All stand up. Pick a partner. One finds or touches an object in the room, the other has to find either a "go-with" (a similar item) or an opposite.

**Pair & share...** All stand up and pick a partner. You can share with your partner any of the following, or your own choice: 1) something you are afraid of in learning 2) something you are unsure about 3) something that you found interesting 4) the idea translated into the vocabulary of a two year old or ten year old.

**Poster mania...** Stand up, find a partner. Look around the room and visually, pick out two or three posters that you like. Take your partner with you and walk over to the posters and tell your partner what they hit home for you. Why are they in particular so meaningful to you?

**Retro games...** all stand up... close eyes... turn the clock back 20, 30 or 50 or 100 years... how would you talk? Discuss topics you would hold conversations about during that era, in the classroom or training room.

**Rock/paper/scissors game...** Everyone picks partners. Pick three ideas from the last hour of class. "Paper" = one idea, "rock" is another and "scissors" the third. Play the game with a partner. Each time someone wins, they get to ask the other a question about that topic... it's a "quiz your partner" review game.

**Role reversals...** Everyone prepares a short talk with a partner. All students by random or volunteer, come up front to teach for 30-60" at a time, then rotate to the next one, all the way through the class.

**Sign language...** You teach or anyone in your group teaches a phrase or word in sign language to the whole group. Add to the phrase each day. Eventually, learn to say a song in sign language... One I especially recommend is "Wonderful World" by "Satchmo."

**Simon Says...** All stand and do only what Simon (you) says to do. Give instructions to follow, some of them prefaced with "Simon says," and others simply given alone. Go at a moderate pace. If they make a mistake, they keep playing. Always make it a win for all, so one's never out of the game. Many variations! You can use it as: 1) A listening game, for following instructions 2) A get to know you game, pointing to or saying or facing a name you call out 3) A geography game..."Simon Says point to the direction of Alaska or point to Australia" 4) A math game... "Simon says use your body to give me the answer to 5 plus 6." 5) Language learning... "Simon says, point to 'su boca' or 'su mano.'" 6) A science game..."Simon says, point to something in this room made of steel... point to something made of glass... made of plastic... that's over twenty years old... that would not have existed 50 years ago..."

**Simple observation game...** All pick a partner, stand up and take 60" to observe all details... then one person turns away, changes one things and the partner tries to guess what the one change was. Variation: change 3 things about your own appearance (with both partners at same time) then each turn around & identify the changes

**Somebody's body...** Everyone stand up. Pair up with a partner. All pairs get five minutes to use some part of the body to measure something in the room. The goal is to invent the most bizarre or fun measuring. At the end of five minutes, the pairs report to the group their results: ("This cabinet is 210 knuckles long")

**Spatial memory...** Teach a move-around system using memory cue words with a different location for each word and number peg.

**Stand-up reviews...** of past content... eyes closed or open, music or not. Make the review interesting and relevant to their lives. Include affirmations.

**Steal the Key...** or "Doggie, Doggie, Who Has the Bone?"- use questioning strategies, reading body language & deductive reasoning skills

**Stretch & breathe...** whole groups stands, the stretching can be a slow movement, can be done to music, can be lead by a student or done to a theme.

**String squares...** put all into groups of four... give each team 10' of string...all stand face each other goal is to make the string into a large square you can all talk, but must keep eyes closed until you're satisfied that you have a perfect square.

**Switch seats...** during breaks - great for exploring the room from a new perspective, switching L & R hemisphere learning

**Team Affirmations...** Read aloud in each team, while standing, a list of team-building, psych-up affirmations (found in the chapter on team-building) that you have already printed & distributed to each team member. Team leader goes first, then, while still standing, they rotate around quickly.

**The good ol days...** Put on old music from the 1920's, 30's or 40's. Do dances from different eras; Charleston, Jitterbug, big band, swing era, etc.

**The world's a stage...** Pause in your lecture. All students stand up. Everyone find 3-5 others to form small groups. The goal of the group is to turn the last hour's of lecture or discussion into a 1-3 minute act (a role play). For example, they become a giant solar system, complete with the sun, planets, moon, debris and comets. Or, they might role-play a discipline policy you just mentioned. They act out a typical rule, a violation, and some solutions. They could Re-enact great moments in history, the news of the day, in poetry, character impersonations.

**Touch & Go...** Get up, in sequence, touch 5 pieces of gold, 4 pieces of silver, 3 of glass, 2 of leather, 1 of clothing label on someone else. All items must be at least 10 or more feet apart. Variations on the game above... instead of touching those items, make the game part of the content you are teaching. Here are some examples: Math: touch right angles, cylinders, cubes, rectangles, a certain total number of objects, length, height. Science: touch textures, colors, weights, rarity, solids. History: touch things that fit a certain time era, things which could be used to... English: touch objects which could be used to... make a sentence, have double meanings, are capitalized Economics: touch items in order of value, cost. Use colors! Get up and touch, around the room, 7 colors in order on seven different objects, using Roy G. Biv in order.

**Traffic Light or "Mother May I"...** can be used for counting skills, estimation and listening skills. You give directions, students ask permission to complete.

**Triangle tag...** requires groups of four... three form a triangle, holding hands, the fourth stands outside the group and tries to tag whoever is "it"... the triangle team keeps spinning to avoid having the "it" person tagged! Fun!

**Tug of war.**...everyone gets a partner and picks a topic from the list that all have been learning. Each person has their own topic and their goal is to convince their partner in an argument why their topic is more important... after the verbal, it has to be settled physically with a giant tug of war, all partners are on opposite sides... Use the power of suggestion to suggest that the audience may find themselves being interested in
energizer activities, and it will be fun & valuable.

**What's in the box?...** You have a real box up front. Others try to guess what's in the box by asking questions that require either a yes or no answer. Uses inductive reasoning, problem-solving, even vocabulary.

**Word for the day...** Announce it early, then others try to catch you using it. Or, you give one to a student and when it's used, all heck breaks loose.

**Writing your name...** with body parts. Students stand up and write their first name with their elbow, their middle name with their other elbow, their last name with their hip, their best friend's name with their other hip and their mom or dad's name with their head.

**Yarn Spider...** get one or two balls of yarn. Group stands in a big circle. The starter holds on to the end of the yarn and tosses the ball to someone across from him or her. That person holds on to the yarn and tosses the ball to another across from him or her. When the ball is unwound, the group has to untangle it all, in order. Celebrate something great about the progress that has been made so far... hi fives, party, dance, etc.

**Variety is the spice.** Every class day or meeting time, each team changes locations - everyone gets up & moves team daily to new place in the room.

## Call-backs & Bring backs

These are actions or activities that can bring a class or group back after a break, lunch or recess. They save you having to play the role of "on-time police."

**"Bring-back" affirmations...** It's usually a good idea to affirm behaviors you like. At the exact moment it's time to start up, raise your own hand as a role model. Then say to the group, "If you made it back on time, raise your hand and say, 'Yes!'"

Use partner to partner or person-to-person or neighbor-to-neighbor affirmations as a call-back. Start out your session by saying, "Turn to the person nearest you and say, 'Welcome back!' or 'I'm glad you're here!'"

**Clapping games...** you stand up front and say, "If you can hear me clap once... and they clap... three seconds later say, "If you can hear me, clap twice." By the second clap, you've usually got just about everyone ready to focus.

Variation on the clapping game above... Keep saying, "If you can hear me, clap once, over and over until you get everyone focused.

Variation on the clapping game above... Face the chalkboard, overhead or flip chart. Start in the center and slowly draw small circles, concentric, getting larger and larger. By the time you get to the boundaries of the paper, you'll have the group's attention. Then say to the group, "Any guesses what I just drew...? It was your attention."

**Foot-stompin' hand clappers...** Use a *"We Will Rock You"* call back routine. One minute before it's time to start up, start foot stomping or desk pounding to the theme of Queen's classic song, *"We Will Rock You."* Encourage everyone to join in until the whole group is in unison. Then it's time to start.

**Music call-backs...** Use a particular song as a call-back idea. Make it a fun, upbeat catchy tune that lasts just 2-3 minutes and ends with a "ta-dah!" Songs like *"Pretty Woman, At The Hop, Chantilly Lace* and *Great Balls of Fire"* are particularly well-suited for these occasions.

**Whistles...** Get a small plastic whistle from a toy store. Many of them have a fun, inviting sound. The first few times you blow it, add the "shhhhh" immediately after it. The group will give you their attention and quiet down. After a few times, you'll never need to add the "shhhhh," since they'll associate quieting down with the whistle. Does the name Pavlov ring a bell? Use a variety of toy store whistles. Have different whistles for different occasions. You might get a classic wooden train whistle or a kids police whistle or even a circus clown whistle.

Take the list above and get together with your staff. Have a brainstorming session where each contributes gaming ideas and the specifics of how to play the games. While it often seems better at first to have a bigger list of games, more is rarely better. It will be more useful to you to have ten games you know well and can adapt, than 100 games you need to learn fresh each time. Some of the best, most adaptable games are role-play, quiz-show, board games, Simon Sez, ball toss and musical chairs.

---

| *Additional Resources for Further Study and Follow up* |
|---|

*Energize!* Carol Apacki Quest Books
*Energizers* by Jones & Bearley
*Brain States* by Kenyon (United States Publishing)*
*Anguished English* by Lederer (Wyrick & Co.)
*The Laughing Classroom* by Loomans & Kolberg (H.J. Kramer Inc.)*
*The New Games Book* by New Games Foundation
*More New Games* by New Games Foundation
*Silver Bullets* by Karl Rohnke
*Free Flight* by Vitale (Jalmar Press)
*Playful Activities for Powerful Presentation* by Williamson (Whole Person Assoc.)*

* These are available in the Appendix.

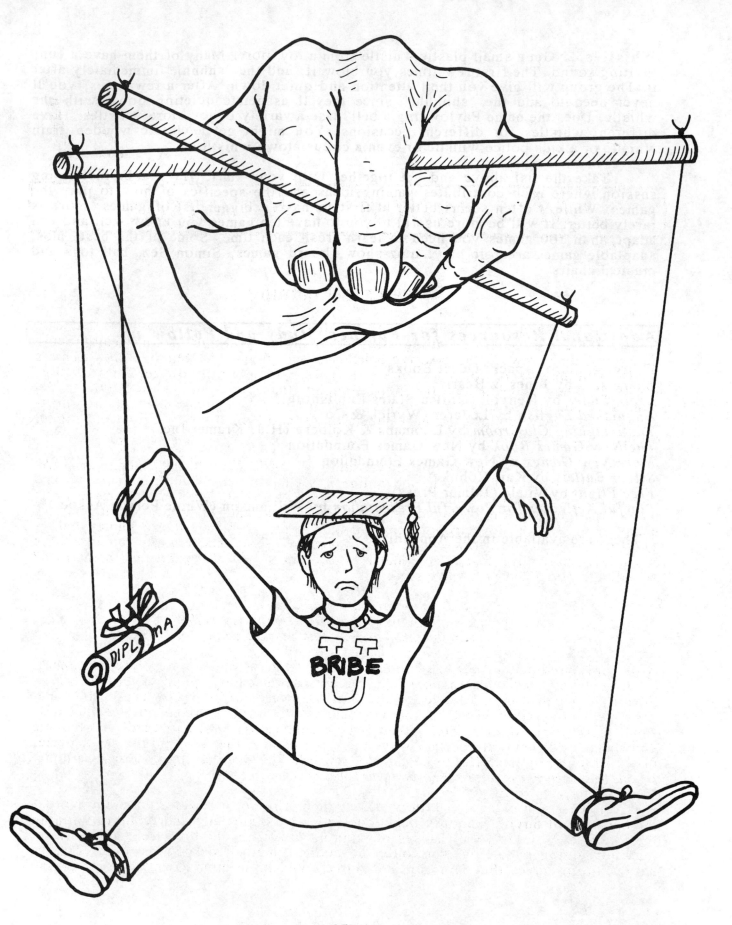

# 21

# Motivation & Rewards

## Rewards in Learning

The old model of teaching was to identify the student behaviors that you wanted (students: on time, sitting still, being quiet, learning, taking tests, being nice, etc.) then, reward the positive behaviors and punish the negative ones. That's the B.F. Skinner theory of behaviorism. It works great on rats. But on human beings it's a disaster. Humans are far more complex than a rat and while you can get humans to do almost anything to gain a reward or avoid punishment in the short-term, you'll never tap into the best human qualities of creativity, civility and higher order-thinking skills. Why?

Rewards create uncertainty in the mind of the learner: "Will I get it or not?" This anxiety causes distress in the brain. It picks the tried and true learning and repeats the predictable, familiar paths. Under this anxiety, the brain's memory is also impaired, so are higher-order thinking skills and creativity. You get the behavior of a lower-level robot, not a magnificent, problem-solving human being. The brain operates in a lower-risk behavior mode. Some teachers use rewards. Are rewards a smart thing to do, considering the brain's natural, operational principles? Absolutely not. First, what is a reward?

*A reward is defined as a*
*compensation or consequence which is both:*
*1) predictable and 2) has market value*

If it's only predictable, but has no market value (e.g., a smile, a hug, a compliment, a long-delayed, low-odds random item, an awards assembly, public approval, etc.), then it is simply an acknowledgment, not a reward. If it has market value, but absolutely **no** predictability (a spontaneous party, pizza, cookies, gift certificates, small gifts, trips, tickets, etc.), then it is a celebration, not a reward. If students know that by behaving a certain way, there's a chance that they might get a prize, that's enough predictability to be called a reward. The determining criteria is simple: *Did the learner change his or her behavior in the hopes of getting the favor?*

If what you offer is a lottery ticket, then it is not a reward. In other words, the behavior of buying a lottery ticket does not have a sufficient correlate to winning the lottery. It's true, your chances of winning are far better by purchasing a ticket than not getting one. However, only the disillusioned or desperate would "behave better" in the hopes that "someone up above" will smile upon them with a winning number. For rewards, the compensation has to have market value (it sure does!) and be predictable (the lottery ticket is not).

If you offer something that has both of those qualities, you are, in fact, bribing the learner. You have a reward system, regardless of what you try to call it. Rewards carry an implicit and covert threat: "If you don't meet the criteria for the reward, some opportunities will be withdrawn from you."

How do you tell which is a reward and which is simply an acknowledgment or celebration? Again, ask the important question: *"Did the learner change behavior based on the possibility of getting something for it?"* In other words, "Did the bribe accidentally or purposely influence or alter the learner's course of action?" As you can tell, the issue has a great deal to do with intent. That's sometimes tough to read.

# Rewards Impair Creativity

The relationship between motivation and rewards has been explored. The research has profound, far-reaching implications for the creative process. It says, "extrinsic motivation inhibits intrinsic motivation." The ability to be creative is strongly linked to intrinsic motivation, since it gives the brain "freedom of intellectual expression," which fuels even more thinking and motivation.

A reward system prevents the establishment of intrinsic motivation because there's rarely an incentive to be creative - only to do the asked for behavior. Creativity is rarely part of any reward system. In fact, the two are usually at far ends of the scale. You get either intrinsically motivated creative thinking or extrinsically motivated repetitive, rote, predictable behaviors.

Caine and Caine say it best: "*[A] system of rewards and punishments can be selectively demotivating in the long term, especially when others have control over the system.*" (Sound like a school or business?) Their contention is that the existence of any behavior-oriented threats and anxiety, coupled with a lack of learner input and control, will "downshift" learner thinking, causing learners to prefer repeated, predictable responses to lower anxiety, and making teachers think the reward system is working. This makes it harder to initiate changes within the system - since any changes in the system will create "threat and anxiety" to both students and teachers, meaning we will get more of the same.

As an example, in kindergarten, many learners get a smiley sticker for good work. By third grade, it's cookies or candies. By fifth grade, the reward is a pizza for a class that behaves well. By eighth grade a student is being bribed by his parents. Is it any wonder that by the time a student reaches eleventh grade, and the teacher wants him to do a research paper, the student response is, "What do I get?" Or he may simply ask, "What for?"

Learners who have been bribed for either good work or good behavior find that soon the last reward wasn't good enough. A bigger and better one is wanted. Soon, all intrinsic motivation has been killed off and the learner is labeled as "unmotivated." Like a rat in a cage pushing a food bar, the learner behavior becomes just good enough to get the reward.

Some, like Kohn, might say that most all rewards are bad. However, Ford argues that it depends on whether the reward creates a conflict with the learner's existing goals. The three most likely times this occurs are:

1. *If the learner feels manipulated by the reward*
"You just want me to give up my guitar lessons."
2. *The reward interferes with the real reason the learner started*
"Now that I'm getting rewarded for getting good grades, I care only about what's on the test, not real learning."
3. *The reward devalues the task and the learner feels bribed*
"This class must be pretty bad if they're giving us a bribe just for attending it."

The three categories above cover most situations where the reward system might be used. It seems that there are few other situations where the need would arise. Let's use as an example, a school that is having problems with truancy and low attendance. The administrative staff decides, as an incentive, to reward those who come every day. Now, each student gets a reward for having a 100% attendance month. The school has worked out an arrangement with local businesses. The reward is a free meal at McDonalds or a pizza at Pizza Hut. Students immediately feel bribed for coming to school. They think, "This must be really bad for them to have to bribe us." But they still do the rewarded behavior. "It's stupid, but we'll play the game," they say. But now school is about "working the system," instead of learning.

## Rewards Perpetuate The Underachievers

In stressful situations, rat behavior becomes rigid and stereotyped with repeated, predictable responses, "completely eliminating the participation of the locale memory system." That's the part of the brain that may be responsible for certain types of memory and spatial mapping. We know from research that the use of rewards increases learner stress.

Other researchers link up the physiological states of anxiety, negative stress and threat with thinking and human performance. The anxiety:

1) reduces the ability to solve complex problems
2) reduces learner responsiveness to the environment
3) increases stereotyped, low-risk behavior
4) increases learner attentiveness to and reliance upon external systems of rewards and punishments

There is evidence linking extrinsic motivation with work involving non-creative tasks, rewards and punishments, memorized skills and repetitive tasks. In order to get learners to be creative and have greater subject interest, higher self-esteem and the ability to be reflective, there must be intrinsic motivation. Reward systems prevent this. Make no mistake about it:

*Learners who are experiencing stress and anxiety
in their environment will prefer external motivation,
meaning a system of reliable rewards*

Paradoxically, *the worse the learner's environment is for intrinsic motivation, the more the learner seeks rewards.* Rewards are initially welcomed by the learner, where predictability and certainty are trade-offs for lowered anxiety. Stressed, anxious learners **are** more likely to look to others for safe, predictable role modeling, to listen to others for goals and to increase their own stereotyped, lower-order thinking. This creates a "Catch-22." Rewards, at a low level, work. So, the teacher continues their usage. The learner now is a victim of the "glass ceiling" principle: he or she learns to perform to the lowest level needed to get the reward.

Caine says, "In effect, they prefer external forms of motivation and lose sight of internal motivation."

Let's use as an example, the learner who has been on a reward system, seems to like it and wants more; he complains when it is dropped and his performance goes down. The teacher uses this as evidence to say, "I know I shouldn't bribe him, but the system works!"

*In the long run, rewards do more damage than good*
*towards motivating the so-called underachiever*

The problem is that the system does work - too well. Then again, holding a gun to someone's head works, too! It will get them to do all kinds of things, but it's not good for the learner's brain (among other things). Rewards lead to learners who become preoccupied with "playing the game" and not really doing quality learning. Why? The ability to alter perceptual maps, to do higher-order thinking and to create complex thematic relationships with the subject is not available to the brain when it experiences the anxiety of a reward system.

Rewards mean: 1) the psychological anxiety of performance increases and 2) every reward carries with it an implied certainty of success or failure - but which one? The learner then wants to reduce the uncertainty, so he picks tasks that have a high degree of predictability (often boring, repetitive skills). The learner also is more likely to pick goals set by others instead of himself (even the goals he does pick are often the basic, overworked, media-reinforced, cliché types).

Replace rewards with positive alternatives. These include: meeting learner goals, peer support, positive rituals, self-assessment, acknowledgments, the love of learning role modeled, enthusiasm, increased feedback, more options for creativity and student control over the work.

Rewards are doing more harm than good by encouraging results other than those originally intended. Phase out reward systems. It makes more sense to make school or work a worthwhile place to be than to try to bribe people to attend or perform. By using the brain-based strategies in this book, rewards will become totally unnecessary.

# Quality Hurt By Rewards

In more than two dozen studies over nearly 20 years gave the same results: in the long run, reward systems lowered the quality of the work and didn't work. Among artists, creativity (as judged by their peers) dropped when they already had signed a contract to sell the work upon completion. The fact that they knew for sure that they were going to be paid for the work lessened their fullest expression. In reading, learners were offered rewards for getting the reading done and for remembering key bits of information. The results were devastating: *learners not only had worse memory for the "key" information, but also the recollection of "incidental" information dropped to almost nothing.*

In terms of reading enjoyment, the incidental and peripheral information is often equally or more important than the key information. It is also considered essential to creativity and understanding because of the contextual base it provides. Reduce or eliminate the use of rewards; they are not worth the cost.

# Rewarded Actions Disappear

In a decade of post-reward research analysis, the conclusions are clear: when the goodies stop, the behavior stops, too. Kazden, *who once was a proponent of rewards*, set up a token economy system in a health care institution. At first, he was excited about the behavior changes. In his first publication, *The Rich Reward of Rewards*, he talked about how much patient behavior had changed. That's what people remembered the most. Ten years later, in *The Token Economy: A Decade Later*, he changes his mind. Kazden says,

> *"Removal of token reinforcement results in decrements in desirable responses and a return to baseline or near-baseline levels of performance"*

Every learner has his or her own bias which they bring to a particular context. The biases constitute personal beliefs, hopes, expectations, fears, values and emotions. These are what hold a behavior in place. In fact, Hart says, "To change the behavior, the biases must be changed, not the behavior directly." The rewards are designed to change the behavior, not the biases. Hence, any reward-driven activity is likely to fail in the long run.

We all know teachers often offer rewards for attendance, homework or discipline. Pizza Hut had a program designed to reward students for reading by offering pizzas. The follow-up may show that the ones who read the most were the ones who were reading already. They just decided to play the game. Many of the readers who were not ordinarily reading before the promotion may not now be readers. Long-term investigation will tell. Many learners could become very intrinsically motivated if given a chance. But as long as a reward system is in place, they'll play the game and undermine their own progress in the long-term. Reduce or eliminate all rewards. Use the alternatives of celebrations, increased variety and quantity of feedback.

# When To Use Rewards

If rewards are counterproductive in so many areas, is there a time and place for them at all? Yes. If your objective is to get people to [temporarily] obey an order, show up on time and do what they're told," rewards can work, researchers says. But, rewards are simply changing the specific, "in the moment" behavior and not the "person." However, if your objective is to achieve any of the following, rewards simply don't work:

- *long-term quality performance*
- *becoming self-directed learners*
- *developing values of caring, respect and friendliness*
- *creativity and higher-order thinking skills*
- *honesty, integrity and self-confidence*
- *inner drive and intrinsic motivation*

In one study, fourth graders were asked what kind of reward they'd like for doing a simple classroom task. They were given that reward for doing it, as promised. Later, when it was time to do the task, *they performed more poorly on the task than the group that was not offered a reward.*

Here's an example of where a reward might be used. You have a bunch of chairs to move to another room. It's the end of the day, you're tired and hungry. You ask a couple of students who stay after class if they'd be willing to help you move them. They say, "No, not really." But you're desperate. You say, "How about if I get you both a Coke?" They change their minds and decide it's worth it. The desks get moved. Everybody's happy. The reward was appropriate. Why? It was for something physical, not intellectual.

## Alternatives Found To Bribes

There are many powerful alternatives to bribing students for intellectual social behaviors. This short-term, narrow-minded Skinnerian approach has been found to do more harm than good. Are there realistic alternatives? Yes, there are. The first and most powerful one is this: make school meaningful, relevant and fun.

Replacing rewards with alternatives gets a bit tricky in two cases. First, in schools, *the entire system of marking and grading is a reward and punishment system*. The rewards are good grades which leads to teacher approval, scholarships and university entry. How can an instructional leader work properly (without bribes and rewards) within a system that is so thoroughly entrenched? Use the options outlined above. What if other teachers use rewards, but you don't? The students will soon discover that your way is not a bribe to learn or behave. Learners will be able to make the distinctions after some time and will prefer your way of learning. Be patient.

Secondly, there are many "gray areas." The getting of a certificate may be just an acknowledgment when you give it, but its role may become complicated. What if the learner takes it home and the parent rewards him with money? Then it becomes a reward in spite of your best intentions. The solution is to try to make parents aware of the destructive effects of rewards at an open house night or by letter. Naturally, schools have to be careful of this "step ladder" effect, where accumulated acknowledgments (certificates, etc.) can lead to a reward.

## The Secrets to Motivation

If you are using any kind of reward system, *let it run its course and end it as soon as you reasonably can*. If you stop it abruptly, you may get a rebellion. The learners will need a "de-tox" or "rehabilitation" time to get off the "reward drug." Remember, the research says:

*Learners who have been on a reward system will*
*become conditioned to prefer it over free choice*

The brain loves to learn. This book is full of alternatives to bribery. At the earliest possible convenience, end the system and replace rewards with alternatives. One of the most commonly asked questions, from both new and experienced teachers, is: "How do I motivate students to learn?" The answer is simple. You don't. The human brain already loves to learn. Your learners have already motivated themselves for much of their life. Their brains have hungrily absorbed information, integrated it, made meaning out of it, remembered it and used it at the appropriate moment thousands of times. In short, any learner who is physically sitting in your class already 1) motivated him or herself to get there 2) has already motivated himself thousands of times 3) may or may not be in a motivated state at the moment.

The secret to remove de-motivating conditions and to do the little things that spark intrinsic motivation.

# Learning Comes First

The question "How do I motivate students?" says more about the asker than the students. It also shows a misunderstanding of the real nature of motivation. All of your students are motivated to learn. In fact, the survival of your students depends on learning (though not necessarily what's taught in school). So, why don't some students seem like they want to learn in your class? Glasser says, it's really about control.

Many teachers are really asking a different question, "How can I control their behavior?" Is your paradigm that your job is to be a learning catalyst (one who lights a fire for learning) or that of a "teacher"(one who stands and delivers - once the students are under control)? In the paradigm of a teacher, there are many ways to "motivate..." temporarily. But it's a dangerous short-term solution.

In the paradigm of a learning catalyst, it's a moot question. After all, in a positive learning environment, the learners are already motivated - just the way they already were before walking to class. Management guru Dr. Deming said that "All human beings are born with intrinsic motivation." They don't need someone to stand over them and motivate them (unless they have a learning-antagonistic environment).

# Avoid Labeling Learners

The unmotivated learner is a myth. Rarely are the most motivating conditions for learning met in a school context. This may explain why so many have been labeled as "underachievers" or "low" students. To arrive at school or a classroom requires some sort of motivation. It may be positive or negative, but it has gotten them there. Once the learner is in the seat, either they are bringing a new strong motivating attitude with them, or the teacher needs to elicit one. The demotivated learner's negative beliefs and behaviors are usually triggered or reinforced by an artificial, unresponsive school environment. Identifying, classifying, grouping, labeling, evaluating, comparing, and assessing these demotivated learners has done little to solve the problem.

*There is no such thing as an unmotivated learner...*
*there are, however, temporary unmotivated states that schools,*
*teachers or students themselves can trigger*

Each learner is either motivated from within (intrinsic) or from the outside (extrinsic). *All of the following de-motivate learners and drive out of them any possibility of intrinsic motivation:*

- Coercion, control and manipulation
- Weak, critical or negatively competitive relationships
- Infrequent or vague feedback
- Outcome-based education (unless learners generate outcomes)
- Inconsistent policies and rules
- Top-down management & policy-making
- Repetitive, rote learning
- Sarcasm, put-downs and criticism
- The perception of irrelevant content

- Boring, single-media presentations
- Reward systems of any kind
- Teaching in just one or two of the multiple intelligences
- Systems that limit reaching personal goals
- Responsibility without authority
- Hopelessness in achieving academic success

Most teachers use both intrinsic and extrinsic forms of motivation. As a result, much of the good things that are done by a teacher are undermined by themselves or others. The obvious choice is to have your learners motivated mostly from within. To do that, it takes a more brain-based approach. The research on motivation is both powerful and persuasive:

*The school environment, for most learners, is quite antagonistic towards motivated learning... educators would literally be astonished by the motivated learning possible in a non-coercive environment*

Should the environment be all smiles, hugs and easy grades? *Absolutely not.* The brain thrives on challenges and variety. Stanford biologists separated amoebae cultures into three petri dishes. One was the control, another gave the amoebae an abundance of food, light and heat. The third gave the amoebae just enough of each while randomly varying the amounts. You might guess the results: the third amoebae culture developed the strongest and lived longest. Can you apply that to our own environment? Many successful teachers already do... they never punish the students nor do they make everything so easy they never grow. When learners are required to figure it out, learning on their own and developing themselves, they grow more.

## Intrinsic vs. Extrinsic Motivation

Much of the extrinsic motivation characteristics originate in the home life. Parents who bribe their children, who role-model laziness, a lack of curiosity and avoid new learning contribute to the problem. While we have little influence on home factors, we can influence others. Researcher Bishop makes the distinction very well:

"Young people are not lazy. In their jobs after school and on the football field, they work very hard. In these environments they are part of a team where individual efforts are visible and appreciated by teammates. Competition and rivalry are not absent, but they are offset by shared goals, shared successes and external measures of achievement... On the sports field, there is no greater sin than giving up, even when the score is hopelessly one-sided. On the job, tasks not done by one worker will generally have to be completed by another...."

When a student drops out of school, he's not unmotivated; he just wants a more responsive environment, *which the world outside of school promises.* If we can make dramatic, positive alterations in the school's climate, policies, teacher methodologies and systems, we can keep the focus on learning and hook learners in for a lifetime.

Let's say a student seems unmotivated all week long. Teachers say that he has no motivation or concentration. But on Saturday, he has his guitar lessons. He practices for hours without any bribe or external motivation. This activity makes quite a statement about how much the student loves to learn.

266

There is a great deal of disagreement among researchers regarding what promotes intrinsic motivation. In fact, an interesting question is, "Should 100% intrinsic motivation even be desired?" Many would say no. Regardless, here are specific ways you can encourage intrinsically motivated learners:

- **help them learn to control their environment**
- **encourage stimulation, activity and incongruities**
- **discourage feelings of inferiority**
- **provide choices that tap into learner goals**
- **build high self-concept and positive beliefs**
- **offer challenges, problems & novelty**
- **have high expectations of success**
- **role-model satisfaction from achievement**
- **create situations where learning is the by-product**
- **stimulate emotional intensity in learning through debates, music, drama, role-play**
- **avoid rewards, role model love of learning**

Other strategies can easily be developed in a learning context and many are relatively simple to do. When students arc given control over the content and process of their learning, motivation goes up. But to motivate learners, it is important to allow them to make choices "about personally relevant aspects of a learning activity." Students need to be able to align self-determination goals with instructional goals.

In addition, learners who tend to focus more on fun and friendships may be able to be engaged when there are ample opportunities for self-determination and peer interaction. These provide ways to meet personal goals and, to some, degree, instructional goals. In other words, the more ways the goals can serve the learner's own agendas, the better.

There are ways to tap into learning, excitement and participation levels for many learners who appear to be unmotivated. Help learners to become more aware of their own personal, academic, health, social, athletic and career goals. A student is often willing to work on a team project because there's another person on the project that he likes and would like to get to know better.

Design instructional experiences that allow for more ways for learners to meet their own goals. They need ways to show off, meet new people, be an expert in something, grow, get in shape or become well-respected. Implement as many of the optimal motivating conditions possible as much of the time as possible. Avoid labeling any learner as "low" or unmotivated. That perception or label alone can demotivate them. Here are some of the best teaching guidelines for bringing out the natural, intrinsic motivation of your learners.

## Use These Motivators

1. **Give learners control & choice**
   Let learners control, at various times, how they will learn a topic, when they lcarn, with whom they learn it and how they'll be assessed. You provide the appropriate structure and guidelines, they get to choose many of the little things. Creativity and choice allow the learner to express & feel valued. The opposite of this is manipulation, coercion and control. Creativity and choice lower stress and draw out what the learner really wants to do and learn.

2. **Make sure your methods and topics meet perceived needs & goals**
The brain is designed biologically to survive. It will learn what it NEEDS to learn to survive. Make it a top priority to discover what needs your learners have and engage those needs. If students need what you have, they're interested. If the content relates to the student's own personal life, they're interested. For example, six year-old students have higher needs for security, predictability and teacher acceptance than a 14 year old student. Their needs are more likely to be peer acceptance, a sense of importance and hope. An 18 year-old learner is more interested in autonomy and independence. Use what's appropriate for the age level of your students.

3. **Engage strong emotions**
Engage emotions productively with compelling stories, games personal examples celebration, role-play, debate, rituals, music. We are driven to act upon our emotions because they are strong forces in compelling decision-making.

4. **Use friendships, partners and group work**
Learners do better in an environment with positive social bonding. The are more motivated when they like the teacher and when the get to work with friends in groups or teams. Again, this interdependence reduces helplessness and stress.

5. **Curiosity**
It's one of the oldest and still the best ways to engage learners. We all know that inquiring minds want to know, that's the nature of the human brain.... Keep engaging curiosity - it works! Newspaper tabloids and electronic tabloids have played off our curiosity for years. Witness all the stories about Elvis, aliens celebrities, freaks of nature and UFOs. In your classroom, use leading questions, mysteries, special hooks and experiments.

6. **Nutrition**
Better nutrition means better mental alertness. Learn about how we think, learn and want to improve. Write up a list of suggestions, give to students or parents or both. Suggest specific brain foods (eggs, fish, nuts, leafy dark green vegetables, apples and bananas). Encourage taking multivitamin & mineral supplements.

7. **Engage more of the multiple intelligences**
They can really hook learners in: spatial, bodily-kinesthetic, interpersonal, verbal-linguistic, intrapersonal, musical-rhythmic, mathematical-logical. When learners get to express what they know and how they know it, they are more motivated to continue to grow.

8. **Your use of success stories**
Tell true stories of particular individuals, yours or others, that overcame obstacles to succeed. Any famous ones? Any who have made a major contribution? These stories form structure that creates a mythology of success.

9. **Acknowledgments**
These include assemblies, certificates, group notices, team reports, peers who give compliments, teachers who praise appropriately. These give learners positive associations which continue to fuel further actions.

10. **Frequency of feedback**
Make it your part-time job to make sure learners get far more feedback each class. Use peers, charts, discussion, peer teaching, projects, role-play, non-verbals, self-assessment and oral games. Make sure that every single learner gets some kind of feedback, from you or someone else, every 30 minutes or less. The all-time best way to motivate the brain is with information - immediately and dramatically. That's what hooks kids into video games and adults into gambling (slot machines, horses, sports, card games, betting, etc.); they continually get feedback. The feedback motivates them to do it again.

**11. Manage learner states**
Role model being in strong, motivated states. Learn to read and manage states. Even good learners can go into unmotivated states. Change activities often, use strong questions and multi-media approaches. Never let a student remain in bad or unmotivated states for long. It creates the wrong precedent.

**12. Provide hope of success**
Learners need to know that it's possible for them to succeed. Regardless of the obstacles or how far behind, hope is essential. Every good game show, from *Jeopardy* to *Wheel of Fortune* keeps the players hooked in with the slim chance of success, even when they're far behind others.

**13. Role model joy of learning**
Enjoy your work and come to your class to share what you have learned every day. Since over 99% of all learning is non conscious, the more you get excited about learning, the more motivated and excited your learners are likely to be.

**14. Celebrations**
These include peer acknowledgment, parties, food, hi-fives, cheers, etc. These create the atmosphere of success and can trigger the release of endorphins that boost further learning. Do not use these as a bribe; they are effective when spontaneous and random.

**15. Make the classroom physically & emotionally safe**
Insure it's emotionally safe to make mistakes and physically safe from hazards or other students. Make it safe to ask any question and safe to make contributions. Insure that physical needs are met for lighting, water, food, movement, seating.

**16. Use learner's learning style**
Do things visually, auditorally and kinesthetically. Provide both choice in how learners learn, and diversity in what you offer. By appealing to the learner's best strategies, you'll make it more accessible.

**17. Instill positive beliefs (capability & context)**
Reinforce to learners that they can succeed and can do this particular task. Discover what those beliefs are as soon as possible and work to affect them positively. Do this through affirmations, success stories, indirect references, posters and how you interact with students.

All of the items mentioned above cost nothing (no rewards or bribes needed). It is certainly more preparation and work initially, to create a climate of intrinsic motivation, but it pays off in the long run. Teachers who rely on extrinsic motivation may be vastly underestimating three things: 1) the power of their influence 2) the desire of the learner to be intrinsically motivated 3) the long term ease in doing it. Take your time. Implement just one motivator per week. Soon, you'll find miracles taking place. You'll have excited, confident and motivated learners everyday.

## Additional Resources for Further Study and Follow up

*Building Your Child's Self-Esteem & Confidence* by Dargatz (Thomas Nelson)
*Motivating Humans* by Ford (Sage)
*Control Theory in the Classroom* by Glasser (Harper Collins)
*Schools Without Failure* by Glasser (Harper Collins)
*Brain-Based Learning & Teaching* by Jensen (Turning Point)*
*The Little Book of Big Motivation* by Jensen (Ballantine)*
*Punished by Rewards* by Alfie Kohn (Houghton-Mifflin)*
*Eager to Learn* by Raymond Wlodkowski (Jossey-Bass)
*Enhancing Adult Motivation to Learn* by Raymond Wlodkowski (Jossey-Bass)

* These are available in the Appendix.

- **CENTER** YOURSELF
- **LISTEN** FOR **FEELINGS**
- **GATHER** INFORMATION
- **MAKE** A **DECISION**
- **RE·ALIGN** WITH STUDENTS
- **FOLLOW THROUGH** AND SUPPORT

# 22

# Discipline Made Easy

## Discipline Can Be Simple

For many teachers, this might be the most important chapter in the book. Yet, the more you get out of the other chapters, the less you'll need this one! Therefore, it is strongly recommended that you read all of the other chapters first. As you'll be discovering, classroom management problems are usually symptoms of mismanagement elsewhere. When the other parts of your teaching are done well, you'll have a bare minimum of discipline problems.

## Problems Are Just Symptoms

Discipline problems are not only NOT the real problem, but they can be a gift to you. If you went to a physician to get a physical and your doctor said you have a calcium deficiency, would you be mad at the doctor? Of course not! In the same way, a student who misbehaves is letting you know of a possible "teaching deficiency." You might think, "No, it's a character deficiency in the student." Mark my words:

*As long as you believe the problem is "out there"*
*it will never, ever get solved*

Quit the "helpless victim" mentality. You can have a class of responsible, engaged learners who enjoy class everyday. Use what's in this book and that dream will become a reality. Guaranteed. Students who "act up" are not a problem. That's simply feedback... essential for your success. What you call problems are the results of gaps in your teaching and give you important information that you can use to be a better teacher.

Have you ever watched a baby play? Learning and curiosity are natural human states. When curiosity is aroused, all our senses are attentive to the task at hand. We are absorbed and nothing else is important. Discipline is unnecessary. In an ideal classroom, discipline problems are minimal. If you do what is suggested in the other chapters in this book, your classroom management problems will virtually disappear. Guaranteed.

## No Such Student as a "Trouble-Maker"

You might be thinking, "You haven't met so and so!" But no student gets up in the morning thinking, "How can I be a real jerk today?" Each person makes the

271

best possible choice, 100% of the time... given the context, the perceived choices available and the outcome desired. In certain states, negative behaviors get chosen. You may recall, from an earlier chapter, a basic premise in learning: all behavior is state-related. Some teachers often label something "problem behavior," or label the student as a "trouble-maker."

Using a label to describe classroom behavior is an injustice to you as well as to the student. There are no unresourceful people, only unresourceful behavioral states. To change the behavior, change their state. In other words, your students all have the capacity to act appropriately, but they access an unresourceful behavioral state at times. Your job is to keep those negative states at a minimum and work towards the positive ones.

# No Tips or Tools Will
# Replace Your Own Growth

Another assumption is that all a teacher needs is a few tips, tools or techniques to manage the classroom better. They won't work. For things to change, you must change. Private victories always precede public victories. Learn to deal with your own "dark side" before you start telling others how to deal with their own. *The fact that you get mad or frustrated at life, a situation or a student does not give you the right to be rude, disrespectful or hurting to another.* Find other outlets for your own stress, anger and frustration. Whatever it takes, learn how to deal with it. Everything you master in your own personal growth makes classroom success much easier.

If you have problems in your classroom the first thing to consider is that you are a co-creator of the mess. If the framework you operate from is that, "I'm not the problem, it's those trouble-makers," *nothing will be ever be resolved.* This is not to say that the students don't have anything to do with it. Of course they do. But, to mobilize your own resources and make the necessary changes, you must accept responsibility for what goes on in your classroom. There are two totally different models and approaches:

## EXISTING BEHAVIORIST MODEL

Student as the subject and problem.
Goal: identify and measure all the desired outcomes...
reward the desired ones and punish the undesired ones

## *MORE USEFUL MODEL*

*Personal responsibility... Ask,
"How can I engage the learner naturally,
intrinsically, to learn best, and what can
I do to encourage more learning?"*

Unless you change your AND their awareness, every conventional method of discipline will fail and fail consistently. Those methods will fail because, for the most part, they don't provide the student with additional resources or choices. In other words, telling a student to quit doing something does not empower him or her, it only frustrates and infuriates.

272

Classroom discipline must be done in a way that supports the dignity of students. Keep their self-esteem intact or you will pay the price. Some studen don't get mad; they get even by being a discipline problem as retribution for you damage to them. The theme of this chapter could as well be to discipline with dignity or to correct with compassion. Your job is to expand students' choices, not shut them down. To accomplish that goal you must be flexible and learn what unfulfilled needs students have. You must dovetail outcomes, find where you have common ground, then design a management strategy. In short, start with a well-defined personal discipline philosophy.

# Discipline Philosophy

## 1. Disruptions are a normal part of living

The normal class disruptions are part of school, of life and of our reality. Treat them as enjoyable challenges & sources of curiosity. It is easier to adapt your understanding of the world to reality, than to try to change the world to your point of view. The message this attitude gives to students is: "School is real life."

## 2. The classroom is a "learning environment"

It's a learning environment in which occasional discipline takes place, NOT a "Well-disciplined class in which learning better occur! (or else!) The worst environment for learning is high fear, high stress. The optimal learning state is "low stress, high challenge." The message this gives to students is: "What we are about is learning."

## 3. Students are all basically good

Students, like you, are just trying to manage their daily lives. No one wakes up in the morning with the sole intent to "get you." However, students do have normal concerns for expression, control, attention & love. They are often just like you, even if they don't seem like it.
The message this attitude gives is: "You and I are both good persons, I respect and appreciate you."

## 4. The best discipline is the kind nobody notices

The less students know they are being disciplined, the better. Keep "learning" as the "class event" by reading states & creating constant novelty & diversity. The more outraged you become about discipline problems, the more they occur. (If you're upset, who's in control?) Remember this: "Where the attention goes, the energy flows!" Keep your attention more focused on the joy & excitement of learning. The message this gives to students is: "The teacher has things handled."

## 5. It's never your class; it's the "group's group"

Your class has it's own culture and they behave according to the rules of their culture, not yours. What rules have you allowed or encouraged to be created by the group? If you over-exert power as a leader without the permission of the group, the group will sabotage you. Position gives you power, but not permission.

## 6. Problems are usually spontaneous expressions

Respond non-verbally, non-traditionally to most of them. Most problem-behaviors originate from the random areas of the brain (reptilian, limbic or right brain). Make your responses appropriate to where the student is really at. Save the lectures & left-brain discussion of rules as a last resort response. The message this gives to students is: "I know exactly where you're at."

# Six Discipline Models

...many ways to approach the issue of discipline. The strategies that ...ng will be an extension of the beliefs and philosophy you have. Which ...  Each one is rated with a star, from a one star P (worst) to a four star ...e best) system. What makes a system better than another? Ease of use, ...erm value to students and emphasis on learning, not intimidation or fear.

**Behavior modification.** Orderly approach based on the sequence "identify, reward and punish." Keeps track of student behavior. Behaviorist theory in action. Example: "Assertive Discipline." P

**Personal Influence.** Based on teacher-student relationships. Build up relationships, then use them to modify behavior. PP

**Logical consequences.** Teacher helps students to understand what they did and why. Then a student explores alternatives and consequences. Teacher role is high. PP

**Self-Awareness Training.** Teacher trains students to observe their own behaviors, so they know when they're behaving counterproductively. Teacher role is active at first, then students get more involved. PP

**Cooperative Discipline.** Use of groups and teams, plus student and teacher relationships. Emphasizing prevention and group norms. PPP

**Brain-Based Discipline.** Teacher emphasizes learning as activities of choice. Does "Invisible discipline" by changing activities, giving students appropriate emotional and linguistic expression. This is the methodology discussed in detail below. PPPP

# Different Strokes

Teachers who have mastered the science and art of classroom management have done it many different ways. Some say, "Don't smile for the first month." Some use sugar, some vinegar. Some follow a system, others say "do whatever works." What is most important when dealing with these issues is that you maintain an atmosphere of love, consistency and integrity. Students need to know they are still good people, it's their behavior that is unacceptable. Students need consistency so they know the framework and boundaries for behavior and don't need to keep testing them to find out how much you'll bend each day. Finally, students need to know that you will keep your word and honor your values. This sets the example for them to do the same and will reduce discipline problems long-term.

# An Ounce of Prevention

While the management of classroom behavior seems like a useful skill, there are some secrets to making it easier. Learn to serve the needs behind the discipline problems and you'll discover that problems disappear quickly. You may have to try several to discover the ones you are most comfortable with but it's well worth it. It's also important to know that these tools are designed to be used only in conjunction with the other tools in the rest of the chapters in this book.

# 33 Simple and Powerful Ways to
# Prevent Discipline Problems

1. **Limit the amount of focused,** directed learning time before switching activities. Suggested time: age of the student in minutes to maximum of 20. With an eight year-old student, teach in a directed, lecture-driven manner for a maximum of eight minutes. Then, move to a more diffused activity like groupwork.

2. **Use baroque music** in the background, at low level to soothe & inspire. Good choices include: Handel's Water Music, Vivaldi's Four Seasons and Bach's Brandenburg Concertos.

3. **Create more "W-I-I-F-M" for the students:** (What's in it for me?). They must generate the reasons to do things...best & worse case scenarios. Ask they what they could get out of learning a new unit.

4. **Make rules fair, clear & enforceable...** fewer the better. Make sure that students know the reasons behind every rule you have.

5. **Put students in cooperative groups or teams** (with accountability!). Use as a source of fun, socialization and positive peer pressure.

6. **Make a positive contact** with each of your students within the first five minutes of class. Over time, connect with parents, if possible.

7. **Boost ways students can have more input** into classroom activities... Ask questions, get input, install a suggestion box... read all, respond to them orally or do them!

8. **More auditory outlets for expression.** The more appropriate forms of noisy, kinesthetic rituals you have the less valuable classtime is stolen. Students teach, "buzz time," partner affirmations, group or team time, discussion, cheers, sharing.

9. **When you present rules,** let students play the "what if" game to find exceptions, or role-play or brainstorm solutions to make rules concrete.

10. **Make the classroom more interesting** to be a student in & change walls often, you or your students make it busy, colorful, fresh, challenging & relevant.

11. **Anticipate, read and respond swiftly to student states...** know that frustration often leads to states of apathy, anger or revenge. Make state management a #1 priority to prevent problems.

12. **Make rapport-building a part-time job.** Start with those you relate to least & do it verbally & non-verbally. If it's broken, repair it ASAP. Know the tendencies of auditory learners who tend to talk a lot and mis-matchers who accidentally disrupt class in an attempt to learn. They're often pointing out what's "off, different, missing or wrong." Use secret signals with them to prevent disruption of whole class.

13. **Keep the physical body moving** many times per hour or brain can switch off... movement, simon sez, hands-on, stretch, or switch activities.

14. **Keep your own stress levels low.** "Download" each school day. Take care of your physical body. Enjoy de-stressing "mindless" relaxing play.

15. **Work on areas of your concern** like parent communications or improving administrative policies or communications to staff.

16. **Give clear, mobilizing directions to students.** Make them consistent, re-check for understanding, then use same congruent call to action.

17. **Give students more control** over their learning through choosing: ways to do things, topics, rules, time, partners, scoring, music, etc.

18. **Get parents involved** in your discipline program from year's start. Send home the plan, the reasons, the excitement & get agreement.

19. **Have lunch with a student** to start, build or maintain relationship

20. **Teach using the multiple intelligences.** Make sure that when you plan out your week, you have covered all of them (every single week).
21. **Provide outlets** for kids to talk about the things that are important to them. Use discussion time, sharing circles, partner or buddy time.
22. **Students can write a monthly letter to teacher & get a response.**
23. **Role play discipline problems** & positive reactions & responses
24. **Peer management** - set up student teams or sets of partners to help them be more aware of unacceptable behavior.
25. **Be consistent and fair** so that students know it's worth following rules. The more consistent you are, the better.
26. **Know when it's time** for a whole class break (to go outside or change plans).
27. **Let students know you care** by attending some kind of outside of class activity that they're in, like a sporting event, a play, a civic event, etc.
28. **Manage the group's leaders** so they'll set the cultural standards for the group

### 29. Develop Sensory Acuity

The periphery of your eye is physiologically built to detect movement far better than the foveal portion of your eye. The way it's constructed, you can gather most of the data you need between a forty-five and a ninety-degree angle. Surprising? You can detect movement, facial responses and changes in breathing on a non-conscious level if you'll just learn to trust that ability. Here are a few other ways:

a. While you are talking to one student, break eye contact, politely, so you can scan the room. Listen for unusual sounds and notice any new movements. This keeps students accountable.

b. Learn to use up what is called "dead time." All the transition time for collecting papers, starting or stopping activities or in between activities is usually a signal for students to begin disruptive activities. The solution? A stretch break or purposeful discussion.

c. If students are restless, give them a break. Have them stand up, inhale, hold their breath for a few seconds, then exhale. Then do some stretching or just a few quick movement exercises to get the circulation going again. Use that time to figure out how you can make the adjustments in your lesson to make learning more valuable, useful, fun or relevant.

### 30. Inclusion - Include Everyone

Most teachers teach to a minority of the students. Give your presentation three or four very different ways so that it reaches more kinds of learners. Explain things auditorally, then show visually, then demonstrate kinesthetically. It means that you give directions several different times, different ways, even with a higher or lower voice, so insure that you included everyone.

### 31. Increase Predictability

One of the ways for your students to access erratic behavior is because of anxiety, confusion and lack of clarity. In earlier chapters, we mentioned the importance of structure and ritual. Students like to know that certain things will happen at certain times.

a. Build in your own ritual. For example, when you are giving directions, always give them with the same pattern. It might be that you first say, then show visually, then demonstrate, then say again, then post them up. This way, the

276

students will learn quickly to pay extra attention during the style of the explanation they understand the best.

b. Post schedules, give schedules. It reduces classroom confusion because a surprising amount of noise and upsets occur over students not knowing what to do.

c. Have variety of options you can use within a predictable structure.

d. Learn to systematically use your own non-verbals. Read the chapter on presentation skills and the one on interactions. The systematic use of non-verbals is one of the real keys to reducing discipline problems and less than 10% of all teachers use it well.

## 32. Create Rapport

This tool is so important it was also mentioned in the chapters on introduction and presentation. Webster's defines rapport as "a relation marked by harmony, conformity, accord or affinity." Do you have that with your students? Only you would know. There are many methods of joining their world and building rapport. You need to choose the ones that are most comfortable for you.

a. Match language-use the same predicate. Listen to how each student represents experiences and match it.

| Visual | Auditory | Kinesthetic |
|---|---|---|
| an eyeful | an earful | a pain in the neck |
| looks like | sounds like | it feels like |
| get the picture | pay attention | get the drift of |
| a dim view | unheard of | underhanded |
| perspective | an account of | get a handle on |

Also match the superlatives that they use. For example, words such as "good, great, excellent, super, or fabulous," are all words which form parts of people's language patterns. Use the same words your students use. Particularly, build relationship with the class leaders. Once you have relationship with them, the rest of the class often follows.

a. Match body movements-with whole body: adjust your body to match stance and posture; with gestures: carefully and subtly match gestures; with face: match their eyebrows, mouth, nose, smile; with their head: match the angle of leaning; with their voice: match tempo, tonality, intensity and volume. With breath: match the rate.

b. You may also increase rapport by discussing, referring to or simply mentioning things that are a large part of your student's world. It may be an upcoming exposition, a rock concert, a holiday, a symphony, a movie, the weather, clothing styles, movie or TV stars.

c. You may also do cross-over mirroring. This is when you use one activity to match a different activity with another. For example, pace a student's eye blinks with your finger tapping or foot tapping or pace the tempo of their voice by scratching or nodding.

With rapport, you're better able to be accepted to and listed to by the learners. You have more influence with them and are better able to understand and enter their world. Of all the tools to reduce discipline problems, the ability to create rapport is certainly of the most important.

277

### 33. Create the Classroom Climate

One of the best ways to start reducing discipline problems is to change the way that you allow yourself to experience others. Avoid seeing students as a problem and start seeing your students as grand possibilities. Refuse to call anyone in your class a "trouble-maker" or "bad kid," or he (or she) will prove you right every time. Instead, refer to the students as "pending miracles" (ones you haven't reached yet, but will). It will make all of the difference in the world.

The old-style quiet classrooms are fast-becoming extinct. Classroom noise is now the pleasant side affect of a highly interactive student learning. Learn to accept a higher level of noise than was common years ago.

## How to Win the Power Game

Below is the triangle structure of power. If I perceive that you are in a position of power (like a student, who thinks of a teacher) and I don't have position, I will use either your time or withhold information. In other words, the more you exert power over your students, the more they will waste your valuable class time or withhold key information from you.

*The more power*
*you give to your students*
*the less they will try*
*to take it away from you*

Here's an example. A student throws a paper airplane behind your back and it hits you. You turn and ask, "Who did it?" No one tells you. Why do they do that? *That's the only power they have over you,* wasting your time or withholding information. As you lower the amount of heavy-handed power you exercise, students perceive that you are less threatening and they offer more information or waste less of your time.

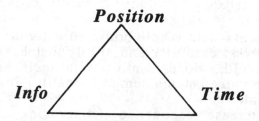

Think about it. Anytime you've been in a position in a organization where you felt powerless, didn't you waste time or withhold key "gossip" or information useful to the hierarchy? Of course. It was your only way to experience power. The way you reduce discipline problems is by understanding this essential "power game" and learning how to meet the needs of your students. The way to "win" the power game is to give away enough power so that others don't want to take it from you. Simple, yet effective. When you empower individuals (whom you used to label as trouble-makers) they won't have to compete with you for power.

## They're in Another World

Before you discipline students, remember they're in another world, separated by age, culture, income, status and maybe gender. One invisible quality of our student's lives is time. Each of your students is "referenced" to a primary time-status. It's either past, present or future. The decisions and behaviors of your students that you might call erratic, negative or undisciplined are often simply a reflection of living out a different time frame. Here's an example.

If your so-called "problem student" is constantly late, it may be because he is present referenced. That means that decisions are made which indicate a primary concern for "How am I feeling right now?" A present-referenced student might be out in the hallways or lockers talking to friends all the way up until the bell rings, then have to come to class late. If he was so "in the moment" of the present time, he's thinking about how much fun he's having, not what he SHOULD DO IN THE FUTURE (like get to class).

This student is not motivated by future rewards (or punishments). He will do his homework if (at the moment he gets around to it), he feels like it. Hence this student is more fun, enjoys spontaneity, lives in the moment and is unpredictable. It would be a mistake to call him "unmotivated or "apathetic" because he turns his homework in late (if at all) or is late for class. He's simply not relating to the future and the consequences you may be wanting him to do.

## Using Rules, Guidelines and Agreements

Studies show that setting limits and successfully enforcing them gives students a sense of stability, structure and self-esteem. Students with clear guidelines seem to behavior better. Make a clear distinction between rules, guidelines and agreements.

- **Rules** - The exercise of authority or control... prescribed guides for conduct or action." Notice that Webster's says nothing about mutually agreed upon standards. Instead, it is the imposition of authority or control. *These are to be put in practice for those actions which need a swift direct response regardless of the student's feelings about the matter.* Examples include assault, property damage, theft, arson, truancy, profanity, a dress code or substance abuse. Everyone must follow these, primarily for the safety of others.

- **Guidelines** - An "indication of policy or conduct." Notice that a guideline itself is not a rule, it merely indicates a rule. This gives a lot of leeway in the interpretation and given teaching situations. Examples might include politeness, noise levels, or raise your hand to speak.

- **Agreements** - A "harmonious accord on a course of action." Notice that the key word in this definition is harmonious. It implies that both parties, on their own free will, and, in fact, with a spirited joyousness, agree upon a common code or plan of behavior. Examples are that you and students agree on a behavior code, seating plan, a homework or testing policy or class procedures.

Make sure you make distinctions for your students and tell why you have each of them. Once you have explained it, most students will know exactly where you are and will not test you continually (provided you enforce them consistently).

## Getting Classroom Agreements

Your students may be ready to help you with the rules. You might say, "Since we want to have our class work well, where everyone is safe, respected and we can learn, let's all agree on some rules. Any suggestions?" Hold a discussion, make it democratic to the degree that is appropriate. You'll want the following:

1. The rule
2. The reason for the rule
3. Any exceptions to the rule
4. The consequences of breaking the rule
5. Post the rules on paper up on the walls

Once discussion completed on each of the rules, get oral and hands up agreement. Say, "All in support and favor, say aye... all opposed, say nay." In general, the fewer the agreements, the better; they are easier to remember and keep.

# Suggested Agreements

1. **Time.** Each student agrees to be seated on time (as determined by the clock on the back wall) for the start of class or the resumption of class after a break. In other words, each student agrees to arrange his circumstances, take care of his needs, and do what has to be done in a way that allows him to be on time.
2. **Safety and Respect.** Students agree to listen while others are talking if the teacher has given permission. Each student agrees to treat other persons and all property safely and harmlessly. (Translated, it means you may not steal, harm, push, shove, destroy, insult, hit, deface, badger, name-call, tease or irritate another student or property.)
3. **Support Learning.** Each student can learn and will also allow others to learn successfully. (Translated: you may not block another's view, disrupt them, throw anything, talk while others are reading or writing).
4. **Respect our Learning Environment.** Keep your classroom clean. Pick up after yourself and keep your own desk area clean. No throwing of objects or tracking in dirt, mud or snow. Take pride in your whole learning environment.
5. **Speak from Your Own Experience.** Use "I" messages. This also means that you can't say, "That guy's a jerk," because the sentence must include the speaker's responsibility for the labeling: What you could say is that, "I didn't like him," or "I couldn't get along with him."

*When you treat*
*your students specially*
*they don't have to act special*

1. Tell students beforehand that you will let them know if they break an agreement and that you will make no concessions or compromises.
2. Be consistent and immediate in your communication to the student. Always let them know when they have broken an agreement and do it immediately. They must know that there is no 'safe time unless specified.
3. Make sure that it's a class agreement that was broken, not just something that you made up or something you just don't like. If you don't have the agreements memorized, you may want to post them up, or reduce the number of them.

# Four Simple Levels

Here are some options for dealing with problems in the moment. Hopefully, you'll take care of most of these through prevention. The ideas are listed in the order of how you can deal with simple, minor infractions to most severe.

## Level #1  Invisible Action

At this first level, nobody knows except the teacher. You are affecting the student's behavior, but he or she doesn't know it. Here, you do whatever it takes to change the physiological state of the student(s). Pick from the examples given below. There are many ways to do "invisible discipline" including:

___ create novelty, switch activities    ___ ask everyone to take in a slow deep breath
___ tonality of voice shift    ___ you or attention drawn away
___ use change of music    ___ you switch places to side or back of room
___ step out of room for 5"    ___ stretching or simon sez game
___ give instructions to all to give to each other a "partner to partner" affirmations
___ simply call on the person NEXT to them. This usually brings their attention back to the room.

## Level #2 Handling the Problem, Not the Person

Here, everyone knows you're doing something to quiet them down, but no one feels singled out or picked on. Class to continues on and you treat it as "no big deal." These strategies get the job done and still avoid the "bad dog" or "shame" strategy.

___ name dropping, use 3 or 4 student names in a single sentence as an example
___ use variety of "shhh" like, You sssssshhhould all be listening right now."
___ gentle touch, if appropriate    ___ proximity....stand near
___ facial expression of curiosity    ___ change of pace activity for all
___ shout out the door, "Hey!"    ___ yell to an object to let off steam
___ ask team/group leader for help    ___ use or point to team class charts
___ send student on errand to another teacher (you've pre-arranged it earlier)
___ give student special class job that allows them to keep busy & avoid distracting others

---

There are many creative ways to discipline students without turning your class into a prison atmosphere where they feel like controlled or coerced inmates. Here are examples that may fit for you:

---

___ admonish the object of noise making problem instead of the student...go up to a student and say, "This is the noisiest pen I've ever heard. Can you keep it under control, otherwise, I have to put it in the bad pen box over there?" That way, the pen is the problem, not the student.
___ use story telling with key "quiet down" phrase for individuals & small groups...Tell pre-planned stories which include expressions you can raise your voice with, as part of the story, such as "Quiet!"

When you say the key word, look right at the noisy students, then continue your story. It's magic! The use of quotes as a tool for classroom management can be a powerful and effective tool. Quotes are a communication tool wherein you are giving a message to others in the form of quoted material. It's much easier and safer to say certain things that way. You can say almost anything you want, with impunity, if you use a quote (you, of course, can make it up) that someone else said. It's especially helpful if you change your tonality during a key part of your quote. The change will alert the listener to the special importance of that phrase. Here are some examples of how to use quotes in the classroom in your everyday presentation to your students:

1. "You know, I was talking to another teacher about his classroom and he was so pleased with his students, you know what he said to them? He shouted, 'You are the greatest group of students I've ever had! You really (raise your voice) pay attention well!' I thought that was pretty nice of him, what do you think?"

2. "Do any of you have a neighbor whose dog is constantly barking? My neighbor's dog really got to me last night so I went out in my yard and shouted over the fence, (raise your voice) SHUT UP! WILL YOU BE QUIET FOR A CHANGE?! You know what? It worked and I felt much better."

3. You can also use quotes to release anger, frustration or edginess. Simply say what you want to say in quotes. For example: "I ran into someone today who was so angry, you know what he said? He said, 'I'm furious! I'm madder than heck and I can't take the noise any more. I'm so frustrated I could scream!' Boy, he must have been mad. Can you imagine someone being that mad?"

___ use consistent "Hot Spot" away from front for disciplining large groups out of control... Never do "heavy disciplining" from the creative, fun front of your room, that "contaminates the area"... move to a special corner that you only use for being "heavy" ...In that corner, be firm, short and congruent... Give eye contact, use same gestures and the same exact key phrase every time (such as "Boys and Girls!" or Exxcuuuse me!")...then walk back to front of room and without adding any sermonizing or lecturing. Continue teaching. It's almost as if you are a Dr. Jekyll and Mr/Ms Hyde. Teacher in front, discipliner in corner.

## Level #3 Student Choice Point

Responsibility, providing choice & consequences are the key. Avoid useless threats you may not want to follow through on. Be straightforward, friendly and matter-of-fact. Use eye contact, ask student to simply choose A behavior or B consequences:

"Kim, you're a responsible person - hold it down for the next 10 minutes & we'll both be happy." Or, "Kenny, by keeping your hands to yourself, we can finish without interruptions & get out on time." Or, "Can you keep it down for the next few minutes? Otherwise we need a serious talk."

## Level #4  Patience is gone

Some learners are motivated more strongly by negatives. Outside of classtime, take strong action by uncovering the underlying cause and negotiating serious changes.
___In private, or with parents, find out what's really behind the behaviors. It could be parent's divorce or loss of a friend or excessive stress or pressure.
___Describe the behaviors, describe the impact on the class, describe how you feel about it, ask student for possible solutions, then you propose solutions. Offer counseling, parent meetings, create agreements that the student can live with, take action to start them.

___ Take strongest measures for repeated, dangerous or special circumstances. The safety of others and the ability of all the others to learn is far more important than trying to "save face" for one student.

# When a Problem Occurs

1. Get centered. Pause, take a breath and relax. Be calm both inside and outside. Anticipate a positive outcome and have a picture and feel for a successful result for both parties.

2. Use one of the strategies mentioned earlier. Do not be confrontive, simply get the job done with minimal fanfare. The bigger the deal you make it, the more you lose. This is not a time to win or "nail" someone. It's simply a way to get the class's energy off the distraction and focused back on learning.

3. If needed, state the facts, and make no judgment about her or him being bad, undependable or disrespectful. You also did not tell how you feel. How you feel when a student is late is your business. Be very careful about **if or how** you express that to the students. Avoid using it as a manipulation. They don't make YOU feel anything, ever. They can trigger a stimulus-response mechanism within you that allows that emotion to occur. But your internal mechanisms are not the creation nor the responsibility of the student.

We started in this chapter talking about some of the underlying assumptions about classroom control. Important issues such as power, control, flexibility and outcomes were dealt with. You also learned ways to empower your students and make them even more resourceful. We saw that creating classroom agreements were important, and learned how 'to deal with those who break them.

And finally, this last section is about how to maintain an climate: which will keep discipline problems to a minimum. Your classroom may not be perfect or have total learning, joy and bliss, but then again, its a lot more possible now than before. You now have the resources to create a well-balanced classroom where students feel safe and trust you. You have rapport with them and they are willing to abide by the agreements for no other reason than it's their word. Having students manage themselves is surely the key to a well disciplined class. Try it and let yourself be pleasantly surprised.

| *Additional Resources for Further Study and Follow up* |
| --- |

*Creating Success* by Akin (Inner Choice Publishing)
*Cooperative Discipline* by Albert American Guidance Service)
*21st Century Discipline* by Bluestein (Instructor Books)
*Teaching the Skills of Conflict Resolution* by Cowan (Innerchoice)
*Discipline With Dignity* by Curwin & Mendler (ASCD)
*Envoy* by Michael Grinder (Metamorphous Press)*
*Righting the Educational Conveyor Belt* by Michael Grinder (Metamorphous)*
*Brain-Based Learning & Teaching* by Eric Jensen (Turning Point)
*Influencing with Integrity* by Laborde (Science & Behavior Books)

* These are available in the Appendix.

# 23

# *Relationships*

## Relationships Make it Happen

By far, the best way you can reduce classroom problems and enhance the learning process is by building strong relationships. The eminent educator, Robert Bills, did a survey of 124,000 students in 315 public and private schools. After gathering thousands of pages of research, *his first and most critical recommendation was that the quality of relationships at school must be improved.* This means primarily the relationships between students and teachers, though others are important, too. Improving the relationships you have is so important that it deserves attention:

> *Your success as an educator*
> *is more dependent on positive, caring,*
> *trustworthy, relationships than on any*
> *skill, idea, tip or tool in this book*

At school, students learn based on four relationships: (1) the relationship with the teacher; (2) the relationship with the subject matter; (3) the relationship the students have with each other; and (4) the one with themselves. The teacher needs to do whatever it takes to build relationships during the first weeks of school and then continue to maintain them on a daily basis. The easiest level at which to build relationships is in the elementary school. Here teachers spend an entire day with their students and can focus on building relationships as a source of support. At the secondary level, this is difficult because departmentalization robs the necessary time to daily build relationships. With 50-55 minutes per class and the pressure of teaching content, your relationship time is minimal. Every move must count. Each activity must serve as a vehicle for building a strong working rapport.

## Rapport with Your Students

There are many building blocks to a strong teacher-student relationship. Here they are:

1. *Love Yourself.* When you care about yourself and respect yourself, your students know that you consider yourself special and worthy of respect. This lets them know that when you respect them, they are worthy judging by your standards. Incidentally, to love yourself does not mean narcissism.
2. *Learn About Your Students.* Find out who your students really are. Have them fill out 3 X 5 cards on themselves telling where they were born, how

many brothers and sisters, pets, and about their mom and dad. What do they like? What do they dislike? What are their fears, concerns, and problems? What's important to them? Ask students what it is like being a student. (It's certainly different from when you and I were in school!)

3. *Appreciate Your Students.* Understand the pressures and difficulties of being a student. Know what kind of effort and courage it takes just to get through the day. Discover how much peer pressure is on your students. Know what kind of academic pressures they feel, too. To do this, it takes a special effort on your part to listen without judging.

4. *Acknowledge Your Students.* Thank them for little things. Thank them for big things. Thank them for being in your life. Appreciate every little thing they do. Give verbal praise, write notes, give hugs, smiles and warm gestures. Let them know that they are special to you and that you really like knowing them.

5. *Listen to Your Students.* Most students feel no one listens to them, not parents, not teachers and not even their friends. Open up class time to let students share about their lives, joys or problems. Even the seemingly little things are big things. If you can be a "no-particular-agenda" set of ears for your students, a real open-minded, open-hearted listener, you will be one of the greatest gifts in students' lives.

6. *Make Small Concessions.* Grant small favors. Bring their popular music to class. Do things that can make a big difference, even if it is letting class out 30 seconds early or giving no homework over the holidays, everything helps.

7. *Include and Empower Your Students.* Ask them what they think. Let them participate in decision-making. Give them options in how to do things as long as they are willing to produce the results. Actively solicit their advice. Have a class advisory board. Help students feel important.

8. *Respect Students.* Never, ever "put down" a student. Avoid all sarcasm. Honor their decisions. As soon as it is appropriate, treat them as adults by giving them more responsibility. Enforce rules, guidelines and agreements exactly as they were set up. Don't bend rules or deny issues where honesty or integrity is involved.

9. *Treat Students as a "Possibility."* This means that each student is treated as a potential success, not as a past record. Treat students as a possibility of their greatness and your job is to have greatness "show up" within the character of each student.

10. *Be Open with Students.* Share about yourself so students get to know you. Talk about your joys, successes and challenges. You provide a great opportunity for students to learn about adult life.

During the first few days of school you must establish the method, manner and structure of relationships that you want with your audience. Create the commonality of relationship that your students need to have in order to feel connected to you. How are you alike? What brings you together? What do you want and what do they want? Do you share common goals? How will you behave toward one another? This important piece of your presentation is the glue that keeps you together in the same room. Take the time to do this well.

## Maintain On-going Rapport

Once you have established initial relationships, you'll still needs to maintain them on a minute-by-minute basis. You'll know what your level of rapport in the audience is by the amount of responsiveness to your presentation. Be aware constantly, using the information gathered to adjust what you're doing. At times, you'll need to make non-verbal changes, and at others, more direct verbal approaches will be necessary.

The most important clues you'll get from your students are non-verbal: posture, breathing, tonality, tempo, tonality, gestures; etc. These behaviors arc critical to monitor because most persons are unaware of them - meaning that they are the most accurate indicators of where you stand with another. Learn to make the following distinctions in your audience so that you'll know when you have the audience in the palm of your hand and when you need to make adjustments.

# Evidence of Rapport

1. **Auditory.** Listen to the questions and responses you are generating. Is the content of the question in line with what you've been saying or counter to it? Listen to the tonality and tempo. A faster paced, fluctuating or emphatic response could indicate you lack rapport unless that's how you speak. The tonality could be saying "Gee, I really like what I'm hearing." Or, it could tell you, "Why in the world are we even studying this?" When you are in total rapport, you may hear some of your pet words, phrases and ideas used. Listen for audience chatter; the content and timing of it in line with your class purposes? If so, chatter could indicate rapport. Otherwise, it may indicate they're bored.

You can increase rapport with those students who are more auditorally inclined very easily. Vary your tonality. Let your tempo fluctuate, and change your volume often. Use other sounds to enhance what you're saying. Remember when you were two years old? You made playful sounds all day long. Sometimes it's just the variety needed to keep the students alert and interested. You may also want to use auditory verbs such as: "Things are clicking. How does this sound? Tune into this. That rings a bell. Here's music to your ears."

2. **Visual.** Wear colors which students can relate to while still dressing professionally. Notice what your students wear - many students will unconsciously begin to wear the same colors you wore the day before. If they do, compliment them. Look for facial expressions that say "I'm confused," or "I want to say something." Move around the class so you can keep taking in everyone in your field of vision from different angles.

Using visually-related verbs means that you'll gain rapport with those in your audience who are visually dominant. "I see what you mean. Take a look at this. From my perspective, you'll get a clearer picture of this." You can also talk more quickly if your usual pace is slower.

3. **Kinesthetic.** Get a sense of their posture. Is it leaning towards you? Do their heads tilt towards you as you speak? Are they nodding in agreement? Are they yawning or looking away? Are their legs or arms crossed? Is their breathing rate the same as yours? How about eye and mouth movements? You've got many indicators, just be sure to check them out-not make assumptions about what they mean.

Those who have kinesthetic as their primary representational system will appreciate two things in your style. First, the pacing of your speech needs to be slower to appeal to the kinesthetic learner. This means... that you may have to... pause a bit... to let things "sit" with your students. The other rapport builder is use of verbs. Use expressions such as "How do you feel about this? What's your sense of this? Let me give you... a couple of concrete examples... so you can better get a handle on things."

# Multiple Rapport Builders

You may be wondering how you could possibly maintain rapport with such varied factions in your audience. It would seem impossible to keep rapport with both the visual, auditory and kinesthetic learners. Yet, it's much easier than it may seem. Your presentation can be varied; speaking quickly, using auditory predicates and maintaining a kinesthetic posture is a simple way. Or, you can speak slowly, use kinesthetic verbs, use lots of visuals, and vary the tonality of your voice. Or, you can use one style for two minutes, then another for two minutes, then switch again. With a subtle "weave," all of your audience can constantly be included.

*Every once in a great while try to truly understand*
*what it must be like to be a student in your own class...*
*you might never teach the same way again.*

If your students were randomly selected, approximately 40% of your audience will process information primarily visually, 40% auditorally, and 213% kinesthetically. This means that regardless of your preferred system, ("Do you see what I mean," or "How does this sound to you?" or "How do you feel about this?"), that if you are committed to reaching all of your students, you need to sprinkle diversity into your predicates.

You might also gauge the effects and responsiveness of your use of predicates by the audience you have. In a group of so-called "Special-Ed" or learning-impaired students, use predominantly kinesthetic predicates and metaphors. In addition, use them in courses where the dominant subject or activity is physical (crafts, sports, home economics, shop, etc.), AND students chose to go on their own volition. In more visually-related courses (art, film, research-related, reading, etc.), use predominantly visual words. And of course, use auditorally-related words when your audience might indicate that as their preference (music, drama, speech, radio, sales, politics).

# Be Responsive

If a student raises his hand, try to acknowledge it right away even if you cannot call on that person. Look at him and say, "I'll be right with you," or "I'll be ready for your question in just a moment." If a student asks you a question, be sure to answer it truthfully and briefly (more on this in an upcoming chapter). If students are restless, get them up for a stretch break. Be sure to use your fullest sensory acuity. It not only builds rapport with students because they feel noticed and heard, but it also makes smart teaching sense.

# Incorporation

You gain rapport with students when you incorporate into your teaching that which goes on in the environment. Students want to know that you and they share the same world. When you include external and internal stimuli in your teachings, they feel closer to you. If an interruption occurs, use it as a positive example of something you are discussing. If a noisy truck or train goes by, use it to your advantage: "We're all on the right track, so let's stay with this." If a student yawns, include: "You may have yawned if you feel you already know this material well enough for a test." Or, if someone drops his books on the floor, say: "A question may have just dropped into your mind, does anyone have one they'd like to ask?"

# Acknowledgments

Learn to acknowledge; give credit to students even when it's marginal. Give it to them when they do what you ask. Thank them if they attempt to do it when you want them to, in the way you want them to. Appreciate all that they do. Respect that they are doing the best they can, given how they see the world. You can turn any situation into an opportunity to acknowledgment, if you are both flexible in your interpretations and committed to empowering others. For example, let's say a student responds to a question with an inaccurate answer. Say, "Thanks for having the courage to offer an answer, I like it when you are willing to go for it."

# Devil's Advocate

When presenting information, be especially tuned in to the possibility of a negative or puzzled response. Then when you get one, USE IT! Change your strategies to either repackage what you just said or play the "devil's advocate" role. If you just said that the moon is made of green cheese and your students smirked, you could say, "now I know some of you may be thinking that's a crazy idea. Truthfully I thought it was, too. But when I heard such and such I changed my mind!" In other words, take the freedom to become the reactive mind of your audience, if need be.

Be flexible and be willing to change points of view as long as you can still get the desired outcome. You might say, "Let's have our class presentation next Friday." To which a student might reply, "Gee, I really couldn't get ready by then." To which you could reply, "On second thought, Friday isn't quite the right day of the week. Which other day did you have in mind?"

# Use Names

If you use names as a manipulative tool for pinpointing the culprits of unresourceful behavior, it breaks up rapport. If you use them as a way to appreciate and make your comments personal, it can build rapport. For example, when someone does something desirable, be sure to use his or her name at least once in your acknowledgment. For example, "I like that idea, Kevin. We can implement that in our next project."

Be sure to refer to what students said before. A great way to build rapport is to use the comments and ideas of your students constantly in your material. For example, "As John mentioned earlier, our balance of trade deficit is getting worse." Or, refer to what the whole class said by taking a poll and using the results. "How many of you think memorizing answers is a key to school success?" Then, later on, "As you all said earlier, memory is important to school success, so let's learn how it works."

# Use Agreement Frames

Differences lose rapport and similarities gain rapport. What happens if a student is responding to you in a way you disagree with? The answer is to use the agreement frames to maintain rapport. Three magic phrases are "I agree, I respect and I appreciate." If you don't agree with someone, you can at least respect the opinion and the right to express it. If you don't agree with someone, you can at least appreciate their willingness to tell you. And if you don't respect someone, at least find a way to agree with the outcome. Here's an example:

STUDENT: "I hate this class, I can't learn anything."
TEACHER: "I certainly appreciate you telling me. What can I do to make it more interesting even if you don't (change your tone) LIKE THE CLASS?"
**OR**
STUDENT: "I don't even care if I do well or not."
TEACHER: "Well, I respect your decision because you usually make good ones. I was wondering what things are important to you?"
**OR**
STUDENT: "Nothing's important to me except motorcycles."
TEACHER: "I agree motorcycles are well worth your time. If I could help you get a handle on your homework to get it done sooner, so you'd have more time for your motorcycle, would you be interested?"
STUDENT: "Yeah, I guess so...."

# Public Honesty

One of the most simple and effective ways to maintain rapport is also one of the easiest to do. Be honest with your students. Tell them the truth about yourself, your world and how things are for you. Let your students know when you are happy, sad, frustrated, anxious or excited. Share your dreams, goals and disappointments. Tell the truth about what policies you have to enforce and which ones you don't. Explain why you do what you do and make sure that you include your students in as much decision making as you can. Students who participate in creating and clarifying policies are more likely to carry them out. Last, do not lie. Even if it's a "white lie," it's never worth it. Your relationship with your students can take months to build and only seconds to destroy, so protect your investment and your integrity by being real and by telling the truth.

*Your success as an educator is more dependent on positive, caring, trustworthy, relationships than on any skill, idea, tip or tool in this book*

One thing about telling the truth is that it can always be "used" to hurt someone. For example, a poor way to reply is: "Your term paper was awful, I liked none of the ideas and it was sloppy, amateurish and lacked conviction." How much better to say, "Here's your paper back. To get a higher grade, I suggest you start with ideas we have talked about in class, rough draft it, write with more enthusiasm, then get someone to read it for you, type it, and proof it before turning it into me. By the way, things I liked were your determination to get it in on time and it was the perfect length. Let me know if I can help." Tell the truth, but be compassionate. Have an appreciation for the personal life of your students and especially for their self-esteem.

291

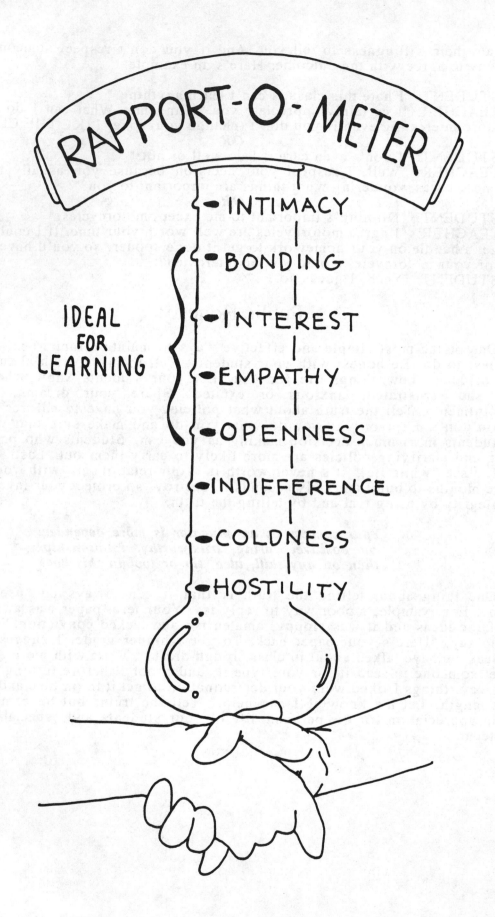

RAPPORT-O-METER

- INTIMACY
- BONDING
- INTEREST
- EMPATHY
- OPENNESS
- INDIFFERENCE
- COLDNESS
- HOSTILITY

IDEAL
FOR
LEARNING

# Student-Subject Matter Relationship

Critical to the success of your students is a positive attitude or relationship with the subject you are teaching. Most of the rest of this book is designed to build that attitude. Here's a summary of some of the points mentioned:

√ Excite your students in a vision about learning
√ Ask students to discover what the subject's possibilities are
√ Have the students create some value or benefits in it
√ Talk about the subject positively
√ Role-model your own interest in the subject
√ Make the subject matter more personal and relevant
√ Make the subject closer to home
√ Utilize a wider variety of learning styles: field trips/guest speakers/hands-on learning
√ Bring humor, songs and games into the classroom
√ Have students visualize liking the subject more
√ Have the students work as a team
√ Appeal to and reach more kinds of learners
√ Create new associations to "re-anchor" the subject
√ Link up the subject with positive emotions and music

# Student-to-Student Relationships

In order to develop powerful inter-student relationships, it will take an extraordinary amount of initial groundwork and constant coaching. Most students at the elementary level are taught to be kind and supportive to their neighbor and help out whenever necessary. Somehow, much of that spirit is usually lost and by the time students are teens, the typical behavior is put-downs, sarcasm and indifference. There are many ways to alter this too-common pattern:

√ Establish a definition and foundation of integrity
√ Ask students to relate to each other in a supportive way
√ See clear class guidelines for behavior
√ Role-model: Relate to other teachers in a supportive way
√ Express your relatedness and commonality to your students.
  Have them do this to each other
√ Declare to them you can be counted on-then role-model it
  Have your students do this to each other
√ Have some out-of-class activities so students can see each other as people, not students
√ Pick a class project that all students can get aligned on and excited about

# Building Student's Relationships

Probably the best way to describe student relationships within themselves is self-esteem. A healthy self-concept means that you "relate" to yourself well. You think of others highly and yourself highly. All persons are of equal value, potential and deserving of respect and compassion. A later chapter describes in detail the conditions for establishing high self-esteem. As a brief preview, some ways for you to enhance student's self esteem are:

√ You, the teacher can role model high self-esteem
√ Let the students discover, list and share their own strengths

293

√ Work with their integrity-it builds self-esteem
√ Build a sense of "family" in the classroom
  Work with partners, teams and as a group
  Give a sense of belonging
  Call absent students, send get well cards to sick ones
√ Honor the uniqueness of each student
  Extra attention, birthdays, compliments
√ Listen to each student with your fullest attention
√ Allow students to share about their family, pets, hobbies
√ Give students more power and control over their life
  Let them make decisions regarding the class
  Teach them how to deal with criticism more resourcefully
  Share with them options for dealing with problems
√ Celebrate the joys and successes of:
  Each individual student, their team, the whole class

In class or out of class, the only things that ultimately matter are relationships. Do what it takes to build relationships early and preserve them. Much of the problem teachers have with students arises from a lack of relationship or a poor relationship. Create an authentic, down-to-earth, honest, and caring relationship with each individual student and base that relationship on mutual respect, love and integrity.

# How to Get Useful Parent Participation

Another important relationship at school is the one you have with the parents of the students you're teaching. You may be interested in these facts about the importance of parent involvement:

•Parents are the #1 influence on a child's life
•90% of teachers say they don't get parent participation
•Parents can provide the individual attention teacher's can't afford
•In 1989 the #1 teacher complaint was lack of parent participation
•Parents can back up their requests for effort with home discipline
•In over 50 parent participation
studies nationwide, the results demonstrate that:
  • kids performed better than non-participating parent groups
  • schools become a greater asset to community
  • failing kids improved dramatically with parent participation
•Research demonstrates only a minority of parents are contacted by teachers with direct specific requests for support (25% But when asked, a whopping 85% responded positively.

## 1. Develop a plan for parental involvement
Your plan needs to be thorough, flexible and well-thought out. Gather resources on parent involvement.

•school materials
•ask other teachers
•district materials
•educational magazines
•educational television
•newsletters

Make your plan based on these things: 1) Your own research, resources and time available 2) The type of parents and children you have 3) What your school has planned, its policies 4) The school calendar 5) Special situations that come up 6) Your own educational philosophy

## 2. Before involving parents... assess things
• Gather all key information about your student's parents/bounce your ideas off other faculty members/learn what they have learned/make plans/do it in writing/use graphics/make it easy to read/get feedback on it from your principal

## 3. Start off on the right foot
• Mail a letter before open house. Start with good public relations. • Opening letter to parents for upcoming school year should say: Who you are/experience/credentials/specialty. Why you are writing: to say hello, to make contact, to reassure, to excite, to share your commitments about education, about working with their child, the joy of learning. • Remind them of upcoming open house ...this is a "pre-invitation". Talk about the importance of the partnership between you and the     parent. Get them excited about it • Give days, time and location of open house. Add a P.S. to the letter "REALLY looking forward to..."

## 4. Make the Open House a spectacular positive event
        This is one of the most important days of the year. This is just as important for secondary as it is for elementary. Put a lot of work into this event, it'll pay off all year long! Here are some suggestions for the event:
• Send personalized invitations designed nicely on the computer - sign each invitation •Involve students in recruiting their parents/decorating the room
• Make it into a game for kids to get parents to be there. Have a contest with no prizes! • Make up a fun event for the night (scavenger hunt, lottery, mystery quest, food, etc.) • Make sure that the invitations are personal and special • Have translators available if needed • Have written materials that are professional and useful • Put up key posters/use name tags/have refreshments/baby-sitting • Include ALL children in your slides, video, music, materials, written pieces • Make sure time is well spent/music choreography for events • Make it well worth their time to do it and a loss if they don't come • End it on a high note.

# Tips for Making It Work

A. Greet every parent by name...listen to them thoughtfully and write down their concerns
B. Talk about what it takes to make their child a success. Talk about partnerships, shared responsibility
C. Talk about your commitment, establish credibility
D. Tell parents specifically what they can do. They can choose from either: (1) support homework and other learning (2) contribute time, ideas and resources as a volunteer.
E. Have a theme and parent philosophy and communicate it
F. Be respectful of parents and proud of yourself and your work. Avoid self-depreciating jokes and put-downs of either education as a whole, the school or your job. Parents want a professional in the classroom, not a victim of circumstances.
G. Make sure the take-home booklet has a response/return portion so you can get feedback from parents ...either they leave it at the open house or return in later. The booklet should include the following:

    •Greetings, positive affirmations
    •School staff names, numbers and class list of kids

- School hours, emergency numbers, school map
- Best nutritional suggestions
- Rules for both the school and classroom
- Curriculum and daily class schedule
- Homework, absentee-make up and medical policies *Calendar, holidays, staff development days
- Study, learning tips, reading lists, resources

## 5. Home support for homework

Talk about homework basics/purpose and types of homework/frequency and amount of it/when and how to complete it/the test schedules and impact on grades/what it should look like and sound like. Talk about the parent's roles to support the doing of homework/what you expect of the parent ways to keep the motivation strong. Talk about your roles/how you reinforce the doing of homework/what you do when it is not done

Write up your homework policy clearly and simply. You give to each of your parents a special letter or flyer. Make it professional, accurate and polished. Send it home to the parent. Have them sign it and return a copy or a lower tear-off piece. If you have decided to give out homework:

- start early in the year with your approach and goals
- keep parents informed
- give clear, reasonable expectations

*follow-up and do what you say you will do

## 6. "On-site" parent participation

Recruitment - how to get parents involved. Sent by letter in native language, include "what's in it for them"... specific benefits to parents and benefits to their child... be blunt about these. List the types of involvement that are possible by parents and don't forget to make it exciting. Put stakes in the game: tell them what could happen if they contribute, what might if they don't! Match volunteers with skills/time/language/resources.

Once begun, make a list duties to be done, ways to communicate, location of supplies, what's OK, what's not OK, how to minimize interruptions, on-going to-do list, folders to complete, on-going assessment, cookies, source of "strokes."

# Types of Tasks for Parents

Provide a variety of ways for parents to help. They can collate papers, write notes to kids, make calls to other parents, cut or paste-up, help with bulletin boards, be a guest speaker, share about cultural background, give library help, do phone calls, help with set- up, put on special events, assist with projects, locate resources, do individual tutoring, give vocational talks or let them offer ideas. Be sure to always have a list waiting for them, so there's no wasted time. They could also help out with:

- Organize school-wide events and fund raisers. Good examples are plays, swap meets, book fairs, bake sales.
- Recruit volunteers from a wide variety of sources
- Provide funding or ideas for in-services
- School Site Council

• Guest speakers could include dentists, doctors, psychologists, drug experts, self-esteem specialists, celebrities, persons with high profiles, discipline specialists, special readers, stories, career day, social services resources, job fair for kids.

Let a parent be a guest speaker in your classroom: cultural-career, utilize their particular expertise. ALWAYS let them do more than just clerical--otherwise it's a waste.

### 7. Ideas for better quality participation
• Homework assistance:  Make policy school-wide. Clarify parent's role, let them know exactly what they can and cannot do. Remember to praise, ask questions, use non-monetary incentives, coach them, monitor the studies, use a study area. Establish after school homework assistance program if needed.

• Communications with parents:  Notes from teachers, report cards, progress reports, phone calls, awards, special projects, newsletter, personal contact, conferences, class participation, survey, make it timely, be friendly, be positive, be complete, give follow-up resources. Keep parents informed as well as report and ask or survey them.

### 8. Personalizing the process
• *For Student Conferences:*
• Do goal-getting conferences at the start of the year.
• Keep a phone log to document the child's progress.
• Always include positives or strokes even for the tougher kids.
• Give a report to each parent on their child's
    strengths/concerns/goals/questions/requests
• Be sure it's sent in their native language. Using the phone is best and
    remember to follow-up on paper.
• Group conferences with key personnel

• *For Parent Education:*
• Do a major push for the education of parents
• Give them school policies, homework and playground rules
• Show office hours, map, personnel, schedules, resources
• Provide newsletters, bulletins, back-to-school night
• Workshops/ESL/nutrition/single parent/etc.

### 9. Making sure parents are acknowledged
    • Parent Recognition:  The little things means the most; especially when they are sincere and continuous. Remember to have students take home projects, holiday goodies, certificates, newsletter recognition, lunch, newspaper stories, praise on phone, praise with notes, a year-end assembly, let them share moment with their children.

---

## *Additional Resources for Further Study and Follow up*

*Parents on Your Side* by Lee Canter (Canter & Associates)
*The Dynamics of Relationships* by Pat Kramer (301) 933-1489;
*Influencing With Integrity* by Laborde (Science & Behavior Books)
*Making Contact* by Satir (Celestial Arts)

\* These are available in the Appendix.

# 24

## Self Esteem Strategies

### We All Like to Feel Good

Take a cross-section of the students at risk in our society (substance abuse, teenage pregnancy, dropouts, low achievement scores, etc.). Compare it with successful students. You'll find one character trait would be dramatically different. It's not income, race, sex or geographical location. It's self-esteem. Students with low self-esteem have a tougher time in life.

Those with a high level of self-esteem consistently make contributions to our society. In your classroom, students with high self-esteem participate more, achieve more, build friendships, complete assignments, score higher, stay in school and feel good about their future. Results of low self-esteem are lower grades, fear of participation, damaging relationships, trouble-making behavior and resignation to a dim future.

*Self-esteem cannot be built directly...*
*you cannot do a self-esteem activity*
*but you can foster conditions for it*

Self-esteem is made of two components: intellectual and emotional That is, being capable and lovable. It is experiencing yourself as being "capable" as in "I am able to do many things now or at least have the capacity to learn them." It also means feeling loved as in "I know I am a unique, special and care-about-able person who is worthy of attention, affection and love." Research demonstrates that 80% of our children enter first grade with high self-esteem and 5% graduate from high school with high self-esteem. Something very damaging affects the well-being of most students between first and twelfth grade.

Self-esteem is really an attitude about yourself and attitudes are a critical part of the learning process. If your students believe they can learn, the job is half done. If you teach curriculum instead of people, you'll always have problems with motivation, self-esteem and performance. By teaching people, modeling and demonstrating useful positive life values becomes as important as the subject for the day. One of your on-going roles is to promote and enhance the self-esteem of your students. It's not a matter of, "Do I have the time?" Or, "Can I afford it?" You cannot afford NOT to do it.

Students who feel good about themselves, value who they are, what they do, and where they're going are a real joy to teach. These students generally contribute more, learn more, are better behaved and easier to get along with. They get along well with other students and they usually have more useful and fulfilling lives. Because you are an important person in each student's life, what you do can and will make a difference in his or her life. In this field, as in others, the myths are rampant.

## Ten Essentials of Self-Esteem

There's no secret formula to building self-esteem. Only you can build it for yourself. You cannot build another's self-esteem, you can *only foster the conditions in which another is likely to build his or her own.* Self-esteem is raised through a series of internal decisions made by the individual, not someone else for him. The student needs to come to the conclusion that he is lovable and capable. That's why giving out "strokes" to students only leads to greater self-esteem IF the student is the one who makes the subsequent decision that HE or
SHE did a great job and THEREFORE is capable. Regardless of what the praise was from another, it's always what we say to ourselves that ultimately determines self-esteem, not what others say.

If there was a secret to building self-esteem in others, it would be to start with yourself. Use everyday as an opportunity to set an example for your students. Be in the discovery process, be a learner and grower. Be the person you would like your students to emulate. Other qualities and behaviors that exemplify high self-esteem are:

1.  *High Personal Integrity.* Tell the truth, always, and tell it with compassion. Keep your word and complete whatever agreements you make. Make a promise and keep it. Make another promise and keep it. That is very powerful!

2.  *Responsibility.* Speak the language of responsibility and be the embodiment of personal accountability. This results in greater personal power and a greater sense of your own ability to make things happen. Use "I" messages, not blame messages.

3.  *Supporting Others.* Be a success by supporting the success of those around you. Speak supportively, praise often and back up other's ideas and work. Find the gifts in the acts of others.

4.  *Self-Discipline.* Do the things that others are unwilling to do. Follow through on promises and projects. Take care of details. Follow a schedule and complete lists. Be meticulous about quality and service. Set a goal and reach it. Set another goal and reach it.

5.  *Build Relationships.* Show you care about others. Tell others you care about them. Do things for others; stick your neck out for others. Remember birthdays, anniversaries, special occasions.

6.  *Know Yourself.* Know your own unique qualities. Know who you are and what you are strong at doing. Know what areas in which you need more work. Know that you are one-of-a-kind and unique in all the universe.

7.  *Vision/Purpose.* Have a dream about what you want to do or have happen in life. Know your life purpose and your steps on its path. Have a grand

vision or dream that inspires you and gets you up each morning. Share it with others and inspire them.

8. *Environment.* Create a specialized living and learning environment that reflects your highest thoughts about yourself and your students. Keep it spotless, up-to-date and rich in meaning.

9. *Excellence.* Give everything your best effort, even a seemingly small insignificant task. Do work with a song in your heart, knowing your purpose and how you fit into the plan.

10. *Health.* Take care of your emotional, mental and physical health. Be proud of your body and do what it takes to have it support your dreams and lifestyles.

Self-esteem takes many forms in the classroom. The least useful form is in content, as in a self-esteem-building exercise. The most useful is to live and embody it so that it forms a weave or a thread throughout the entire school year. Self-esteem is so delicate that it can be damaged with just one off-purpose comment. Yet it may take many dozens of comments to raise it.

You want to build up a reserve of positive self-esteem feelings within each of your students. In the case of a mistake, you can simply apologize and move on without any permanent damage. That's why self-esteem needs to be your way of being, not a task you do to get it over with.

# Seven Keys For Building Self-Esteem

## 1. Create a Sense of Purpose With Your Students
Share your vision for yourself or the world. Convey expectations, elicit student goals and assist them in setting realistic ones. Share your own life purpose and personal goals. Build confidence and faith in them by sharing how you connect with your own purpose and mission in life.

## 2. Convey a Sense of Control and Personal Power
Make sure that your students know they have a choice over their feelings; that others don't make them angry or upset or happy, that they can control feelings themselves. Give them control over dozens of daily decisions. Avoid manipulating and managing every single action they make. The more power your students have, the happier, more confident, and more secure they'll be. Could you think of a better combination for a learner? Some options are:

- Help them set their own limits... let them be responsible for their own behavior.
- Show them ways to influence others... teach them communication tools that will increase their ability to get what they want.
- Ask lots of probing questions... about how to solve problems instead of doing it for them. Let them learn to come up with answers. And listen carefully to what your students say.
- Provide students with more choices... the process mentioned earlier in the chapter for broken agreements is an example of providing more choices.
- Teach them how to make better decisions... give them tools for problem-solving and teach them how adults make decisions continually.
- Confront cause and effect... give them lots of opportunities to see the cause and effect they generate. It begins the responsibility process.

Invest the time with your students to do goal-setting and goal-getting exercises. Help them make milestones for reaching their sub-goals. Help them learn the skills to reach their goals. Acknowledge them as they reach their goals.

## 3. Establish a Sense of Security

Develop self-respect through words and actions. Build trust, set realistic rules and limits. Enforce rules consistently. Create classroom predictability through opening and closing rituals. See the chapter on rituals for more information on how to set them up and maintain them.

## 4. Create a Democratic Atmosphere

When appropriate, allow students to make choices and feel more powerful. Give freedom when possible and allow students to participate in decisions. Ask their opinion often. Use their names when discussing topics, "As Jeff said earlier...." Allow them to have input on planning... or just simple ideas that you use. Let them know that they have a part of the show.

## 5. Create a Sense of Belonging and Connectedness

Have students feel part of the learning family. Be warm, loving and accepting. Create responsibilities of group membership. Encourage the acceptance and inclusion of others.

Students who feel a part of what's going on are more likely to pay attention to what's being presented. To create greater feelings of belonging and connectedness, here are some possibilities:

- Include individual students in more of your teachings... use their names in examples, point out things that they have done, refer to their part of the room.
- Do something special for them... bring them a card, write them a note on their paper, or on a separate paper, offer them a special activity or privilege.
- Listen without judging... allow them to be who they are without having suggestions for change.
- Show more expressions... smile, laugh, wink, a touch of the hand on the shoulder, a pat, a hug.
- Be specific in praise... tell them exactly what they did, what your reaction was, use clear words, and praise them for just being in your class.
- Share personal thoughts... talk to them about your dreams, goals, interests, hobbies, encourage the same.
- Let them know how the material relates to their world... make it relevant to their lives, constantly.

## 6. Create a Sense of Uniqueness and Identity

Make sure that students know who they are, their strengths, their uniqueness and specialties. Aid them in assessing their qualities and provide unconditional acceptance and love. Students who feel special and unique usually do not need to get negative attention in the classroom. Everyone needs to feel special in some way and the more you can let students know just how important and special they are to you, the better they will feel about themselves. When students are made to feel special, they don't have to act special. Good advice for any teacher!

1. Encourage expression... let them have ways and outlets of self-expression. Allow the set-up of special projects and classroom activities.

2. Communicate acceptance to them... make sure students know that you accept them for who they are. Use their names, refer to them specifically. Greet them with a big smile and hug at the door.
3. Notice your students, know who got a new dress, jacket, who got a haircut, earrings, etc. and be sure to let them know that you noticed.
4. Private time... be sure to make the time for private discussions with each student, even if it's just a few minutes after class.
5. Allow them to do special projects. Give them all the chances possible for creativity, let them make class announcements or share with the group.
6. Acknowledge special days. For example, always ask who has a birthday each day. If someone is sick for a week or more, send them a get-well card signed by the whole class.

## 7. Create a Sense of Competence

Have students learn and do tasks they consider important. Provide encouragement, strokes and support. Aid them in self-evaluation and provide recognition and acknowledgments. Of all the things you can do in the classroom, one of the easiest and most powerful ways to weave in healthy self-esteem is with appreciation and acknowledgment. Why acknowledgment? Quite simply, it works.

No single tool in this entire book is as powerful as acknowledgment for raising self-esteem, creating more confident and resourceful students and boosting productivity. Yet, in spite of what it can do for others, acknowledgment is really about oneself. To notice the good in others is to notice the good in ourselves. Conversely, the better we feel about ourselves, the more good we'll notice in others. Our wants and needs are similar. Our dreams and hopes are similar. Our talents and abilities are similar. We all need reinforcement and approval for improvement as well as for just being ourselves.

With the apparent deficiency of strokes, approval and acknowledgment in learners' lives, there are superb opportunities for teachers to fill in the gaps. Teachers spend many hours with students and have the capacity to immerse them in an environment of support, acknowledgment and validation. Through so doing, teachers help make their students better human beings.

The first place to start is with you. Begin to acknowledge yourself for little things as well as the larger ones. Learn to acknowledge and love yourself for just being you. Appreciate yourself for being the courageous growing person you are. Appreciate yourself for just being alive. Embrace yourself and hold appreciative thoughts of yourself. Say to yourself, "I love you!" and mean it. Know that all love starts from within. You are the source of all good in your own world. Since you are the source of all good, that's a great reason to acknowledge yourself!

The next place to start acknowledging is with those closest to you. When was the last time you thanked or acknowledged your spouse or other family members? Do you recall the last time you appreciated the janitor, school secretary, other teachers or your supervisor? There have been dozens of persons who have contributed to your success as a teacher and to whom an acknowledgment would be immediately appropriate. Guess what? The more you acknowledge them for what they've done, the stronger you feel and the better they feel. How about the obvious... your students? There is no shortage of persons to acknowledge or places to start. Make it a goal to acknowledge ten people per day. The sooner you start, the easier it becomes.

# How to Acknowledge Successfully

First, what makes one person develop a better self concept might make no impression on another. Second, teachers must have the sensory acuity to be able to tell if an acknowledgment has "landed" and have the resources to change their behavior as needed. There are those who try to deflect validation. The better prepared you are for that outcome, the better you can deal with it.

In one sense, there could hardly be anything simpler. However, as we found out earlier in the book, there are a lot of different kinds of people in this world and you can be sure you'll have diversity in your classroom. To be a master at delivering acknowledgments, you need just three things:

1. To be committed to the outcome that your acknowledgment will be received with the same meaning with which it is delivered.
2. To have the sensory acuity to know if it actually did "land" in the way you intended.
3. To have the behavioral flexibility to be able to make the necessary adjustments instantly so that the intended outcome is reached.

**Follow These Simple Steps:**

1. Check your physiology. Hold the posture and breathing that could be labeled as "open, warm and safe" by others. It will vary. For some, the hands will be behind the back; for others, open palms extended; for all, a smile! You'll know what feels most comfortable.
2. Get the attention of the person. The most common ways are through eye contact, a hand on the shoulder, your position and posture or through a simple spoken word ("John...?").
3. Say what you want to say. Be brief and to the point. Share feelings, observations or expressions with all your energy and intention behind it. Say it without strings attached and use the person's name. ("John...it's been a real joy having you in class, thanks!") Use any gestures, eye movements, breathing and posture that corroborate the verbal message. Be sure that your non-verbal message matches your verbal message.
4. Pause. Let the message stay with the student for a moment by continuing to maintain some form of contact (eyes, hand, etc.) while keeping silent. Observe the reactions and quickly assess body language for signs that the message "landed" or did not.
5. Respond. At this time, you have two possibilities. If the acknowledgment did not "land", you'll need to develop a different approach for the next time. If it did land, continue with whatever feels appropriate. That may include more conversation, a hug, a smile, a handshake.

# Group Acknowledgments

Nearly anytime is a great time to appreciate and acknowledge your students. Do it before class, "I love how all of you are dressed today - great flashy colors!" Do it at the start of class, "I consider it a privilege to be here in class with you - your time is valuable and I hope to do my best to make it worthwhile." Or, "Thanks for being on time. In fact, I'm glad just to have you all in my class. It makes me feel lucky!" Do it during the class, "Thanks for really participating today." Or, "You know what? Class is more fun with you in it!"

*Teaching is not a job or a duty to perform...*
*it is, rather, a privilege to be accepted by those able to be*
*responsible   and with hearts big enough to love enough*

At test time, say, "Thanks for staying quiet and respecting your neighbor." In the middle of class, "Boy, I sure have a lot of fun with you!" As the class closes, "It's students like you who make my job so great. Thanks for really participating and going for it!" There's no maximum or minimum, but you should be able to find ways to acknowledge your students dozens of times in every class. One of the best results is that students often begin to live up to our acknowledgments and standards of performance increase.

# Important Distinctions

Distinguish between appreciative acknowledgments, descriptive praise and evaluative praise. The first two are healthy, the last is not. The first two are unconditional, the last is not. The first two are non-judgmental, the last is not. An evaluative praise is a performance-oriented judgment, the kind that an unaware boss (or teacher) gives an employee (or student). It consists of evaluating character traits or actions and often creates anxiety, defensiveness or dependency. For example, "You're a great student" is a performance-oriented remark which is vague. Better than nothing to be sure, but far from the optimum.

It is healthier to say, "You're a pleasure to have in class... and thanks for turning in your assignment on time." Instead of saying to a student, "You are so good," say, "Thank you for returning the lost wallet. I appreciate it very much." Don't say, "Good job, David. Keep up the good work." Instead, say, "I feel really blessed just to have you in my class. It's a great feeling!" Notice that there are no strings attached to an appreciative acknowledgment. It's just a straight-from-the-heart, "Thanks."

**Praise**

1. *Evaluative.* (Reduce or avoid this type!) It is judgmental. It is based on a powerful-powerless role of teacher-student. It is manipulative, stressful and often does NOT get the job done. By using this kind "praise" you plant conclusions in the student's mind about the quality of the job or the quality of the character. How much better to have the student come up with the conclusion for him or herself.

   EXAMPLES:   "Good job, Johnny!"
   "Your homework was excellent, Susie."
   "You did great today, Jeff."

2. *Descriptive.* (Very useful) This is a statement in simple words that tells what occurred. It states the event, acknowledges it and affirms it. What's effective about this type of praise is that the student hears you state what occurred and can conclude for himself that she (or he) is a capable human being.

   EXAMPLES:   "Your handwriting was perfectly within the lines, the
   letters were evenly formed and everything was
   capitalized exactly according to the rules we talked
   about."

"Your skit was on exactly the subject matter requested. It brought up all the key points and was finished on time."

"Your question is most relevant..."

3. *Appreciative.* (most useful) This type of praise tells how you REACT to what was done. It's really your response to the event, rather than the event itself. It comes from the heart and lets the student know that he is special and makes a difference. But most importantly, after you make these statements to a student, HE or SHE can make conclusions such as, "I am lovable" or "I am capable." When the student arrives at those conclusions, it is much more powerful and likely to last as an acknowledgment and self-esteem builder.

EXAMPLES: "I loved your skit, Ellen. I never laughed so hard." "I was really inspired by the last couple of questions you've asked."

"I really appreciate the way you got your homework done. I am really proud for you and the progress you've made."

# Reaching the "Hard to Reach"

Students use three tools to form their internal "map" of the world: deletion, generalization and distortion. These tools may also prevent your acknowledgment from being received. A deletion is made when part of an experience is left out of the interaction. A generalization occurs when a student takes a conclusion which is true for a specific incident and assumes it can be applied to others. A distortion occurs when a speaker changes the content or meaning of the experience to make it say something different from what was intended. Redefining is a distortion method that people use to alter communications to fit their frame of reference.

Everybody distorts, deletes and generalizes. Those are the essential coping skills for life. People who have low self-esteem delete and distort and generalize just as much as those with high self-esteem. However, those with high self esteem "warp" the world in their favor, for themselves. They "preserve their esteem" through manipulation of the world. The difference is that those who have low-self-esteem, "warp" *against* themselves. Here are examples of how a someone with low self-esteem deals with a simple acknowledgment. Here it is not received; and here's how you can re-phrase, by trying it again.

1. *Teacher:* "You're real special, thanks for being in my life."
   *Student distortion:* "What are you trying to get from me?"
   *Solution:* "You're right, I'm sorry. I guess sometimes I just don't know how to tell you how much you mean to me. Any suggestions?"

2. *Teacher:* "Wow, what a class we had and you really contributed!"
   *Student redefining:* "How do you expect me to believe that?"
   *Solution:* "Actually I don't. What I should have said was that I had a good time and felt good about having you as part of it."

3. *Teacher:* "Hey, David. Thanks for helping with the set-up before class."
   *Student deletion:* "You gotta be kidding, that was nothing."
   *Solution:* "Have you ever had someone do a small favor to you, and yet it really meant a lot to you? I feel that same way. You did make things easier for me this morning and I just wanted you to know that, so thanks again."

4. *Teacher:* "I've felt great having you in my class."
   *Student generalization:* "But you say everything's great. Are you ever serious?"
   *Solution:* "You're right, I do use that word a lot. Guess I should have used a different way to let you know it's really made a positive difference having you in my class."

Another set of tools that prevent acknowledgments from "landing" are actually subtle variations on the ones mentioned earlier. They are discounts, denials, throwbacks, and "marshmallowing." Discounting is the process used to make a compliment worth less, hence to "discount" it. Denial is the method used to refute the validation, and throwback is the process of giving the compliment back to the sender. Marshmallowing is the appearance of support but is actually the subtle message, "You're going to fail."

# Discounts

*Teacher:* "Thanks for joining us today, you made real contributions and it felt great just having you around."
*Student discount:* "I actually didn't do that much at all. I just came and sat around."
*Solution:* "That's true and I agree that physically you didn't do a lot. I guess what made it worthwhile for me was just knowing you were in my class and enjoying your presence."

# Denials

*Teacher:* "What a blessing to have you in class - you really got everyone participating!"
*Student denial:* "You're far too generous with your compliments - I couldn't take credit for what went on today."
*Solution:* "I respect your modesty and at the same time, I was just letting you know how much you mean to me. Thanks!"

# Throwbacks

*Teacher:* "It's been a real joy to have you in class. Thanks."
*Student distortion:* "Hold it. You're the one who should get all the credit. It wasn't possible without all you did."
*Solution:* "I appreciate that you noticed what I contributed. Mostly I wanted you to know that it makes me feel good just having you in class. Thanks."

# Marshmallowing (avoid this)

*Teacher:* "I know you're a good student. I called your folks to make sure you brought your homework because you're so important to me that I didn't want to take a chance that you'd forget it. I'll stay after class today to make sure that you understand today's assignment and help you all I can."
*Student response:* "I think can handle it on my own."

**Note:** In the above comment the teacher is giving a "marshmallow" acknowledgment. Is not useful because it: 1) invites dependency 2) gives permission to be irresponsible 3) doesn't allow the student to learn the consequences of his own actions 4) implies that the student can't make it without you.

# Reading Your Students

You need to know if your acknowledgments are getting through for two reasons. One, if the other person did not get the message, your appreciation wasn't felt so you must re-package it. Two, you might be speaking "different languages" and have poor rapport.

Most of the time, the body is a visible indicator of the subconscious. Body language will show you first, and most accurately, if the compliment is being received. If it's about to be turned away with one or more of the tools mentioned in this chapter, the body will show it even before the words do. Here's how to find out if your acknowledgment has been heard, felt and landed successfully:

**Head** - nodding in agreement. **Eyes** - opening wider and blinking less, perhaps looking from side-to-side or down. **Facial tones** - usually become fuller. **Eyebrows** - raised. **Shoulders** - squared and fuller. **Breathing** - pauses, then becomes stronger, lower in the chest. **Hands and arms** - unfolded and still. **Voice** - varies, you must calibrate it with previous event.

Certainly there's no shortage of people to acknowledge and you've always got yourself! Now that you know how to give acknowledgments successfully, to insure that they "land" and know how to make changes if they don't, start today! You can expect some positive, noticeable changes in your students and you'll enjoy teaching more yourself.

# Quality Role Models

One of the major problems for students is the lack of quality role models. Students have role model selections from magazines, television commercials, billboards and MTV. Where are they going to get the behavior model that you want in your classroom? From you! If you are committed to mastery in teaching and are on the path to mastery, you will be setting a good example for your students. There are some other ways to provide modeling for your students:

1. Understanding... help your students understand why they are doing what they are doing. It gives them a mechanism for re-creating success.
2. Share your philosophy... in this case, quality is better than quantity, let them know what moves you, and how you achieve the successes you have.
3. Set goals... help your students understand the power of setting goals, how to do it and the value in it.
4. Staying on purpose... help your students see the cause and effects of behavior, being clear on the outcome you want.
5. Trigger their thinking... get your students to think about why they do things. Help them notice the discrepancies between what others say and what they do. Allow them to sort out false claims or other challenges.
6. Model-building... talk to them about how people build models of their world in their mind by taking sensory input and generalizing, distorting and deleting. Show them how to do that more usefully.
7. Allow some of the better students to do some sharing in the role of a student assistant.

308

As we mentioned at the start of the chapter, you cannot teach or build self-esteem directly. It is a by-product of how your life unfolds. While you can't control every event, every interaction in the classroom, you can certainly influence them. For example, after students work with a partner and before they move onto something else, have them turn to their working partner and say, "Thanks!" It's small, simple and it works.

People like to feel appreciated. Self-esteem building is an on-going climate... done all the time, within every hour, within every day of the school year. Holding a single self-esteem day, then going back to damaging patterns is, of course, useless. Make positive affirmation, trust, support, acceptance and recognition an everyday climate and your students will want to come to class.

## Additional Resources for Further Study and Follow up

*Thinking, Changing & Rearranging* by Anderson (Metamorphous)
*Esteem Builders* by Michelle Borba (Jalmar)
*Freedom to Fly* by Chris Brewer (Zephyr)
*100 Ways to Enhance Self-Concept in the Classroom* by Jack Canfield (Allyn & Bacon)
*Building Your Child's Self-Esteem & Confidence* by Dargatz (Thomas Nelson)
*Me!* by Jo Ellen Hartline
*Project Self-Esteem* by Sandy McDaniel & Peggy Bielen
*6 Vital Ingredients of Self-Esteem* by Bettie B. Youngs
*101 Activities for Building Self-worth* (Zephyr)

* These are available in the Appendix.

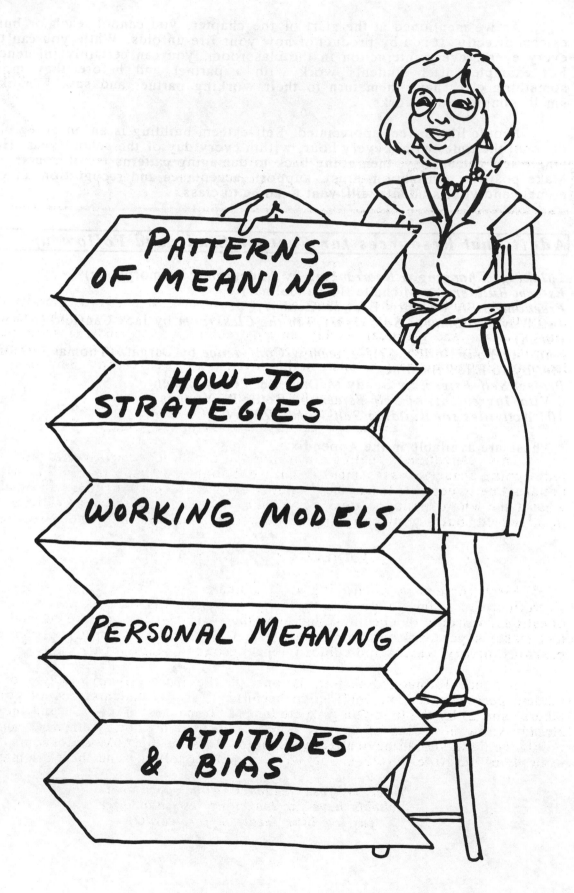

310

# 25

## Better Assessment

### Is There a Better Way?

Tests, much like the weather, get plenty of criticism. Are they really different today than they were fifty years ago? Yes, they are. Fortunately they are getting more realistic and practical. Today, in most schools, you can find some variety of assessment for nearly anything and everything. Yet, the experts on the brain and learning, the top neuroscientists see the problem quite differently. To them:

*Most of what we can measure now,*
*behaviorally, is neurologically immaterial*
*to the optimal development of the brain*

This realization is fueling a massive and urgent movement worldwide in redesigning academic assessment. What we thought was important in the past, may not at all be important. It may have simply been *more measurable!* In other words, what if the whole testing system was wrong? You can have the most efficient oil rig in the world, but if you're digging in the wrong area, you'll still not strike oil.

### Objective vs. Subjective

First, there is no such thing as an objective test. All tests are subjective, and all reflect the value judgments, priority systems, likes and dislikes. Choice of questions, wording of questions and even the format of the test are formed from the test maker's personal history. Even a test written by a committee brings to it the previous history, values and subjective background of individuals.

Second, formalized testing is one of the least effective ways to evaluate student performance. It's ineffective because 1) many students are not good "test-takers" and 2) by the time you give students a formal test, both you and they should already know how each of you are doing. You should know your weak and strong points well and should have already begun to work on them. Most tests are a perfect example of too little, too late. Yet, you still need a solution and there are many.

*Never confuse feedback with assessment...*
*schools have far too many tests and offer*
*far too little feedback for learners*

311

Dipsticking gives you immediate and accurate feedback on your student's level of understanding at the moment of presentation. The way to do it is simple. Set up a system with your students of various hand signals which represent answers. You might have a sign for more, less, higher, lower, multiply, divide, useful, not, etc. Then you can use these immediate digital feedback signals during your presentation so that you know how much is being understood. It's a signal system which allows every teacher to get constant feedback on his or her presentation. Then, changes and corrections can be made right on the spot when they're needed, not at a test two weeks later.

## Present Your Evaluations

What you say and how you say it will determine students' test-taking attitudes. An evaluation is a feedback mechanism for the teacher. If the teacher designs it well, it can also serve as a feedback mechanism for the students. Simply tell your sudents that the tests will measure how well you taught instead of how much they learned. It takes the pressure off each student and reduces the incentive to use the success strategy called cheating. Turn evaluations into a game and make it fun-one that the students wanted to play. Rename your tests. Call them something else more fun (like a "loop," as in feedback loop)

## Reminders

**Assess often!** Based on study results, direct observation and personal experience, it's been discovered that for feedback to be useful, it must be constant. Testing during every class is useful. The tests do not have to be written. It's just as easy to create class exercises in which students can respond orally, in unison drills or informal feedback systems. Probably the best "signal system" is a hand response or lap board. Set up a reply system so you get immediate answers from every student on every question. By using creative response-systems, you are constantly updated on how well each student is learning.

*Avoid motivating your students,*
*instead, lead them to an addiction*
*of their own greatness*

Students who get infrequent testing experience anxiety, disassociation, fears, lowered interest and participation levels. Daily testing creates more of a relationship with the subject matter, more interest in it and lowers stress about grades because each test is less significant.

**Keep them light!** Who says assessing should be painful and tramautic? Find ways to allow the students to devalue the test score, but still learn from the experience. Possible ways are including some questions which are silly or giveaways, making the test itself full of cartoons, allowing students to contribute questions, allowing them to take the test with partners, or to develop a new scoring system.

**Use a variety of testing methods.** You may recall from your own experience that some students best express themselves in writing, others talking, others by demonstrating, others on special projects, and others love a basic, standard written test. The greater the variety of testing forms you usc, the greater the chances your students will have for success. That's why a hand or hoard signal system is an excellent quick feedback system for neary any age student.

**Be on the student's side.** Allow students to be successful. Tell them ahead of time when you will test, what kinds of test methods you'll use, and the grading system. Help them choose the testing varieties. Ask them to get involved in the process. Many master teachers test only when they feel students are ready and likely to be high scorers. Put instructions in the middle of the test to stand up and stretch or take a deep breath.

**Give immediatate feedback.** Score the tests as soon as possiblke. Scoring is what students and teachers need for feedback and course correction. The easiest way is to have students grade their own test as soon as they are completed. "What if they cheat?", you may ask. Somehow, when you do the things that this book talks about, kids don't cheat. If you make students more resourceful, and give them the learning strategies that they need to succeed, cheating becomes extinct. Correct tests in class with lightness and humor, then celebrate each right answer with group applause or cheers.

**Collect and record tests intermittently.** The consistent patterned scores become too ritualized and eventually ignored. Some teachers disagree and claim that reinforcement must be consistent to provide the information that both teacher and student need. Combine the best of both: test often, record scores less frequently.

**Use the portfolio and processfolio method.** This means that you keep a file for each student which does two important things. First, it contains the history of the learning process the learner is going through. Second, it provides a wide variety of assessments methods. The folder is accessible to the learners and it constantly keep up-to-date.

## Many Ways to Assess

To repeat something mentioned earlier, there isn't a single best kind of test because different students have different learning strategies. As a result, students test differently. If some of your students were color-blind and you gave them a test which asked them to distinguish colors, you might notice a high failure rate from that group. Does that mean that your students are "slow?" Of course not. They simply never had a chance to succeed. It makes more sense to offer assessment in two ways: provide variety in your methods and provide choice in your methods. Why? Your goal is to help provide students with a way to demonstrate what they have learned. It is not to embarrass them or point out what they have missed.

## Quick Feedback

Some students will want this evaluation type all the time. Create a balance by teaching mastery of other test types. Also, you must give to the students a clear criteria for feedback. Here are some examples:

1. **Lap boards:** small notebook-sized cardboards with a vinyl covering on them. They are cheap, easily used and effective. Basically, they are miniature chalkboards using quick-erase pens instead of chalk. You simply ask a question. Each student writes the answer and holds up the hoard for you to see. With these boards, students can give immediate, personal and private answers to any question you have. Plus, you can quickly scan the classroom to find students whose answer is different and follow up on them.

2. **Non-verbals.** Watch for smiles, nods of the head, students who sit back in their chairs with theor hands clasped behind the head. Pay attention to changes in breathing patterns, in conversations and noise level.

3. **Hand and Body Signals.** This system is based on the old "thumbs up or thumbs down" signal as an answer to questions the teacher asks. Have students use dozens of different hand responses which include using different letters of the alphabet, pointing to different parts of the room, using body parts or partners. It's easy to imagine this working perfectly well in math classes, especially when students can make function signals easily such as add, subtract, multiply or divide. Yet, with some creativity, many other feedbacks can be developed. The desired outcome is to create a quick, easy, workable system to give immediate feedback. These signals have been described in detail in the chapter on presentation and evaluation.

# Homework: Yes or No?

Probably the most common form of written evaluation is homework. First, consider the purpose in assigning homework. If it's busywork, don't assign it. If the assignment can be done in class just as well do it in class. Your classroom is a controlled environment. You can observe, support, give reinforcement and make the learning process more useful and fun for the student. Early steps in a learning process are like a cake making and you want to have the corrections made in the batter, not when it's in the oven!

**Shorten it.** Minimize the homework, make it shorter, more meaningful. Have it be consistent, useful and fun. Let it increase fluency and proficiency of classwork. Vary it and involve as much creativity. Ask students to read a short synopsis just before going to sleep with a classical music concert as the background. This allows the mind to integrate and store the material for maximum usage. Be sure to follow through during the next class.

**Consider the team approach.** Here, students support each other instead of competing. Have them work on an assignment in teams of five which you have set up to have the greatest academic diversity. Use the group score as the score for each individual. Allow students to network with phone calls to learn the material. Have students bring homework into class early then work in groups to learn it. They can use synergy to come up with a "group version" of the homework which increases the understanding and interest.

**Formats.** One of the best homework assignments is to create a format (such as the mind map introduced in the chapter on planning) to be used, then have students fill in what went on in class that day. It serves as a review, it increases recall, it may bring up questions that otherwise would not have risen and it's fun to do. Encourage students to share phone numbers and trade ideas for homework. Students should have every possible opportunity to learn. If they turn in something that has an unacceptable quantity of mistakes on it, give them no grade until they fix it and bring it back to you. Remind them that they can use anyone else's help. The reading assigned should be short passages, not 20 or 50 page chunks to do overnight. Consistency is of more value than large chunks all at once.

**Relevancy.** Make it something that they can easily transfer to real life. You have many possibilities for "home learning." Consider the following:

- Interviews of parents, siblings or neighboors
  their past, their opinions, knowledge, etc.
- Use of television
  tie in with news, movies, science, people, process
- Use of the house and neighboorhood
  measuring, identifying, analyzing, grouping
- Individual learning can be simple:
  journals, visualizing, model-building, experiments

The point is simple. If you're going to assign homework, make it short, realistic, practical and meaningful. Busywork is out, genuine learning is in. Re-assess what, how and why you assign it. It may be time for a change.

## Informal Assessment

**Use observation in problem-solving.** Give students a problem to solve which can be solved many different ways. For example, the one about the man and the woman starting out walking from the same place. The man takes two steps for every three the woman takes. They start out together, and immediately lose synchronization. After how many steps will they be back in "sync" again? That problem can be solved using just about every one of the seven intelligences. Which one is chosen by the students?

**Give students a choice in activities and games to play and watch.** Discover which ones they pick: *Pictionary, Monopoly,* crossword puzzles, manipulative puzzles, charades, music recognition, etc. Then observe what they do during that game.

**Use discussion, and reflection after a play, movie or musical.** After students watch one of these, ask which parts struck them most and were really memorable - was it the music, the action, the relationships, etc.?

**Watch the type of learning and intelligence used the most.** Students tend to do what they like or are most successful at doing. Find out who are the questioners, the noise and music-makers, the artists, doodlers, the active learners, the talkers, the loners, etc.

**Your observation in inventions & model-building.** Give students a chance to design, build and use some kind of a physical representation of the topic learned. Observe what parts of the task they like and excel in most easily. You'll learn a great deal about how each learner learns.

**Allow for the use of music and sounds.** Students create jingles or songs about a unit. They create a song and sing or perform it. They could re-do the lyrics to a song with the new key words.

## Keys are Choice & Variety

Remember, choice and variety are the key for better ways to assess students. The form of assessment that could be used is unlimited. Many staff and administrators have developed better benchmarks and criteria to measure each early through mastery level in learning. While some will argue that *just one* of the criteria below is most important, all three really are equal. You'll want to find a way to provide feedback on:

**End result.** What is it that students are creating? What kind of quality is it? The student asks: "What do I know? What do I do with it?"

**Learning Process.** Many educators feel that the journey, the process of how the learner got to the product is as, if not more important, than the product.

**Learner Skills.** This is often referred to as the "improvement gain." The question is more how far has the student come, given the circumstances?

Keeping in mind that much of what's really important cannot be easily measured, at least some progress has been made. The basic value of this is not for the schools to be able to compare students, but for learners to have feedback on the milestones in their learning. You might have three categories:

**NY** - Not yet...entry level; this means the student has *just started learning* in an agreed-upon area or discipline. No progress yet.
**DEV** - Developing; this means that the student is *in process of developing* the key skills and information needed for basic competence. This has stages, so that progress can be noted.
**EX** - Extending; means that the learner has *already met the criteria* for learning in that particular subject or skill and is exploring it further.

In primary and secondary schools, this means that every single unit will need to have each of the above three categories detailed. It is a time-consuming process, but it will provide more stability, fairness and accuracy in the long run. It insures that when a student switches from one school to another, the assessment will help accurately determine where the learner is really at, not solely a subjective opinion.

| Not Yet: | Developing | Extending |
|---|---|---|
| counts 1-5 | counts 1-10 | counts 20+ |
| skips #s | errors at 11-20 | forward & |
| needs help | needs prompt | backwards |
|  | sometimes | oral or written |

Is this better than a letter grade? It certainly provides more information. It certainly is less judgmental. It certainly provides a more standard understanding of a learner's progress. Yes, it is better than just a letter grade, as long as it is used properly. Remember, the learner's brains may be as much as three years apart, developmentally, and still be normal. There is no allocation in this assessment for that. As long as it is used for feedback and teacher information, not for comparison, it's acceptable.

# Does a Rubric Make Sense?

It does for many. Another system of assessing the learner progress is to use a runbric... A rubric is simply a matrix developed by someone which lists the criteria for measuring what you want. If your criteria is out of date, the use of a rubric won't help, either. A rubric is an attempt to get more objective about the "subjective." Often the rubric will have the following:

**Topic:** (Let's say it's process writing)

**Primary & peripheral intelligence** types utilized: verbal/linguistic also... interpersonal, vspatial, musical/rhythmic and intrapersonal

**Targeted standard:** mctacognition of writing standards

**Indicators** of each level are the following: After completing a writing assignment, a student completes a 1-2 page self-assessment of how they planned, monitored and assessed their own work.

*"Not yet:"* Indicated by numerous spelling & grammar errors, jumbled sentence structure, no clear beginning, middle or end, unable to identify plusses or minuses.

*"Developing:"* Indicated by occasional spelling & grammar errors. Clear beginning, middle and end, one or two examples, self-assessments notes both plusses and minuses.

**"Extending:"** Indicated by no spelling or grammar errors, clear transitions, lucid & ample examples, clear structure and strong insights into plusses and minuses. To create your own rubrics for assessment, you might take the following seven steps:

- **Explore & gather ideas from other rubrics**
- **Find work samples and explore the range of quality**
- **Discuss the qualities & characteristics of excellent work**
- **Prioritize the list of qualities**
- **Make a sample rubric**
- **Test it with a sample of student work**
- **Revise as needed**

The idea of a rubric is simple: Take all the those ideas, intuitions, beliefs and opinions about what is excellent and do your best to objectify them. Many teachers find that the use of rubrics can make the assessment easier, even when you're using such diverse methods. A rubric is simply a criteria-based grid which uses specific and defined guidelines to assess learning evidence. It might look like a box with 5 lines across and 5 high.

Everything your students submit for assessment ought to have clearly defined success parameters. No more "teacher's intuition" or a vaguely defined opinion about what is or is not quality. It's time to invite student input on what they think constitutes quality. Your first rubric for assessment may be rough, but it will evolve over time to become a better way to discover what learners know, feel and can do.

With each of these, you can set a standard, from one to five. "1" is lowest quality, "5" is highest. To get all 5's on a project would be the highest possible. By making your criteria for quality specific, you get better quality work from your students. Your criteria may be "1" is the work turned in late or the wrong assignment. "2" can be on time, accurate content and sloppy throughout. A "5" might be on time, visually appealing, the right topic, in-depth, meaningful and reflective. It's up to you and the students (if the age is appropriate). The point is, you can create a fairly objective set of standards for what is seemingly a subjective student effort. Remember though; if the criteria used for assessment are still the old fashioned lists of facts, a rubric won't make your system any better. What you should be asssessing is:

- **Patterns of meaning**
- **Strategies & how-to skills**
- **Personal biases; what and why**
- **Working models of systems**
- **Personal meaning**

Granted, those a a bit tougher to quantify. But it sure beats the ols tyle of testing that simply became a game for the students to play and try to beat. There's got to be mnore to school than playing advesarial games.

# The Role of Personal Meaning

The concept is simple: make it a priority that the demonstration of the learning has to be related to one's own life. In short, it is not a question of information, *it has to integrate personal meaning into it*. Only when the learning becomes woven into the fabric of one's own life does it become genuinely, internally, meaningfully learned. And it will last! Here are the criteria important to personal meaning concept:

1. Evidence of progress towards multiple learning goals - a timeline
2. Ability to transfer the subject knowledge to other subjects
3. An indication of transfer of learning from school to life
4. Evidence of self-reflection and self-awareness on a topic
5. Items that convey understanding of the basics of that topic as well as details or trivia
6. Something that conveys the relevance and meaning of that topic in a local or global context (as well as personal)
7. Demonstration of use of a related skill, problem-solving or ability to produce a model or an artifact in that topic

The concepts behind personal meaning are simple: 1) the learning must be related to the students' personal life and be found to be an extension of everyday naturally-acquired knowledge; 2) the learner always gets choice in which of the 20 mediums can be used for assessment; 3) each level of assessment requires that students use a greater number of options available for demonstration; 4) students are not graded on a curve or compared to other students; 5) grading is done both by the teacher and the students, using criteria for mastery that has been agreed upon by both teachers and the students. It insures that the following will occur:

1. Students will have a way to express what they know, in the way that they know it best.
2. Students will be measured by consistent standards, ones on which they had some input.
3. All learners will have equal chance to succeed.
4. Learners will be encouraged to learn in a meaningful way.

How do you use everyday learning opportunities as forms for personal meaning? First, set up activities that allow you time to observe and listen. Secondly, involve the students in self-assessments. Thirdly, you may want to find alternative time management strategies to free up time for more productive assessing.

*Personal meaning virtually guarantees that the learning will come alive for the learner and that it will be a part of his or her life for the long term*

For example, once a week or once a month, can you double up with another teacher at your grade level? Can you utilize volunteer support staff to free up your time? This will allow you to be more thorough in the support of student learning. Here are some ways that students can be learning while you are observing.

**1. Newspaper article** Let students create their own mock-up front page of some learning topic. They take many points of view and each has to be related to their own life. That way it could be covered from personal, financial, sociological, historical, literary or scientific aspects.

**3. Commercials** Students take their subject matter and turn it into a commercial. It could be a written one for the print media, a tape to be played on the radio or a video. Make it personal to the student's interests.

**4. Student teaching** Allow the students time to think it out first, then make their own notes or mind-maps on it. The more props, music and visual aids used, the more meaning the presentation may have. Keep them fun by providing choice in the topic selection and a low-risk peer support environment. Then give them time to teach it to the class.

**5. Model-making** In some cases, students can build a scaled-down or working-size model of the material. That can be particularly useful in demonstrating their understanding of the material when it is physical and involves steps or processes.

**6. Performance** Let students do drama or theater on the material. Some material, especially literature, lends itself to being performed. Allow students time to do a quality job, then make a fun "stage" for them to perform on.

**7. Music** Most material can be set to music, written about in music, performed as rap or opera. It can also be used as the key words to re-write an already familiar song and then performed as a musical.

**8. Interview** Many kinds of material can be assessed if students simply have time to talk freely about it. Casual, unstressed discussion-interview time is rarely used and can be of great benefit. The ability to formulate questions and to extrapolate hypothetical answers becomes important here.

**9. Artwork/Drawing** Let students have a chance to express themselves in art. Many types of material can be best understood in the form of a drawing. Give students a large piece of paper and let them express what it means to them. You may be surprised at some of the great examples you get.

**10. Journals/Learning Logs** For students that are more private and intrapersonal, you may learn much about what the student knows through this reflective medium. In these journals, the content is specific to learning and students can create or answer questions about what and how they learned, add their own feelings and possible applications of the learning.

**11. Sculpture** Some learning can be represented as a physical object or a sculpture. If it is appropriate, many students would love to be able to let out their own "Michaelangelo" and express themselves.

**12. Debates** These can come in many forms. Half of the value is in preparing for the debates. You may want to make your criteria for assessment very specific, so that they know how they'll be appraised.

**13. Mind-mapping** Let students create huge, poster-sized maps of what they know. These webbed, thematic graphic organizers offer colorful peripheral thoughts organized around a key idea. They were popularized by Tony Buzan, Michael Gelb and Nancy Margulies. These provide an excellent vehicle for understanding relationships, themes and associations of ideas.

**14. Game design** Learners know many games, most of them from their culture of growing up. Allow your learners to take any game, such as simon sez, *Monopoly*, *Jeopardy*, *Wheel of Fortune*, *Concentration*, card games, ball toss, poker and others, then re-design it using alternative content.

**15. Montage/collage** This format provides a vehicle for collecting and assembling thoughts and ideas in art. It's actually a combination between a mind map, a sculpture and a drawing. The more choice and freedom you offer your learners, the more likely you are to get something really innovative.

**16. Multi-media** Students can make a video, cassette tape or CD. Insist that it be quality and help provide access to the necessary resources. Your rubric will help you and your students evaluate these so-called "subjective" mediums.

**17. Students write test** Let students figure out what's important and what's not. Then ask them to create their own test. You can set some basic criteria, but keep plenty of room for creativity.

**18. Timelines, Diorama** These can be a great way to demonstrate an idea. The idea comes alive in a chronological graphic description. The goals, processes, resources and players are included along with the content learned.

**19. Personal Goals Checklist** Students set original learning goals, interim goals, then they revise them as time goes on. Goals are self-assessed: if reached, when reached, how reached and when re-assessed. Each student shares this analysis with the teacher.

**20. Attitudinal Surveys** You design them, students fill them out. Use both box-checking and short essay. Ask questions such as "how did you feel about this subject when we first started?" Then ask progressive ones to find out if the learners have changed their feelings about it.

**21. Plan & Produce a Mini-Party or Conference** Students plan an "experts" gathering on the topic. They gather up speakers, plan the talks, organize the logistics and put it on. Can either be just planned or actually carried out.

**22. Prepare an encyclopedia, journal, book, album or yearbook** Brainstorm possibilities. Research the topic. Gather articles, photos, create drawings. Prioritize ideas, plan and produce.

**23. Create a wall-sized mural** Can be done as a school or civic project. The planning, producing and documentation of this project can bring tremendous results.

**24. Create story boards** Disney cartoonists pioneered the concept of storyboarding: start with a sequence of roughly drawn pictures that capture each key moment. Put them up on a wall to create and trace the history of the project.

**25. Write a story** The story could be either fiction or non-fiction. The point of it would be to make the information personally meaningful to the creator of the project and the other learners.

**26. Student Choice** Allow the student to select an example, process or product for evaluation. It could be something that was originally developed outside of class time like an organizing system, a hobby or unusual collection. This can work only if you provide the acceptable criteria for it in advance.

With variety and choice, you can now have a model which honors and respects all of your learner's gifts. You can focus less on "how smart" a student is and focus more on "how is he smart?" By using the concept of profound assessment, your learners are more likely to feel fairly treated and fairly assessed. They'll be more willing to submit their learning to you or their peers for review.

## Working Towards Mastery

The mastery concept means that every student works towards successful completion of the unit of learning. Once mastered, he has earned an A. Either a student has an incomplete or an A, then he moves on. It's the simplest, makes the most sense, and avoids the entire issue of grouping and prescriptive labeling. It also allows students to learn at their own rates which is important for self-esteem and competency. It is, in the author's estimation, the best of available evaluation methods. Any way that a teacher can implement it is well worthwhile.

The mastery concept is brilliant - in concept. It takes good teaching to make it work, and fortunately you qualify! The mastery concept states that clear specific criteria be set for student competency in a subject area, and that each student is responsible for achieving mastery, at his own pace. To be fully effective, students need a full toolbag of resources for mastering the material, PLUS the commitment and drive to carry it out.

## Grading Solutions

The ways to grade successfully are: (1) set up a system that includes many kinds of input: attendance, class participation, daily sub-quizzes, portfolios, weekly quizzes, demonstrations, debates, monthly exams, models, projects or papers. (2) set up ways for students to make up absences or lower scores (3) tell students exactly how to get a top score in your class, and remove the much of the threat of failure - it's counter-productive to learning (4) give constant feedback to the students (5) the more the feedback you get and give, the better your students will learn (6) treat the whole grading system lightly, and still respect its meaning to the students.

## Testing Environment

Everard Blanchard of Villa Educational Research Associates has done some excellent work in the area of the actual testing environment. To put it briefly, environment matters. The tone of your voice, the tempo, the content, the expectations, all matter. Think carefully in terms of your purpose and intended result. In addition, Everhard confirmed that students who take exams with a light classical music background scored higher than those who took the exam in silence. The lesson? Improve the aesthetic and emotional atmosphere in your testing situations.

## Cheating Solutions

For many students, cheating is an often-used and best success strategy. Students who cheat well may be smart. Dr. Wayne Dyer, author and teacher says:

*"How could anybody cheat? I saw a study which tested chickens to see which ones were dumb and which ones were smart. A length of chicken wire was set up in front of their feed and the ones you eventually*

*labeled dumb just sat and died of starvation. The chickens you labeled smart walked around the barrier and got at their food. Now when chickens go around barriers for rewards, they're labeled smart, but when students do the same thing, you label it cheating."*

It's so curious in our culture that if a student gets answers from a teacher or a textbook, its OK. But when students get an answer from another student, we call it cheating! This is not to justify cheating. Cheting is wrong. It's just that a high percentage of students cheat and there are some better ways to deal with it.

1.  Provide more clearly stated objectives... insure that the students have a sure idea of what you want
2.  Increase feedback - more consistent and better quality feedback...every day at least once per student, per one hour of learning time
3.  Provide learn-to-learn skills... teach your students how to find information, how to learn better and give themclass time for specific practice
4.  Provide tutoring or some kind of extra help... maybe it comes from students at an grade lebvel above
5.  Give students more opportunities to work in groups... the more they work in groups the more they will want to be tested by themselves...most students will want to know how they really are doing in your class
6.  Give each student a "study-buddy"...make it formal or informal... everyone needs some support
7.  Offer help during "down" times so that you catch the gaps in learning and they are less like to cheat
8.  Give better directions at test time so they don't have to ask others for them
9.  Have a clear policy about what is cheating and what is not
10. Be consistent, fair and firm in dealing with cheaters.
11. Provide plenty of space around each student at test time.
12. State your own personal views, rules and class policiy on it

## Follow Up

One of the most difficult moments for a student is when a test result is below expectations. It is possible to reframe the student's experience. Find a different way of integrating the test experience so that each and every test causes the student to feel resourceful rather than a beaten down failure. What if you kept presenting to your students the following:

*   A low score indicates a gap in teaching effectiveness
*   There's no such thing as a failure or a mistake
*   What is called a failure is an outcome that we've prejudged as bad
*   Every outcome gives the information you need to succeed next time
*   Each experience is part of a larger success
*   With every adversity comes the seed of an equal or greater benefit

These beliefs may or may not be true, but you'll produce more confident students by applying them. These new beliefs create the willingness to gain something from each setback. Imagine the change in feelings in your students when they call a test a result or a grade simply an outcome! Or, if each time you give test scores, your students were asked to come up with a decision about their results that would allow them to be even better learners. After all, one of the major differences between kinds of learners is the strategy used. Successful learners include, as part of their strategy, a decision about the learning event that makes them:

322

- Have more resources, more choices for the next time
- Feel stronger and better it elicits positive emotions
- Appreciate the valuable feedback
- Re-evaluate ineffective strategies for next time

Another important role for teachers is to teach the necessary study skills. It's easy to assume that someone else has prepared your students for studying successfully, but that's usually not the case. Unless you are well-versed in the latest study strategies and have the time to teach them to your students, have your students get a copy of *Student Success Secrets*. It's listed in the bibliography and provides the fundamentals as well as the specifics for learning material better.

You may recall a statement that was made earlier along the lines of, "The better you do, the better your students do." With that in mind, you might already know what will be presented about grades: that it's not only possible, but desirable to be giving out all As in your class. All As would mean that you did a great job.

Remember that as you continue to increase your ability to communicate effectively and bring out the best in your students (who are all of approximate equal ability), the results will be that their best is an "A" and since they are all equal in ability, all of them will deserve one. If you are mandated to give out a certain number of Bs, Cs, Ds or Fs, or if you have been grading on the curve, you might want to re-examine that procedure and ask yourself why would you want to guarantee that a certain number of students do poorly?

# Affirm the Positive

*"A little girl came up to me one day and said, 'Mr. Jensen, Mr. Jensen, look at my paper.' She showed me her paper, and **every single word on it was misspelled**. I looked at her and said, 'Maureen, I really like your paper - the margins are nice and neat, and your printing is clean and readable.' And she said, 'Thank you, Mr. Jensen - I've really been working hard on it. Next, I'm going to work on my spelling.'"*

The ultimate success as a teacher in the classroom is to have ALL of your students succeed. If half of them do well, you didn't reach the other half and that could be your goal next time. It should be the dream of every teacher-to have every student in your class succeed. If any of them don't, adjust the variables: your teaching, the tests, the grading system, etc. Behavioral flexibility, teaching skills, rapport, presentation methods all can bring you closer to the 100% goal.

---

### *Additional Resources for Further Study and Follow up*

*Multiple Assessments for Multiple Intelligences* by Bellanca (Skylight)*
*A Practical Guide to Alternative Assessment* by Joan Herman (ASCD)
*Brain-Based Learning & Teaching* by Jensen (Turning Point)*
*Graduation by Exhibition* by Joseph MacDonald, et. al.
*Assessing Student Outcomes* by Marzano (ASCD)
*Expanding Student Assessment* by Vito Perrone(ASCD)

* These are available in the Appendix.

# 26

# From Surviving to Thriving

## A New Way of Thinking

Almost anyone can survive the day. All you need to do is to do is drag yourself through the day and by the end of it, still be breathing. But what a waste! We want much more out of life than just surviving. We all want to have life be rich, meaningful and fun. We want to thrive! This chapter is chock-full of the tools, tricks and strategies that can get you thrive through the day. Whether it's dealing with energy levels, hassles, parents, reports cards or yourself, you'll find ideas you can use immediately.

If you find yourself having a tough time motivating yourself to go to work, use it as a wake up call! Find out what the problems is and deal with it. Is it an irritating colleague, a frustrating student or unresponsive administration? Is it a particular parent or is it everything? Your first choice is to isolate the problem and deal with it. If you successfully handle problem after problem and you still have a tough time getting motivated to go to work, you may need a leave of absence or even a new career! But most of the time, one of these suggestions will work for you:

## How to Motivate Yourself

1. Make a special personal highlight for yourself every day - some fun, interesting activity or appointment.
2. Think of the difference you make in the lives of others. If you can't come up with that difference, start doing something different.
3. Start each day with a simple, short task that you can get success.
4. Set goals for yourself every day. Poorly sized goals may be too big, others too small. Vary the size of them until you find the size that is most motivating.
5. Meet with another person who is an expert in a field you want to learn more about  learning can be very motivating and inspiring.
6. Improve your work environment add: plants, an ionizer, pictures, fresh air, an aquarium or flowers.
7. Start an attitude of gratitude; think of how fortunate you are to haveyour work or any kind of work at all.
8. Think of what gets you motivated in other areas and use that strategy.
9. Make time predictions for your tasks. Then try to beat your own predicted goals...make it fun and challenging.
10. Teach another person something that you are learning, something that you'd like to be better at doing.

11. Call a local newspaper and tell them about something wonderfully positive at your school that has just enough of a twist to it that it warrants attention.
12. Hang around more excited and enthusiastic friends.
13. Find three people each day to give a compliment to - it's inspiring. Then, finish the day by complimenting another person; especially a "down" one.
14. Rearrange your time & do fun things to start & end the day.
15. Go for a passion walk. Use the time to work yourself up into a bubbling passion about something big in your life.
16. Celebrate your successes every day - even the little ones.
17. Chunk your tasks into smaller more manageable, motivating ones.
18. Make a list of everyone you support & those who support you, have a talk with those who support you about your job.
19. Read inspiring biographies or listen to inspiring people.

# How to Deal with
# Unlikeable Colleagues

1. **Start with what's in common...** Seek first to understand, then to be understood. Start talking at any chance you get. In conversations, be interested in & curious about their world. Begin conversations about what you both share: work, supervisor, stress, weather, etc.

2. **Get-to-know each other...** beyond professional side. Find the softer side: ask about children, hobbies, hopes, dreams, retirement, etc.

3. **Reach through whom the student considers highly or values...** Influence his or her mentor or find something about his mentor you can connect with. Can you influence this person through his or her friends?

4. **While in conversation, do the following:**
   a) change your conversational "buts" to "and" The buts are a negation that rarely feels positive or good. Instead of saying, "I know it's a hassle, BUT there's another consideration..." You say, "While it's true that... it's also true that..."
   b) match verbals - voice-tempo/tonality/volume. If he or she talks fast, you can pick up pace a bit...do the same with volume....
   c) match non-verbals--breathing/gestures. When done in a very subtle way, the other can feel like you're "like him."
   d) match superlatives used. With discretion, use the same words like "amazing" or "super."
   e) match Visual-Auditory-Kinesthetic modalities with predicates. If he says, "I see what you mean," you verify by saying, "So, youunderstand my point of view?" For auditory predicates (that sounds good) you can match. Same with kinesthetic: "That feels right."

5. **When you very much disagree, disagree through 3 magic words...** Use the words, "respect, appreciate & agree." Regardless of the topic, there is something you can agree with, respect or appreciate.

6. **When you have discussions...** change from "I, you," words to "We" and "us." That keeps it friendly. Also, you can get "yes" sets by seeking agreement on easy or obvious topics.

7. **Low key...** Do your best to have conversations in casual, non-confrontive postures or locations. You might match physical height in conversation if there's a big difference, one of you can sit on a table.

8. **Use his or her ideas in conversation...** Refer to their ideas (positively) and let them know you listen. In general, keep asking for his or her opinion. Asking doesn't mean you have to agree or use it.

9. **Venue change...** Can you interact outside of work? Maybe a more relaxed, less stressed venue would help - a school picnic, a game, a barbecue. Does he or she have any hobbies that might benefit the school? Software programming, building, electronics, stamps, race cars?

10. **When all else fails...** Ignore the problem for awhile. It may cease to be an issue over time. Otherwise you can either apply for a transfer to another school (it might even pay more!) or very respectfully ask your colleague if he or she may want to switch to another school. Until that time, keep your mouth shut, avoid that person and still be supportive.

## The High-Energy Teaching Diet

Teaching requires a great deal of energy. Your body cannot run on inadequate or poor nutrition without you paying the price. When you abuse your health, you'll feel run-down, get irritable, get sick more often and even depressed. When you take care of your health, you have more energy, less stress and feel good about yourself and life.

A good deal of research has been done on the affects of food on your mind and mood. For more information, there are several suggested resources at the end of this chapter. For now, here are the highlights of years of scientific research on maintaining alert, low stress, high-energy diets.

## High Alertness

To boost your alertness and mental performance, include a natural source of tyrosine : eggs, fish, turkey, tofu, pork, chicken, and yogurt. It's available in capsule form: Ginkgo biloba extract is known for increasing the flow of nutrients and oxygen to the brain, available at fitness and natural health food stores. Many now carry a whole product line of neural or neuro-supplements. Many have strong advocates. Experiment with them.

Proteins early, carbos later in the day. Eat foods low in refined carbohydrates - it promotes relaxation. Avoid high sugar & high carbohydrates combo - sugar is utilized differently by the brain when "carried in" with protein. Eat carbohydrates with protein for a better nutrient balance to the brain. Eat multivitamin supplements, especially the B vitamins. Thiamin may be able to increase visual acuity, reactive time and fine motor control.

Lecithin, found in egg yolks and wheat germ can boost memory. Folic acid was discovered to reduce depression and boost learning performance. Folic acid is found in leafy green vegetables, beef liver and beans. Selenium improves memory and concentration. It is a mineral found most concentrated in seafood, whole grain breads, Brazil nuts and white meat tuna. Boron supplements improved mental activity. The trace mineral boron is found in broccoli, apples, pairs, peaches, grapes, nuts and dried beans. Use zinc supplements for short term memory and attention span. Better yet, zinc can be found in fish, beans, whole grains and dark meat turkey. Eat iron-rich foods like dark-green vegetables, meat, beans & fish for improved attention, memory, perception and visual-motor coordination.

## Extra Eating Tips

Drink pure, fresh water. Brain specialists recommend from 8-12 glasses per day. Cut the bad fat. Good fat is the omega-3 fatty molecules. Those are the unsaturated ones found in fish oil, cottonseed oil, even butter is better than margarine (same calories & fat, but butter is unsaturated). Subjects on a diet of polyunsaturated fats learned 20% faster than those on a saturated fat diet. They also retained the information longer. The brain runs best on a "nibbling diet". Studies showed increased learning and performance when subjects ate from 5-9 small snacks or meals per day. Bring snacks to your classroom. Eat often through the day, even if it's just a piece of fruit. Buy foods in bulk like those small juice containers with built-in straws, fruit, seeds or nuts.

**Summary:** *For breakfast:* fresh juice, fruit & boiled eggs plus multivitamin supplements. Snack on fruits, nuts & drink water. *Lunch:* dark green salad. Snack on fruits, pure yogurt, nuts & water. *Dinner:* pasta, or potatoes, brown rice, beans, lean meats, plus dark green vegetables & multivitamin supplements. Make dessert an exception and drink alcohol in moderation (weekends only).

## Energy Management

We've all had the experience of coming home from wok so utterly drained, you wonder if you can make it back the next day. Here's a secret: You can have positive, uplifting, high-energy days, every day. Here are the tips to managing your own health and energy levels:

**1. Start your day strong.** Wake up to positive imaging of the day. See and believe you'll reach your goals for the day.

**2. Avoid the sleep trap.** Some think that sleep will restore your energy. It does, *but only to a point.* Doing what you love to do, doing a variety of things is more restorative than longer sleep times.

**3. Learn to enjoy the little things.** A favor, a smile, a puffy cloud, a favorite food, a short line or warm breeze. Not only enjoy them once, but keep drawing attention to them repeatedly to gain extra pleasure and energy.

**4. Pick out personal revitalizers.** Listen to a favorite song. Have a cup of your favorite tea. Visualize yourself playing a sport successfully. Get a cold drink. Read the comics. Browse through a catalog. Play a desktop toy such as a yo-yo or use a dart board. Walk around the block. Go outside and watch the weather. Write in a journal. Look at old photographs that mean a lot to you. Call your parents. Plan your next vacation.

**5. Learn to say no.** Say no to a committee you don't really want to join. Say no to an extra luncheon you might dislike. Say no to a favor that you can't do without tremendous resentment.

**6. Understand how you relate to others.** You'll want to have a person in your life that is a real "upper." That's the high energy positive person who inspires you. You'll want to have someone whom you can "dump your emotional refuse... the disappointments, upsets and complaints that all of us can build up on. Learn what people combination recharges your batteries. It is usually being by yourself or being with others. Once you know what it is, be purposeful in applying that strategy to gain personal energy.

**7. Take "power naps."** These are short (10-30 minute) naps during the day. Block out distractions, close the door, turn down the lights, prop your feet up and put on a meditative tape. Or, simply enjoy the quiet. Learn to put yourself into a brief sleep (take a self-hypnosis course) and you'll be able to refresh yourself throughout the day. Famous inventors, writers, executives use this strategy--you can too.

# Knowledge and Skill Base

The whole concept of thriving means that you are not staying the same, you're stretching and growing. Your greatest asset is your ability to learn and communicate what you have learned. If you are in education, chances are good that you value learning very highly. If so, what have you done lately to boost your own knowledge and skill base? The average teacher reads three books a year, two fiction and one non-fiction. Less than 30% of all teachers read professional journals. Fewer than 15% of all teachers attend a professional development seminar outside of what is offered by their school or district. If you were having surgery, would you want to be operated on by a physician who had not upgraded to the latest knowledge and procedures? It's doubtful. Are your students any less important?

Make a commitment to yourself to continuous improvement. Read a book a month and if you like fiction, at least alternate with some nonfiction. Attend seminars, workshops and summer institutes. Find out what is in your school or district's staff development library. You say there isn't one? That's a good project to get started! Set up at your school, a meeting... at least once a month of the shakers and movers to discuss what's new. At one school, there's a Friday afternoon Happy Hour group that meets at a local restaurant for drinks and success stories from the week. That's one way to keep up the collegial sharing. The knowledge about the brain and learning is exploding dramatically. If you're not keeping up, you're falling behind. And if you're not building your knowledge and skill base, your market value may drop precariously low. Learning keeps you excited, motivated and thriving.

# How to Make Extra Money
## (and Stay in Education)

There are hundreds of ways to do what you love to do and earn an extra $500-$50,000 a year. Each carries its own risks and rewards. The key is to know yourself well enough to realize 1) What are your best gifts and talents? What does the marketplace need more of? 2) Would this have a negative impact on your work or family? and 3) Realistically, how much or little time and money you're willing to put in? If you're ready to get serious, here's how others have done it:

1. Teach evenings or weekends at a local junior college university.
2. Create a simple product (like this one!) and sell it at educator conventions or by mail in magazines. The easiest one is to create a great picture, drawing or slogan and put it on a sweatshirt or T-shirt. They sell like crazy at educational conferences!
3. Write yourself into a grant proposal. Be the director of a project for extra income. Make it a 3-5 year grant.
4. Become a weekend or evening salesperson for educational products.
5. Design educational software & sell the rights to a company.
6. Organize weekend study skills programs at your school that parents pay for to get extra help for their kids. You put it on & get paid.
7. Research nearby districts who have a higher pay scale. It may be well worth it to transfer.
8. Get summer work for the Defense Department teaching overseas.
9. Your employer may have a higher grade pay scale available if you upgrade your educational credentials.
10. Teach classes for a local vocational/trade/technical school.

11. Start up a home educational business: writing, teaching, consulting. It'll increase deductions, and help earn extra money.
12. Become a coach or assistant coach where they actually pay.
13. Write a book, sell it and collect royalties. If it won't sell, then either edit it to make it better or self-publish (sounds like *SuperTeaching*, doesn't it?)
14. Be a consultant and do work in other counties, districts & states.
15. House-sit for parents who have students in your school.
16. Tutor students after school, 4 at a time @ $15/hr = $60 hour.
17. Get work at a summer camp. If you're very, very good at teaching, call Learning Forum's SuperCamp at 619-722-0072.
18. Contribute to magazines or journals who pay per article.
19. Do a video on something others want to know more about that's unusual at your school or something you have done special and market it by mail order or at educational conventions.

## Additional Resources for Further Study and Follow up

*Parents on Your Side* by Canter (Canter & Associates)
*Seven Habits of Highly Successful People* by Covey (Simon & Schuster)
*Seeing with Magic Glasses* by Ellison (Great Ocean)
*Influencing With Integrity* by Laborde (Science & Behavior Books)
*You Don't Have to Go Home Exhausted* by McGee-Cooper (Bowen & Rodgers)
*Mind Food & Smart Pills* by Ross Pelton (Doubleday)
*Million-Dollar Habits* by Robert Ringer
*Awaken the Giant Within* by Anthony Robbins (Simon & Schuster)
*Unlimited Power* by Anthony Robbins (Simon & Schuster)
*The Skillful Teacher* by Saphier and Gower (Research for Better Teaching)
*Getting Organized* by Winston (Warner Books)
*Managing Your Mind & Mood Through Food* by Wurtman (Perennial)

* Items marked with an asterisk are available in the Appendix.

# WHAT'S NEXT?

CONTAINS:

New Possibilities
Networking
New Paradigms
Leadership
Anticipation

# 27

# *What's Next?*

## Being Part of the Solution

What will it take to make education work in the way we all know it can? Let's not kid ourselves. It will take plenty. We will need to be re-inventing the way we teach, educate, run systems and administrate. It will take one of the most purposeful, courageous and sustained commitments ever made. It will take an unrivaled ability to bring forth your vision on a daily basis. It will require an relentless insistence on seeing beyond the problems, circumstances and complaints that make up much of the current conversation about education. It will take a whole new set of skills, many of which we haven't yet imagined.

We will be going into new areas; some not even yet imagined. It will take stronger, new partnerships and relationships in every area of our professional and personal lives. It will take more focused planning and insightful thinking than ever done before. It will necessitate knowledge of new paradigms about the brain and how we learn. It will require a rediscovery and realigning of values and a certain ruthlessness to tell the truth. Finally, it will require that each individual teacher bring forth every last bit of integrity, personal power and ability to manage than ever before. It means being willing to live and teach only in its best and brightest vision. The job to take on education as a possibility and as something you are responsible for improving is quite a task. But it's worth it. Here are the words of the great philosopher De Ropp:

> *"Seek, above all, a game worth playing... Having found the game, play it with intensity-play it as if your life and sanity depended upon it. (They do depend on it.)... Though nothing means anything and all roads are marked "No Exit", move as if your movements had some purpose... For it must be clear, even to the most clouded intelligence, that any game is better than no game.*

> *"But although it is safe to play the Master Game, this has not served to make it popular. It remains the most demanding and difficult of games, and in our society, there are few who play.... Once a person has... (decided to play), he is no longer able to sleep comfortably. A new appetite develops within him, the hunger for a real awakening.*

> *"Here, it is sufficient to say that the Master Game can NEVER be made easy to play. It demands all that a man (or woman) has, all his feelings, all his thoughts, his entire resources, physical and spiritual. If he tries*

*to play it in a halfhearted way or tries to get results by unlawful means, he runs the risk of destroying his own potential. For this reason it is better not to embark on the game at all than to play halfheartedly."*

Choosing to make a difference, as you may have guessed, is metaphorically "the crossing of the Rubicon." It's a commitment on par with the most difficult on earth. No awards are likely to be given. Expect no grand monument for all your efforts. Expect no hero's welcome for playing the game or even winning the game. Expect criticism, difficulty and unthinkable challenges. Your prize, your reward and monument for all of your efforts is likely to be quite simple. Education will work. Our children will be empowered, enriched and opened to the grand possibilities of who they truly are.

## Start With Your Passion

Where do we start? Pick the area below that you care the most about. Why start with an area that you're passionate about? This way, you'll have the energy to do it when you're tired, when your getting criticized and when you run into stumbling blocks.

First, let's start with a global overview of the tasks at hand. What are the key areas of instructional reform? They are a brain-based approach, thematic curriculum, environments for learning, multiple intelligences, relevant assessment and systems thinking. These elements are among the ones that you have the most control over and can also make the greatest contribution to the success of your learners. In addition, they are likely to make your job more fun, keep you motivated and your stress low.

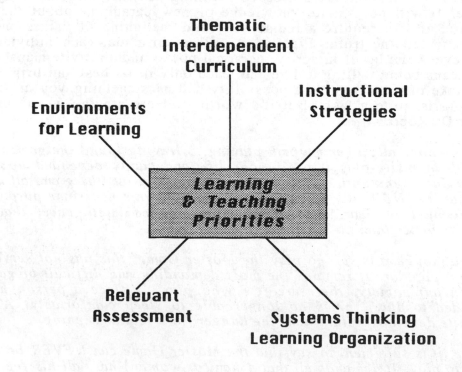

Which of the areas above are your passion? Pick the area that you care about the most, and commit to yourself to being a leader in that area. In what ways can you be a leader? There are many. There are some recommended books at the end of this chapter. You can attend workshops and seminars. You can also get started, just by reading the next few pages.

# Building Leadership

To make this work, no matter what your role, you'll need to be a leader. The differences between leaders in any organization become more and more obvious, the more you are around them. You feel good being around leaders; there's a sense of vitality and hope. A good leader does not boss you around. Instead, a leaders inspires you to be your best. Here's some important distinctions.

| Leader speaks mostly about: POSSIBILITIES | Non-leader speaks mostly about: CIRCUMSTANCES |
|---|---|
| speaks about vision | talks about obstacles |
| keeps the dream alive | keeps the problems alive |
| talk generates action | talk generates resignation, |
| ownership & commitments | blaming & avoidance |

Leaders recognize that schools are about learning. And if they aren't learning, they need to either make learning a new priority or find another job. To create a school of learners and a staff of learner leaders, you'll want everyone to work together to make your organization a learning organization. How do you know whether you're in one or not? Do you hear any of these comments?

| Learning Organization | Traditional Bureaucracy |
|---|---|
| "I am a catalyst" | "I teach, they better learn" |
| "We are all part of it" | "The solution is out there" |
| "We stop mid-stream to ask" ask what's working" | "We assume we're going right" |
| "Learning means creative skills in achieving both process & results" | "Tests tell the final story" |
| "The greater the rate at which we learn | "If we could just solve this problem" the more fun we'll have while solving life's infinite problems" |

# Role Model Your Leadership

Your leadership is evident in many ways. Role modeling and professionalism is an easy example. Do you speak highly of the profession or do you make jokes about it, put it down, demean it and complain about it? Do you know some teacher keep track of the number of days left until a vacation (like a convict, counting days in prison)?

"Tired of school - get a real job"
"You got problems? Shoot yourself!"
"Wake me up when it's Friday"
"School is what we sandwich in between weekends"

"I hate Mondays"
"Teacher's two favorite words are Saturday & Sunday
"Teacher's Three Favorite Words: June, July & August
"Homework causes brain damage"
"I'm the boss. When in doubt, reread first sentence."

Some have T-shirts or mugs have those types of sayings, and they should be banned from school. Why? They are all intended to be humorous. We all would say we have a sense of humor, but what's left after the joke? The residue is a cutting remark and sarcastic comment that degrades the profession, implies the job is distasteful and puts out negative suggestions and attitudes to the students and other faculty. Get rid of them!

As an instructional or staff leader, it takes much more sense to be a source of inspiration and positive energy. Turn your faculty lounge into a "staff revitalization center" with fun and relaxing ways for teachers to unwind and stay positive. Some staff lounges have positive signs up, like these:

"Never give up on anybody; miracles happen everyday"
"Expect others to follow your example & ignore your advice"
"Give yourself time to cool before responding"
"Never deprive someone of hope - it might be all they have"
"The true joy in life is lighting a spark and feeding the flames of learning"
"Every student has a right to succeed"
"The relentless pursuit of excellence"
"Teaching - you gotta love it!"
"I teach... I touch the future"

## Leaders Communicate Vision

If you haven't already done so, develop your vision. You will only be as powerful in life as that which you are willing to speak about and be responsible for. Your vision is necessary for others to take you more seriously and for you to excite them to become mobilized to support your dream.

*My vision is a world of confident and*
*capable learners who love to learn and have fair,*
*unlimited and equal access to learning*

A vision is two things-what you would like to have happen and your commitment in the face of that vision. In other words, the vision is a possibility of how things could be. What is also needed is your authorship of the vision and a relationship with that vision, making it powerful. You must take a stand for the vision. Then, communicate your vision to as many people as possible. Speak to individuals, groups, young and old. Bring forth vision that excites people and gets them thinking about possibilities, not complaints. Once you have a vision, you'll need a mission. That's the "job" needed to be done to make the vision happen.

*My own mission is to make a significant, positive*
*and lasting impact on the way the world learns*

Act as if you are the secretary of education and your actions alone determine the fate of education in this country. If you bring that quality of presence to your work, things will change. They have to change with that kind of momentum. Once you've done ABC, the wheels are set in motion for the next step.

# Become Part of the Planning Process

Once your vision and mission for education is clear, your value as a contributor increases dramatically. Bring your vision to every group you join. Inspire others to share your vision. Assist in the planning for tomorrow's schools in any way you can.

To take part in the planning process means that you are taking on the role of responsibility. No one can assign that to you. No one can assign or "fix" responsibility to another. Responsibility is something that an individual "takes on" for him or herself. It always comes from within. It's a gift and best described as a privilege, not a weight. There's no guilt or burden in responsibility, only an opportunity to step out and be courageous. It allows you to be at the cause of things, not the effect. And best of all, it empowers you to be your best. You are only as "big" in life as the responsibilities you are willing to accept.

# Commitment for Reform

One of the things that does not work in education is empty opinions about how to fix it. Opinions are relatively useless in the face of what's required to make education work. Opinions come across like a cabby's babble or the "guy in a diner" who has an opinion about everything. The problem with opinions is simple: they're vapid, cheap and irresponsible. What's needed is not some half-informed prognosis and dime-store conclusion, but rather some real honest-to-goodness commitments.

Let's quit talking about what needs to be done and start committing to doing what needs to be done. Your commitment is the stand, the position you take and the place from which you can operate. You need that stand, that backdrop of grounding from which to express yourself. So the next time someone has a great idea about how to fix something in education, ask them what they personally would like to commit to insure that the changes happen.

*Instead of only preaching what changes*
*you'd like your school to make, announce what*
*you're personally going to do right away*

In addition to depth of commitment, it also takes depth. Start being committed to reform at every level until the vision becomes reality. Have a concrete plan, find those who will listen, speak about your plan with such a level of commitment and empowerment that others become excited about your vision, too. There will be many changes in education in the next few years and many of them are exciting!

Teachers will become co-explorers with students because no one person can know it all. It will be a high-tech and high-touch partnership with interchanging roles. Because so much learning will occur at home, it will become a new center of learning. In a curious reversal, younger students will come to school to play more than learn. Elementary students who will have already learned reading, writing and math on television or home computers, will need to interact with other students and play. School will become the place for social skills, field trips, experiments, plays, dance, music, and nurturing human contact.

It's clear that what we have done before will fail because we have been working on symptoms, not causes. Let's review what causal-level changes we are dealing with in our society. These are the underlying issues that, if left unattended, will result in behavior problems, low test scores or drug abuse. Unless we prepare our educators to deal with these, the money spent on symptomatic relief will continue to be wasted. These causal changes or trends must be addressed, for they are at the core of education's current difficulties.

The key is that *the game has changed.* To be effective, to be pro-active (as opposed to reactive), we must have some awareness of what's going on so we can begin to predict what's needed. If you want to make a real difference in education, what are some of the key areas you can impact? Here are list of projects you can take on. Which are of most interest to you?

**Staff Development.** Increase preparation to deal with more areas relative to students' lives. Boost training in counseling, listening, conflict resolution and facilitation skills.

**New Skills.** Prepare students with more strategies and tools. Teach more HOW to learn, and less WHAT to learn. Work in class using a greater variety of learning styles. Teach students how they learn and how to become more accountable for their own learning process.

**Role Changes.** Ask teachers to relinquish the role as the only source of information. Have students take on additional roles, becoming more responsible for their learning. Use textbooks as reference books, not as standard issues for every student. Rely more on magazine subscriptions, computers, video and television.

**Time Management.** Creatively, find ways to allow teachers more planning time, more collegial discussion time and more staff development time. Do this with doubling up on classes once a week, better use of support staff and other creative systems.

**Brain-Based Approach.** Learn more about the brain. Attend courses, watch videos and read books. Begin to design learning more the way the brain is best designed to learn. You'll find that your learners become more motivated, learn more and recall information longer. They will apply their learning better and will be more capable citizens in the community.

**Resource Sharing.** Find a way to inventory all the school resources, including supplies, rooms, machinery, talent, creativity, parents, hobbies, contacts, speakers, curriculum and teaching strategies. Next, find a way to share all this so that it is available to all staff. You have an amazing amount of resources, but you've got to discover them and share them.

**Scheduling.** Change secondary-level school schedules to match the elementary model of one teacher, all-day. Rotate schedules so that students would have one class, such as history, with one teacher, all day. Schedule a physical education break each day. It refreshes students' brains and gives the teacher planning time. Students would have one subject one day, another the next. Same teacher all day. Have teachers stay with the same group of students all the way through schooling.

In elementary, make it six years. In secondary, make it either three or six years depending on if there's a change in schools. This builds long term understanding and prevents a teacher from being sent someone else's "problem." This provides the opportunity for building better relationships between student and teacher - a significant step towards reducing absenteeism, discipline problems, improperly diagnosed learning problems, vandalism, alienation and dropouts.

**Communications.** Re-structure the school's lines of communications, support and accountability for teachers. Create new positions for the coaching and support of teachers. (This role would be separate from a principal's role.) Teachers need constant, direct, qualified coaching on what they are doing and what can be improved. They also need daily, weekly and monthly systems set up to acknowledge and support that growth. There also needs to be greater measurable accountability on the part of teachers for the progress of their students. Not solely in the form of test scores, but also in the form of self-esteem, participation, breakthroughs and increases of growth.

**Respect.** Set up specific pathways and vehicles where teachers can have their concerns heard, acted upon and acknowledged. Create ways for teachers to fully participate in the processes affecting them the most, such as teacher-student ratio, class hours, curriculum and classroom design. Increase the salary incentives for mastery-level teaching.

**Parent relationships.** Find a way to create communication lines with parents. Use telephone hot lines, newsletters, students, events and the media.

**Cultural awareness.** Train teachers in how to build student acceptance and self-esteem. Train teachers in more team building activities. Have qualified organizations train teachers in cultural similarities and differences. Contact San Diego City School's Race and Human Relations Department to learn how to raise cultural awareness.

**Community ties.** Find greater openness for sources of funding. Create better partnerships with the military or national service organizations for students who want to quit school. Create new, more effective partnerships with business. Less regulation regarding private enterprise's relationships with schools.

**Educational activism.** Other activities needed are the following: your state legislators need to know what kinds of curriculum should be included or deleted to make things work. Your schools need to know the specific kinds of teacher training you need to make your school a total success. Parents must be included in many more ways. Your community needs to know that you would like to make a shift in the quality of education and you must invite citizens to give input. Your school board needs to re-prioritize teacher needs so that you can get the job done. This means less red-tape, more administrative support, less mandated curriculum, more acknowledgment for work well done and more "say-so" in how the system is set up. School monies invested in teachers are better spent because the effect is multiplied: one teacher affects many students. Whereas monies spent on students are dead-end funds; the effect stops with the students.

You'll discover that there are both adapters and innovators. The adapter is right at home in a bureaucracy and tends to try to make the existing system make do. The innovator sees that behavior as dogmatic and inflexible and wants to do things differently. The innovator breaks accepted patterns and the adapter accepts the old framework. It will take both to make education work. As you find out who wants to join you, keep in mind that your game is not the only game in town. This means that when it's not right for others, don't force them into your game or get righteous about it.

# Build Partnerships

We may think of ourselves as just one, but our effects move like the ripples on a pond. So what would happen if we began to work with other teachers and began networking? Do you wonder what's possible if we began to share ourselves and our mastery with other teachers and administrators? If we teachers are going to continue to grow, we have to do it together. There is little growth in isolation and the gifts you have must be distributed in order to have impact.

All you have to do is make a commitment. Tell the teachers around you what you intend to have happen. "I'm committed to helping make this school work for the students and me." Just by saying it, your words begin to make it happen.

Fortunately, there will be those teachers who immediately want to jump on the bandwagon to join you. Others may not be interested at all. Include those interested and allow the others to go their own way. Eventually, they may discover that what you've got provides fulfillment, joy and satisfaction.

The next step, once you have networked and gained supporters, is to create leaderships, agendas and items to do. Get parent support and community input. Choose a grand goal and make it happen. Once you have that grand goal as a beacon or mission, roll up your sleeves and start in on the little things. Concentrate on getting many small successes. This builds credibility, energy and elicits support for your work. Ideas for teacher network groups include: support meetings, acknowledgment ceremonies, a gala teacher barbecue or fund raisers for classroom supplies.

Include other teachers who want to get involved. The better you make the "game" of transforming education, the more others will want to join. Make it light, make it fun, and get things done! One of the things Walt Disney credited to his success was the notion that one must "do what you do so well that when people come to see you, they'll get excited and want to bring back their friends; and those people will get excited and bring their friends." That's what many schools have done. In fact, the Key School in Indianapolis has a waiting list for visitors, it's such an attraction. That's how good you must make the game of transformation in education.

# Maintain Relationships

The key to being successful at creating transformation is rapport. Rapport means that you make friends, not enemies. You will get nowhere if you start by making other teachers wrong or blaming them for not supporting you. Each person can accomplish what they do given their personal history, resources and intended outcome. Include everyone you can in your group because you need their support. Include parents, students, administrators, and anyone else who will listen. Include their ideas and find out how you can make the system work for everyone. Support others in helping them get what they want. A fundamental law of humanity is when you help others get what they need, they can better help you get what you need.

Even if you think someone is way off the track, you can appreciate their good intentions, respect their interest and agree with their need to live their own dreams. And, at the same time, you may feel that what they are doing is inappropriate for your needs. Never humiliate or antagonize the opposition. Instead find ways to educate, learn from them or include them. Be sensitive to the beliefs, positions and judgments of others - not in the form of taking them personally, but in the form of listening and understanding them.

You may need a public relations person in your teacher's support group. Someone who will put cut the news, create news letters and let everyone know what you are doing. The more others know about what you are doing, the more support you'll receive. Then, if you need to take any corrective action, do it with the intention of keeping rapport in mind. Your path to mastery requires organization, involvement of others via networking, and the creation of support groups. It's much earlier when we all pull from the same end of the rope!

# Where to Start Now

There are many, many "right" ways to get started with a better schools. Nobody has the answer for you because *the answer needs be a local solution*. In a year-long study of successful schools, it was found that all successful transformations had the following characteristics:

**1. SEARCH** - *"What else is out there?"* The staff searched near, far and wide for successes and solutions. Read, network, call other schools, attend conferences, check out books, buy newsletters and hold discussion groups.

**2. CONSOLIDATE** - *"What do we have so far?"* Analyze & modify the solutions for your own needs & culture. Commit to building on existing strengths.

**3. UNIFY** - *"Can we all agree on what we want?"* Get complete input and "buy-in" on the vision and steps to make... Develop a complete staff unity of purpose.

**4. SOLIDIFY** - *"If this is good, then let's make it policy"* Make your ideas into *policy*, not just another good idea. Willingly assume responsibility, but with corresponding amounts of authority to act on what was needed at the time.

**5. COMMIT** - *"If we believe in it, let's stick with it!"* Commit to staying with it until it works. No excuses. Emphasize the positives and celebrate the successes. Learned to communicate what isn't working and fix it. Take on reform as a permanent on-going process, not some one or two year gimmick to quiet critics. Quality is an endless process.

If you were to get a closing "homework assignment" from this book, it would be like this: Do what you do so well, set such a good example, that the enthusiasm, the shouts of aliveness and joy (from your work area) reaches out to others and wakes them up. Be so committed and so purposeful and so excited about what you do that others either want to join you or are embarrassed by the high standard you set and want to leave the profession for some other job more suited to their commitments.

Go out and teach so well that you literally reinvent it. Re-create it the way that Picasso redefined painting. Start over the way that Julius Erving and Michael Jordan reinvented the game of basketball. The way Casio re-invented the wristwatch and Apple reinvented the computer with the MacIntosh. Be creative. Be outrageous. Somehow, get out the message about your commitment to make education work and most importantly, LIVE IT. Futurist Marilyn Ferguson says:

> *"Our past is not our potential. In any hour, with all the stubborn teachers and healers of history who called us to our best selves, we can liberate the future. You are not just you. You are a seed, a silent promise. You are the conspiracy."*

The end of this book is just the beginning for you. There is a new you who turned the last few pages of this book, far different from the one who opened it. May you grow and reach as you never previously thought possible. You have been an inspiration for me and you are the person from whom this book was written.

> *You have taught well if ten years later*
> *your students forgot who you were and remember*
> *who they became in your class*

You knew there was more to education than showing up and waiting for the last bell. Teaching is so much more than that. It is discovery, sharing, growing, excitement and love. It's not a burden, it's a joy. And it's like a consuming, fulfilling bonfire that provides you with a glow of warmth and a blaze of passion. You've already demonstrated a commitment to education by reading this book. The intention to grow and willingness to improve sets you well above and beyond most other educators. Keep growing! There's no such thing as standing still; we are either expanding or contracting.

Commit yourselves not only to your cause, crusade or mission, but to your own aliveness and self-expression. If you have a commitment to education with anything less than your life, it will be insufficient to the task at hand. Keep taking on more responsibility and more challenges. I know you might be tired. I know you have given a lot already. It's been great, but the results say that it's not enough. We must all recommit to vision and the work that needs to be done.

It is you, and the choices you make in the classroom that will make a difference in this world. Each move you make, each class you give, and thought you think is shaping our tomorrows. So don't worry about how or why or when, begin now. Begin with your commitment. The possibilities are more grand than we have yet imagined. Take that first step now. There is a lot riding on our jobs as educators. If you stumble or fall, there are plenty of us who will reach to pull you up on your feet again. We know what kind of journey we are beginning and we are already taking the first and most important step. One last closing story for you:

> *There was a wise old man who always knew the answers. People came from far and away to ask him things and he always knew the right answer. Then an envious village smart-aleck decided to trick him. He decided to hold a live butterfly in his hands behind his back and ask the wise man what was in his hands. When the wise man got that correct, the smart-aleck would then ask if the butterfly was alive or dead. If the wise man said dead, he would show the living butterfly, and if he said alive, he would kill the butterfly and show him the dead one.*

*The day of the test came, and the smart-aleck went before the wise man with his plan, holding the butterfly behind his back. He then asked the old man what he was holding and the wise man answered, "a butterfly." Then the smart-aleck asked if it was alive or dead, and the wise man gave an answer which just might also apply to you right now in terms of education, "It is in your hands now."*

---

## Additional Resources for Further Study and Follow up

*Readings From Educational Leadership: Restructuring Schools* by Brandt (ASCD)
*The Learning Revolution* by Dryden & Vos (Jalmar Press)*
*Mindshifts* by Caine, Caine & Crowell (Zephyr)*
*Changing School Culture Through Staff Development* by Joyce (ASCD)
*School Success* by Kline & Martel (Great Ocean)*
*Ten Steps to a Learning Organization* by Kline & Martel (Great Ocean)*
*Fifth Discipline Fieldbook* by Senge (Doubleday)

* Items marked with an asterisk are available in the Appendix.

# Appendix

# Index

348

# Bibliography &
# Further Readings

Amabile, Teresa (1989).*Growing Up Creative.* New York: Crown Publishing.

Ames, Carole. (1992). Achievement Goals and the Classroom Motivational Climate. *Student Perceptions in the Classroom.* (Ed. Dale Schunk and Judith Meece). Hillsdale, NJ: Erlbaum.

Ames, Carole. (1992). Classrooms: Goals, Structures, and Student Motivation. *Journal of Educational Psychology* 84, 261-71.

Ames, Carole. (1987).The Enhancement of Student Motivation. *Advances in Motivation and Achievement.* Eds. Maeher and Kleiber (Vol. 5, pp.123-148). Greenwich, CT: JAI.

Apacki, Carol. (1991). *Energize!* Granville, OH: Quest Books.

Armbruster, B. and Anderson, T. (1980). "The Effect of Mapping." *Center for the Study of Reading* 182735th ed. Urbana, IL: University of Illinois.

Armstrong, Thomas. (1987). *In Their Own Way.* Los Angeles, CA:Jeremy Tarcher Publishing.

Bandler, R. (1988). *Learning Strategies: Acquisition and Conviction.* (Videotape). Boulder, CO: NLP Comprehensive.

Barkley R. (1988, September). *Attention-Deficit Hyperactivity Disorder.* (Lecture at conference) The Many Faces of Intelligence. Washington, D.C.

Barrett, Susan. (1992). *It's All in Your Head.* Minneapolis, MN: Free Spirit Publishing.

Baumeister, R. F. (1984). Choking Under Pressure: Self-Consciousness and Paradoxical Effects of Incentives on Skillful Performance. *Journal of Personality and Social Psychology* 46, 610-20.

Baumeister, R. F., Heatherton, T. F. & Tice, D. M. (1993). When Ego Threats Lead to Self-Regulation Failure: Negative Consequences of High Self-Esteem. *Journal of Personality and Social Psychology* 64.1, 141-56.

Benton, D., & Roberts, G. (1988). Effect of Vitamin and Mineral Supplementation on Intelligence of a Sample of Schoolchildren. *The Lancet,* 140-143.

Bergin, D. (1989). Student Goals for Out-of-School-Learning Activities. *Journal of Adolescent Research* 4, 92-109.

Berliner, D. C. (1984). The Half-Full Glass: A Review of Research on Teaching. *Using What We Know About Teaching.* (Hosford, P.L., Ed.). Alexandria, VA: Association for Supervision and Curriculum Development.

Biggee, Al. (1982). *Learning Theories for Teachers* (4th ed.). New York, NY: Harper & Row.

Black J. E., et al. (1990, July). Learning Causes Synaptogenesis, Whereas Motor Activity Causes Angiogenesis, in Cerebral Cortex of Adult Rats. (Proc. of a conference of the National Academy of Sciences). 87.14, 5568-72.

Blackman, et al. (1982). Cognitive Styles and Learning Disabilities. *Journal of Learning Disabilities* n2 15, 106-115.

Blakemore, Colin. (1990).*The Mind Machine.* (with Richard Hutton & Martin Freeth). London, England: BBC Books.

Bloom, et al. (1988).*Brain, Mind and Behavior.* W. H. Freeman and Co.

Bourre, J. M., et al. (1993). *Brainfood.* Translated from French. Boston, MA: Little, Brown & Co.

Bower, G. H. & Mann, T. (1992). Improving Recall by Recoding Interfering Material at the Time of Retrieval. *Journal of Experimental Psychology* 18.6, 1310-20.

Bower, G. H., Mann, T.D., & Morrow, G. (1990). Mental Models in Narrative Comprehension. *Science* 247.4938, 44-8.

Brewer, C. and D. Campbell. (1991). *Rhythms of Learning.* Tucson, AZ: Zephyr Press.

Bricker, William, McLoughlin & Caven. (1982). Exploration of Parental Teaching Style: Technical Note. *Perceptual & Motor Skills* Pt. 2 55, 1174.

Brophy, J. (1981). Teacher Praise: A Functional Analysis. *Review of Educational Research* 51, 5-32.

Brophy, J. (1987). Socializing Student's Motivation to Learn. *Advances in Motivation and Achievement* (Maeher & Kleiber. Eds.) Vol.3, pp. 181-210. Greenwich, CT: JAI.

Burton, L. A. & Levy, J. (1989). Sex Differences in the Lateralized Processing of Facial Emotion. *Brain and Cognition* 11.2, 210-28.

Butler, R. (1988). Enhancing and Undermining Intrinsic Motivation. *British Journal of Educational Psychology* 58, 1-14

Butler, R., & Nissan, M. (1986). Effects of No Feedback, Task-Related Comments, and Grades on Intrinsic Motivation and Performance. *Journal of Educational Psychology* 78, 210-216.

Buzan, Tony. (1993). *The Mind Map Book: Radiant Thinking.* London, England: BBC Books.

Caine, G., Caine, R.N., & Crowell, S. (1994). *Mindshifts.* Tuscon, AZ: Zephyr Press.

Caine, G., & Caine, R.N. (1990). Downshifting: A Hidden Condition That Frustrates Learning & Change *Instructional Leader* VI 3, 1-3, 12.

351

Caine, G., & Caine, R.N., Eds. (1993). Understanding a Brain-Based Approach to Learning and Teaching. *Educational Leadership* 48: 2,66-70.

Caine, G., & Caine, R.N., Eds. (1994). Making Connections: *Teaching and the Human Brain*. Menlo Park, CA: Addison-Wesley.

Calvin, William & Ojemann, George. (1994). *Conversations with Neil's Brain*. Reading, MA: Addison-Wesley Publishing Co.

Campbell, D. (1983). *Introduction to The Musical Brain*. St. Louis, MO: Magnamusic.

Campbell, D. (1992). *100 Ways to Improve Your Teaching Using Your Voice & Music*. Tucson: Zephyr Press.

Campbell, D. Ed. (1992). *Music and Miracles*. Wheaton, IL: Quest Books.

Carbo, M., Dunn, R., & Dunn, K. (1986). *Teaching Students to Read Through their Individual Learning Styles*. Englewood Cliffs, NJ: Prentice-Hall.

Carper, Jean. (1993). *Food: Your Miracle Medicine*. New York, NY: Harper Collins Publishers.

Chapman, Carolyn. (1993). *If the Shoe Fits*. Palatine, IL: Skylight Publishing.

Cherry, C., Godwin, D., & Staples, J. (1989). *Is The Left Brain Always Right?* Sydney, Australia: Hawker & Brownlow.

Christianson, S. (1992). Emotional Stress and Eyewitness Memory: A Critical Review. *Psychological Bulletin* 112.2, 284-309.

Chugani, H. T. (1991). Imaging Human Brain Development with Positron Emission Tomography. *Journal of Nuclear Medicine* 32.1, 23-6.

Clynes, Manfred, Ed. (1982). *Music, Mind and Brain*. New York, NY: Plenum Press.

Clynes, Manfred, Ed. (1982). Neurobiologic Functions of Rhythm, Time, and Pulse in Music. *Music, Mind and Brain*. New York, NY: Plenum Press.

Cohen, E.G. (1990). Treating Status Problems in the Cooperative Classroom. *Cooperative Learning: Research and Theory*. (Sharan, S., Ed.) New York, NY: Praeger Press.

Connors, Keith. (1980). *Food Additives and Hyperactive Children*. New York, NY: Plenum Press.

Connors, Keith. (1989). *Feeding the Brain*. New York, NY: Plenum Press.

Covington, M.V. (1991). Motivation, Self-Worth, and the Myth of Instensification. (Paper presented at annual meeting of the American Psychological Association). San Francisco, CA.

Coward, Andrew. (1990). *Pattern Thinking*. New York, NY: Praeger Publishers.

Csikszentmihalyi, M. & Isabella. (1990). *Flow: The Psychology of Optimal Experience*. New York, NY: Harper & Row.

Czeisler, C. A. (1986). Arousal Cycles Can Be Reset. *Science* 233, 667-71.

Damasio, Antonio. (1994) *Descartes' Error*. New York, NY. Putnam & Sons.

Dartigues, Jean-Francois. (1994, February). Use It or Lose It. *Omni*. p. 34.

DeBello, T. (1985). A Critical Analysis of the Achievement and Attitude Effects of Administrative Assignments to Social Studies Writing Instruction Based on Identified, Eighth-Grade Students' Learning Style Preferences for Learning Alone, With Peers, or With Teachers. *Dissertation*. St. John's University.

DeBono, Edward. (1993) *Six Thinking Hats*. New York, NY.Harper & Row.

Deci, E. and R. M. Ryan. (1985). *Intrinsic Motivation and Self-Determination in Human Behavior*. New York, NY: Plenum.

Deci, E., et al. (1992). Autonomy and Competence as Motivational Factors in Students with Learning Disabilities and Emotional Handicaps. *Journal of Learning Disabilities* 25, 457-71.

Deci, E., et al. (1991). Motivation and Education: The Self-Determination Perspective. *Educational Psychologist* 26, 325-46.

Della Valle, J., et al. (1986). The Effects of Matching and Mismatching Student's Mobility Preferences on Recognition and Memory Tasks. *Journal of Educational Research* 79.5, 267-72.

Dennison, Paul, & Dennison, Gail. (1988). *Brain Gym.*. (Teacher's Ed.) Ventura, CA: Edu-kinesthetics.

Dhority, Lynn. (1992). *The ACT Approach. The Use of Suggestion for Integrative Learning*. Philadelphia, PA: Gordon & Breach Science Publishers.

Diamond, Marian. (1988). *Enriching Heredity: The Impact of the Environment on the Brain*. New York, NY: Free Press.

Dienstbier, R. (1989). Periodic Adrenalin Arousal Boosts Health, Coping. *Brain-Mind Bulletin* 14.9A.

Dixon, N. (1981). *Preconscious Processing*. New York, NY: Wiley.

Doll, W.E.J. (1989). Complexity in the Classroom. *Educational Leadership* 47.1, 65-70.

Dossey, Larry. (1993) Healing Words. San Francisco, CA: HarperCollins Publishers

Drucker, Peter. (1994, November).The Age of Social Transformation. *Atlantic Monthly*, 274,(5) pp. 53-80.

Dryden, Gordon & Vos, Jeannette. (1994). *The Learning Revolution.*. Rolling Hills, CA: Jalmar Press.

Dunn, R. & Dunn, K. (1987). Dispelling Outmoded Beliefs About Student Learning. *Educational Leadership* 44.6, 55-61.

Dunn, Kenneth & Rita. (1992). *Bringing Out The Giftedness In Your Child*, New York, NY: John Wiley.

Edelman, G. *Bright Air, Brilliant Fire*. (1992). New York, NY: Basic Books.

Efron, R. (1990).*The Decline and Fall of Hemispheric Specialization*. Hillsdale, NJ. Lawerence Erlbaum and Associates.

Ellison, Launa. (1993). *Seeing With Magic Glasses*. Great Ocean Publishers, Arlington, VA.

Emery, Charles. (1986, October). Exercise Keeps the Mind Young. *American Health*.

Feingold, D. (1985). *Why Your Child is Hyperactive*. New York, NY: Random House.

Feldman, R.G. & White, R.F. (1992). Lead Neurotoxicity and Disorders in Learning. *Journal of Child Neurology* 7.4, 354-9.

Felix, Uschi. (1993).The Contribution of Background Music to the Enhancement of Learning in Suggestopedia: A Critical Review of the Literature. *Journal of the Society for Accelerative Learning and Teaching* 18.3-4, 277-303.

Feuerstein, Reuven, Klein, Pnina, Tannenbaum, Abraham. (1991). *Mediated Learning Experience*. London, UK: Freund Publishing House Ltd.

Ford, Martin. (1992). *Motivating Humans*. Newbury Park, CA: Sage Publications.

Freeley, M.E. (1984). An Experimental Investigation of the Relationships Among Teacher's Individual Time Preferences, Inservice Workshop Schedules, and Instructional Techniques and the Subsequent Implementation of Learning Style Strategies in Participant's Classroom. *Dissertation*. St. John's University.

Frijda, N.H. (1988). The Laws of Emotion. *American Psychologist* 43, 349-58.

Gardner, Howard. (1993). *Multiple Intelligences: The Theory in Practice*. New York, NY: Basic Books.

Gazzaniga, M. (1992). *Nature's Mind*. New York, NY: Basic Books.

Gelb, Michael. (1981). *Body Learning*. New York, NY: Delilah Books.

Gelb, Michael. (1988). *Present Yourself*. Rolling Hills, CA: Jalmar Press.

Glasscr, William. (1981). *Stations of the Mind*. New York: Harper & Row.

Glasser, William. (1985). *Control Theory*. New York, NY: Harper Collins.

Gleik, J. (1987). *Making a New Science*. New York, NY: Viking.

Gratton, G., Coles, M. G., & Donchin, E. (1992). Optimizing the Use of Information: Strategic Control of Activation of Responses. *Journal of Experimental Psychology* 121.4, 480-506.

Green, K.P., et al. (1991). Integrating Speech Information Across Talkers, Gender and Sensory Modality: Female Faces and Male Voices in the McGurk Effect. *Perception and Psychophysics* 50.6, 524-36.

Greenough, W.T., & Anderson, B.J. (1991). Cerebellar Synaptic Plasticity: Relation to Learning Versus Neural Activity. *Annals of the New York Academy of Science* 627, 231-47.

Greenough, W.T., and B. Anderson. (1991). Cerebellar Synaptic Plasticity. *Annals of the New York Academy of Sciences* 627, 231-47.Grinder, Michael. (1989). *Righting the Educational Conveyor Belt*. Portland, OR: Metamorphous Press.

Grinder, Michael. (1989). *Righting the Educational Conveyor Belt* Battle Ground, WA: Michael Grinder & Associates.

Grinder, Michael. (1993). *Envoy*. Battle Ground, WA: Michael Grinder & Associates.

Grunwald, L., & Goldberg, J. (1993, July). Babies Are Smarter Than You Think. *Life Magazine*, 45-60.

Harmon, D.B. (1991). The Coordinated Classroom. Grand Rapids, MI: [In Liberman, Jacob, *Light: Medicine of The Future*] Santa Fe, NM.

Harper, A.E., & Peters, J.C. (1989). Protein Intake, Brain Amino Acid and Serontonin Concentration and Protein Self-Selection. *Journal of Nutrition* 119.5, 677-89.

Hart, Leslie. (1983). *Human Brain and Human Learning*. White Plains, NY: Longman Publishing.

Healy, Alice & Lyle Bourne. (1995) *Learning and Memory of Knowledge and Skills*. Thousand Oaks, CA. Sage Publications.

Healy, J. (1990). *Endangered Minds: Why Our Children Can't Think*. New York, NY: Simon and Schuster.

Healy, J. (1987).*Your Child's Growing Mind*. New York, NY: Doubleday.

Hermann, D.J. & Hanwood, J.R. (1980). More evidence for the Existence of the Separate Semantic and Episodic Stores in Long-Term Memory. Journal of Experimental Psychology: Human Learning and Memory 6 & 5, 467-478.

Herrmann, Ned. *The Creative Brain*. Lake Lure, NC: Brain Books, 1988.

Herrnstein & Murray. (1994). A Bell-Shaped Curve. New York, NY: The Free Press.

Hirsch, A. (1993). Floral Odor Increases Learning Ability. Presentation at annual conference of American Academy of Neurological & Orthopedic Surgery. Contact: Allan Hirsch, Smell & Taste Treatment Foundation, Chicago, IL.

Hooper J., & Teresi, D. (1986). *The Three Pound Universe: The Brain, from Chemistry of the Mind to New Frontiers of the Soul*. New York, NY: Dell Publishing.

Hopfield, J., Feinstein, D., & Palmer, R. (1983, July). Unlearning Has a Stabilizing Effect in Collective Memories. *Nature*. pp. 158-59.

Horn, G. (1991). Learning, Memory and the Brain. *Indian Journal of Physiology and Pharmacology* 35.1, 3-9.

Horne J. (1989). Sleep Loss and Divergent Thinking Ability. *Sleep* 11.6, 528-36.

Horne J. (1992, October 15). Human Slow Wave Sleep: A Review and Appraisal of Recent Findings, with Implications for Sleep Functions and Psychiatric Illness. *Experientia* pp. 941-54.

Houston, Jean. *The Possible Human: A Course in Enhancing Your Physical, Mantal and Creative Abilities.* Los Angeles, CA: Jeremy Tarcher, 1982.

Huchinson, Michael. (1986). *Megabrain.* New York, NY: Beech Tree Books.

Hynd, G.W., et al. (1991). Attention-Deficit Disorder Without Hyperactivity: A Distinct Behavioral and Cognitive Syndrome. *Journal of Child Neurology* 6, S37-43.

Hynd, G.W., et al. (1991). Corpus Callosum Morphology in Attention Deficit-Hyperactivity Disorder: Morphometric Analysis of MRI. *Journal of Learning Disabilities* 24.3, 141-6.

Iaccino, James. (1993). *Left Brain-Right Brain Differences: Inquiries, Evidence, and New Approaches.* Hillsdale, NJ: Lawrence Erlbaum & Associates.

Jacobs, W.J., & Nadel, L. (1985).Stress-Induced Recovery of Fears and Phobias. *Psychological Review* 92.4, 512-531.

James, Tad. (1989). *The Secret of Creating Your Future.* Honolulu, HI: Advanced NeuroDynamics.

James, T., Woodsmall, and Wyatt. (1988). *Timeline and the Basis of Personality.* Cupertino, CA: Meta Publications.

Jenkins, D.J., et al. (1989). Nibbling Versus Gorging: Metabolic Advantages of Increased Meal Frequency. *New England Journal of Medicine* 321.14, 929-34.

Jensen, Eric. (1994).*The Learning Brain.* Del Mar, CA: Turning Point Publishing.

Jensen, Eric. (1994).*The Little Book of Big Motivation.* New York, NY: Ballantine.

Kage, M. (1991). The Effects of Evaluation on Intrinsic Motivation. (Paper presented at the meeting of the Japan Associaiton of Educational Psychology). Joetsu Japan.

Kandel, M. & Kandel, E. (1994, May). Flights of Memory. *Discover Magazine,* 32-38.

Kandel, E. & Hawkins, R. (1992, September). The Biological Basis of Learning and Individuality. *Scientific American* pp. 79-86.

Kaplan, R. (1983). Reader's Visual Fields Increase with Color Therapy. *Brain Mind Bulletin* 8.14F.

Karkowski, W., Marek, T., & Noworol, C. (1989). Stimulating Work Found to Boost Pain Perception. *Work and Stress* 2, 133-37.

Kavet, R., & Tell, R.A. (1991). VDT's: Field Levels, Epidemiology, and Laboratory Studies."*Health Physics* 61.1, 47-57.

Kenyon, Thomas. (1994). *Brain States.* Naples, FL: U.S. Publishing.

Khalsa, D., Ziegler, M., & Kennedy, B. (1986). Body Sides Switch Dominance. *Life Sciences* 38, 1203-14.

Kimura, D. (1992, September). Sex Differences in the Brain. *Scientific American* pp. 119-25.

King, Jeff. (1991). Comparing Alpha Induction Differences Between Two Music Samples. Abstract from the Center for Research on Learning and Cognition, University of North Texas, TX.

Klein & Armitage. (1979). Brainwave Cycle Fluctuations. *Science* 204, 1326-28.

Kline, Peter. (1990). *Everyday Genius: Restoring Your Children's Natural Joy of Learning - And Yours, Too.* Arlington, VA: Great Ocean Publishers.

Kline, Peter & Martel, Laurence. (1992). *School Success: The Inside Story.* Arlington, VA: Great Ocean Publishers.

Kline, Peter & Saunders, Bernard. (1993). *Ten Steps to a Learning Organization.* Arlington, VA: Great Ocean Publishers.

Klivington, Kenneth, Ed. (1989). *The Science of Mind.* Cambridge, MA: MIT Press.

Klutky, N. (1990). Sex Differences in Memory Performance for Odors, on Sequences and Colors. *Zeitscrift fur Experimentelle und Angewandte Psychologie* 37.3, 437-46.

Kohn, Alfie. (1987). *No Contest: The Case Against Competition.* New York, NY: Houghton-Mifflin.Kohn, Alfie. (1993, September). Choices for Children: Why and How to Let Students Decide. *Phi Delta Kappan,* 8-20

Kohn, A. (1994, October). Grading: the Issue Is Not How But Why. *Educational Leadership* Volume 52, 2, 38-41.

Kohn, A. (1993). *Punished by Rewards.* New York, NY: Houghton Mifflin.

Kopera, H. (1980). Female Hormones and Brain Function. *Hormones and the Brain.* (de Wied & Van Keep, Eds.) Lancaster, England: MTP Press. pp. 189-203.

Kosmarskaya, E.N. (1963). The Influence of Peripheral Stimuli on Development of Nerve Cells. [In The Development of the Brain and its Disturbance by Harmful Factors, Klosovski, B.N., Ed.] New York, NY: Macmillian Publishing.

Kotulak, Ronald. Unraveling Hidden Mysteries of the Brain. (1993, 11-16 April).*Chicago Tribune.*

Krashen, S. & Terrell, T. (1983). *The Natural Approach.* San Francisco, CA: Alemany Press.

Krimsky, J.S. (1982). A Comparitive Analysis of the Effects of Matching and Mismatching Fourth Grade Students With Their Learning Styles Preferences for the Environmental Element of Light and Their Subsequent Reading Speed and Accuracy Scores. Dissertation. St. John's University.

Lavabre, Marcel. (1990). *Aromatherapy Workbook.* Rochester, VT: Healing Arts Press.

LeDoux, J., & Hirst, W. (1986). Attention. *Mind and Brain: Dialogues in Cognitive Neuroscience.* New York, NY: Cambridge. pp. 105-85.

Leff, H. & Nevin, A. (1994).*Turning Learning Inside Out.* Tucson, AZ: Zephyr Press.

Levine, S.C., Jordan, N.C., & Huttenlocher, J. (1992). Development of Calculation Abilities in Young Children. *Journal of Experimental Child Psychology* 53.1, Ú72-103.

Levinson, H. (1991). Why Johnny Can't Pay Attention. *Bottom Line Personal* 12.20, 11.

Levinthal, C. (1988). *Messengers of Paradise: Opiates and the Brain.* New York, NY: Doubleday.

Levy, J. (1983). Research Synthesis on Right and Left Hemispheres: We Think With Both Sides of the Brain. *Educational Leadership* 40.4, 66-71.

Levy, J. (1985, May). Right Brain, Left Brain: Fact and Fiction. *Psychology Today.* p. 38.

Lewicki, P., Hill, T., & Czyzewska, M. (1992). Nonconscious Acquisition of Information. *American Psychologist* 47.6, 796-801.

Lieberman, H.R., Wurtman, J.J., & Teicher, M.H. (1989). Circadian Rhythms in Healthy Young and Elderly Humans. *Neurobiology of Aging* 10.3, 259-65.

Lloyd, Linda. (1990). *Classroom Magic.* Portland, OR: Metamorphous Press.

Lozanov, Georgi. (1979). *Suggestology and Outlines of Suggestopedia.* New York, NY: Gordon & Breach.

Lozanov, Georgi. (1991). On Some Problems of the Anatomy, Physiology and Biochemistry of Cerebral Activities in the Global-Artistic Approach in Modern Suggestopedagogic Training. *The Journal of the Society for Accelerative Learning and Teaching* 16.2, 101-16.

MacLean, Paul. (1978). A Mind of Three Minds: Educating the Triune Brain. *77th Yearbook of the National Society for the Study of Education.* Chicago, IL: University of Chicago Press. pp. 308-42.

MacLean, Paul. (1990). *The Triune Brain in Education.* New York, NY: Plenum Press.

MacMurren, H. (1985). A Comparative Study of the Effects of Matching and Mismatching Sixth Grade Students With Their Learning Style Preferences for the Physical Element of Intake and Their Subsequent Reading Speed and Accuracy Scores. *Dissertation.* St. John's University.

Malone, T., & Lepper, M. (1987). Making Learning Fun: A Semanticomy of Intrinsic Motivations for Learning. *Aptitude, Learning and Instruction III: Cognitive and Affective Process Analyses.* (Snow & Farr, Eds.) Hillsdale, NJ: Lawerence Erlbaum & Assoc. pp. 223-53.

Mandler, G. (1983). The Nature of Emotions. *States of Mind.* (Miller. J., Ed.) New York, NY: Pantheon Books.

Mark, Vernon. (1989). *Brain Power.* Boston, MA: Houghton-Mifflin.

Marzolla, Jean & Lloyd, Janice. (1972). *Learning Through Play.* New York, NY: Harper & Row.

Marzano, Robert. (1992). *A Different Kind of Classroom.* Alexandria, VA: ASCD.

McCarthy, B. (1990). Using the 4MAT System to Bring Learning Styles to Schools. *Educational Leadership* 48.2, 31-37.

McGuiness, D. (1985). *When Children Don't Learn.* New York, NY: Basic Books.

Michaud, E., & Wild, R. (1991). *Boost Your Brain Power.* Emmaus, PA: Rodale Press.

Milich, R., & Pelham, W.E. (1986). The Effects of Sugar Ingestion on the Classroom and Playgroup Behavior. *Journal of Consulting & Clinical Psychology* 54, 1-5.

Mills, R.C. (1987, April). Relationship Between School Motivational Climate, Teacher Attitudes, Student Mental Health, School Failure and Health Damaging Behavior. (Paper at Annual Conference of the American Educational Research Association). Washington, D.C.

Moir, Anne, & Jessel, D. (1991). *Brainsex.* New York, NY: Dell.

Morgan, Brian, & Morgan, Roberta. (1987). *Brainfood.* Los Angeles, CA: Price, Stern, Sloan.

Neve, C.D., Hart, L., & Thomas, E. (1986, October). Huge Learning Jumps Show Potency of Brain-Based Instruction. *Phi Delta Kappan* pp. 143-8.

Nummela, R., & Rosengren, T. (1986). What's Happening in Student's Brain's May Redefine Teaching *Educational Leadrship* 43.8, 49-53.

Nummela, R., & Rosengren, T. The Brain's Routes and Maps: Vital Connections in Learning. *NAASP Bulletin* 72: 83-86.

Oakhill, J. (1988). Time of Day Affects Aspects of Memory. *Applied Cognitive Psychology* 2, 203-12.

Olds, James. (1992). Mapping the Mind onto the Brain. *The Neurosciences: Paths of Discovery.* (Worden, F., Swazey, J., & Adelman, G., Eds.) Boston, MA: Birkhauser.

Orlock, Carol. (1993). *Inner Time.* New York, NY: Birch Lane Press, Carol Publishing.

Ornstein, Robert. (1986). *Multimind.* Boston, MA: Houghton-Mifflin.

Ornstein, Robert. (1991). *The Evolution of Consciousness.* New York, NY: Simon & Schuster.

Ornstein, Robert, & Thompson, Richard. (1986). *The Amazing Brain.* Boston, MA: Houghton-Mifflin.

Ostrander, Sheila & Schroeder, Lynn. (1991). *SuperMemory.* , New York, NY: Carroll & Graf Publishers.

Pearce, Joseph Chilton. (1992) *Evolution's End.* San Francisco. HarperCollins.

Pelton, Ross. (1989). *Mind Food & Smart Pills.* New York, NY: Bantam Doubleday.

Pintrich, P.R., & Garcia, T. (1991). Student Goal Orientation and Self-Regulation in the College Classroom. *Advances in Motivation and Achievement.* (Maeher & Pintrich, Eds.) Vol. 7. Greenwich, CT: JAI. pp. 371-402.

Pizzo, J. (1981). An Investigation of the Relationships Between Selected Acoustic Environments and Sound, an Element of Learning Style, as They Affect Sixth Grade Students' Reading Achievement and Attitudes. *Dissertation.* St. John's University.

Price, G. (1980). Which Learning Style Elements are Stable and Which End to Change? *Learning Styles Network Newsletter* 4.2, 38-40.

Restak, R. (1988).*The Brain*. New York, NY: Warner Books.

Restak, R. (1988). *The Mind*. New York, NY: Bantam Books.

Restak, R. (1991). *The Brain Has a Mind of its Own*. New York, NY: Harmony Books, .

Restak, R. (1994). *Receptors*. New York, NY: Bantam Books.

Restak, R. (1994) *The Modular Brain*. Charles Scribner's Sons. New York, NY.

Rose, Colin. (1986). *Accelerated Learning*. New York, NY: Dell Publishing.

Rose, Steven. (1992). *The Making of Memory*. New York, NY. Anchor/Doubleday.

Rosenfield, I. (1988). *The Invention of Memory*. New York, NY: Basic Books.

Rosenthal, R. & Jacobsen, L. (1968). *Pygmalion in the Classroom*. New York, NY: Rinehart & Winston.

Rossi, A.S., & Rossi, P.E. (1980). Body Time and Social Time: Mood Patterns by Cycle Phase and Day of the Week. *The Psychobiology of Sex Differences and Sex Roles*. (Parsons, J.E., Ed.) London, England: Hemisphere. pp. 269-301.

Rozanski, Alan. (1988, April 21). Mental Stress and the Induction of Silent Ischmia in Patients with Coronary Artery Disease. *New England Journal of Medicine* Vol 318, 16. pp.1005-12.

Ryan, R.M., & Stiller, J. (1991). The Social Contexts of Internalization: Parent and Teacher Influences on Autonomy, Motivation, and Learning. *Advances in Motivation and Achievement*. (Maeher, M.L., & Pintrich, R., Eds.) Vol. 7. Greenwich, CT: JAI. pp. 115-49.

Samples, Bob. (1987). *Open Mind/Whole Mind*. Rolling Hills, CA: Jalmar Press.

Schatz, C.J. (1992, September) The Developing Brain. *Scientific American*. pp. 60-7.

Schiffler, Ludger. (1992). *Suggestopedic Methods and Applications*. Philadelphia, PA: Gordon & Breach.

Scholz, J. (1990). Cultural Expressions Affecting Patient Care. *Dimensions in Oncology Nursing* 4.1, 16-26.

Schunk, D.H. (1990). Goal Setting and Self-Efficacy During Self-Regulated Learning. *Educational Psychologist* 25.1, 71-86.

Seligman, Martin. (1992). *Learned Optimism*. New York, NY: Pocket Books.

Senge, P., Kleiner, A., Roberts, C., Ross, R. & Smith, B. (1994). *The Fifth Discipline Fieldbook*. New York, NY: Currency/Doubleday.

Silverstein, Alvin, & Silverstein,Virginia. (1986). *The World of the Brain*. New York, NY: Morrow Jr. Books.

Soloveichik, Simon. (1979, May). Odd Way to Teach, But It Works. *Soviet Life Magazine*.

Sternberg, Robert. *Beyond I.Q.: A Triarchical Theory of Human Intelligence*.

Sternberg, Robert & Wagner, Richard. (1994). *Mind in Context*. New York, NY: Cambridge University Press.

Sylwester, Robert. (1993, December - 1994, January). What the Biology of the Brain Tells Us About Learning. *Educational Leadership*. pp. 46-51.

Sylwester, Robert. (1994, October). How Emotions Affect Learning. *Educational Leadership* Volume 52, 2, 60-65.

Sylwester, R. & Cho, J. (1993 January). What Brain Research Says About Paying Attention. *Educational Leadership*. pp. 71-5.

Thayer, R. (1986). Time of Day Affects Energy Levels. *Brain-Mind Bulletin* 12, 3D.

Thayer, R. (1989). *The Biopsychology of Mood and Arousal*. New York, NY: Oxford University Press.

Trautman, P. (1979). An Investigation of the Relationship Between Selected Instructional Techniques and Identified Cognitive Style. *Dissertation*. St. John's University.

Verlee Williams, Linda. (1983). *Teaching for the Two-Sided Mind*. New York, NY: Simon & Schuster/Touchstone.

Vincent, J-D. (1990). *The Biology of Emotions*. Cambridge, MA: Basil Blackwell.

Vos-Groenendal, Jeannete. (1991).An Accelerated/Integrative Learning Model Program Evaluation: Based on Participant Perceptions of Student Attitudinal and Achievement Changes. *Unpublished Dissertation*. Flagstaff, AZ: ERIC & NAU.

Walker, Morton. (1991). *The Power of Color*. Avery Publishing, Garden City Park, NY.

Ward, C., & Jaley, Jan. (1993). *Learning to Learn*.. New Zealand: A&H Print Consultants.

Webb, D., & Webb, T. (1990). *Accelerated Learning with Music*. Norcross, GA: Accelerated Learning Systems.

Wenger, Win. (1992). *Beyond Teaching & Learning*. Singapore. Project Renaissance.

Whitleson, S. Sex Differences in the Neurology of Cognition: Social, Educational and Clinical Implications. *Le Fait Femenin*.

Wlodkowski, R. (1985). *Enhancing Adult Motivation to Learn*. San Francisco, CA: Jossey-Bass Publishers.

Wurtman, J. *Managing Your Mind & Mood Through Food*. New York, NY: Harper/Collins, 1986.

Zalewski, L.J., Sink, & Yachimowicz, D.J. (1992). Using Cerebral Dominance for Education Programs. *Journal of General Psychology* 119.1, 45-57.

# In-Depth Follow-Up Resources

# *Recommended Resources:*

Here are the resources most recommended by the author. These are available by mail order. Order using the toll-free number below.

| *Title:* | *Author:* |
| --- | --- |
| 4-Mat System book | Bernice McCarthy |
| 12 Brain-Booster Posters | Eric Jensen |
| Student Success System | Eric Jensen |
| Accelerated Learning Book | Colin Rose |
| Accelerated Learning Audiotapes | Eric Jensen |
| Act Approach book | Dr. Lynn Dhority |
| Brain Gym book | Paul & Gail Dennison |
| Brain-Based Learning & Teaching Video | Eric Jensen |
| The Creative Brain book | Ned Herrmann |
| EnVoy book | Michael Grinder |
| The Everyday Genius book | Peter Kline |
| Focused Learning States Audio | Eric Jensen |
| If the Shoe Fits book | Carolyn Chapman |
| Introduction to Accelerated Learning | Eric Jensen |
| The Learning Brain (book, tapes & video) | Eric Jensen |
| Learning & Teaching Styles book | Kathleen Butler |
| Learning Modalities audiotapes | Eric Jensen |
| Learning Revolution book | Dryden & Vos |
| Learning Styles of the 1990's audio | Eric Jensen |
| Little Book of Big Motivation | Eric Jensen |
| Making Connections book | Nummela Caine & Caine |
| Managing Your Mind & Mood Through Food book | Judith J. Wurtman, Ph.D. |
| Mapping Innerspace book | Nancy Marguiles |
| Mind Food & Smart Pills book | Ross Pelton |
| Multiple Assessments for Multiple Intelligences book | Carolyn Chapman, et al. |
| Nurturing Intelligences book | Brian A. Haggerty |
| Power of Color book | Dr. Morton Walker |
| Punished by Rewards book | Alfie Kohn |
| Righting the Educational Conveyer Belt book | Michael Grinder |
| Rhythms of Learning book | Campbell & Brewer |
| School Success book | Kline & Mart |
| Seeing with Magic Glasses book | Launa Ellison |
| Seven Ways of Teaching book | David Lazear |
| Ten Steps to a Learning Organization book | Kline & Saunders |

Overnight and 2nd Day delivery available. Call 800-325-4769 or fax 619-792-2858. Or, call for FREE catalog included. Satisfaction or money-back guarantee.

# SuperTeaching Resources

**For a Speaker or Trainer Contact:** For district programs, conference speaking, train-the-trainer programs, district or school inservices and workshops, phone (619) 755-6670 or fax (619) 792-2858. Address: Box 2551, Del Mar, California 92014 USA.

**For Certification Training** as a master-level trainer or teacher, a 6-day immersion training is held each year. This book is just the beginning! See information elsewhere in this appendix for details and registration.

**Distributor Inquiries Welcome:** If you distribute a catalogue or do workshops, your audience may be interested in learning more about these practical teaching & learning-strategies. To provide a valuable service and earn additional income, contact our publishing office for distributor price list. Call (619) 755-6670 or fax inquiries to: (619) 792-2858.

**Feedback, Suggestions and Corrections:** Please feel free to write, call or fax the author with any information that might be useful for upcoming revisions: P.O. Box 2551, Del Mar, CA 92014 USA

**For a FREE Catalogue** of SuperTeaching, Brain-based Learning Products for teaching, training and personal use, including:

* Books          * Videos
* Audiotapes     * Special Reports
* Bulletins      * Kits & Programs

Call (800) 325-4769 or (619) 755-6670, fax (619) 792-2858 or mail your name and address to: Turning Point, P.O. Box 2551, Del Mar, CA 92014 USA

# *Amazing 6-Day Certification*
# *21st Century Teaching Skills*
# *Learn the Brain-Based Approach*

- **Learn how to inservice your staff & others**
- **Gain university credits for pay increases**
- **Discover dramatic & powerful ways to learn**
- **Increase your market value & boost income**
- **Boost your self-confidence & self-esteem**
- **Learn over 100 specific, practical ideas**
- **Make a bigger difference & feel good about it**
- **Learn an "in-demand" cutting edge skill**

If you enjoyed this book, you may want to take the training that goes with it! Are you a teacher, trainer or administrator? Do you now, or would you like to make your living as a presenter? Would you like to master the art of using all these brain-based strategies? Would you like to be able to consistently get audience participation, engage meaning and motivate for lasting changes? You would? Good, then keep reading, because you're about to learn exactly how to do it. You're about to learn why taking a 6-day brain-based training may be the absolutely best thing you can possibly do for yourself (and your audience).

- **Discover easy ways to use hot strategies**
- **Boost attention, learning, recall & usage**
- **100% Satisfaction guaranteed**

There's a surging tidal wave sweeping the country and some say, the world. It's the not just the current or trendy thing, it's a virtual explosion in neuroscience discoveries. In the last few years, maverick researchers have uncovered astonishing details about the brain and learning... and they're already being implemented in technology, medicine and business. Learn how to apply them now, and you'll possess rare, powerful and highly marketable 21st century skills that can transform the very foundations of the educational system. You will become more than a contributor, you'll become a "key player" to global learning transformation.

*As we move towards the next century, you'll*
*either be part of the new learning revolution*
*or left behind wondering "What happened?"*

I should know; as a former classroom teacher, a world-wide staff developer and corporate trainer with over 15 years of successful brain-based training experience, I have successfully trained over 5,000 teens and 10,000 adults. I've been a key part of two of the largest brain-based programs in the world. I'm not bragging, this has been my passion for years and I like to share it. Wouldn't you want to tap into that kind of experience? I'll bet you would. Here's what one participant from this 6-day train-the-trainer seminar said:

*"Simply mind-boggling... learned more in 6 days than in twenty years*
*in education"* P. Kohlbacher, IL
*"So much useful information that would solve many of our problems*
*in education...how can this be disseminated faster?* H. Bridges

Would you like to know what we cover? I'll bet you're curious like me. Just for fun, read the course items below that you'd like to learn & experience:

* **How to design and conduct a workshop or training based on the brain**
* **What are the 12 super-essentials to know about the brain**
* **How to permanently boost persuasiveness, congruency and impact**
* **The newest learning styles you don't know about but should**

If you could successfully do those things, would your work be easier, more effective? Of course. Yet, why take my word for it when you can get it straight from past course participants:

*"You've inspired me to succeed in areas I've only tasted before."* B. Degelsmith
*"Never been to a course that gave me so many ideas that were so specific."* K. Norman
*"I wish I had learned this stuff in college... it should be a graduate requirement."*
     J. Murphy

I could give you countless testimonials. But let's get back to the curriculum of the six-day San Diego course. You can also expect to learn the answers to these topics:

* **How to deal with troublemakers & hecklers with ease & confidence**
* **What is the perfect learning and thinking diet**
* **How to translate information into "deeply felt" meaning**
* **How to build and maintain high-performance teams**

Those are just some of the more powerful skills and ideas which you can expect to learn. What happens when you implement the results of this course? I can cite you example after example of how participants from my courses have gone on to become highly requested speakers, presenters and even experts in their field. Sometimes I smile with pride when I see conferences with two, three and in one case FOUR speakers, ALL who have been trained by me. But please, don't get me wrong. I don't mean to brag. The *participants* did all the hard work to get good. But I do have a knack for lighting a professional fire and opening up minds. Read what this next participant said. Could you be the next one to give the course rave reviews?

*"It was a professionally mind-blowing experience."* D. Hennesey.
*"Your workshop positively and dramatically changed my teaching forever...*
*I have so many parents coming to me and telling me what a difference I've made in their*
     *children's lives."* I. Forber.

There are more; I'll save them for later. Since you're probably an insatiable learner like myself, you might be interested in what else is offered in this workshop:

* **19 Rituals which boost learning and maintain optimal states**
* **How specifically to teach to the brain as a learning organ**
* **Which types of music are best for learning and when to use them**
* **How to make best use of the 7 Multiple Intelligences**
* **The 5 secrets to permanently eliminating discipline problems**

You may be wondering how in the world can we do all of those things in just 6 short days. The answer is simple. Using the powerful strategies of accelerated learning, we'll be able to enhance absorption, speed up the pace and still absorb far more than you ever believed possible. This methodology, combined with the sizzling cutting-edge neuroscience discoveries will help you learn faster. These breakthroughs will help you discover:

* **What are the real learning differences between males and females**
* **The 7 secrets to boost concentration and attention in learning**
* **How to guarantee that your audience will recall & use what they learn**
* **The 6 types of memory & which one to reduce the use of dramatically**
* **What are the most amazing facts about the brain you MUST know**

In addition, you'll learn through one of the all-time best methods ever: my role modeling. The workshop is meticulously planned so that you get a real experience of HOW all these brain-based strategies actually work. To put it blunt, I am one of the few that actually practice what I preach:

*"It was the most valuable presentation for me in my professional experience... your demonstrations were the greatest single influence on me."* M. Ball
*"Loved the way you modeled the strategies."* L. Vardenega
*"The fact that you modeled what you were doing made it so worthwhile."* T. Mills

Those are just some of the more powerful things you'll learn. My goodness, there's going to be a lot of shakin' and moving in that course! One lady (D. Morgan) said, *"I have not expended this much energy in ages! I can now see how reluctant students can get caught up in this."* By the way, have you decided to attend yet? I hope so.

As you can tell, I'm not shy about asking you to enroll. Why should I be shy? It's the best investment you can make in yourself and your future. You've got a satisfaction or money back guarantee. After this workshop, your first paid presentation you make, will probably return your investment immediately. And your referral business will astonish you. By the way, are there any other reasons you might want to enroll? Of course!

* **Network with "like-minded" people**
* **Gain learning & workplace efficiency**
* **Discover best brain-based resources**
* **Get ready for the 21st century**

Let's take care of the details. It begins the second Monday, (8:30am-5pm) in July each year in San Diego, California. The course takes place at a beautiful harborside location with colorful yachts and great seafood nearby. You can walk from your hotel to the training... no rental car needed. During the course you'll also get great summer weather (average July temperature is 76 degrees, with no rain).

We'll also provide a virtual supermarket of the best set of brain-based resources anywhere on this planet! This is going to be some kind of special event....You ARE planning on being a part of it, aren't you?

The tuition costs $675. Can you afford it? It just may be a case of "Can you afford NOT to register?" If you've read this far, you KNOW it's for you. Get your school or district to pay for it. Put it on your credit card, use your savings or get a grant. It's a tax deduction! But move fast. You and I know, if you want anything badly enough, you'll find a way.

---

The demand for those who understand the brain is growing faster than the supply! This can be for your school, business or your next career. So, go for it. You've got a satisfaction or money back guarantee. The registration form is on the following page. Fill it out, copy, mail or fax it. today. While it's fresh on your mind, and there are still spaces left in this sock-hopping, idea-packed, transformational training, go ahead and register. Your future is important and this can positively and fundamentally alter its course. Do it now. You'll be glad you did. I promise....

---

# Registration

✔ **YES!** *I'd like to register. Here's my $95 deposit on the $675 tuition.*
Tuition includes course workbook, certification, all special activities and supplies.
Remember...transportation to the event, meals and lodging are extra. Send me
confirmation, travel, lodging, course details and confirmation kit by first class mail.
Held several times each July in San Diego, California. June and August locations
usually include the East Coast, Midwest or Texas. Call for this year's exact dates
and locations. *(Prices and locations valid thru September 1997)*

**Circle Payment Form:** VISA/MC    wire transfer    check    purchase order
I understand the complete balance ($580) is due no later than 2 weeks prior to event.
**Free!** With my $95 deposit, send me the amazing, exclusive book "Brain Facts."
**Credits:** SDSU extension credits available for an additional fee.
**Hotel:** Call the hotel direct for reservations. We'll give you that information when you call.
We'll suggest an affordable hotel within walking distance. Register early, rooms go fast!

Name (print)

School or Company Name                          Role/Title

Home Address                                    City

State & Zip Code                                Country

Phone (include area code)                       Fax (include area code)

VISA or Master card number                      Expiration date

**Group Discounts:** *Group price for schools, businesses and other groups of three (3) or more. Details available by phone or in registration kit. Sorry, no group discounts allowed on registration day (the first day of the course)*

**Cancellation Policy:** *All monies paid are refundable except a $25 registration fee. To qualify, you must contact us by phone, fax or letter prior to course start date.*

**Guarantee Policy:** *You can be assured of a first-class workshop. After completion of the six-day course, if you don't feel you got your money's worth, you may request & receive a refund (minus the $95 materials and registration fee). Refund requests honored up to, but not exceeding 90 days following the course.*

*call:* **1 (800) 325-4769 or (619) 546-7555**
*fax:* **1 (619) 546-7560**
*mail:* **TURNING POINT, Box 2551 Del Mar, CA 92014**

See more information on the following page

How do you know this video will fit your needs? Four good reasons. 1) It's the source for this book. If you like this book, you'll like the video. 2) It's got a satisfaction, money-back guarantee. 3) It's got a fool-proof guidebook with it to keep your worries low and help make your presentation job easy. 4) It's proven; here's what other have said: *"Absolutely outstanding..couldn't take my eyes off it."* Mary Francis, N.J. *"I can't say enough good things... all my expectations were met & exceeded..."* T.Johnson, Principal, NJ *"The whole course was so valuable & enlightening, I can't wait to start using it."* Staff Developer, Austin, TX. You can easily lower stress, save money, bring fresh ideas in and get motivated, enthusiastic staff members with this exciting product. Next-day and 2-day delivery service available. Here's what to do...

# How To Order

❏ **YES!** Send me my **Personal Copy** of the exciting two part 76 min. "Brain-Based Learning & Teaching" Video. I understand my satisfaction is guaranteed with a full 90 days satisfaction or money back guarantee. Here's my $89 (U.S.Dollars) + $7.95 postage and handling(continental U.S. only).

❏ **YES!** I'd like the $99 **Staff Development** Budget Package. Includes facilitator's Manual for conducting a terrific staff development session. Two exciting 38min. color sessions which can be used as a 2-hour to full-day inservice. **Item #094-801 only $99**

❏ **YES!** I'd like the **Deluxe $375 Staff Development Package.** It's an budget-stretching $500 value: It's a fail-safe, lock-step staff-development kit in a box! First, you get a master-designed approach to easily help you plan your training to make it a total success. Secondly, you get the two-part, 76min. video, a facilitator's guidebook, overheads, handouts, posters for the faculty lounge and two of the best "Brain-based Learning" books ever written. **Item #094-802, well worth $375**

U.S. Orders add $7.95 for shipping & handling. Fast 2-day and express overnight delivery available. Overseas orders add $35 for shipping (U.S.funds only). **Total Enclosed: $ \_\_\_\_\_**

*Circle one:*　　　　check　　　purchase order　　VISA　　Mastercard
*Format requested:*　　　VHS　　　　　　　　PAL version

_____　　_____
VISA or Mastercard credit card number　　　　　　　expiration date

Name (print) _____ Occupation _____
Shipping Address _____City _____
State/Postal Code _____Country _____
Phone(\_\_\_\_) _____ Fax (\_\_\_\_) _____

## Ordering is easy!

*By Phone:*　Call FREE 800-325-4769 or 619-755-6670
*By Fax:*　　(619) 792-2858 M-F 9am-5pm PST. Overnight and 2nd
　　　　　　day delivery available.
*By Mail:*　Send this form or a copy of it to: Turning Point, Box 2551,
　　　　　　Del Mar, CA 92014...Satisfaction guaranteed!

# The Author

Eric Jensen is a former reading teacher who has taught elementary, middle school, high school level students. He remains deeply committed to making a positive, significant, lasting difference in the way the world learns. He received his B.A. in English from San Diego State University and M.A. in Psychology from the University of California. He has taught as adjunct faculty at the University of California at San Diego, National University and the University of San Diego. He's listed in "Who's Who" and is a former Outstanding Young Man of America selection.

Jensen was the co-founder of SuperCamp, the nation's first and largest accelerated learning program for teens. He authored the bestselling *Student Success Secrets, The Little Book of Big Motivation, 30 Days to Bs and As, You Can Succeed, The Learning Brain* and *Brain-Based Learning and Teaching.*

He was a key part of Australia's Accelerated Learning Initiative, one of the largest (over 4,000 teachers trained) brain-based teacher training programs in the world. Trainers from AT & T, Disney, IBM, Digital, GTE, Hewlitt-Packard, ICA, Burroughs, Atlantic Bell, SAS and three branches of the military have used his methods. Jensen provides successful trainings for conferences, schools, organizations, and Fortune 500 corporations, and is an international speaker, writer and consultant.

**For a speaker or trainer, contact the author:** For brain-based trainings, conference speaking, corporate trainings, district or school inservices and workshops, phone (619) 755-6670 or fax (619) 792-2858. Address: Box 2551, Del Mar, California 92014 USA.

**For a FREE Catalogue** of Brain-Based Learning Products for Teaching and Training, call (800) 325-4769 or (619) 755-6670 or mail your name and address to: Turning Point, P.O. Box 2551, Del Mar, CA 92014 USA

**Overseas Inquiries Welcome.** If you are a publisher in U.K., France, Germany, Spain, Mexico, Canada, Asia, Australia, or elsewhere, please contact our office. Our fax is (619) 792-2858. Address: Box 2551, Del Mar, California 92014 USA.

**Distributor Inquiries Welcome:** If you distribute a catalogue or do workshops, your audience may be interested in learning more about these practical brain-based strategies. To offer a catalog and earn additional income, contact our publishing office for distributor price list. Call (619) 755-6670 or mail your name and address to: Turning Point, P.O. Box 2551, Del Mar, CA 92014 USA.

# Notes, Thoughts and Author Feedback

All feedback, positive or not, is welcomed. If you have any comments, corrections, additions or suggestions for the next printing of this book, please fax or write to the author at the address on the previous page. Thank you very much. You make a difference.

370